WOODWORKER'S GUIDE TO
HANDPLANES

WOODWORKER'S GUIDE TO
HANDPLANES

How to Choose, Set Up, and Master the Most Useful Planes for Today's Workshop

By Scott Wynn

FOX CHAPEL
PUBLISHING

All illustrations by Scott Wynn.

All photos by Rick Mastelli and Scott Wynn.

© 2010 by Scott Wynn and Fox Chapel Publishing Company, Inc.

Woodworker's Guide to Handplanes is an original work, first published in 2010 by Fox Chapel
Publishing Company, Inc. The patterns contained herein are copyrighted by the author. Readers
may make copies of these patterns for personal use. The patterns themselves, however, are not to
be duplicated for resale or distribution under any circumstances. Any such copying is a violation of
copyright law.

ISBN 978-1-56523-453-6

Library of Congress Cataloging-in-Publication Data

Wynn, Scott.
Woodworker's guide to handplanes / by Scott Wynn.
    p. cm.
Includes index.
ISBN 978-1-56523-453-6
1. Planes (Hand tools) 2. Woodwork. I. Title.
TT186.W96 2010
684'.082--dc22
                        2010013091

To learn more about the other great books from Fox Chapel Publishing, or to find a retailer near
you, call toll-free 800-457-9112 or visit us at *www.FoxChapelPublishing.com*.

Note to Authors: We are always looking for talented authors to write new books
in our area of woodworking, design, and related crafts. Please send a brief letter
describing your idea to Acquisition Editor, 1970 Broad Street, East Petersburg, PA 17520.

Printed in China
First printing: August 2010

ACKNOWLEDGMENTS

To my father, Jerry, who taught me always to watch and listen; and to my daughter, Josephine, who stands on her grandfather's shoulders watching, listening, and learning—and teaching all of us.

I would also like to acknowledge the untiring support of my partner Kathy Tam, and the helpful guidance of technical editor Rick Mastelli, which made this book possible.

CONTENTS

INTRODUCTION *1*

CHAPTER 1: SMOOTH
What to Use, When, and Why 6
   Understanding is Essential 8
      The Challenge of Grit .... .12

CHAPTER 2: SHARP
The Cutting Edge 14
   Beyond Mystique .... .16
   Anatomy of Steel .... .17
      The Ideal Edge .... .18
      Hardening, Tempering, and Annealing .... .20
   Types of Edge Steel .... .21
      Alloy Ingredients .... .21

CHAPTER 3: PLANE ANATOMY
Tactics for Achieving Best Performance 30
   The Angle of the Blade .... .33
      Traditional Blade Angles .... .33
      The Best Blade Angle .... .35
      Blade Angle and the Task .... .38
      Custom Blade Angles .... .39
   Mouth Opening .... .41
   Chipbreaker .... .45
      Setting the Chipbreaker .... .48
      Plane Geometry, a Summary .... .49
   Bevel Angle .... .52
      The Correct Bevel Angle .... .52
      How an Edge Dulls .... .53
   Shape of the Blade Edge .... .54
   Length of Plane/Width of Blade .... .55
      How Flat is "Flat" .... .57

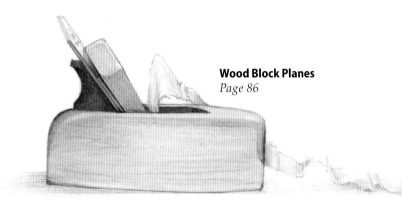

Wood Block Planes
Page 86

CHAPTER 4: BENCH PLANES
Traditional Solutions: the Jack, Jointer,
and Smoothing Planes 58
   The Jack Plane .... .60
      The Fore Plane .... .62
      Jack Variations .... .62
   The Jointer Plane .... .63
      The Correct Blade Shape .... .63
   Smoothing Planes .... .67

CHAPTER 5: THREE MORE PLANES
Strategies for Speeding the Work 70
   The Panel Plane .... .72
   The Scrub Plane .... .75
   The Block Plane .... .76
      Market Block Planes .... .77
      Adjusting the Throat .... .78

CHAPTER 6: STYLES OF PLANES
A Wealth of Traditions 80
   The Bailey Plane .... .82
      Anatomy of the Bailey-Style Plane .... .83
   Wood Block Planes .... .86
      Anatomy of the Wood Block Plane .... .87
   The Norris Plane .... .89
      Anatomy of the Norris-Style Plane .... .90
   Horned Planes .... .91
      Anatomy of the Horned Plane .... .92
   Japanese Planes .... .95
      Anatomy of the Japanese Plane .... .95
   Chinese Planes .... .98
      Anatomy of a Chinese Plane .... .99

CHAPTER 7: JOINERY PLANES
Tools & Techniques for Making & Fitting Joints **100**

   Rabbet Planes 102

   Fillister Planes 105

      Using the Fillister Plane 106

   The Dovetail Plane 108

      Sliding Dovetail........................109

   Shoulder Planes............................110

   Bull-nose/Chisel Planes 112

   The Router Plane...........................113

      Using a Bridge Board 114

      Using the Router Plane....................115

   Side-Rabbet Planes 116

   The Mortise Plane..........................118

CHAPTER 8: PLANES FOR SHAPING WOOD
Specialty Planes that Form and Refine **122**

   Compass Planes............................124

      The Correct Sole Configuration 125

      Western Versus Japanese Planes for Curves 127

   Hollows & Rounds 128

   Other Shaping Planes 129

CHAPTER 9: CHOOSING YOUR FIRST PLANES
A Guide to a Suitable Toolkit **134**

   First Things First...........................136

   Beyond the Basics 140

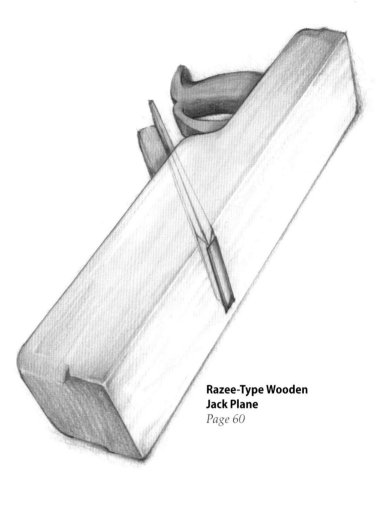

Razee-Type Wooden Jack Plane
Page 60

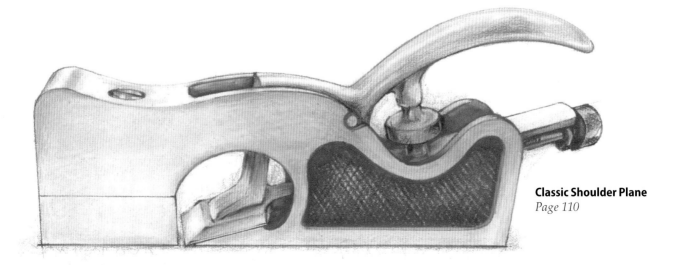

Classic Shoulder Plane
Page 110

CONTENTS

CHAPTER 10: PLANE SETUP
And Tuning Your Plane to Work Right **144**

  Preparing the Blade. 146

  Preparing the Chipbreaker .146

  Flattening the Back of a Plane Blade 148

  General Techniques for Adjusting the Plane Blade. . .152

  Setting Up the Bailey/Stanley Plane 153

    Inspect the Plane 154

    Prepare the Blade and Chipbreaker 155

    Bed the Blade Properly .155

    Configure the Sole. 157

    Adjust the Mouth 161

    Attend to the Details of the Body and Sole 162

    Attend to the Details of the Grip and Finish 162

    Adjusting the Bailey-Style Plane 163

  Setting Up Wood-body Planes 163

    Inspect the Plane: Old Planes 163

    Tapered Blades. 164

    Inspect the Plane: New Planes 165

    Prepare the Blade and Chipbreaker 165

    Bed the Blade Properly .166

    Checking for a Custom Fit 166

    Configure the Sole. 168

    Adjusting Wedged, Tapered Blades. 171

    Attend to the Details of the Body and Soul 173

    Attend to the Details of the Grip and Finish 173

  Setting Up Chinese Planes .173

    Inspect the Plane 173

    Configure the Sole. 174

    Adjust the Mouth 175

    Attend to the Details of the Body and Sole 175

    Attend to the Details of the Grip and Finish 176

  Setting Up Japanese Planes 177

    Inspect the Plane 177

    Tapping Out a Japanese Plane. 178

    Prepare the Blade. 179

    Prepare and Fit the Chipbreaker 180

    Bed the Blade Properly .181

    Configure the Sole. 184

    Adjust the Mouth 186

    Adjusting a Japanese Plane 187

    Attend to the Details of the Grip and Finish 188

Norris-Style Coffin-Sided Smooth Plane
Page 89

  Setting Up Rabbet Planes 188

    Inspect the Plane 188

    Japanese Skew-Bladed Rabbet Plane 189

    Prepare the Blade. 190

    Prepare and Fit the Chipbreaker. 190

    Bed the Blade Properly .190

    Configure the Sole. 190

    Adjust the Mouth 191

    Attend to the Details of the Body and Sole 192

  Setting Up Fillister and Moving-Fillister Planes. 193

  Setting Up Hollows & Rounds. 194

  Troubleshooting 197

CHAPTER 11: SHARPENING PLANE BLADES
A Basic Skill that Leads to Others **202**

  Sharpening Fundamentals .204

    Jig Drawbacks 204

  Bevel Shape 205

  Grinding. 207

  Sharpening Stones 209

    Using and Maintaining Waterstones 211

  Technique. 212

    Sharpening 213

CHAPTER 12: BENCH WORK
Of Slaves, Dogs, and Deadmen 216

A Simple Bench. 220
Deadmen and Helper Boys 223
Bench Dogs 224
Shooting Board 225
Dimensioning Stock 225
  Winding Sticks 226
  Preparing the First Face: Scrub and Jack Planes . . .226
  Continuing With the Jointer Plane 230
  Smoothing the First Face 232
  Planing the Edges and Second Side 233
Other Handplane Preparatory Work 234
Shooting an Edge. 235
  Techniques for Shooting an Edge. 236

CHAPTER 13:
MAKING & USING SHOOTING BOARDS
Invaluable, Often-Overlooked Tools 238

Types of Shooting Boards. 240
Shooting End Grain 243
Making a Shooting Board. 244

Long Plane
Page 55

CHAPTER 14: MAKING & MODIFYING PLANES
Expanding Your Options 256

Making Traditional Wood-body Planes 258
  Materials 259
  Preliminary Work 276
  Rough-Shaping the Blocks 280
  Fitting the Sole Plate, Cross Pin, and Wedge 281
  Shaping the Smoothing Planes. 283
  Handle Shape. 284
  Finishing Touches 285
Making a Japanese-Style Plane 286
  Laying Out a Block for a Japanese Plane 288
  Chiseling the Chipwell, Mouth & Blade Seat 290
Making Chibi-Kanna 295
Making a Compass Plane 298
Hollowing, Rounding & Spoonbottom Planes 301
  Laying Out & Cutting the
    Mouth Opening for Different Blade Shapes. 302
Fitting a Sole Plate at the Mouth of a Plane 306
Fitting a Moveable Sole Plate. 309
Fitting a Moveable Sole Plate when
  Making a Krenov-style Plane 313

INDEX. 314

Classic Simple Moving-Fillister Plane
Page 105

INTRODUCTION

I cannot think of anyone who has made a shaving with a plane and not been seduced by the sight, sound, and feel of the emerging shaving. It is a tool of enormous satisfaction. However, it is far more than the pleasure of using a plane that makes it important.

The handplane quickly and effectively does things other tools cannot. Power tools have redefined and often supplanted the handplane's traditional role but not replaced it. And for those who have experienced frustration with the handplane, this knowledge will finally allow you to experience the enormous satisfaction intrinsic to this most essential woodworking tool.

Development peaked during the late-nineteenth century, as great numbers of planes, some of them highly esoteric, were available to woodworkers, professionals, and hobbyists.

Some handplanes were works of art, some mechanical marvels, and some both. Ironically, the mechanization that enabled production of vast numbers of handplanes led to its decline. Mechanization brought mass production and development of woodworking machines, making power tools increasingly available and affordable. The changes reduced demand for handplanes in general and specialty planes in particular. In a culture of mass production,

These hollowing and rounding planes, basically unchanged since the eighteenth century, are still useful today and can be the fastest way to fair a curve or restore a short section of molding. Above, one plane is used to tune-up its mate.

reduced demand often means eventual disappearance, as a product falls below the threshold where development, manufacturing, and distribution costs make economic sense. The economics result in gradual elimination of all but those few models appealing to the broadest market, leaving everything else behind. And typically, the products that do remain are slowly simplified in order to reduce manufacturing costs and further extend market reach, often resulting in a gradual deterioration in the quality of the product.

The gradual decline in the quality and variety of handplanes, and hand tools in general, began around the turn of the twentieth century. For a period, we had the best of both worlds: increased production brought on by the availability of power tools and access to skills nurtured by tradition and the tutelage of a declining apprentice system.

FROM PAST TO PRESENT

With growing industrialization, an emerging global economy, and increasing entrepreneurship creating new fortunes, the newly rich, the established peerage of Europe, and a growing upper-middle class of managers and investors competed to have the first and the best of the latest styles. The quality of production furniture toward the end of the nineteenth century was quite high. While you can argue about the quality of design, the execution was impressive. Mass production made elaborate styles available to a broader clientele than would otherwise have been able to afford them.

However, the world continued to change, and the brief union of patrons, skilled workers, and machine production ended in the Art Deco era with the closing of the shops of Ruhlman, Dunand, and their contemporaries. The shops produced what I believe was some of the best furniture ever made using a combination of machines and hand tools.

The Great Depression brought the end of patronage while World War II and its aftermath brought the mechanization of life. With a need for massive rebuilding and a reduced workforce available in Europe, mechanization seemed the only way to create shelter for those devastated by war, though retention of trade traditions and integration of them into modern life were considerations.

The United States, having built immense production systems during the war, was not about to look back, and handwork was subtly discouraged. Non-essential trades, never fully established as the institutions they were in Europe and elsewhere, and, I believe, a subconscious reminder of the servitude our immigrant fathers had fled, slowly became a curiosity. Training programs, other than the trade unions (and even those declined in quality), lost support and became fewer and farther in-between.

By the time interest in woodworking was renewed—not coincidentally at about the time *Fine Woodworking* magazine began publication in the mid-1970s, the first of a renaissance of books and magazines on the subject—the economic pressures of mass production and a declining market reduced both the number and quality of hand tools. Only the Bailey/Stanley-style plane and basic hand tools were widely available.

The hand tools were not great quality and little information on setup and use of any of the tools was available. I began woodworking in the late-1960s, picking up what tools I could from the local hardware store, and what tips I could from relatives and a few scattered written sources. The tools were an immediate disappointment. Where were the tools that built the works of art in the museums?

Certainly during 3,000 or more years of woodworking, our predecessors, who did all work by hand, had developed effective ways to maximize their efforts to produce flawless work. The modern tools were not capable of flawless work, and what they could do took backbreaking, hand-blistering effort.

I began to look further afield, searching available sources. In the early-1970s, I drove across the country from my home in Ohio to Berkeley, California, to search out a then-obscure Japanese-tool dealer to look at what were then exotic tools. (The drawings of them in the *Whole Earth Catalog* looked too bizarre to be real.)

The tools were a revelation—and a validation. Well-made hand tools *could* be a joy to use and highly productive. I began looking at tools from all woodworking traditions, experimenting with any I could find, identifying strengths and weaknesses, and the work for which they were best suited. I used them daily to make my living.

CHOICES TODAY

The world has changed again. The Information Age has made a galaxy of new tools available. Clearly, I was not alone in my frustration with the quality and availability of tools during that rebirth. Catalogs now offer an array of hand tools from a variety of cultures and times with uses that may be applicable or arcane. Sometimes we have little knowledge of the intended use of these tools, their maintenance, the materials they worked, or the objects they helped to make.

Often, there are only the seller's descriptions for this information. Handplanes in particular show a disparity in form that suggests they perform tasks differently. However, a systematic look at the anatomy of the handplane and how planes were traditionally used shows that despite differences in form, solutions to woodworking problems have a certain similarity from tool to tool, and culture to culture, from which we can learn.

Today we can choose parts and pieces from a variety of woodworking traditions to fit our style of work—and our style of working wood. Coupled with the tremendous accessibility to machine tools, we have an advantage not enjoyed previously.

To maximize the advantage, woodworkers must consider the type of work they do. Some will derive more benefit from the handplane and hand tools in general. A machine might best accomplish a repeated task (you decide how many justifies automation). Hand tools can efficiently assist or accomplish short runs, one-of-a-kind, prototypes, and variations on a theme. I find one of the main advantages to

proficiency with hand tools is fewer limitations in the types of projects I am able to tackle—projects otherwise too small or too big, projects too complex, and projects whose form is evolving even as they're being produced. Even if you are working in production or large millwork situations, handplane skills can be a godsend.

In addition to extending the range of projects you can tackle, the handplane is demonstrably faster for some tasks, including smoothing small parts. A well-set handplane can smooth a side of a leg, for instance, smoother than 1000-grit sandpaper in two or three strokes, with none of the rounding or waviness you might get with sanding. A few strokes of a handplane can likewise remove the saw marks and tearing you get on end grain. A follow-up of a few strokes with 220-grit sandpaper and you get quick, baby-bottom smoothness. The best tool to remove snipe and power-planer variations is the handplane, as its flat sole flattens the board in removing the snipe. It is fast, and it is accurate.

THE RESULTS

The results you get with a handplane are different from those with sandpaper. Assuming the blade is correctly shaped, a handplaned piece is going to be flatter and straighter than all but the work produced with the best wide-belt sanders. Less expensive wide-belt sanders can leave ripples, as can planers. Belt and orbit sanders leave a gently wavy surface like calm water that shows up especially after applying finish, most noticeably on horizontal surfaces. If you have a flat-grain piece, say in oak or pine, sanding removes more softer spring growth than denser late-season growth, resulting in a gently rippling surface following the grain. This will not happen with a handplane. Power sanding, particularly with the random-orbit sander, tends to slightly round over work in general, but especially smaller pieces, sometimes giving the work a doughy look. Handplaning also provides a better surface for gluing.

Besides the difference in surface quality, there is a subtle but palpable difference in the look and character between pieces shaped and smoothed by edge tools and those prepared by sanding. The crispness and flow suggestive of the sweep of the cutting edge is not present in work abraded to shape. That is an important critical lesson for woodworkers. This is not to say one or another piece would be inferior, but there are differences in the look and feel of the piece. Understanding the difference helps you choose the correct tool.

YOUR HEALTH

Also important to consider in the choice between power tools and handplanes is exposure to dust. Long underestimated, the dangers of dust are now becoming more apparent. The U.S. government has officially identified wood dust as a carcinogen. The modern production shop produces large quantities of it. The one-man shop, with its orbital, belt, stationary, spindle, disk, and thickness sanders can produce choking amounts of it.

The widespread use of abrasives is relatively new, so the long-term effects of inhaling their dust are not fully known, nor are the effects of the many compounds in wood—many of them toxic, allergenic, or simply irritating. These include those associated with any rot-resistant wood and many tropical hardwoods. We know they can cause rashes and other skin reactions. Particles inhaled deeply into the lungs can cause permanent lung damage. The smallest dust particles sanding produces are the most dangerous.

Some particles are so small they pass through the best filters. Read the product specifications— no filtration system, no dust mask is 100% effective. A dust collector can actually make things worse. Anything not collected by the filter (particles from 30 microns to less than 1 micron, depending on your filter) will be blown back into the air, continually suspended, and circulated by the collector until you turn it off. Even if the filtration material in a dust mask were better, no dust mask fits airtight, especially if worn over a beard.

Concern extends beyond the lungs. Long-term dust exposure can cause nasal polyps, which can be pre-cancerous. There also is the very real risk of hearing loss from machine noise. Many woodworkers I know who are my age have suffered some hearing loss.

Therefore, woodworkers should approach sanding with more awareness, and take steps to limit and control their exposure to dust and noise. They should also consider methods beyond a sander to achieve a shape or surface. Perhaps the image of the woodworker quietly planing wood, listening for the sound of a well-cut shaving, the floor littered with (dust-free) streams of shavings, and the bench and tools so free of dust you could wear black clothes to work and leave without a mark, is less romantic and more serious than it would seem. It certainly represents a better quality of life than standing over a screaming, dust-spewing sander for hours on end.

YOUR WALLET

And what about the economics? The handplane can be more cost-effective than sandpaper. Look at the costs of a random-orbit sander. You have the initial investment, less probably than for a good plane, but not cheap. You have the cost of sandpaper: use the sander all day long and you can easily burn through $20 to $30 worth of sandpaper.

Three or four days of that and you just bought yourself a handplane. You have down time when the machine is sidelined for repairs. You are not going to be doing any sanding with it, and when you are not sanding with it, you are not making money.

Then there is the cost of repairs: replace the bearings, brushes, and hook-and-loop pad (which also wears out), and you have just about bought yourself another sander. In addition, no matter what, eventually the machine wears out and must be replaced.

If you were to use a random orbit sander every day, all day, you would wear it out in a year after having the machine repaired twice. Use a handplane all day, every day, and you have worn maybe a half-inch off the blade. You would be able to get another two maybe three years out of that $40 blade.

Assuming you make the correct decisions as to the appropriate tool to use as you work, the *efficiency* of each tool becomes equal, but the *cost* of the sander is many times higher.

There are, of course, costs associated with the handplane, but they compare favorably. Once you have set up the plane, which may

or may not require much time, maintenance is minimal. Sharpening can be a pain, but with some practice and decent technique, you can be back to work in five minutes or less.

REWARDS

The learning curve for the handplane is higher, but woodworking requires the continual acquisition and advancement of skill. That is the essence of the craft. You do not have to leap into the most challenging uses of the plane right at the beginning. Expand your handplane skills gradually as your skill progresses. The information in this book will greatly shorten the learning curve.

Abrasives are here to stay and are an important part of woodworking. To not use all of the skills and techniques available, or to not acquire the knowledge that will help you choose the appropriate technique and the skill to follow through, limits the scope of your work, creativity, and growth.

Knowledgeable use of both power and hand tools leads to better, more rewarding work, and the handplane, always the premier woodworking instrument, remains one of the most useful tools available. By temperament, and perhaps because of how you see your pieces, you will naturally favor hand tools over power tools, or vice versa, but it is important you make a reasoned decision. The first step to understanding the effectiveness of a technology—in this case woodworking handplanes—is to fully understand the capabilities and limitations of the tool. That is what this book aims to accomplish.

1

SMOOTH

What to Use, When, and Why

Different tools leave different surfaces, discernible by eye, hand, or both. While the differences may be subtle, they still are often immediately recognizable. End users, in particular, can respond quite strongly, even without fully understanding why. Such subtle differences distinguish craftwork from production work and make it sought out by potential buyers, whether consciously or not, and can literally close the sale.

The handplane is unmatched in its ability to get a crisp, clean, clear surface on wood.

Figure 1-1.
The grit in sandpaper acts like a series of minute pointed scrapers, removing wood by compression failure at the points of the abrasive. It is a reliable way to smooth wood, but in some ways, it is as if you are using an uneven bed of nails. It leaves a series of erratic uneven grooves across the board, often leaves little balls of wood fiber at the end of the grooves, and tears the edges of the wood pores and fills them with dust. Clarity of the wood's grain and figure is compromised for reliability.

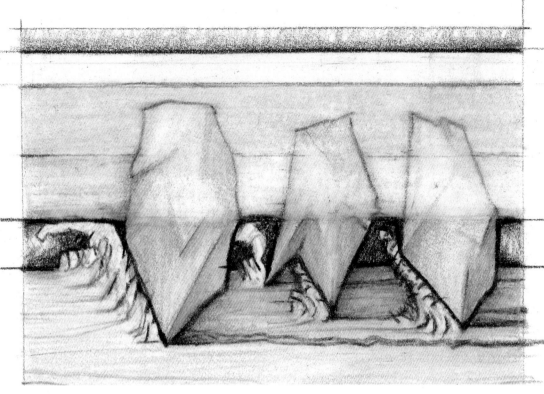

Understanding is Essential

To get to that level of finesse—of craftsmanship—the use, position, and intended finish of a piece, or parts of a piece, all will have to be considered when deciding on the best tools to use for a project. To make informed decisions, understanding the nature of the different surfaces different tools produce is essential.

The three ways to smooth wood—sanding, scraping, and planing—all leave a different kind of surface.

SANDING

Sanding abrades the surface, leaving a series of irregular microscopic grooves with slightly fuzzy edges. Sandpaper, which consists of randomly distributed abrasive particles of irregular size, shape, and orientation, tears and scrapes the wood fibers. The points and edges of the particles project and wear unevenly, cutting to different depths. The result is most noticeable when starting with coarse sandpaper and then skipping grits, because coarser grits leave deep scratches finer grits will not reach (Figure 1-1).

Sanding also leaves a myriad of microscopic torn fibers hanging onto the surface. And even though you may be meticulous, sanding thoroughly through progressive grits, you still have to sand to a grit finer than 600 to get light to penetrate the torn fibers with enough clarity to bring out the grain of a figured wood.

SCRAPING

Scraping, using the burr turned on the edge or a sharpened blade held at a high angle, tears the wood fibers as well, removing wood essentially by compression failure at the edge of the burr (Figure 1-2). The burr is a relatively blunt cutting edge that establishes a point where compression failure begins, rather than actually cutting or shearing the wood.

Hard tropical woods scrape cleanly, I suppose, because scoring the wood fibers with a blunt edge is more effective on hard, brittle wood. But the softer the species, the less cleanly the burr-edge pulls wood away, often causing the chip to collapse upon itself, while tearing the fibers from the surface being smoothed. The surface of pine, for instance, can be shaped with a scraper, but ends up fuzzy.

The big advantage the scraper has over sandpaper is that on most hardwoods, it removes wood as fast as 60-grit paper and leaves a finish like 400-grit, all with one tool that will probably last a lifetime and cost less than a single package of sandpaper.

Moreover, unlike a plane, it is virtually impossible to get any major tearout with a scraper, though on some woods the resulting fuzziness confirms surface tears. Nor is the scraper unidirectional, as some believe. It cuts better in one direction than the other, though cutting in the wrong direction does not usually result in the disastrous tearout you might get with a plane.

Both sanding and scraping leave the edges of the wood pores ragged, though technically the results are slightly different. With

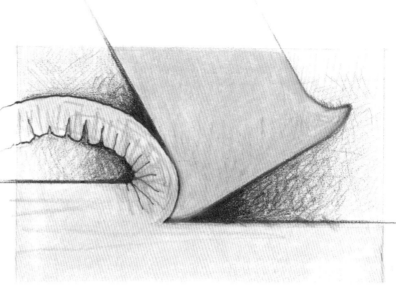

Figure 1-2. *A cabinet scraper removes wood by compression failure parallel to the grain at the edge of the burr. While it can give dependable results, a heavy cut can result in erratic failure both in front of and below the edge, snowpiling the chip and reducing the quality of the surface. Making a light cut attains best results.*

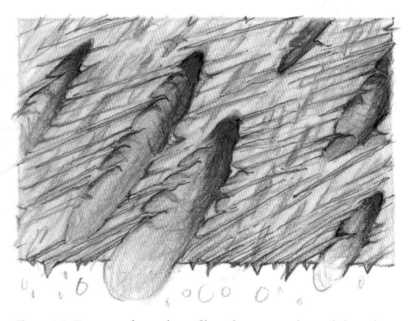

Figure 1-3. *Deep scratches and torn fibers characterize the sanded wood surface. Sanding tears fibers in the surface of wood, while scraping leaves behind fewer ragged fibers that tend to be longer.*

sanding, the last grit used determines the size of the ragged fibers. Whatever the grit, however, torn fibers are plentiful (Figure 1-3). With scraping, the ragged fibers are fewer and longer. In both cases, the fibers lie flat until finish is applied, and then stand up, swollen and stiffened with the finish.

Figure 1-4.
A handplane removes wood by shearing the fibers right at the point of its thin, sharp edge. Though the results can be less dependable (unless the cut is controlled by the methods described in Chapter 3), the remaining surface is not torn by abrasion or compression failure, revealing the beauty of the wood's grain and figure.

PLANING

A sharpened plane cuts by shearing the fibers off cleanly. The lower the angle of the cut, the cleaner the shear; the higher the angle, the more the blade scrapes. The shearing cut is clean—the surface is not torn by abrasion or compression failure—and light penetrates the surface structure, refracting through the changes in direction of the wood grain, and revealing the dazzling beauty of the wood's figure (Figure 1-4).

The surface, however, deserves further consideration. Most woods display wonderful clarity with a little raggedness at the end of the pores (Figure 1-5). The residue rises when applying finish and stiffens when it dries, resulting in a rough surface. Removing the tails to achieve a smooth surface creates a conundrum: in order to get the smoothest surface you must risk compromising clarity by lightly roughing it up.

ADDING FINISH

There are a couple of ways to approach the issue. The first is to consider the planned finish. *Penetrating finishes*, such as oil, raise the grain less and bring out the figure of the grain more than surface finishes.

On some woods, vigorous application and removal of the oil eliminates the tails, especially if the last step is buffing with a wool rag.

Some woods require rubbing with steel wool after the first or second coat of oil. Steel wool hooks the hanging fibers and pulls them off. Polish some surfaces by rubbing them hard with shavings before applying oil.

I go over broad and/or horizontal surfaces, after planing to a fine finish and applying the first coat of oil, with 1000-grit or finer sandpaper, working either wet or dry for the second coat. The grade of sandpaper I use may vary according to the type of oil I am using and other factors.

Surface finishes, such as varnish or lacquer, do not bring out the figure as well as oil for two reasons: (1) the finish does not penetrate as deeply and (2) light must travel through a thickness of film before striking the wood and bouncing back through again. The clean shear you get from planing is muted, and, therefore, probably less critical. I have also had feedback from finishers that (in one case anyway) the plane left the surface too smooth without enough tooth for the finish to adhere.

To prepare for a heavy surface finish, such as brushed varnish, catalyzed varnish and lacquer, or nitrocellulose lacquer, my general procedure is to remove the machining marks, snipe, and such with a plane. If the plane leaves minor tearout, I remove it with a card scraper. If the project or parts of it (such as shelving) are less sensitive—and especially if the wood is difficult—I may remove the mill marks with a handled scraper, such as the Stanley 80, followed by the card scraper.

A handled scraper is faster than sanding through three or four grits of sandpaper. I follow the planing (or scraping) with a quick, light pass with 220-grit sandpaper to even out any minor irregularities or any traces of the plane or scraper. If the finish is to be shellac, I will follow the planing (and scraping if necessary) with 320- or 400-grit sandpaper. (Follow that procedure for shellac applications except for French polishing, which has its own set of procedures.)

Shellac does not seem to flow out as well as lacquer, even when applied thickly or repeatedly. Shellac seems to benefit from extra sanding. The catalyzed finishes flow out wonderfully and cover a multitude of sins. Unfortunately, catalyzed finishes can also make a closed-pore wood like cherry look like plastic laminate.

Figure 1-5. *Scraping often leaves a tail at the end of the wood pore the length of which varies from species to species. Planing also can sometimes result in a tail, depending on the species, but it is usually much smaller. A coat of finish raises and stiffens the tails and other irregularities, making the surface look and feel rough.*

FLAT AND SMOOTH

On broad horizontal surfaces, take special care to prepare the surface, no matter what the finish. Once the light glances across the surface, variations in flatness will literally be glaring. Sanding a horizontal surface flat will not yield satisfactory results. Belt sanders and orbital sanders used directly after power planing will result in a surface that looks like a calm pond in a slight breeze when the light reflects across it. I have found most stationary thickness sanders do not give satisfactory results, either. Only the top-end industrial sanders used to finish plywood sheets give anything close to acceptable results.

Hand planing yields flat surfaces, especially if the handplanes used are the correct size for the work. Unfortunately, large surface handplaning is one of the hardest skills to master, though the results can be quite rewarding. Using the tools, techniques, and information presented in this book can accelerate your efforts to acquire these skills. Flattening and smoothing a horizontal surface requires a series of handplanes. If tearout or minor imperfections remain, follow with one or two scrapers. Use a handled scraper, such as a scraping plane (not the Stanley 80) to maintain flatness if tearout is extensive. Use a card scraper over the whole surface for minor tearout. Usually this leaves the surface sufficiently flat and smooth so that, depending on the finish, a light sanding with 220-grit or finer is all that is needed. Often I can even skip this step and have to sand only lightly after the sealer coat of finish.

If I am not satisfied the surface is flat, I may sand using 220-grit or finer with a half-sheet sanding block to remove any slight ridges or any minor unevenness left between the cuts of the plane or scraper. The ridges or unevenness will not telegraph through visually upon completion of the finish, or physically while sanding between coats.

That is particularly important with a brushed-on varnish finish. The coats do not blend, so cutting through a coat will leave a ring, necessitating removing the finish and starting over. (You can usually avoid cutting through to minor high spots, by either hand sanding without a block, or using a soft block, after the first coat of finish.)

HANDLING EDGES

There is another often-underestimated subtle difference more than one client has pointed out to me. While the handplane leaves a surface whose visual and tactile quality is usually unsurpassed, the surface it leaves

THE CHALLENGE OF GRIT

The grit size on sandpaper refers to the maximum size contained. On most papers, up to 65% of the abrasive is smaller than the listed grit size, some quite a bit smaller. This means the scratch pattern will be inconsistent, with the listed grit size making deeper scratches than the remaining abrasive. This inconsistent scratch pattern will then have to be reduced by the inconsistent scratch pattern of the next finer grit, and so forth, until the scratch pattern is fine enough not to be easily discerned by the eye or hand. That is why you should not skip grades when sanding. Some of the new premium papers have a more consistent grit size with as much as 95% of the abrasive being of the listed size, so attaining good results should be easier.

on an arris (a corner where two faces come together) usually can be improved.

If you watch clients study pieces of furniture, they will always—consciously or not—run their hand along the edges, making the edges of a piece among its most important features. The edges can clinch the deal—or break it. Knocking the edges off with a handplane will leave a somewhat harsh, unfriendly quality to the piece, even if done with a round-blade chamfer plane. Follow the final touches of a plane with a light sanding to soften the edges, usually with 220-grit sandpaper (or finer if the chamfer was well cut). This will make the all-important edges satisfying to the touch.

SUBTLE DIFFERENCES

So *smooth* is both visual and tactile, looking and feeling differently in different places, with different results from different tools, and sometimes different results with the same tools—in different woods. How do we use that information effectively?

I have come to a number of conclusions through my experience working with planes. For one, removing a lot of wood by sanding is, in most situations, a poor and inefficient choice. Bring wood as closely as possible to its final shape and finish with a cutting edge—a plane, scraper, or power tool.

After grinding the work with abrasives, sanding with succeeding grits to eliminate the deep scratches from the coarse shaping grit is expensive and time-consuming, and raises excessive fine dust. Sandpaper's first use was as a final step in polishing the work, and at its

most aggressive, removing minor tool marks. I think that remains its best use.

Another important point: Wood shaped by abrasives, rather than by a cutting edge, results in both the shape and surface being different. The differences are subtle, but important. The cut pieces reflect the crispness of the edge used to shape them, and the sweep of the stroke the artisan used to make the cut. Sanded pieces feel and look ground down, reflecting the back-and-forth scrubbing or rotary movement of the abrasives used. The artisan must be aware of the differences and how they will affect the final product.

In summary, on a piece where you want to bring out the figure and texture (grain) of the wood—a piece that is to have no finish or only a light finish such as linseed, lemon, or tung oil, wax, or shellac—smoothing with a clean-cutting plane gives spectacular results and brings out the beauty of the wood.

With some difficult-to-plane woods, however, taking the surface all the way down to a polish with a plane can be demanding and not necessarily efficient. On some special pieces, the extra effort may be worth it. That is an individual decision.

For most work, however, leveling with a plane, smoothing (if required) with a scraper, and a final polishing with sandpaper will be the most efficient procedure. This technique is especially applicable if a heavy surface finish, such as lacquer, brushed varnish, or a catalyzed finish, is to be applied.

2

SHARP
The Cutting Edge

The blade is the heart of any plane. An exotic, expensive hardwood, or marvelously machined bronze and iron may hold it in place, but it is the blade that does the work. If the blade is not up to the job, the plane becomes more of a curious decoration than a valued tool.

The claims tool manufacturers make about their blades are often confusing and contradictory, sometimes invoking near-mystical qualities rather than offering real information. At times, the claims tout qualities applicable to industrial performance and are not meaningful to woodworkers. It was not always this way. Until about World War II, woodworkers had little choice in the material used for blades. Carbon steel was the sole option. The only question was what quality could be afforded. The purchase was often made based on the manufacturer's reputation. Today's manufacturers promote new industrial steels and processes as the next best thing. To make matters more difficult, the differences in blade quality are often subtle and hard to discern under many working conditions.

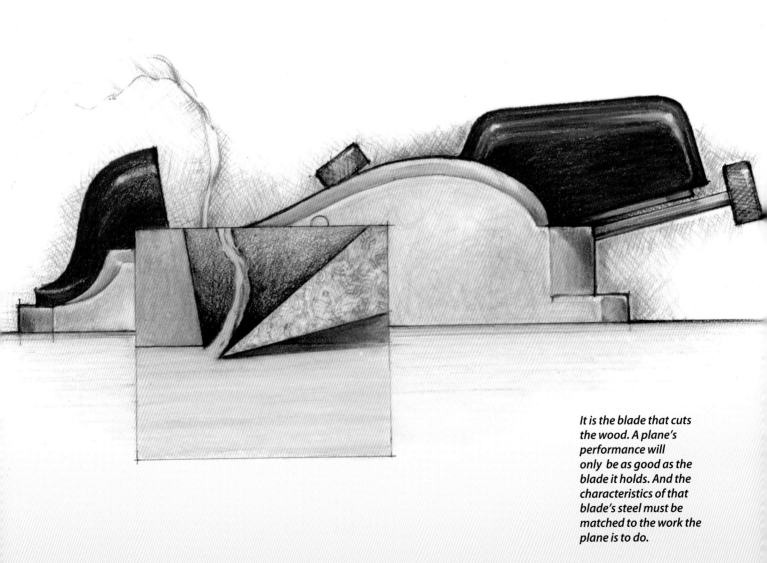

It is the blade that cuts the wood. A plane's performance will only be as good as the blade it holds. And the characteristics of that blade's steel must be matched to the work the plane is to do.

Beyond Mystique

Given such confusing information, it is tempting to ignore it, use the blade that comes with the plane, or buy the most expensive blade and hope. Doing so ignores a critical link in the chain of knowledge required to do the best woodworking.

Steel is the interface between wood and woodworker, transmitting your concepts while shaping, smoothing, and transforming the wood. The interface—concentrated at the cutting edge—and the feedback it gives you, provide invaluable input affecting the finish, fit, form, and feeling of the final product as it goes from concept to reality. Understanding the complexities of the steel used for the cutting edge helps you make decisions.

Many woodworkers have only indirect interest in blade steel. Having used a variety of blades over the years and researched the results, I have found cutting edge steel to be complex and possessed of art and nuance. Steel seems to be simple, cold, and aloof, but those qualities disguise its complexity. Mystique surrounds the making of edge steel. Despite several hundred years of industry and science, making steel into blades for cutting wood relies heavily on experience, judgment, and skill.

A blade demonstrates the effort put into its creation—be it a little or a lot. Blade steel— especially forged blade steel—is alive with energy the smith put into making it and the fire used to shape it. A woodworker should understand and appreciate the individuality of blades, learn what they do, and apply the knowledge for greatest effect.

BASIC BLADE CRITERIA

The woodworker needs the edge on the hand-tool blade to do three basic things: get sharp, stay sharp, and re-sharpen easily. The three qualities usually exist in balance with one another. Increasing one probably decreases one or both of the others. In many applications, one quality may be most important, so understanding the strengths and weaknesses of different steels is valuable.

There are additional considerations when selecting a blade. The first is the type of wood being cut. Softwoods and some softer hardwoods prefer an edge that is thin and sharp. Only some steels can get really sharp, to a thinner bevel, and still hold an edge. As the wood gets harder, however, the steel's toughness becomes more important. Secondly, edge requirements vary with the job. A blade required to remove a lot of wood needs an edge that holds up well under heat build-up and impact.

SHARPENING VERSUS RE-SHARPENING

I use *re-sharpen* here rather than *sharpen* because re-sharpen properly evokes the time and repetition involved that the other two words do not. I believe many woodworkers (myself included) do not keep their blades sharp enough, and I want to encourage them to change their habits. Many woodworkers believe sharpening is like cleaning the house: do it once and you are good for the week, or at least for the next few days. However, in reality, if you are using your plane all day, you will need to re-sharpen many times that day. Re-sharpening becomes the nuisance chore that keeps you from doing woodworking until it is done. *Easy* has a different meaning when it is done twenty times (or more) a week instead of just once.

Anatomy of Steel

The key to understanding edge steel is in its anatomy. I approach the anatomy of steel as a woodworker. The metallurgist or machinist will see things differently. For the needs of the woodworker, three characteristics define steel's anatomy—grain, structure, and hardness.

GRAIN

For woodworking hand tools, the grain of the steel is the most important characteristic of a blade. Ordered, repetitive arrangements of iron and alloy atoms in a crystalline structure comprise steel. The crystals can be small and fine or large and coarse. They can be consistent in size (evenly grained) or vary widely, with odd shapes and outsized clusters in among the rest. The steel's grain affects how finely the blade sharpens and how quickly it dulls. Generally, the finer and more consistent the grain, the more finely it sharpens, the slower it dulls, and the better the blade performs.

Grain is a function of the initial quality of the steel used, the alloys added, and how the steel is worked or formed. In addition to the average size of the crystals, the initial quality of the steel may include impurities, called *inclusions*, which may persist throughout refining. Inclusions add large irregularities to the grain. Irregularities sometimes are used to good effect in swords and perhaps axes, but except for the backing steel on laminated blades, impurities are a detriment to a plane blade. Sharpening impurities out

to the edge causes them to break off easily, causing chipping and rapid dulling of the edge. The dirtier the steel, the more rapidly it dulls. This fine chipping will not affect the performance of an edge used for chopping wood. Depending on the inclusion, it can add tensile, shock-resisting strength to the blade. But for fine woodworking, such as planing a surface, even fine inclusions prevent sharpening the blade fully and shorten the edge's life.

Alloys change the texture of the grain. They may be part of the steel's original composition (though usually in small amounts), or added in a recipe to increase the steel's resistance to shock and heat. Alloys often coarsen the grain, so there is a trade-off. While the edge of an alloy blade may be more durable, especially under adverse working conditions, it may not sharpen as well as an unalloyed blade. To shear wood cleanly, no other attribute of an edge is more important than fineness.

STRUCTURE

Structure, the second most important aspect of a woodworking blade, results from changes in the original composition of the steel due to heating it and changing its shape with a hammer (or rollers), often called *hot work*.

Heat causes the crystals of the steel to grow. Hammering steel when it is hot causes its crystalline structures to fracture and impedes growth as the grains fracture into smaller crystals. Before being hot-worked, the crystals of steel are randomly oriented, and frequently inconsistent in size.

Through forging (repeatedly re-shaping with a hammer while the steel is hot), the grain aligns and knits together in the direction of the metal flow. Proper forging increases grain structure consistency. When exposed at the edge through sharpening, crystals consistent in size and orientation break off one at a time as the blade dulls, rather than breaking off randomly in big clumps. The consistency of the crystals allows for a sharper blade that stays sharp longer.

The techniques used in preparing steel for woodworking tools are hammer forging, drop forging, and no forging. Hammer forging, where repeated hammer blows shape the steel, is the most desirable because it aligns the grain particles (or crystals) of the steel. It is a time-consuming, skillful process and therefore expensive. If improperly done, hammer forging stresses the steel, reducing, rather than increasing, reliability. With the general decline in hand-woodworking skills during the last century, and the increased reliance on power tools, the discriminating market that would appreciate the difference forging makes has shrunk considerably. As a result, hand-forged tools are not commonly manufactured or available in the United States.

Drop forging verges on die cutting. A large mechanized hammer called the punch drops on the heated blank, smashing it into a die (mold), giving the tool blade its rough shape, often in just one blow. For tools that vary considerably in cross-section, this method may be more desirable than grinding

THE IDEAL EDGE

The edge requirements for cutting different materials vary widely. The most obvious example is the edge required on a kitchen knife. Meat and vegetables are cut by the sawing action of drawing a coarse edge through them. The sawing action of drawing a coarse edge through meat and vegetables cuts them. A properly sharpened kitchen knife has what under a microscope would look like a series of small saw teeth, which result from sharpening it with an 800- or 1200-grit stone. If you are skeptical, sharpen your best kitchen knife with a #8000 stone and try to cut a potato. It will stop cutting halfway through and jam. While the knife is sharp enough to cut transparent shavings in wood, it will not cut halfway through a root vegetable. The lesson is that demonstrations of sharpness using other materials and claims of qualities originating in other trades and uses, such as industry or surgery, are not particularly useful in evaluating a woodworking blade.

Conceptually, for a blade to be perfect for woodworking, it must be possible to polish it down to single-crystal uniformity across its entire edge, with the crystals all lined up neatly, oriented the same direction, all very small and of the same size, equally hard, and tightly bonded to one another so they will not break off. In reality, several types of crystals comprise a cutting edge. The crystals are greatly different in size and hardness and grouped together so they tend to present themselves at the cutting edge, and break off in clusters, leaving voids and dull spots. The finest blades, however, have the qualities that enable something approaching the ideal edge.

or cutting from stock because the heat of grinding or cutting can cause some minor negative alteration in the grain structure at those areas. Drop forging imparts a marginally more consistent structure than a blade cut or ground from stock, because the steel often elongates in the process resulting in some improvement in the crystalline structure alignment.

Drop forging is preferable to no forging at all when shaping is done by grinding bar stock. No forging is an oversimplification because all tool steel receives some hot work during reshaping. Bar stock is hot-formed by rolling or extruding the ingot into lengths of consistent cross section. The process rearranges the crystalline structure and the crystals tend to align in the direction of the flow as the steel lengthens.

The arrangement is not very refined compared with the structure resulting when steel is hot-worked further at the forge. Modern Western chisel blades are frequently drop-forged (though some new premium chisels are being ground from A2 bar stock). Modern Western plane blades, even many after-market premium blades, are usually ground from unworked, rolled stock.

HARDNESS

Hardness is a major selling point in the advertising of woodworking tools. However, as explained earlier, grain and structure are the most important factors in the performance of a blade. A plane blade soft enough to shape with a file (for instance, made from a piece of a good old handsaw blade) will give excellent

'KEEPING THE CUTTING EDGE' ON DISSTON SAWS

"Disston saw steel was heat treated in the plant and was harder than competitive saws. We rolled our own saw sheets on a sheet mill so we could control the direction of grain within a sheet, enabling us to set the teeth at that hardness without their breaking. Disston saws were of a hardness that read 52–54 on the Rockwell C scale, and competitive saws were 46–48—about 10–15% softer than Disston's. They did not know the secret of how to roll a new saw sheet so the teeth would not break during setting at that hardness"

From a letter written by Bill Disston, great-grandson of Henry Disston, to Harold Payson, as excerpted in Payson's book, *Keeping the Cutting Edge: Setting and Sharpening Hand and Power Saws* (Wooden Boat Books, 1988).

results if the fineness of its grain allows it to be sharpened well and its structure allows the edge to break off finely and evenly. I knew a boat builder who preferred plane blades made from good quality saw blades. The blades made it easy for him to file out nicks when his plane hit unexpected metal in the boat structure.

At the other end of the hardness spectrum is carbide, used on power tool blades. Hard and brittle, carbide is unsuitable for the body of the tool blade because it would shatter. While carbide is extremely hard, the particles are also extremely large. They do not break off easily, but when they do, they break off in clumps so big they are nearly visible to the naked eye. Carbide also cannot be made nearly as sharp as steel. A sharp steel saw or router blade cuts much more cleanly than a sharp carbide blade. Unfortunately, the steel dulls quicker than the carbide, especially when subjected to the glues in plywood and particleboard.

HARDENING, TEMPERING, AND ANNEALING

The hardness and ductility (the extent to which it can be stretched or bent without breaking) of steel depends on its exact carbon-to-iron ratio and its thermal processing. Different temperatures are associated with different crystal structures, or *phases*, of the iron and carbon atoms. When steel with a carbon content above 0.4% (the minimum amount required for steel to harden) is heated beyond its *critical temperature* of around 750°C, it enters what is called the *austenite phase*. Austenite has a crystal structure that opens to allow the carbon atoms present to combine with the iron.

When austenite is cooled quickly (by quenching), its structure changes to a needlelike crystalline form called *martensite*. Martensite locks in the carbon atom, *hardening* the steel. In this state, the steel is at its hardest and is under a great deal of internal stress and brittle. The more carbon the steel had to begin with, the more of it will be martensite and the harder it will be. As the carbon goes over 0.8%, however, the steel does not become any harder, but rather grows more brittle. In order for the steel to be usable as a blade, it must be softened to reduce the brittleness to a workable degree. This process is called *tempering*.

Tempering is a compromise, meant to balance hardness and ductility, and is definitely a judgment call made by the one doing the tempering, based both on experience and the intended use of the blade. To temper a blade, after hardening, the blade is reheated, this time to a lower temperature, perhaps 175°C (depending on the type of steel and the blade's intended use), and quenched again.

There is a third process, done after the blade has been hot-worked to shape, but before hardening and tempering, and that is *annealing*. Here the blade is heated red hot and allowed to cool *without* quenching. This softens the blade and removes stresses that may have resulted from its being hot-worked. Usually at this point, the blade is then ground to final (or near final) shape—easily done, since it is now soft—and then hardened and finally tempered.

Hardness must be in balance with intended tool use. High-impact hand tools should be softer than plane blades. Otherwise, the edge fractures quickly under hard use. Blades for fine work can be very hard, but if their hardness exceeds the ability of the steel to flex without breaking at the microscopic edge, the tool will be next to worthless.

The Rockwell C (Rc) scale measures the hardness of woodworking blades. This is a unit of measurement determined by the impact of a ball-shaped point into the steel, measured in terms of the depth of the resulting impression. Japanese saws (harder than Western saws) are roughly in the 50–58 Rc range. This is on the cusp of what a file will cut. Decent plane and chisel blades are in the range of 58–66 Rc range.

Only some finely wrought steels work effectively in the upper-half of this range, principally high-quality hand-forged Japanese blades, and some high-alloy steels. In carbon steels, Rc 66 seems to be a limit above which the edge breaks down too rapidly in use.

In summary, grain, structure, and hardness are the characteristics of tool steel important to the woodworker using hand tools. Other tool users may emphasize other characteristics—primarily because they are working in other materials or using other methods. The cutting of wood fibers is a very particular application with very specific requirements. The right combination of grain, structure, and hardness—and method— provides good results.

Types of Edge Steel

Steel for hand tool blades can be roughly divided into two categories: carbon steel and alloyed steel. All tool steels contain carbon, which makes it possible to harden the metal. Processed from iron and iron ore, carbon steel contains at least 0.5% carbon and traces of other elements. Alloyed steel is carbon steel with small amounts of other elements added to improve performance under certain conditions and for specific uses.

Steel manufacturers have specific guidelines for nomenclature with regard to the percentages of alloys used. Manufacturers of woodworking tools, have no such guidelines and may at their discretion emphasize or de-emphasize any or all included alloys and their relative amounts, depending on what they may think is most marketable. Focusing on the commercial or idiomatic names of blade steel helps clarify the nature of the various steels and reduce confusion.

CARBON STEEL

Carbon steel is the longstanding workhorse for manufacturing hand tools for woodworking. Carbon steel's qualities ideally meet the demands of hand tools for woodworking. When manufactured properly, carbon steel sharpens optimally, holds a sharp edge, and re-sharpens easily—the three basic requirements of a woodworking blade. In addition, its manufacture can be varied slightly to accommodate different woodworking tasks. Many variations exist, based mostly on the quality of ingredients and manufacture, how much it has been

ALLOY INGREDIENTS

Carbon added to iron makes it harder and more wear resistant. Carbon content of about 0.5% to 0.6% is about the lowest amount found in tool steel. This low-carbon steel is used for hammers, blacksmith tools, etc. A carbon content of about 0.8% makes a steel file hard (about Rc 56-58). Carbon above that level does not increase the steel's hardness, but raises its wear resistance. A carbon content of 1.3% is about the highest. This highest-carbon steel is used for razors, engraving tools, etc. A carbon content of about 1.05% is a good average—hard with good wear resistance, yet not fussy or sensitive to heat.

Tungsten, added in small quantities, can impart a tight, small, dense grain structure and the ability to attain a keen cutting edge. It enables steel to retain its hardness at higher temperatures but is detrimental to the steel's forgeability. A tungsten content of 4% (with 1.3% carbon) is so hard it is difficult to grind with an emery wheel.

Manganese makes steel sound when first cast into ingots, and easier to hot roll or forge. Practically all tool steel has at least 0.2% of manganese. Steel can contain up to 0.5% manganese before it is considered alloy steel.

Silicon facilitates casting and hot work. It is usually used in combination with manganese, molybdenum, or chromium. All steel has 0.1% to 0.3% silicon. Steel with 0.5% to 2% silicon content is considered an alloy.

Chromium increases the hardness penetration of the steel. A thick bar of plain carbon steel will be hardened to a depth of only ³⁄₁₆" (5mm) from its face during heat treatment. Adding chromium allows the bar to harden all of the way through. But, because most hand tool blades are less than ⅜" (10mm) thick, this not really an issue for woodworkers. Chromium increases the steel's wear resistance under impact and heat, but does not necessarily increase its hardness. Steel with chromium content of 4% and higher is called high-speed steel.

hot-worked, and what incidental alloys may be included. The quantity of alloys present may be more than incidental and not mentioned because the hand tool manufacturer has decided to present its steel or allow it to be perceived as carbon steel. Lumped into this general category are a number of types you will encounter commercially. Besides plain high-carbon steel, you will encounter (among others) *white steel*, *blue steel*, and *cast steel*.

White and blue steel are associated with Japanese tools. They derive their name from the color of the identifying paper label applied by the steel maker (usually Hitachi). Both have carbon in the 1% to 1.4% range with 0.1% to 0.2% silica and 0.2% to 0.3% manganese. *Blue paper steels* additionally have 0.2 % to 0.5% chromium and 1% to 1.5% tungsten, with up to 2.25% tungsten in the *super blue steel*. The tungsten makes the blue steel harder to forge but increases its wear resistance when cutting difficult woods. On the other hand, adding tungsten

Figure 2-1. *A cast steel blade is usually marked* Cast Steel *or* Warranted Cast Steel.

widens the critical temperature range needed for hardening the steel, and makes this step a little easier for the blacksmith. In contrast, some white steels are fussy about their hardening temperatures. White steel is easier to sharpen, and takes the keen edge necessary for soft woods.

The difference between white and blue steel is not very obvious. A Japanese woodworker I know makes an enlightened distinction between the two. He describes white steel as having a sharp, angular grain structure, and blue steel as having smaller, rounded grains. This allows the white steel to be sharpened a nuance sharper but under harsh conditions or with difficult woods, white steel's grain structure breaks off a little quicker and in slightly larger clumps.

For that reason, dealers often recommend blue steel for working hard, abrasive, or difficult tropical woods. I think it is worth noting that Japanese blacksmiths seem to be increasing production of blue steel tools, at least for the U.S. market. The increase may be because blue steel is more tolerant of minor misuse than white steel and workers with less skill are more likely to misuse their tools.

Cast steel, also called crucible steel, is high-quality steel made in small tightly controlled batches, an expensive process developed in Europe and America when producing quality steel was more of a craft than a manufacturing method. Over the years, as production methods improved, ever larger, cheaper, and more consistent batches of steel became possible. As the number of demanding craftsmen dropped, along with

Figure 2-2. *A polished bevel on a cast-steel blade reveals the lamination of the two steels; the dark area across the edge of the blade at left is the edge steel, while the lighter area is the softer backing steel. At right is an unlaminated modern blade ground from bar stock.*

their market, particularly during the Great Depression, so, too, did the necessity for cast steel. With World War II and a changing world economy, cast steel all but disappeared and is now produced in only very small quantities (Figure 2-1).

With its fine grain, cast steel takes and holds an edge far superior to most steels available today. Its qualities seem ideally suited to the demands of fine woodworking as it developed in the West prior to World War II, though its attributes can be appreciated by demanding and discerning craftsman today. I take every opportunity to replace my modern blades with blades made of cast steel.

The edge steel of Japanese and cast-steel blades is too hard, susceptible to shock, prone to cracking during use, and expensive to use alone in a blade. Instead of compromising the edge's hardness by tempering the steel, a thin layer of it is forge-welded (laminated) to softer steel that has more tensile strength. The combination is better able to absorb shock without breaking (Figure 2-2).

Backing steel is low in carbon, softer, and more flexible. Impurities in backing

Figure 2-3. *The traditional Japanese blade is always laminated with hard edge steel and softer backing steel. If you look closely at the backing steel here, you can see some layering and variations that reveal its handworked origins.*

steel can be an advantage. For instance, in Japan before the mid-nineteenth century, smelting techniques allowed the inclusion of impurities, which in the grain structure appear as strands, similar to the glass in Fiberglass. The impurity increased the steel's flexibility and resistance to breaking—both desirable qualities.

Because the smelting process improved after the 1850s, steel produced since then lacks the impurities. Scrap iron produced earlier is highly coveted by Japanese blacksmiths who stockpile such treasures as pre-1850 anchor chain for future use as backing steel for the edge steel in laminated blades (Figure 2-3).

Another option is plain carbon steel blades, usually cut from bar stock as it comes from the manufacturer, with no additional hot work done to improve its structure. Plain carbon blades will probably offer disappointing performance. In addition, while many premium after-market blades advertise a higher degree of hardness than competitors, unless the blades are forged, they will not have the improved grain structure resulting from additional hot work (Figure 2-4).

Figure 2-4. *I thought these blades from a set of planes from Thailand were low quality, cut from bar stock, until I sharpened one of them and saw the lamination. They have given good service, though the chipbreaker was not usable.*

ALLOY STEEL

Alloy steel was developed by and for industry, mostly in the mid-twentieth century, to cost-effectively produce large numbers of precisely engineered parts as might be used in cars—and nearly everything else we use now. I suspect the demands of World Wars I and II speeded development of these steels. While an alloy steel blade can be useful in some handplanes and woodworking hand tools, makers use cheaper mass-manufacturing processes mostly to imitate (with generally limited success) the quality blades previously achieved through skilled hot work of high-quality carbon steel.

Carbon steel has shortcomings in industrial production. It hardens only to a depth of about 3/16" (5mm). Pieces of thick cross section do not harden all of the way through and their internal structure remains different from their surface structure. The differences compromise virtually any large machine application. As well, the hardening process to produce this less-than-adequate structure requires quenching the red-hot steel in cold water.

The shock of quenching usually distorts the object, and is at least unpredictable. If, after considerable time and effort milling a piece precisely to within a tolerance of several thousandths of an inch, the product is rendered unusable. Lastly, when carbon steel is used for cutting tools to make other objects, especially out of metal or steel themselves, the speed of the cutter (or the object in relation to the cutter, as on a lathe) will overheat the blade, soften it, and cause it to lose its cutting ability within seconds.

Eliminating Problems

Industry discovered adding small amounts of alloys eliminated many problems. The addition of chromium, for instance, allows steel of large cross-section to be hardened all the way through. Chromium and other alloys also produce steel that can be hardened in an oil bath, which is less shocking than water, and thus reduces dimensional distortion.

Even better, some combinations of alloys allow the steel to harden in air, a slower, less-shocking process resulting in virtually no distortion. Many alloys produce steel that can be red hard; that is, even when heated by the friction of the cut to red hot, the steel will not lose its hardness, obviously very desirable in the manufacture of metal-cutting tools.

Eventually, a large number of recipes evolved to produce different steels for a variety of conditions. However, as the requirements of manufacturing metal parts for cars are different from those for woodworking hand tools, few alloy steels are useful to woodworkers. A small number are worth considering.

FORGEABILTY

Because they remain hard while red hot, many alloy steels cannot be hot-worked (forged) or are forged only with great difficulty, and must be ground to shape. Many of the varieties, though, would not benefit from being forged.

Grain Structure

The main difficulty when deciding whether to use alloyed steel is adding alloys usually coarsens the steel's grain and structure. Cutting wood cleanly and efficiently requires a fine blade edge. Coarsening the grain and structure of a handtool blade reduces its effectiveness. Casual use of the few alloy steels used in hand tool blades will not show much difference between them and unalloyed blades. However, there is a difference more obvious in some woods and applications that suggests the blades have special usefulness different from unalloyed carbon-steel blades.

Alloy steels are particularly suited for hard-use conditions. While they may not get as keen an edge as a finely wrought carbon-steel blade, their capacity for keeping their edge is excellent. As a result, they are a viable choice for spokeshaves, jack planes, and carpentry chisels, where the stress of deep, repetitive cuts, grit, adhesives, and impact all take a toll on the edge. The steel can be a good choice for versatile tools such as the block plane, which may chamfer edges, remove glue, shape the edges of plywood, and smooth various surfaces, all on the same project.

Because alloyed steels cannot achieve the sharpness of carbon steel, I believe they are more suited to harder hardwoods, particularly tropicals, than to softwoods and softer hardwoods. Softwoods require a keen edge, though as the types of wood being worked increase in hardness and density, the importance of edge toughness increases. Tropical hardwoods require a combination of keenness and toughness in equal proportions.

Sharpening Methods

As to the third requirement for woodworking hand tool blades—being easy to re-sharpen—alloyed steels can be difficult and require different sharpening methods, increasingly so as the alloy content grows. The greater the alloy content, the less effective are water and oilstones, necessitating a diamond stone or paste. The technique and the amount of time is about the same once the different abrasives are employed

Some of the more common alloy steels woodworkers encounter are chrome vanadium, tungsten vanadium, O1, and A2. In the latter two, the *O* stands for *oil hardening*, the *A* for *air hardening*. O1 and A2 are two of only a few oil- and air-hardening steels that actually have an O or A in their name. The numbers complete the name of that particular steel.

Chrome vanadium and tungsten vanadium often are clearly marked on German plane blades. Occasionally, you find the blades of Stanley/Bailey-style planes marked as containing one of these vanadium alloys.

Both chrome vanadium and tungsten vanadium are workhorses, not given to much subtlety, but proving quite durable. They are well suited to the heavy work horned planes often perform. While chrome vanadium and tungsten vanadium are suitable for many miscellaneous tasks around the shop, both are coarser grained, making fine, tearout-free shavings in many woods difficult to achieve (Figure 2-5).

A2 steel blades have gained prominence as the apparent answer to the desire of manufacturers for affordable quality and consistency, and the woodworker's interest in satisfactory performance. A2 steel is more finely grained than chrome vanadium and tungsten vanadium blades, and rivals their durability.

Figure 2-5. *Blades of alloyed steel are often marked, but not consistently so.*

Cryogenics

Additionally, higher-end A-2 blades are cryogenically treated. In theory, the cryogenic process hardens the blade similar to heat-treating by causing the growth of carbides (crystals that cause steel to harden), but without enlarging the crystal structure, as can happen during heat treatment.

Actual evidence this is happening is inconclusive, and anecdotal evidence from woodworkers suggests it is difficult to tell any difference between cryogenically treated and untreated blades.

Regardless of whether they are cryogenically treated or not, the sharpenability of the blades varies by manufacturer. I have one blade I sharpen on waterstones, while another requires diamond stones. You will have to discover what works best for your blades (Figure 2-6).

A2 blades promise performance across a spectrum of tasks and difficult woods, and may become the new industry standard. Aiming toward a least common denominator, however, compromises performance at both ends of the spectrum.

Fine smoothing in softwoods and many hardwoods is not as effective with an A2 blade because it does not take a small bevel well, and a blade with higher alloy content better handles heavy work in tropical hardwoods.

Figure 2-6. *Blades of A2 steel are usually marked. The one at left was cryogenically treated and is labeled as such.*

O1 tool steel is another alloy blade now available. O1 has one-tenth the chromium of A2. I have not worked with O1. I suspect its lower chromium content makes it easier to sharpen and probably (depending on quality) will take a keener edge than A2. Because it has some tungsten and vanadium in it, it will probably show greater endurance in shaping tasks than carbon steel.

I have tungsten vanadium blades in my jack planes and A2 in my block planes, and they perform well. I have a high-alloy blade in my Chinese smoothing plane, which has a high cutting angle that's effective for tropical hardwoods. For my best smoothing planes, from which I expect tearout-free performance, I prefer a good quality hand-forged carbon blade.

Figure 2-7. *The blade from this small Chinese-style plane at left is high-speed steel, as is the blade from the finger plane next to it. The traditional-style blade at right has a piece of high-alloy steel brazed on the end of a longer blank.*

Changing Market

I believe the increased use of alloy steels was the hand-tool manufacturers' response to a changing market. To a casual user, the qualities of an alloy blade mimic those of good carbon-steel blade, without the difficult and expensive handwork in carefully controlled steps its manufacture requires.

To a professional using a plane every day for hours, the differences are more apparent. The industry's largest market for hand tools is now the occasional user, who is typically less skilled than a professional of 100 years ago. A chrome vanadium blade is much more tolerant of abuse such as crashing your plane into a knot, planing lesser quality or dirty wood, or jabbing the stroke, the technique of an inexperienced woodworker that subjects the blade to rapid heat build-up and edge flex.

While alloy-steel blades will not get as sharp as good carbon-steel blades, they also will not lose their edge as rapidly under these conditions and require less sharpening. The fact alloy-steel will not get as sharp as a good carbon-steel is, unfortunately, not a consideration for a large number of woodworkers today, and, more unfortunately, a quality that many may not even notice.

HIGH-SPEED STEEL

Further yet out on the scale of alloy steels is high-speed steel (HSS), which has chromium, vanadium, tungsten, and others (but mainly chromium) added in relatively high percentages. HSS is essentially the same steel used in drill and other power-driven bits, and is very hard and tough. Industry originally developed HSS to work at red-hot temperatures while remaining hard enough to maintain its cutting edge.

For the woodworker, there are two main problems with the use of HSS, the same problems associated with the alloy steels, only multiplied several times over.

The first is the difficulty in sharpening. While alloy steels are difficult to hone on the more common sharpening stone, HSS is next to impossible. A diamond stone or diamond paste is a necessity, which is more a nuisance than a problem.

The second problem with HSS is it does not get as sharp as carbon steel or even alloy steel. The grain of HSS is coarser than alloy steel—so it has limitations.

HSS has found favor among woodturners. A lathe tool, especially when aggressively used, can build up a lot of heat, causing a carbon-steel blade edge to degrade fast. However, arguments in favor of both steels exist here as well. A carbon-steel tool used with rhythm and sensitivity at the lathe will be sharper starting out, and will shear cleaner longer than a HSS tool. Developing and maintaining a more refined technique (shearing rather than scraping, in this case) in order to produce higher quality work using more finely suited tools is the challenge all woodworkers face as they advance in the craft.

I also have seen modern Chinese-style planes use HSS blades. The blades in other traditional Chinese planes also appear to have high alloy content. HSS blades are used with rosewoods and other difficult woods because the cutting action of most Chinese-style planes, with their steeply bedded blade, is more like scraping. Coupled with the heat generated by the hardness and abrasive quality of the woods, HSS is a logical choice (Figure 2-7).

The woodworker must decide if, for a particular task, the sharpness of HSS is adequate. In my experience, there are a limited number of such tasks. Once you have experienced the true sharpness of a finely made blade, it is difficult to take a step down to anything less.

The option to choose a blade of one type of steel or another is one of the great advantages woodworkers have today. Understanding the qualities of each in the face of contradictory claims and explanations allows us to choose one over another and expedite the work. Knowledge and practice allows us to match the blade to the tool and the tool to the work.

3

PLANE ANATOMY
Tactics for Achieving Best Performance

Over centuries, literally hundreds of planes were developed to speed specialized tasks. Even bench planes, used to create the flat faces and straight edges of wood parts, evolved through scores of variations intended to increase productivity. As different cultures pursued different solutions to common woodworking problems, some proved more successful than others. Though the planes may look different, they do share a common anatomy. Understanding the anatomical similarities and differences, both individually and in combination, is key to getting the most out of your handplane.

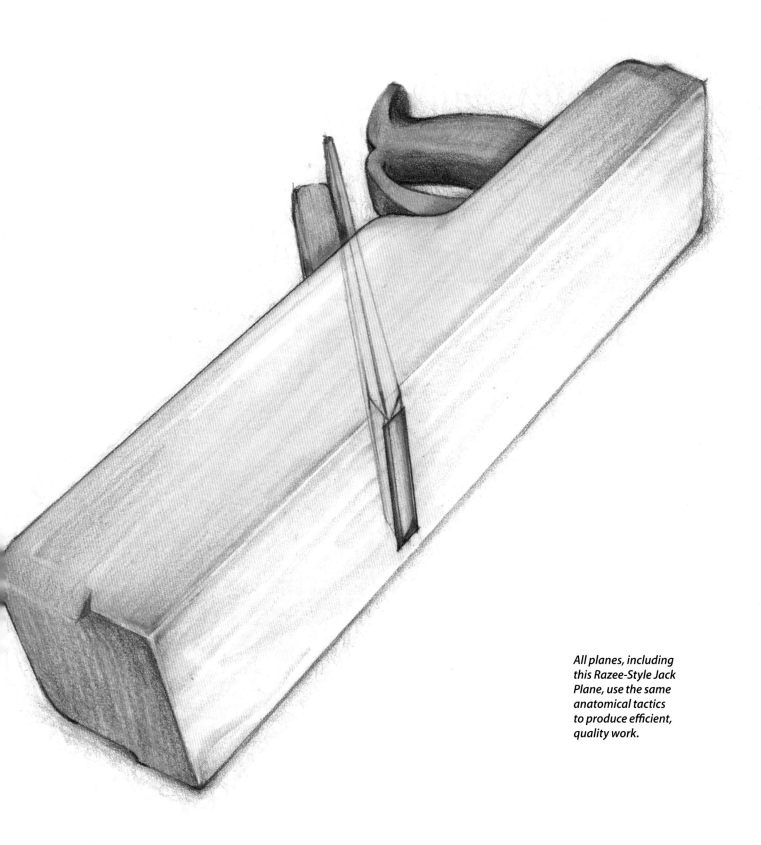

All planes, including this Razee-Style Jack Plane, use the same anatomical tactics to produce efficient, quality work.

Chapter 3 discusses the anatomy of handplanes in detail—and the tactics for optimal quality and efficiency they make possible—both individually and in their interaction with one another. Later chapters demonstrate how these tactics traditionally were employed in various combinations to dimension, join, and smooth lumber by using the jack, jointer, and smoothing planes; their use in other types of planes; and how a modern user can put his or her own combination of tactics together to achieve fast and effective results.

HOW TO USE THIS CHAPTER

The information throughout this book should serve beginner and experienced woodworkers alike. For some beginners, however, this chapter might be too much information. Glance over it and absorb what you can.

If it seems too much, rather than risk frustration, it may be better to set up your plane as best you can, following the basic guidelines set out in the following chapter on bench planes, and begin work. After you have used your plane for a while, Chapter 3 will make more sense, and you will be better able to apply its advice. You will have to read Chapter 3 eventually, because the information here is fundamental to setting up, tuning, modifying, and troubleshooting your plane.

THE TACTICS

For most of the twentieth century, woodworkers were mostly limited to the Stanley-style handplane (originally patented by Leonard Bailey). Options have increased, allowing us to buy or even construct planes that make possible combinations of tactics that most effectively suit our work. With some variations in approach, these same tactics are used in handplanes across the spectrum of woodworking, in all cultures. The core tactics for effective performance involve six common anatomical features:

1. **Angle of the blade to the work.** Using planes with blade angles suited to the wood or task increases reliability and efficiency.

2. **Clearance of the mouth through which the shaving passes.** Little understood and often abused, a suitable mouth opening controls, if not eliminates, tearout.

3. **The use of a chipbreaker.** A recent invention that nearly eliminates tearout while increasing a plane's versatility.

4. **Angle of the blade's bevel.** An incorrect blade bevel angle causes many headaches.

5. **Shape of the blade edge.** The re-sharpened edge of a plane's blade is not always straight—in fact, it seldom is.

6. **Length of the plane body and width of the blade.** The two have a relationship to each other and define a plane's intended use.

The Angle of the Blade

To be more accurate, the *angle of the blade* (Figure 3-1) should be called the *angle of the cutting edge*. It is the angle at which the cutting edge is presented to the work. On blades with the bevel down toward the work, it is the angle of the blade as positioned in the plane. On blades with the bevel up, it is the bedding angle plus the angle of the bevel (Figure 3-2).

Most woodworkers take this aspect of the handplane for granted because it is built into the plane and the availability of new planes with different blade angles has been limited.

The response of different woods to different blade angles is not necessarily pronounced, except with extremely hard and extremely soft woods. For many woodworkers, the Bailey plane with its blade angle of 45° will be satisfactory for most work. Move from the middling ground to demanding projects in difficult woods, and matching the blade angle to the work becomes a powerful asset.

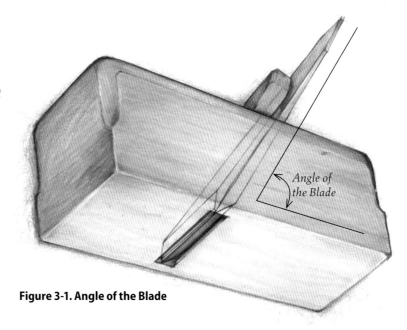

Figure 3-1. Angle of the Blade

TRADITIONAL BLADE ANGLES

Looking at traditional tools, beyond the Stanley/Bailey-style handplanes commonly available, you can see that using planes with different blade angles (or *pitch*, as it is called in Britain) was a common practice. Variations in blade angles among traditional tools are large and obvious, within the tradition of a particular culture and from culture to culture.

For instance, the difference in blade angles between a classic Chinese furniture plane and a traditional Japanese carpenter's plane, is striking, and very unlike the 45° blade angle

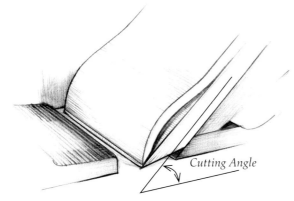

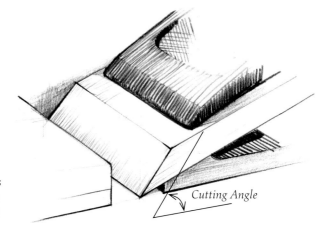

Figure 3-2. *The cutting angle is the angle that the cutting edge presents to the work. On blades with the bevel down (above), it is the angle of the blade in the plane (the bedding angle). On blades with the bevel up, it is the angle of the blade in the plane plus the angle of the bevel (right).*

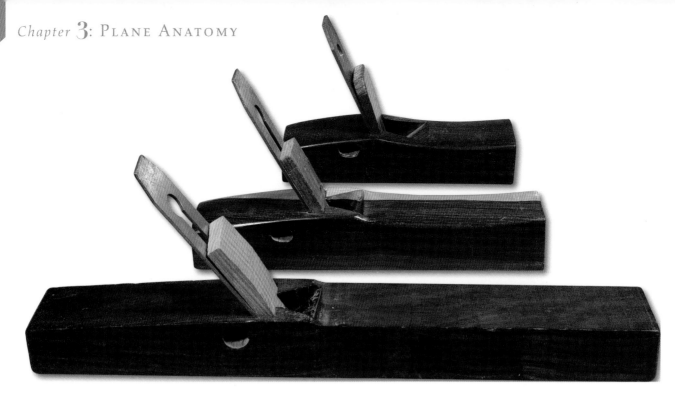

Figure 3-3. *A set of Chinese cabinet-makers planes, front to back: jointer with a 55° pitch; intermediate smoother with a 60° pitch; smoother with a 65° pitch. The size of the intermediate smoother varies from woodworker to woodworker. Sometimes it is about the same size as the jointer but with a higher pitch and finer setup. Sometimes it is about the size of a Western jack plane, as shown here.*

PITCH ANGLES

While Western blade angles are usually measured in degrees, the pitch of a Japanese plane blade is determined using a rise/run scale based on 10 rather than degrees. That is why you will sometimes come across such apparently odd pitches as 47½°, which is actually a rise of 11 in a run of 10. Curiously, these pitches can be found also in English planes. Norris planes often had a pitch of 47½°, and I have an American razee try plane with a 43° blade angle (a 9 in 10 pitch). As it turns out, these are my favorite blade angles for smoothing wood; 43° does a nice job on many of the softer hardwoods, as well as maple, and 47½° works well on many of the harder hardwoods. The latter pitch also seems to be a critical angle around which the geometry of the cut begins to change.

USE THE LOWEST EFFECTIVE CUTTING ANGLE

The lower the angle, the cleaner the shear. The higher the angle (increasingly above 47½°), the more it cuts like a scraper. At an angle around 75° or 80°, the tool is best regarded as a scraper.

of the ubiquitous Bailey plane, no matter what the particular plane's length or intended purpose.

I believe such differences exist because individual woodworking trades within each culture tended to work on a limited number of typically indigenous woods. Over time, woodworkers discovered certain cutting angles worked better on these woods, so blade angles on the tools within these trades usually spanned a narrow range.

Additionally, you see similarities in the blade angles of tools within the same trades right across different cultures, as they often used similar species of wood. Finally, historically, you can see the changes the introduction of new woods through international trade brought to the tools.

This effect on plane anatomy attributable to the material being worked is most striking in the planes of Chinese and Southeast Asian furniture makers (Figure 3-3). Traditional furniture in these cultures is typically made of rosewood or some similar tropical hardwood. The cutting angle of these planes is very high. Truing planes, usually the first to be used and making the heaviest cut, have cutting angles around 55°. Intermediate smoothing planes have angles around 60°. The cutting angle of the final plane is often over 65°.

Northern Europeans, working with indigenous hardwoods such as oak, birch, and walnut, and using deal (pine or fir) and other species as secondary woods, have planes with cutting angles ranging from about 40° for preliminary to about 55° for finish planes, with 60° and 64° often used for molding planes (Figure 3-4).

The carpentry tradition of Japan is exquisitely refined and sophisticated, and most of the tools imported from there reflect it. The woods worked are largely softwoods such as cedar, with elm and some similar woods also encountered. The majority of planes commonly imported have an angle of 40° (Figure 3-5), though in response to the American market, planes with higher blade angles are now occasionally brought in (Figure 3-6).

THE BEST BLADE ANGLE

The inference of all this, and a fact borne out in practice, is that softer woods take a lower cutting angle than the harder woods. Conversely, the harder the wood, the higher the angle. This is not always true, but it is a good starting point. I would add: Use the lowest cutting angle that remains effective. There are two reasons: the lower angle shears rather than scrapes wood fibers,

Figure 3-4. *In this set of Western-style planes, the higher the pitch, the smoother the surface produced. From top to bottom: try plane with a 43° pitch; jointer with a 47½° pitch; smoother with a 50° pitch.*

Figure 3-5. *This is a particularly fine example of an 8/10- (40°-) pitch Japanese-style smoothing plane with 70mm-wide, hand-forged, acid-etched blade and chipbreaker. The acid etch brings out the grain pattern of the softer backing steel.*

BLADE ANGLES FOR DIFFERENT WOODS

As a general rule of thumb, the plane-blade angle for softwoods varies from 35° to around 45°, with the lower end working best. Blade angles for hardwoods run the gamut from about 40° to 55° and higher, though the majority works well in the 45° to 50° range. Tropical hardwood blade angles ranges from about 50° to over 65°.

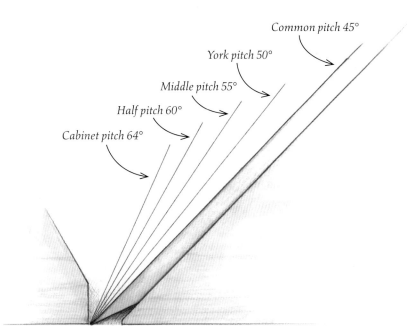

Common pitch 45°
York pitch 50°
Middle pitch 55°
Half pitch 60°
Cabinet pitch 64°

Figure 3-6. British Nomenclature for Common Blade Angles (Pitch).

WHY 45°?

Because the majority of woodworkers work in hardwoods, the question arises—why do manufacturers use a softwood angle for their planes? I think the answer lies in the evolution of the tool. The Bailey-type plane is a general-use plane, for carpentry as well as cabinetwork, meant to perform a variety of tasks—a least common denominator that appeals to the widest market. The 45° blade angle allows use of the plane for the widest variety of woods. The 45° angle is low enough that it will cut softwoods but not so low it cannot deal with many of the more common hardwoods. It is a compromise angle—it cuts well in a few woods, and with serviceable mediocrity in all the rest.

CUTTING END GRAIN

End grain is best cut at the lowest possible angle: in practice about 22°—or about the size of the bevel of a paring chisel—which works quite well for shearing end grain, but is hard to control. The traditional solution, rather than using a blade with one face flush to the work as a paring chisel would be, was to mount a blade in a plane at a low angle (12° to 18°) with the bevel up. The arrangement, somewhat compromising of performance on end grain, gains the advantages of control, adjustability, jigging (provided by the sole of the plane), and the ability to plane long grain with some reliability.

A number of planes are set up like this, the most familiar being the Stanley 60½, which can be used on a shooting board to plane board ends, as well as perform the multitude of other tasks it is often called on to do (see "Wood Block Planes" on page 86 for a more thorough discussion). Another plane of note was the Stanley 62 low-angle jack plane (now remade by Lie-Nielsen and Veritas), whose original purpose was to flatten badly worn end-grain butcher blocks. Shoulder planes, a joint-making plane discussed in Chapter 7, developed mainly from a need to even out the end grain of poorly cut tenon shoulders.

producing a better surface; and the lower angle involves less work.

It is, of course, not quite that straightforward. A number of factors interplay with this rule of thumb. First, softwoods, hardwoods, and tropical hardwoods each respond differently to the cutting action of the blade. Second, end grain cuts are different than long grain.

Softwoods require cutting, not scraping. The higher cutting angles that, in hardwoods, produce successful compression failure (Type-II chips, as per Bruce Hoadly in *Understanding Wood*) will only tear the fibers in softwoods, causing the chip to crumple into a bunch (Figure 3-7). A scraper will shape, but not actually smooth, softwood.

Hardwoods are somewhat on the cusp between softwoods and tropical hardwoods.

Figure 3-7. Blade Angle and Wood Species.
Within the range for each wood, the lower angles are generally for preparatory planes. The higher angles are for smoothing planes.

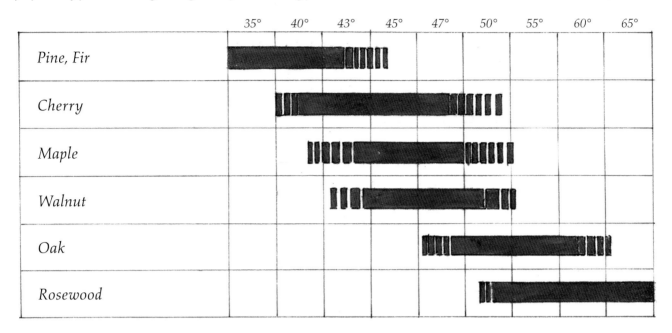

Hardwoods often respond well to a sharp low-angle blade. Smoothing is possible with just a scraper.

The variety of grain structures and hardness within hardwoods suggests using a variety of cutting angles. Low-to-medium blade angles work well, though higher blade angles are sometimes safer and more predictable, producing less tearout with less adjustment, maintenance, and sharpening. The resulting surface, though, is not as smooth or clear as with a lower-angle cut.

Tropical hardwoods respond well to scraping, conversely tearing out disastrously at low and intermediate blade angles. Traditional blade angles for tropicals often are quite high—at what would be a scraping angle in a softer wood. Despite the high angle, the plane blade leaves a clean-cut surface with good clarity.

There is a great deal of overlap where angles work well in a particular wood. Often

BLADE STEELS FOR DIFFERENT WOODS

Softwoods respond best to a fine-grained steel blade sharpened to a thin, sharp edge, mounted at a low angle for a shearing cut. For this reason, a high-quality hand-forged carbon-steel blade is the best choice for smoothing softwood.

Though the sharpness of a fine-grained edge is not as critical, North American and European hardwoods respond best to a sharp edge. For final tearout-free smoothing, a finely wrought carbon-steel blade remains the best choice, though an A2 blade often yields satisfactory results.

Tropical hardwoods are less sensitive to the thinness of the cutting edge. Tropical hardwoods do not demand the sharpness required by the softwoods and most hardwoods for good results. They cut best with a high-angle blade—more of a scraping cut. The wood's hardness generates a fair amount of heat at the blade's edge. Under such conditions, and considering the abrasive nature of some of these woods, a thin edge is more susceptible to rapid dulling, minor chipping, or other damage. Using a good fine-grained alloy steel blade makes sense here.

MOLDING PLANES

The traditional practice of often using higher blade angles on molding planes than smoothing planes reinforces two ideas:

• increasing the blade angle increases reliability of the cut; and

• increasing the blade's pitch above the normal range used for that wood reduces cut quality.

Increasing the blade angle is the default for reducing tearout on a molding plane.

Many molding planes use pitches in excess of the normal range for hardwoods—often as high as 64°. Experience with molding planes confirms that while this may produce a surface with minor roughness, it largely avoids more disastrous forms of tearout. A reduced-quality cut was the better choice for the eighteenth-century craftsman who used these tools, than a higher-quality cut punctuated with deep tearout. Look at the alternatives available to eighteenth-century craftsmen.

The goal of smoothing work for the eighteenth-century craftsmen was to achieve an acceptable surface straight from the plane or scraper, and to absolutely minimize the use of glasspaper. Glasspaper, the precursor to sandpaper, was usually made by the craftsman himself, by pulverizing a piece of expensive glass, sieving, and sifting it onto paper coated with hide glue. It worked slowly, wore out quickly, and was effective only for polishing—not removing anything more than minor imperfections. The craftsman aimed for a surface from his molding plane that required only minor, if any, glass papering. Moldings produced by high-pitch molding planes would generally be acceptable.

To further reduce demands on planning and increase the chances of getting an acceptable surface, craftsmen carefully selected molding stock for straight grain and even texture. Also, moldings were often used in millwork that was painted or of such size (or height) as to further obscure a less than polished surface.

THE JAPANESE BLADE

The Japanese believe a low shearing cut with an extremely sharp blade is the best approach to a smooth cut. They depend heavily on the quality of their blades, their ability to get them sharp, and their technique in planing. The plane I use most is a 40° 70mm (2¾") Japanese plane that works well on woods most Westerners would not touch with a plane having such a low blade angle. This capability is attributable to the quality of the blade and how sharp it can be made.

the same angle seems less effective from one board to another in the same species, or even from one part of a board to another. Because of such variations, most woodworkers use more conservative angles—slightly steeper but within the acceptable range—for more predictable results and little or no tearout.

The Japanese are an exception to this thinking. (See "The Japanese Blade" at left, below). In practice, I prepare a piece with a 40° Japanese plane to see how the board responds and step up to a steeper-angle plane if the wood requires it.

Finally, you will find some blade angles cannot be used on some woods. It is not that they do not cut well, but that they nearly do not cut at all. Pine, for instance, seems to crumple as the blade angle increases over 45°. Results can be disastrous with some tropical hardwoods at even intermediate blade angles.

BLADE ANGLE AND THE TASK

Studying traditional tools also shows the task defines the cutting angle of a plane blade. Because a lower-angle blade presents less resistance in cutting than a higher-angle blade with its scraping cut, planes used for shaping or preparing stock tend to have lower angles. Lower-cutting angles are less fatiguing because the plane requires less effort to push. At this stage, stock removal is more important than smoothness, which can be accomplished with succeeding planes. Traditionally, craftsmen use several planes to take a board from initial surfacing to final smoothing. (For more on this see Chapter 4 and "Dimensioning Stock" on page 225.)

CUSTOM BLADE ANGLES

If you utilize wood you suspect would work more easily or predictably with a blade angle different from what is commonly available, you have several choices. The first is to make your own. If you have not made a plane of your own, it may sound intimidating. Do not let it be.

A Krenov-style plane is simple to make generally, and easier still with certain machinery. An intermediate woodworker can readily make a Western wood-block plane or a Japanese plane (Figure 3-8). With a little extra time, a novice can make one as well. The trick is to know the simple technique.

With some practice, a single-blade Japanese plane with a 45mm (1¾") blade (no chipbreaker) takes about 1½ to 2 hours (the first one will take longer). Moreover, it is usable the same day, because you do not have to wait for the glue to dry. (See "Making a Japanese-Style Plane" on page 286.)

Making your own planes expands your options. You can customize the blade angle and match the blade to the work as well. For instance, you can use:

- a modern manufactured blade,
- a premium modern blade,
- a high-quality antique laminated blade (which can often be purchased for less than after-market premium blades),
- a high-alloy, or high-speed-steel blade, or
- a variety of Japanese blades.

Once you have the confidence to make a plane, you can experiment making specialty planes to solve specific problems. I have made simple molding planes to match antique work where I needed only a few feet of molding.

Figure 3-8. *Here are three custom planes, left to right: 70mm blade at 47½° pitch; 70mm blade at 43° pitch; 55mm blade at 53° pitch.*

Figure 3-9. *These chibi-kannas, or finger planes, were very effective in fairing out the long sweeping curves of this carving.*

In addition, I have made planes to assist in effects on carved work (Figure 3-9).

Alternatively, you can still find many antique block planes—a blade in a block of wood, not the modern steel block plane—at very reasonable prices. The blades in them are often very good laminated cast steel. The range of blade angles is limited, but often outside what is available in a newly manufactured plane. To get a sense of what you are looking for, see "Setting Up Wood-body Planes" on page 163.

Another way is to alter the angle of the bevel on the blade itself, which is easiest in planes with the bevel of the blade mounted up. Examples include the modern metal block plane like the Stanley 60½ or any of the new bevel-up planes made by Lie-Nielsen or Veritas. Because the bevel is mounted up, any change in its angle changes the cutting angle.

The disadvantage is that increasing the bevel angle often results in an angle blunter than normally desirable. With the blunter angle, cutting action is reduced, the surface is not cut as cleanly, the edge may dull quicker (it was blunter to begin with), and the plane requires greater effort to push. (See "Bevel Angle" on page 52.)

In planes with the bevel mounted down, you can back-bevel a blade. This is where you put a second bevel on the top side of the blade, opposite to the main bevel. This is usually a small bevel established by honing

rather than by grinding. I would do this only for the occasional piece. If you find yourself working repeatedly with woods that require a different angle, it will be more efficient to make a plane to that angle. This is because when you work much with a plane, you should sharpen frequently. Accurately repeating a finely angled back-bevel becomes a problem. In addition, back beveling may require the bevel to be reground, because the bevel is larger and more blunt, which reduces the blade's cutting action. When you finally remove the back-bevel, you have to grind that much of the blade away to restore the original edge. But, back beveling can be an efficient solution for less frequent plane users or for those occasional situations.

Skewing the plane in use is another way to vary the blade angle. Craftsmen who plane a lot do it instinctively in response to the feedback from the wood. They may do it over the whole board or only those sections of it that respond better to the technique. Skewing the plane effectively lowers the blade angle, and presents a thinner bevel to the wood (Figure 3-10).

It works sometimes for these reasons, but I think it is successful more because you are approaching a section of difficult grain from a more successful direction. I usually skew the plane only to change the angle of attack. Keeping the blade sharp usually works better. I would not substitute this tactic for a plane built with the correct blade angle.

A surprising amount of tearout at any angle is avoidable by having an extremely sharp blade.

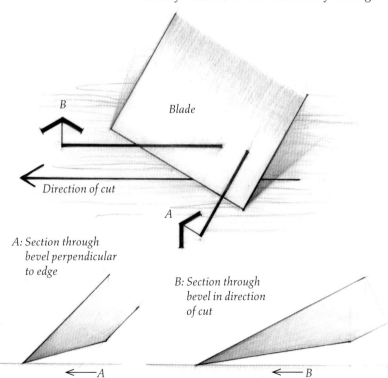

Figure 3-10. *If the blade is skewed when planing, the effective bevel angle (as presented to the wood) is smaller than the actual ground bevel.*

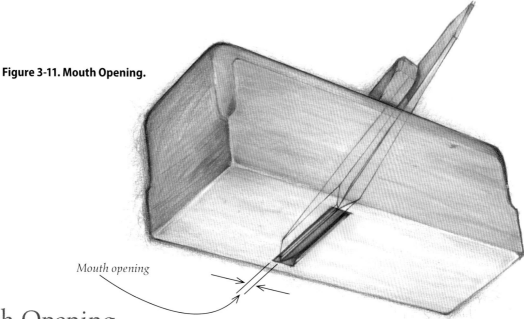

Figure 3-11. Mouth Opening.

Mouth opening

Mouth Opening

Controlling the shaving as it passes through the opening in the bottom of the plane is probably the second-most basic technique for controlling tearout, but one that is not well understood (Figure 3-11). Restricting the throat opening works to reduce tearout (Figure 3-12) by compressing the wood fibers immediately in front of the blade, thus keeping them from splitting out ahead of the cut (Figure 3-13). While it is an effective tactic, it has become a less popular one for a number of reasons.

For one, the amount of openness is a dynamic factor, affected by the combination of blade angle, chipbreaker bevel angle, and escape angle of the throat.

The result of such complexity is easy to misjudge, and can be frustrating. If the mouth is too small for the cut, the shavings jam in the throat, which can damage the edge of the mouth and sometimes the blade (Figure 3-14).

Restricting the chip at the mouth of the plane definitely increases stress on the blade, as both pressure and heat build. The increased downward pressure on the blade due to the chip being constricted as it passes through

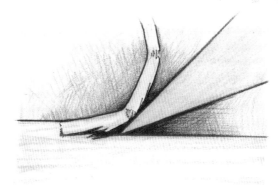

Figure 3-12. *Unrestrained shaving splits out ahead of cut, causing tearout.*

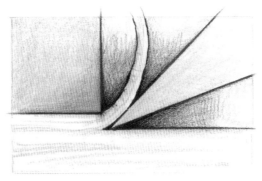

Figure 3-13. *Shaving restrained by a tight mouth opening prevents shaving from lifting ahead of the cut, reducing or eliminating tearout.*

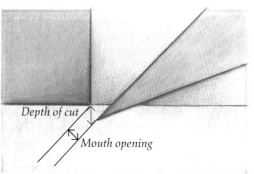

Depth of cut

Mouth opening

Figure 3-14. *For maximum effectiveness against tearout, the mouth opening is equal to the depth of cut. In the real world, the mouth may have to be ever so slightly larger, but definitely no less than, the depth of cut.*

the mouth—made even greater at the higher blade angles—increases the importance of the correct bevel angle, as the blade edge is liable to flex (see "Bevel Angle" on page 52). When this happens, it flexes deeper into the cut, taking a slightly thicker chip (Figure 3-15). The result is one of three things: tearout, a chattering cut (as the blade flexes back and forth), or a chip too large for the opening.

Closing the mouth down also increases the wear on the edge of the mouth itself. For maximum effectiveness, the edge of the mouth should be crisp. Sharp is even better. The increased pressure from constricting the chip rounds the edge over pretty fast, and the rounder it gets, the less effective it is. Ideally, the material at the mouth of a finish plane should be at least as hard as brass. Many old planes incorporate a restricted mouth opening employing a brass or iron piece let into the sole of the plane to close the throat opening (Figure 3-16).

Alternatively, a piece of hardwood can be dovetailed into the chipwell so its end grain closes the mouth opening, giving a hardwearing surface where it is needed. This is easier to do in Japanese planes, as the blocks are not as thick, and is a common repair in Japan. New Japanese planes and plane blocks can be bought with this feature installed. This dovetailed piece is often called a *kuchi-ire* in catalogs (Figure 3-17); Toshio Odate refers to it as a *koppa-gaeshi*. Even with an iron plane, the mouth occasionally needs to be filed.

Increased heat build-up at the mouth is palpable. The oils in the wood being planed vaporize and condense on the top edge of the blade, causing a superficial discoloration of the blade just above the edge (Figure 3-18).

Though work hardening of a plane blade seems like a woodworking myth, when you see evidence of this kind of heat, you begin to think that perhaps some change in the steel might be occurring. Increased heat build-up speeds deterioration of the edge. I believe this is one of the main reasons Chinese planes, which have a high-angle blade (more heat-

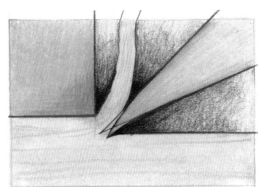

Figure 3-15. *A mouth opening or bevel angle that is too small can cause the edge to flex.*

Figure 3-16. *The mouth on this old coffin-sided smoother—repurposed as a spoon-bottom smoother—has been closed down with a brass piece let into the sole.*

inducing) and a narrow throat, tend to use a higher alloy steel in their blades (see "Alloy Steel" on page 24).

The interrelationship of the mouth opening to other anatomical tactics is dynamic. The effectiveness of restricting the opening varies according to blade angle. While effective at lower angles, it seems more so at higher blade angles (50°-plus) and practice confirms it.

The chipbreaker, however, seems to be less effective on higher-angle planes and increasingly effective as blade angle drops below 50°. On planes with angles greater than 50°, I rely on a small mouth opening alone to control tearout.

Without an adjustable mouth, finish planing is the only task you can do with a plane so configured because the mouth is too narrow for even intermediate work. You will need more planes because a single tool will not do a variety of tasks as designed. But, I believe you will find the setup and maintenance of a fine finish plane does not lend itself to the plane doing less-refined tasks, mouth opening or not, intended versatility or not. Fine-finish planing is demanding and having dedicated planes set up for it is a timesaver.

ADJUSTING THE MOUTH OPENING

Woodworkers have developed ways to match the mouth opening to the work. The first is to have different planes dedicated to different tasks, each with a matching mouth opening. If you are doing a lot of such work, it is the most-efficient method.

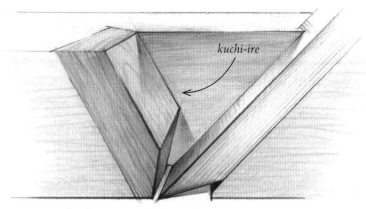

Figure 3-17. *A kuchi-ire installed as a repair to close the mouth on a wooden plane. Because end grain bears on the work, this is a durable (and re-adjustable) repair.*

Figure 3-18. *You can see the brown discoloration from heat build-up on the face of the blade, right; it follows the silhouette of the bottom edge of the wedge.*

A second method is to alter the plane's mouth by inserting a piece of metal or wood to close the opening. Insertion repairs a plane with a mouth worn open or modifies the mouth for a different use. This, of course, can only be done on a wooden plane.

A modern invention that increases a plane's versatility is a method for adjusting the mouth opening. Two ways have been developed to do this.

Figure 3-19. *Moving the frog forward on a Stanley-style plane to close the mouth will leave the edge unsupported—on some models by nearly ¼" (6mm).*

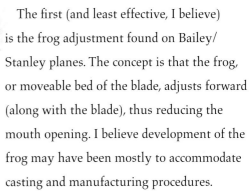

The first (and least effective, I believe) is the frog adjustment found on Bailey/Stanley planes. The concept is that the frog, or moveable bed of the blade, adjusts forward (along with the blade), thus reducing the mouth opening. I believe development of the frog may have been mostly to accommodate casting and manufacturing procedures.

In modern metal frames, with the exception of the Bedrock models, the blade cantilevers nearly ¼" (6mm) off the frog (Figure 3-19). Combine that with a blade about ¹⁄₁₆" (2mm) thick, and you usually get a blade that flaps around in the breeze when called upon to do serious work. On the Bedrock models, the frog slides down and forward, supporting the blade closer to the edge. With this configuration, a precise mouth opening still requires some fiddling back and forth with both the blade and frog adjustments.

The best method for adjusting the mouth is the sliding mouthpiece, set into the sole of the plane in front of the blade. Most commonly found on metal block planes (Figure 3-20) and other low-angle metal planes, as well as the German reform (improved) wooden planes, this is a very effective, quick, and easy method for adjusting the throat while the blade remains firmly bedded (Figure 3-21).

Figure 3-20.
Like many (but not all) block planes, the Veritas has an adjustable mouth.

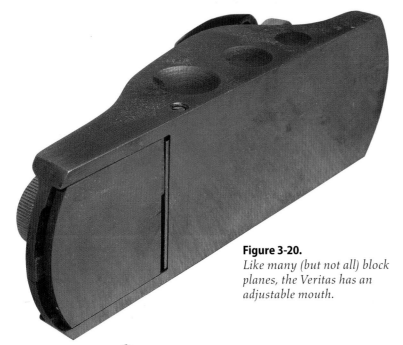

Figure 3-21.
This is the sole of the Ulmia reform smoothing plane with its adjustable throat plate. It is adjusted with two screws: one on top that loosens the plate, and one in front that moves the plate forward or backward.

Chipbreaker

The chipbreaker (Figure 3-22) is a 300- to 400-year-old invention that has increased the reliability of the handplane in getting consistently smooth results. The chipbreaker accomplishes it through one main mechanism and some secondary ones. The primary mechanism for improving consistency of the cut gives the piece its name. By sharpening the bevel on the chipbreaker and placing it directly behind the cutting edge (Figure 3-23), the chip is broken backward before it has a chance to lift and split ahead of the cut (Figure 3-24). This has proven to be a highly effective method of reducing tearout, especially when coupled with a small mouth opening at lower-to-medium blade angles.

JAPANESE CHIPBREAKERS

Good-quality Japanese planes have chipbreakers and main blades laminated with a hard steel edge. Sometimes on the lesser-quality Japanese planes, the chipbreaker is tempered, not laminated. You might think this is excessive, but it is not. Using a chipbreaker in a position tight to the cutting edge subjects it to a lot of impact and heat. It will dull and needs to be resharpened over time, and if it is not, it may begin to trap chips. I have seen soft chipbreakers get a multitude of tiny dents from just the impact of the shaving. I also have seen the discoloration on the edge from when the oils in the wood vaporize from the heat of the cut. Having a hard chipbreaker reduces maintenance and improves reliability.

There are at least three distinct shapes of chipbreaker. One, typical on older, wooden planes, Japanese planes, and now Lie-Nielsen planes, consists of a large flat bevel ground at about 25° (measured when mounted to the blade), with a secondary, smaller bevel that does the work (Figure 3-25).

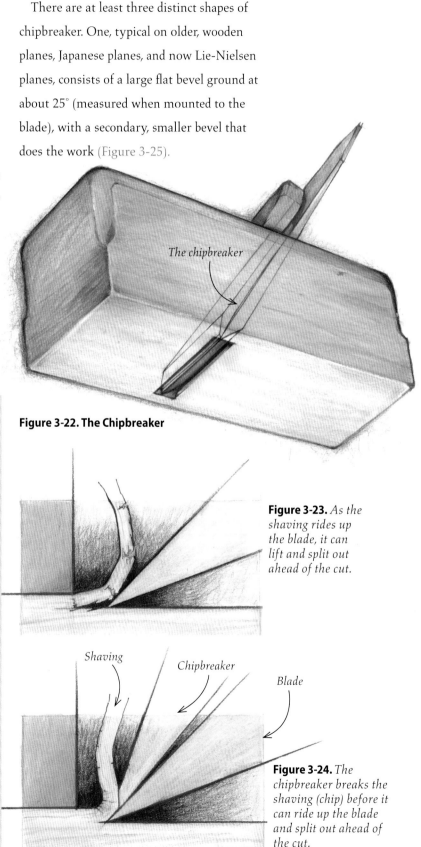

The chipbreaker

Figure 3-22. The Chipbreaker

Figure 3-23. *As the shaving rides up the blade, it can lift and split out ahead of the cut.*

Shaving

Chipbreaker

Blade

Figure 3-24. *The chipbreaker breaks the shaving (chip) before it can ride up the blade and split out ahead of the cut.*

Figure 3-25. Flat Bevel-Style Chipbreaker with Secondary Bevel.

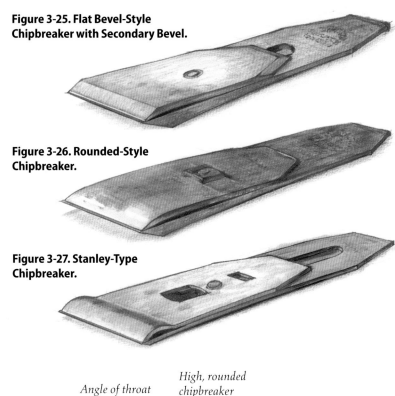

Figure 3-26. Rounded-Style Chipbreaker.

Figure 3-27. Stanley-Type Chipbreaker.

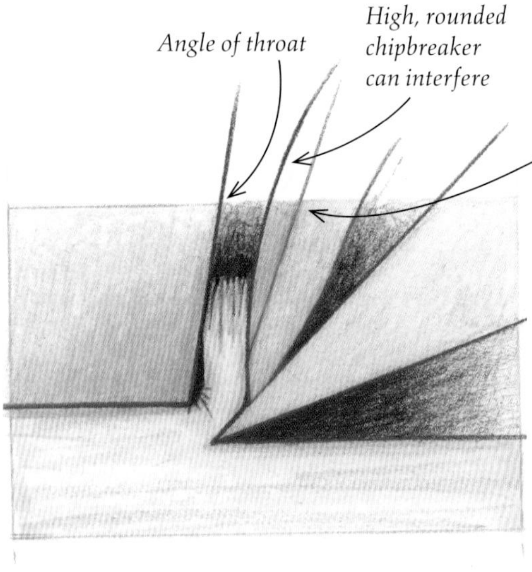

Angle of throat

High, rounded chipbreaker can interfere

Line of flat-bevel chipbreaker

Figure 3-28. *To allow the shaving to pass unobstructed, the throat of the plane should be wider at all points than the thickness of the shaving. On some planes, the high, rounded type of chipbreaker will obstruct the throat.*

Figure 3-29. *The Sta-Set chipbreaker with its edge-piece removed so the blade can be sharpened. Reassembly does not require readjustment, as the part of the chipbreaker that is screwed to the blade has an interlocking groove and a small pin that aligns with a matching hole in the edge-piece. The edge-piece is then held in place by the lever cap.*

A second shape, seen on both new and old manufactured planes, is similar in profile, only slightly rounded, rather than beveled (Figure 3-26).

The third shape, most often seen on the Stanley/Bailey planes, is a bulbous, almost semicircular curve near the blade edge (Figure 3-27).

The first shape is probably the most versatile, because the large, low bevel provides more clearance for the shaving broken by the smaller bevel. Rounded chipbreakers constrict the throat more, resulting in a greater chance the shavings will jam. (See "Plane Geometry, A Summary" on page 49.)

The second type, slightly rounded, will often work satisfactorily, but if you have problems with jamming, consider filing the rounded shape to a flat secondary bevel (assuming you are left with enough material not to weaken the chipbreaker itself). I would try this fix before opening the throat angle.

The third type, with its bulbous rounding, perhaps meant to provide better pressure distribution under the lever cap, often takes up too much room to allow chips to pass when the frog is moved forward and the mouth closes down (Figure 3-28).In many cases, the chipbreaker and mouth must be relieved before chips will pass. This is another indication the frog concept is not a serious effort at solving the problem of closing down the Stanley/Bailey mouth.

In the Sta-Set, a new two-part chipbreaker by Clifton, the lower part where the chip is actually broken removes and reinstalls without unscrewing the main body of the chipbreaker from the blade. This is a great timesaver when sharpening. You have to be careful, though, when using waterstones, because water can get between the main body of the chipbreaker and the blade and cause rust. The Sta-Set is rounded, though low, in profile. It fits flat to the blade, rather than arching above it, and is quite a bit thicker than most modern chipbreakers, adding considerable stiffness to the blade (Figure 3-29).

The chipbreaker introduces interesting dynamics into blade functioning. With the exception of the Japanese-style and the Sta-Set, screwing the chipbreaker to the blade firmly to ensure tight contact arcs the blade.

On early planes, when used with a heavy, handmade tapered blade fixed with a wedge, this was an advantage. It nearly guaranteed the blade would contact the bed at the heel (right behind the bevel)and at the top. This eliminated the need to custom-fit the bed of each plane to the varyingly thick blade, and simplified any fine-tuning of the bed by the user as well. I have even seen the bed of an old plane cut concave to guarantee this fit (Figure 3-30).

Relieving the bed this way is less successful with thin modern untapered blades because they are not stiff enough. I believe the strategy relies on a thick blade, assisted by an equally massive chipbreaker. Old tapered blades are nearly ¼" (6mm) at their thickest. Together with the chipbreaker the assembly is almost ⅜" (10mm) thick. Contemporary blade/chipbreaker assemblies together are

barely the thickness of an old tapered blade by itself, not much more than ⅛" (3mm). The modern Bailey/Stanley chipbreaker appears to be designed to compensate with its rounded shape, which seems to put pressure on the blade a little farther up as well as on the edge when the lever cap is tightened down. However, trying to force the blade into full contact with the bed does not often work (Figure 3-31).

Using a thin blade not bedded for its full length is asking for trouble. If the frog is

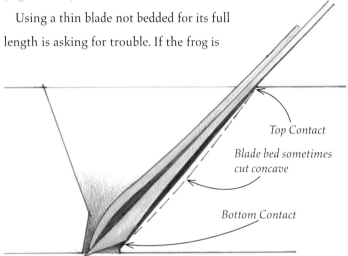

Top Contact

Blade bed sometimes cut concave

Bottom Contact

Figure 3-30. Section Through an Antique Wooden Plane with a Tapered Blade *The blade contacts the blade bed only at the top and bottom, but across its full width.*

Figure 3-31. A Bailey Frog-and-Blade Assembly *If you hold this up to the light, you can see the blade is arched and not making contact with the bed at the center of its length.*

MILLERS FALLS LEVER CAP

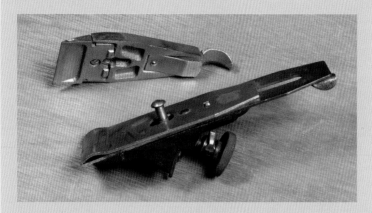

The assembly from a Millers Falls plane includes a double-action pivoting lever cap that puts pressure on the blade at three points, flattening out the blade assembly and securely bedding the blade. However, this is exceptional, and I have never seen another lever cap like it.

not carefully seated on the plane's body, not aligned with the back edge of the blade opening, or moved forward to close the mouth, the blade will likely chatter.

If your blade chatters, inspect these possible reasons and correct. If the blade still chatters, try a Sta-Set chipbreaker that does not arch the blade when installed, a thicker blade, or both. Be careful when buying a thicker blade, however, because some are too thick to fit into the mouth opening.

Another type of chattering happens because the bevel angle is too small (and thus the material immediately behind the edge too thin). Some woodworkers believe the chipbreaker can correct this situation by *pre-tensioning* the cutting edge. I would not rely on the chipbreaker to correct for a too-small bevel. It is better to give the edge its proper bevel angle. (See "Bevel Angle" on page 52.)

SETTING THE CHIPBREAKER

The chipbreaker increases a plane's versatility. Setting the chipbreaker close to the edge reduces tearout and allows a more finished cut. Setting the chipbreaker back allows the blade to be more deeply set to hog off wood. (A similar versatility is provided by the adjustable throat of the small metal block plane.) Backing off the chipbreaker on most planes requires disassembly and a screwdriver, but it still is the better alternative to moving the frog.

How close should the chipbreaker be set to the edge? Generally, the chipbreaker is set back from the edge a distance equal to the maximum thickness of the shaving you expect to make with that plane. This is also usually equal to the amount of curve honed into the edge of the blade. (See "Shape of the Blade Edge" on page 54.)

You do not want the chipbreaker set below the corners of the blade. For the finest finish work, I set the chipbreaker down until there is only the barest glint of light left on the top (back) of the blade. This is much less than $\frac{1}{64}$" (0.4mm). Only that fine line of light tells me there is still some blade exposed.

For coarse work, the chipbreaker can be set well back, though it is usually not necessary to set it back much more than $\frac{1}{16}$" (2mm). On planes used to prepare stock, such as the jack, the chipbreaker is usually set back a little more than the arc of the blade edge.

PLANE GEOMETRY, A SUMMARY

The interrelationship between blade angle, mouth opening, chipbreaker, throat angle, and bevel angle is dynamic (**Figure 1**). When constructing or tuning a plane, keep the interplay in mind and adjust each element according to the other.

Figure 1. Definitions

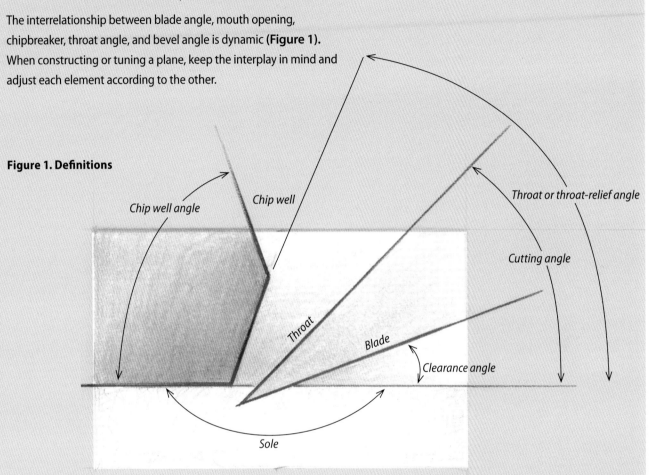

Chip well angle

Chip well

Throat or throat-relief angle

Cutting angle

Throat

Blade

Clearance angle

Sole

PLANES WITHOUT A CHIPBREAKER

On planes without a chipbreaker, the mouth opening should be the same size or perhaps slightly larger than the thickest shaving you intend to make with that plane. On roughing out and dimensioning planes, the opening could be ⅟₃₂" to ⅟₁₆" (0.8mm to 2mm) or greater (**Figure 2**). (The scrub plane has a throat of about ¼" (6mm).) On intermediate smoothing planes, a mouth opening of 0.01" (0.25mm) or less is expected (**Figure 3**). On your finest finish planes, the mouth opening could be just several thousandths of an inch (**Figure 4**).

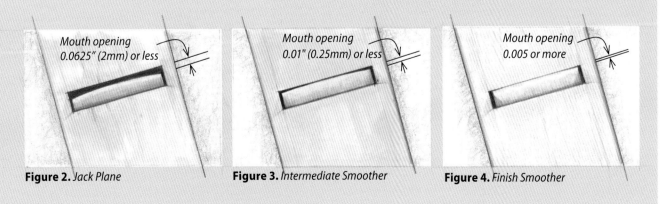

Mouth opening 0.0625" (2mm) or less

Mouth opening 0.01" (0.25mm) or less

Mouth opening 0.005 or more

Figure 2. *Jack Plane*

Figure 3. *Intermediate Smoother*

Figure 4. *Finish Smoother*

PLANES WITHOUT A CHIPBREAKER *continued*

The angle of the throat opening need be only 15° to 20° greater than the cutting angle, but usually not less than 70° (**Figure 5**).

You want to keep the throat angle as small as possible because as the plane wears and the bottom is trued repeatedly, the mouth opens (**Figure 6**). Keeping the angle as small as possible slows this process and delays mouth repair. If your plane has a moveable mouth plate, you avoid the problem.

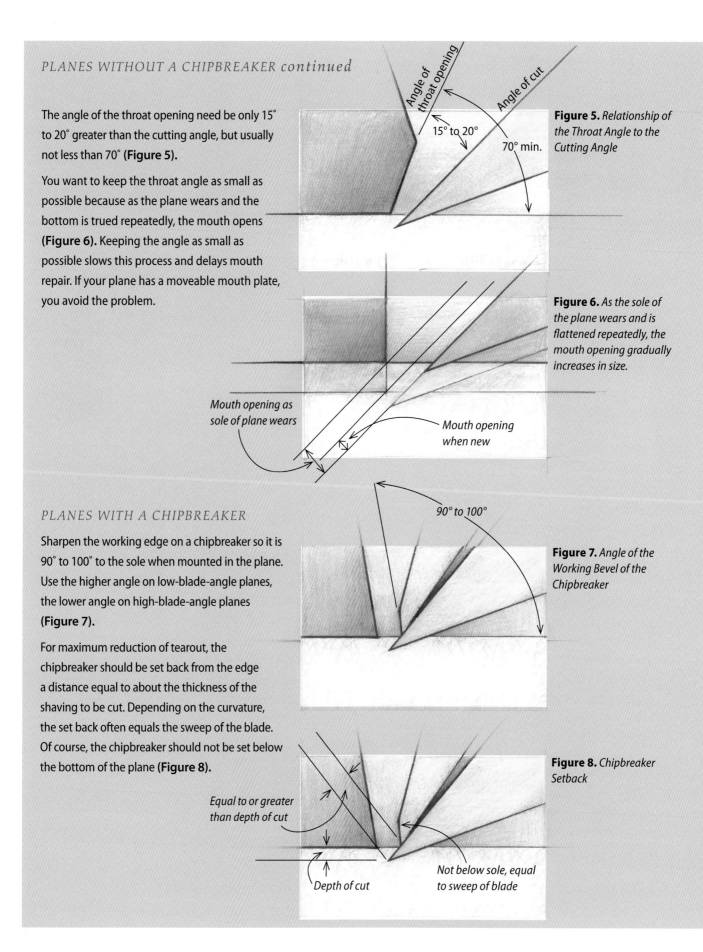

Figure 5. *Relationship of the Throat Angle to the Cutting Angle*

Angle of throat opening

Angle of cut

15° to 20°

70° min.

Figure 6. *As the sole of the plane wears and is flattened repeatedly, the mouth opening gradually increases in size.*

Mouth opening as sole of plane wears

Mouth opening when new

PLANES WITH A CHIPBREAKER

Sharpen the working edge on a chipbreaker so it is 90° to 100° to the sole when mounted in the plane. Use the higher angle on low-blade-angle planes, the lower angle on high-blade-angle planes (**Figure 7**).

For maximum reduction of tearout, the chipbreaker should be set back from the edge a distance equal to about the thickness of the shaving to be cut. Depending on the curvature, the set back often equals the sweep of the blade. Of course, the chipbreaker should not be set below the bottom of the plane (**Figure 8**).

90° to 100°

Figure 7. *Angle of the Working Bevel of the Chipbreaker*

Equal to or greater than depth of cut

Figure 8. *Chipbreaker Setback*

Depth of cut

Not below sole, equal to sweep of blade

At all points, the opening for the shaving to pass must be greater than the thickness of the shaving itself. To maximize the effect of a small mouth opening in combination with a chipbreaker, the throat angle must be equal to, or preferably greater than, the combined angle of the blade and chipbreaker bevel, or between 90° and 100°—maybe slightly more (**Figure 9**).

Any more, however, and the edge of the mouth can become too thin, wearing extremely quickly and sometimes even flexing under the pressure of the constrained shaving, causing the shaving to jam the throat. As the sole of the plane flattens, the mouth also wears open quickly.

A plane set up with the smallest mouth opening and tightest chipbreaker setting can make only the finest, thinnest of cuts. For smoothing planes requiring more versatility, especially in the low-to-intermediate blade angles, it is more practical to rely mostly on the chipbreaker to eliminate tearout, with the mouth opening in a supporting role. Such a strategy allows a reduced throat angle that will slow the gradual enlargement of the mouth opening as the sole is conditioned. The mouth opening would be no more than ¼₄" (0.4mm). Clearance for the shaving through the throat must be maintained, however.

Because the throat angle in this setup is not parallel to the working edge of the chipbreaker, the high point of the chipbreaker is where the shaving tends to jam (**Figure 10**). Have the edge of the chipbreaker ground with a second, main bevel of about 25°, with the working edge shaped to a microbevel of about ¼₃₂" (0.8mm), rather than the more rounded profile seen on many chipbreakers. In preparing Stanley-type chipbreakers, be certain they are not rounded over more than their original shape.

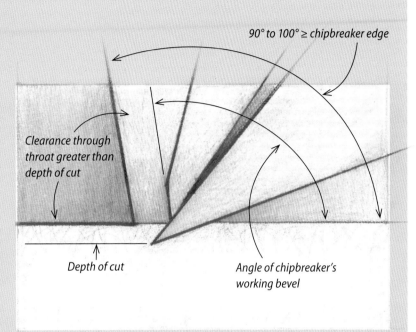

Figure 9. *The angle of the chipbreaker's working bevel.*

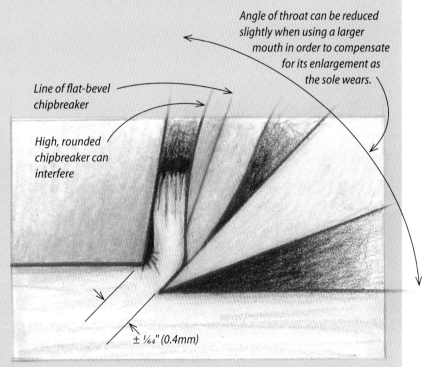

Figure 10. *To increase a plane's versatility, especially in planes with a blade angle of 47½° or less, it's more practical to rely on the chipbreaker than the mouth opening to reduce tearout. On a smoothing plane, however, you'll still want a mouth opening of about ¼₄" (0.4mm).*

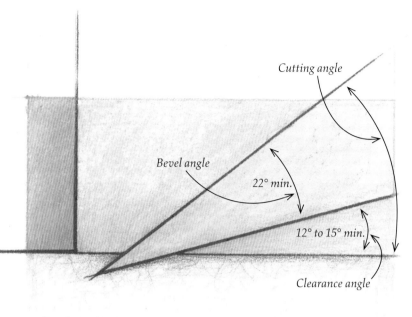

Cutting angle

Bevel angle

22° min.

12° to 15° min.

Clearance angle

Figure 3-32. Practical Minimum Bevel Angle and Clearance Angle

THE CORRECT BEVEL ANGLE

There are limits and ranges you can use as rules of thumb in correcting bevel angle. The minimum clearance angle on a bevel-down blade should be about 12°, though 15° would be better. This parameter limits the size of the bevel angle on low-angle planes. If you have a plane with a 35°-cutting angle, the bevel angle of the blade is limited to a maximum of 23° (35°-12°=23°). The lower limit of the bevel for most blades is about 22°—any smaller and the blade usually crumples at the edge. Some blade steels such as A2 may have trouble at small bevel angles. Also, the bevel angle varies according to the bedding angle of the blade. The steeper the bedding angle, the greater the bevel angle should be. A plane with bedding angle of 40° could have a bevel angle of 22°; 25° to 28° would probably be more serviceable. A 45° plane would have a bevel angle of 25° to 30°. A plane with a bedding angle of 55° could have a bevel angle of 30° to 32°, to perhaps as much as 35°. A bedding angle of 65° could have a bevel angle of as much as 38° to 40°.

Bevel Angle

The bevel angle is the angle to which the blade is sharpened. Most blades leave the factory with a 25° or 30° bevel angle—though Japanese blades often come with a 22° bevel. To bring a plane to its finest performance, the bevel angle may well need further attention (Figure 3-32).

If the bevel angle is too small, the edge flexes under the load, bending down until the chip releases, and then springing up to its original position (Figure 3-16 on page 42). It may do this repeatedly, resulting in chatter.

Or, the blade may flex under the stress of cutting the shaving, especially if it hits a harder part of the board, diving down into the wood and cutting a chip thicker than it was set for. If the plane has a very fine mouth, instead of springing back up, the thicker chip may jam the mouth. Therefore, even though the plane is otherwise finely tuned, the mouth can continue to jam with chips.

As a rule of thumb, the bevel angle should be as small as will cut without chattering. Larger angles and a restricted mouth opening place increased stress on the blade edge, causing it to deflect in use. Increasing the bevel angle alleviates the problem. Increase the bevel angle only enough to eliminate chattering. Any more increases resistance and may reduce the smoothness of the cut.

Begin with the factory angle and see how it performs. If you suspect it is too small and diagnostics described in "Troubleshooting" on page 197 indicate that is the problem, increase the bevel angle until achieving the desired performance.

HONING A HOLLOW-GROUND BEVEL

An argument against hollow grinding is that it thins the metal immediately behind the edge and produces a bevel angle that is too small. This happens because even though the edge is honed at the proper angle, the steel right behind that honed edge that should support it has been removed—hollowed out to the curve of the grinding wheel. If you were to draw a tangent to the curve of the grind in the area immediately behind the honed edge, you would see this is a much smaller angle than the honing angle, and could allow the blade to flex. (See Chapter 11 "Sharpening Plane Blades" for a discussion of the types of bevel configurations.)

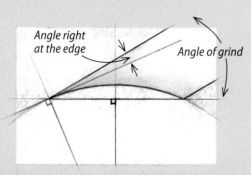

Figure 1. *The angle near the edge on a hollow-ground blade (shown here exaggerated for clarity) is much less than the overall angle to which the blade has been ground. On a ⅜"-thick blade, such as a Japanese blade, ground to 30° on a 6"-diameter wheel, the angle is roughly 7° less at the edge than the grind angle.*

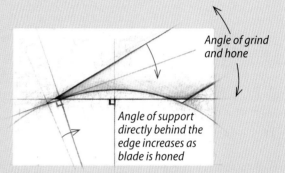

Figure 2. *As the blade is honed, the hollow decreases with each sharpening, and the angle directly behind the honed edge increases. Eventually, when the bevel has been honed flat, it equals the grind angle.*

HOW AN EDGE DULLS

To understand why you would want the bevel angle as small as possible, study how an edge dulls. The gradual effect is that the edge rounds over. If the bevel angle is too large, the worn edge retreats from the work and the main bevel begins rubbing, which prevents the edge from contacting the work. This is exacerbated by the natural tendency of the wood to spring back slightly after the cut. The larger the bevel (on a bevel-down blade), the less the clearance angle to the work, and the sooner the action happens.

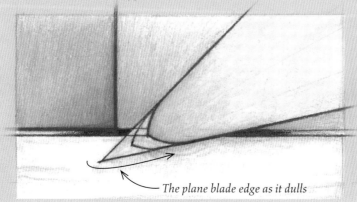

The plane blade edge as it dulls

FACTORY-GROUND BLADE ANGLES

Japanese blades often come sharpened to 22°, even on higher-angle planes. This is very small and may be a source of flex or exceptional wear in planes with higher bedding angles. European tradition suggests sharpening blades to 25° for softwoods and 30° for hardwoods. In some high-angle smoothing planes, especially those with a small throat, even 30° may not be enough. My traditional Chinese plane came with the bevel angle sharpened to over 35°.

Shape of the Blade Edge

Shaping the blade edge (Figure 3-33) is a traditional technique not well understood today, but one that greatly increases the effectiveness of the handplane. The basic concept is that roughing and shaping planes have blades of significant curvature across their width, smoothing and finishing planes have blades with decreasing curvature, and the final plane has a nearly straight edge. In theory, on all three planes, the curvature equals the maximum thickness of the shaving to be taken (Figure 3-34). This strategy is effective for a number of reasons.

On all planes, it keeps the blade's corners from digging in and tearing up the wood. On roughing-out planes properly used diagonally to the grain it reduces tearout and chip jamming at the most likely spot—the corners of the blade. On finish planes, it eliminates steps or ridges between cuts, producing a smoother surface. On jointer planes, the slight curvature can speed up jointing edges and strengthen the edge joint (see "The Jointer Plane" on page 63).

A few planes should have a straight edge, most notably rabbet planes. Planes used on a shooting board need a blade with a straight edge.

Figure 3-33. Shape of the Blade Edge

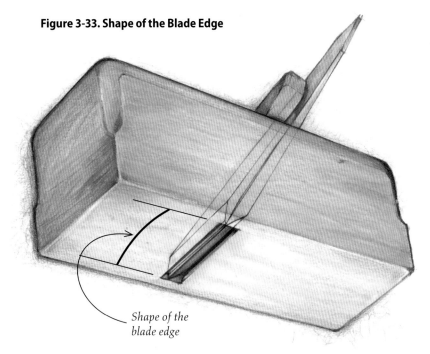

Shape of the blade edge

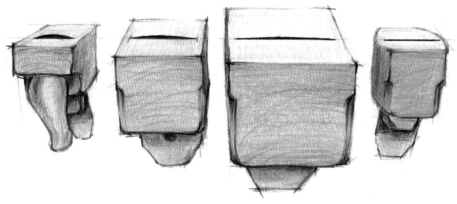

Figure 3-34. *The progression of the curvature of the blades of a set of traditional Western planes, used in order from left to right, rough lumber to smooth. On the far left, the blade of the scrub plane has a curve of ⅛" (3mm) or less; next to it, the jack plane blade has a curve of 1/16" (2mm) or less; the jointer plane blade a curve of 1/32" (0.8mm) or less; and the smoothing plane blade a curve of less than several 0.001" (0.025mm).*

Length of Plane/ Width of Blade

The length of a plane determines its intended function (Figure 3-35).

Long planes true (straighten) surfaces. Their long length bridges low spots, with the blade cutting the high spots down and lowering all surface points to the same plane (Figure 3-36).

Intermediate-length planes handle initial stock preparation. A longer plane for truing often follows, or they follow a longer plane as a preparatory plane before finish smoothing. Appropriate setup and blade shape accompanies either use.

The shortest planes are for final smoothing. They are short for the opposite reason truing planes are long—to follow low spots. Because of the fine tolerance of their setup and use, variations in the surface of only a few ten-thousandths of an inch may cause the plane to skip over the low spots. On difficult woods, setting the blade deeper to cut to low spots is not an option because a deeper setting may cause tearout. Shortening the plane's length helps reduce bridging.

A corollary to the length of the plane is the configuration of the bottom of the plane. Western tradition has the bottom of all planes dead flat. However, what is flat? Is within 0.01" (0.25mm) good enough? 0.001" (0.025mm)? 0.0001" (0.0025mm)? In addition, on what areas on the bottom of the plane would variation be allowed?

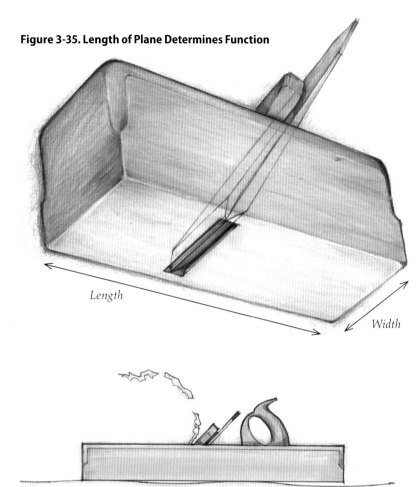

Figure 3-35. Length of Plane Determines Function

Length

Width

Figure 3-36. *Longer planes bridge the low spots, cut the high spots, giving a truer surface.*

THE PROPORTION OF LENGTH TO WIDTH

In full-size planes, a truing plane ranges from about 18" to 30" (457mm to 762mm). Both preparation and intermediate smoothing planes range in length from about 13" to 18" (330mm to 457mm). Smoothing planes range in length anywhere from 6" to 12" (152mm to 305mm). However, it is up to the crafter to decide the best use for planes of particular lengths. The decision may have more to do with blade shape and bottom configuration than length. A plane disproportionately short for its width of blade can be useful for difficult wood. It allows a fine setting of the blade while reaching into slight hollows left from the preparatory planes. The proportion of plane length to blade width used in full-size planes can also be scaled down to the smaller planes used in smaller-scale work.

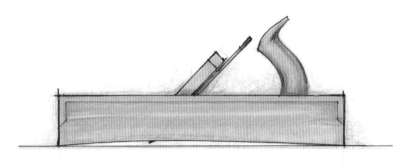

Figure 3-37. *Even though you can see the blade is adjusted to a cutting depth, it may be held off the work and prevented from cutting by the amount the sole is out of true.*

Contact areas behind the blade vary in location and number depending on the intended use of the plane.

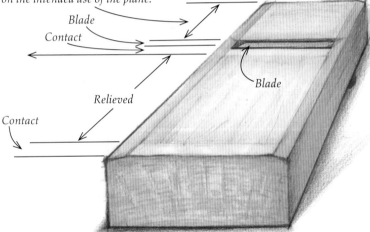

Blade
Contact
Blade
Relieved
Contact

Figure 3-38. *The sole of a Japanese plane is traditionally relieved in strategic areas to simplify maintenance.*

Figure 3-39. *Right, a so-called flat sole may not be contacting the work correctly. Below, the sole is relieved to ensure correct contact.*

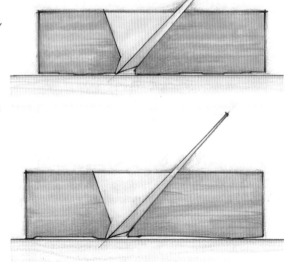

The plane must be as flat as the finest shaving you expect to make with that plane. If you intend the plane to produce shavings only 9 microns thick, as sometimes happens in Japanese planing competitions, then the bottom of the plane must be within 9 microns of flat; otherwise, the blade may be held off the work by the bottom and will not cut (Figure 3-37).

If you are making a cut ¹⁄₁₆" (2mm) thick with a jack plane, then the bottom needs to be only less than ¹⁄₁₆" (2mm) out of flat (though it will work better if it is flatter).

If you are heading for very fine work, this can be a daunting proposition conceptually; practically, it is downright frightening. To flatten 16 square inches consistently to within 9 microns is meticulous, nearly perpetual work.

The Japanese have a practical answer to flattening the bottom of a plane that I use now. The concept is only two (or three or four, depending on the type of plane or its intended use) areas need to be in a flat plane, about the width of the blade extending across the sole, and about ¼" (6mm) long (Figure 3-38). Other areas are relieved so they do not contact the work or need constant attention. This simplifies *flattening* and maintaining the sole (Figure 3-39). The contact areas are then configured for the intended use.

To facilitate rapid stock removal, the contact areas of dimensioning planes are relieved in the area following the blade perhaps 0.01" (0.25mm) (Figure 3-40). Truing planes will have all contact areas along the length of the plane in a line, to ensure stock being planed comes out straight. Smoothing planes will have the contact area behind the blade slightly relieved—usually less than the desired thickness of the shaving (0.005" or 0.125mm)—to help maintain flatness and enable a finely set blade to contact the work.

The width of the blade also varies according to the plane's intended use. The blade of the truing plane (the longest plane) also tends to be the widest, in the Western tradition about 2⅜" to 2¾" (60mm to 69mm) wide. This helps produce the flattest surface.

Planes for stock preparation, such as the jack, have the narrowest blades, from about 1¼" to 1⅞" (31mm to 47mm). Because they are used to remove large amounts of wood, a wide cut would be too much work.

Smoothing planes tend to be wider than the stock-removal planes, but just how wide is up to the craftsman. The wider the blade, the less pronounced the faint scallops, which are a result of the faint curvature of the blade edge. A wider blade, however, involves more setup, maintenance, and work. Smoothing planes, especially for hardwood, are in the range of 2" to 2⅜" (50mm to 60mm) wide, though 2¾" (69mm) is not uncommon.

AND REMEMBER...

There is an additional aspect of effective plane work that tends to be overlooked—the sharpness of the blade. No planing operation will be very effective unless the blade is *really* sharp.

HOW FLAT IS "FLAT"

One of the rationales for development of the metal plane is it comes out of the box flat and is easier to keep flat, although anyone who has tried to flatten a metal plane knows neither is true. The end user can go to great lengths to ensure the bottom of a plane is flat to within a thousandth of an inch. Practically speaking, this is a backbreaking proposition, and a great obstacle to properly setting up a handplane. Even with a milling machine, true flatness is hard to achieve, as the necessary clamping process often distorts the plane, so when it is removed from the clamps it springs back out of true.

However, it is mainly a maintenance problem. Just like wood, iron moves. It needs to age for at least six months after casting so the cast-in stresses can relax. It still moves, albeit a lot less, for quite a time after that. Additionally, various stresses can cause it to move, not the least of which would be if dropped. However, even the constant pressure of the cap-iron screw can distort the body. In addition, it wears. While it may wear more slowly than wood, it just takes cast iron much more effort to flatten it.

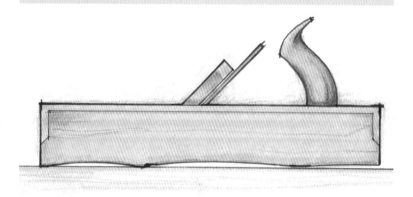

Figure 3-40. *The jack plane may have its sole slightly relieved behind the blade to facilitate access to a rough surface when first preparing a board.*

Beginners often find sharpness difficult to judge; it can seem to be a fleeting thing. But woodworkers must always seek to improve their skill, striving to make sharpness a constant in their work. As your woodworking skills grow, you will come to accept only true sharpness. You will realize too, that without a blade sharp enough for the task, all the other strategies for effective planing will not work.

4

BENCH PLANES
Traditional Solutions: the Jack, Jointer, and Smoothing Planes

Bench planes perform three basic functions in woodworking: shaping and dimensioning lumber, truing and preparing pieces for gluing, and smoothing surfaces. The correct application of the anatomical tactics discussed in Chapter 3 is critical to effectively performing these tasks. Because each task requires a significantly different combination of tactics, traditionally a different plane was developed and used for each: the jack, the jointer, and the smoothing plane. They are visually distinguished from each other primarily by their length relative to the width of their blade, and by the shape of the blade's edge. Varying other techniques as well maximizes work efficiency.

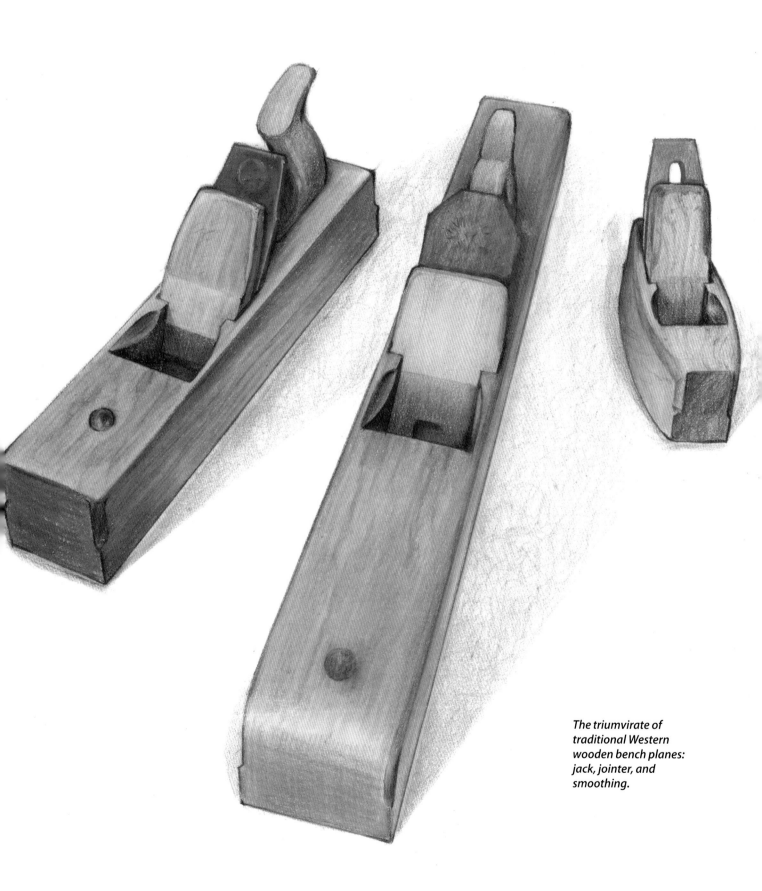

The triumvirate of traditional Western wooden bench planes: jack, jointer, and smoothing.

Figure 4-1. Razee-Type Wooden Jack Plane
Razee Planes have the body cut away behind the blade and alongside the handle.

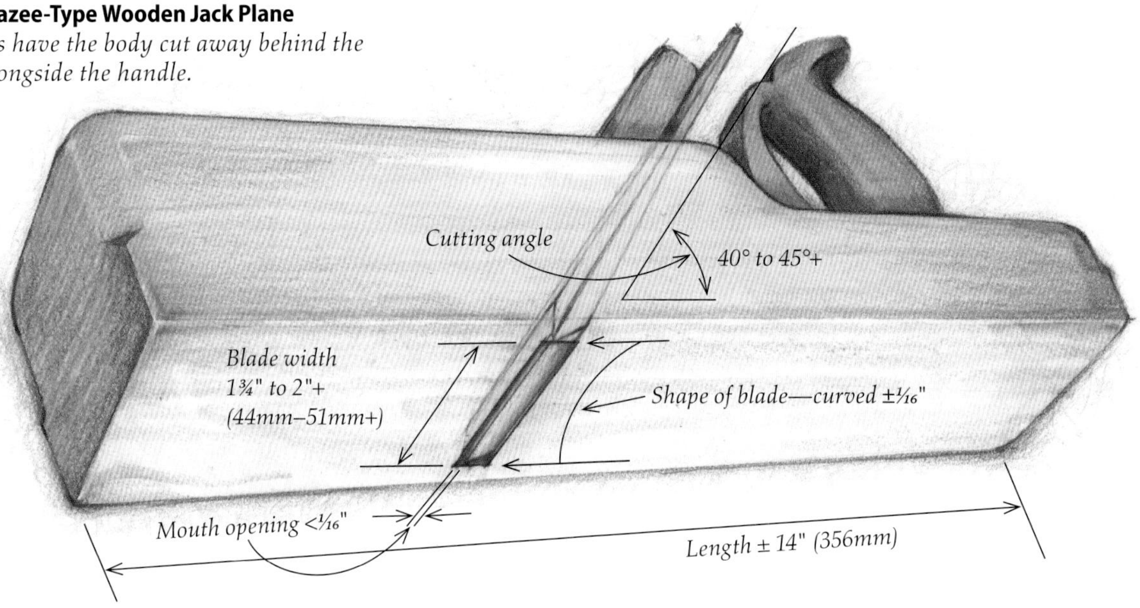

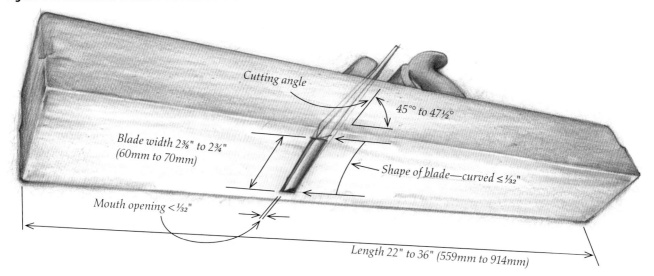

Cutting angle

40° to 45°+

Blade width
1¾" to 2"+
(44mm–51mm+)

Shape of blade—curved ±¹⁄₁₆"

Mouth opening <¹⁄₁₆"

Length ± 14" (356mm)

Figure 4-2. Traditional Western Wooden Jointer Plane

Cutting angle

45°° to 47½°

Blade width 2⅜" to 2¾"
(60mm to 70mm)

Shape of blade—curved ≤¹⁄₃₂"

Mouth opening <¹⁄₃₂"

Length 22" to 36" (559mm to 914mm)

I informally call these three types of planes the *triumvirate*—from the old Roman phrase *the three who jointly rule*. Additional planes assist these and fill various particular needs. However, these three planes are basic and, for centuries, have formed the core of the broad spectrum of handplanes.

While you may only rarely dimension lumber or true an edge with handplanes, understanding the the jack, jointer, and smoother, and how they work allows you to effectively use handplanes in your own work.

The Jack Plane

Most closely identified with shaping and dimensioning lumber is the jack plane (Figure 4-1). It is traditionally used to remove a fair amount of wood quickly to bring a piece to rough shape and dimension after being rough-sawn, split, or hewn from the log. It usually is about 14" (356mm) long (though the horned German jack is about 10" (254mm) long), its length—longer than a smoothing plane but shorter than the jointer—aids in the initial straightening and leveling of stock from the rough (Figure 4-2). For rapid stock removal, and to reduce tearout and resistance, the edge of the blade sharpens to a curve, projecting as much as ⅟₁₆" (2mm) (Figure 4-3).

The chipbreaker, if used, is set back from the edge—a minimum of ⅟₁₆" (2mm). It engages the blade-adjustment mechanism more than to reduce tearout (Figure 4-4). To minimize effort in using the plane, the blade is narrow, about 1¾" (44mm) up to 2¼" (57mm), and set at the lowest angle among the three planes of the triumvirate.

In the European tradition—generally for hardwoods—the blade angle is as low as 40°, though 43° or 45° is more common. As well, 47½° and 50°, intended for particularly hard wood, are also found, as are planes with a higher angle. In working with tropical hardwoods, such as in the Chinese tradition, the blade angle generally is 50° to 60°. In softwoods, 35° and 40° are used. The sole is configured straight or slightly convex over its length, with contact behind the blade relieved perhaps 0.01" (0.25mm). Because it is a rough plane and makes a deep cut, maintenance of a flat bottom is less critical.

The jack is a real workhorse. Before power tools were common, the jack did the bulk of dimensioning and surfacing in the woodshop. The plane is typically used along the grain diagonally resulting in the curved blade making a nice *downhill* shearing cut with the grain, reducing both effort and tearout in all but the most difficult-grained woods.

We all start with the jack plane, in our toolkit as well as at the bench. We commonly

purchase and use a single plane for a long time to shape, dimension, and smooth work—the job of the jack. As your skills improve, you become more demanding and look for more specialized tools to address specific tasks. Nevertheless, the traditional use of the jack in the multi-step process of stock preparation remains relevant.

Stock too large for your equipment need not intimidate you. Proper use of the jack and the others in the triumvirate makes work go quickly. Understanding the jack allows

Figure 4-3. Jack Plane Mouth Opening

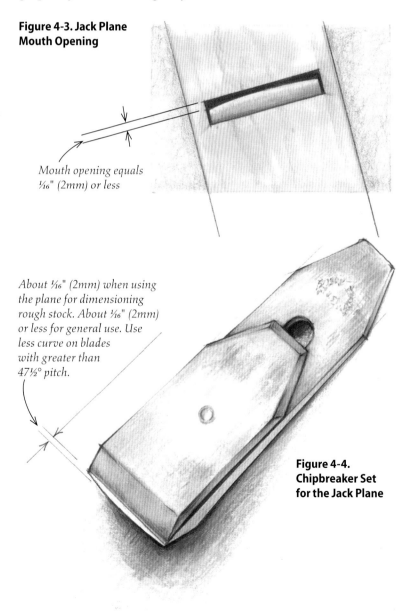

Mouth opening equals ⅟₁₆" (2mm) or less

About ⅟₁₆" (2mm) when using the plane for dimensioning rough stock. About ⅟₁₆" (2mm) or less for general use. Use less curve on blades with greater than 47½° pitch.

Figure 4-4. Chipbreaker Set for the Jack Plane

Figure 4-5. *The English pattern jack (left), and the German-style horned plane (right), are lighter and more comfortable than their metal cousins*

JACK VARIATIONS

Strictly speaking nowadays, any plane used for roughing out stock could be called a jack plane. For instance, I have a couple of small planes, both Japanese, which I use for shaping. The coarsest one has a blade 1¼" (32mm) wide and is about 8" (203mm) long. Because I use this for smaller and narrower pieces, the blade is rather straight across its width, but the sole of the plane is shaped to a slight curve. The slight curve allows me to use it to shape pieces with a long sweep, or simply to get in there and remove a lot of stock without it bridging the low spots. The throat is large. The second plane is slightly wider, about the same length as the first and flat on the bottom. I use the second plane to shape mostly flat stock, or perhaps experiment with a convex curve or twist in a piece. I also often use this one to shape convex curves and have since fitted an adjustable block on the end to assist in this.

A couple of Japanese planes *approximately 8" (203mm) long, set up to do many of the same functions as a jack plane.*

THE FORE PLANE

In a time when most stock was prepared by hand, another plane was often used: the fore plane, 14" to 17" (356mm to 432mm) long. It was often set up like a jack plane, with significant curvature to the blade, and was generally used to prepare larger stock or rough down a long edge in preparation for shooting it with the jointer or long plane. Its actual setup would vary with the craftsman's particular needs. The fore plane could also be followed by the try plane, about 22" (559mm) long and used to prepare an edge for trial fitting (thus its name) before being finally shot true with the jointer or long plane.

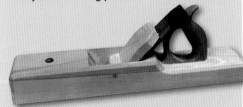

Razee fore plane, 15" (381mm) long. *The term* razee *derives from the French* vaisseau rasé, *a wooden warship with the upper deck cut away. Razee planes have the top of the body cut away behind the blade, lowering the handle and reducing the weight.*

you to choose aspects of its anatomy for customizing other planes for other purposes.

If you know why the blade curves, you can decide if use requires a blade with curvature, and if so, how much. From experience with the jack, you can reference how big a throat opening or chipbreaker setback, or what sole configuration another plane requires. You can modify different planes for shaping or preparing pieces not going through the jointer or planer. You are faster, more efficient, and not limited by your power tools.

WHAT TO LOOK FOR IN A JACK

The jack plane should be light because you will be lifting and moving it a lot. It should be capable of hard work without causing blisters. For this reason, traditionally, a wooden plane is often preferred (Figure 4-5).

Having a blade mechanism that quickly and easily adjusts the blade as work progresses is advantageous. It is often necessary to retract the blade as the work becomes smoother, and readjust from one piece to another.

Because you are removing a lot of wood, which subjects the blade to heat and stress, a blade of alloy steel, such as chrome-vanadium, tungsten vanadium, or A2, is a good choice for a jack plane. If you are using an older plane with a laminated blade in good shape, change it only if you are dissatisfied with its performance.

The Jointer Plane

After generally straightening and roughly dimensioning the stock with the jack, use the jointer to remove roughness left by the jack and to true surfaces and edges in preparation for final smoothing.

Today, the jointer plane (Figure 4-6), in the European tradition, most commonly is about 22" (559mm) long (the Stanley #07). In the past, longer planes of 24" to 30" (610mm to 762mm)—the Stanley #08, no longer in production, is 24" (610mm) long—were used. Its long length and greater width—the blade is usually 2⅜" (60mm) to 2¾" (70mm) wide—results in a flat surface overall. Its wide blade, traditionally sharpened to a gentle curvature of about ⅟₃₂" (1mm) or less—takes

out the ridges left by the coarsely set jack, and aids in squaring board edges (Figure 4-7).

The chipbreaker is set back from the blade edge the distance of the thickest shaving. The blade angle is intermediate to reduce tearout and the effort needed to work the plane, which often makes thick shavings.

THE CORRECT BLADE SHAPE

While the amount of curvature of the edge is at the discretion of the woodworker, it is important that a sweep to the edge tapers off the corners of the blade because it allows you to adjust the edge of the board being planed to square while the plane itself remains in solid contact with the work (see "Shooting an Edge" on page 235). The edge of a jointer-plane blade is not sharpened straight unless it is used with a shooting board.

TRYING, LONG, AND JOINTER

We classify any plane 20" to 30" (508mm to 762mm) long as a jointer plane. Up until about the 1870s, however, three distinct planes occupied this range: the trying (or try) plane, 20" to 22" (508mm to 559mm) long; the long plane, 24" to 26" (610mm to 660mm) long; and the jointer plane, 28" to 30" (711mm to 762mm) long. After 1870, use of these planes began to diminish, as did the distinction between them.

Figure 4-6. Jointer Plane Mouth Opening

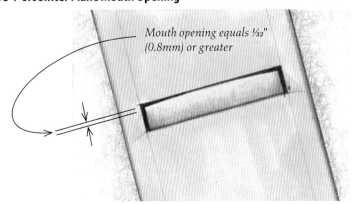

Mouth opening equals ⅟₃₂"
(0.8mm) or greater

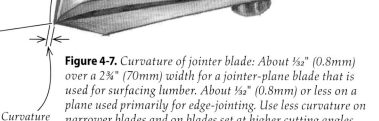

Figure 4-7. *Curvature of jointer blade: About ⅓₂" (0.8mm) over a 2¾" (70mm) width for a jointer-plane blade that is used for surfacing lumber. About ⅓₂" (0.8mm) or less on a plane used primarily for edge-jointing. Use less curvature on narrower blades and on blades set at higher cutting angles.*

Curvature of blade

JAPANESE AND CHINESE JOINTERS

Japanese carpenters and Chinese furniture makers can use their jointers in a different sequence than their Western counterparts, indicative of valuable techniques Western woodworkers can use to improve the speed and quality of their own work.

The Japanese carpenter will use one or two planes to remove roughness and prepare boards for smoothing (Figure 4-8). These planes will be about 12" (305mm) to 14" (356mm) long with blades around 60mm (2⅜") wide.

The coarsest plane will often be single-bladed without a chipbreaker. The blade is sharpened to a good curvature similar to, but not as pronounced as, that of the Western jack. The second plane may be slightly wider, the blade sharpened to less of a curvature and capped with a chipbreaker to reduce tearout.

Once the surface has been prepared, a truing plane is used. Unlike the previous two planes, which will in effect have their soles shaped slightly convex along their length (by maybe less than 0.01" or 0.25mm), the sole of the truing plane will have at least three, but more probably four or five, areas of contact.

These form a straight line and a true plane. The areas in between are relieved to simplify maintenance of the contact surfaces. This plane is about 16" to 18" (406mm to 457mm) long with perhaps a 70mm (2¾")-wide blade sharpened to the curvature similar to a smoothing plane. In practice, the plane is more of a preliminary smoothing plane—what I have come to call a *panel plane* (more in the next chapter). At the artisan's discretion, one or more smoothing planes follow the panel plane.

It is common in the woodworking trades in Japan, to the best of my knowledge, to edge-join boards similarly to the way Westerners do using a shooting board. A plane is laid on its side on a ledge fixed to the side of the bench, and the piece to be joined is laid flat on the bench with the edge to be joined projecting slightly.

The plane is run along the edge of the piece, planing it straight and square. Slightly different from the one used for truing surfaces, this plane is typically about 18" (457mm) long, and the side of the plane that rests on the ledge is thicker than the other side. This is so the plane does not wear out prematurely while removing material in the course of maintaining square between this side and the sole. The blade in this plane is sharpened straight across.

Chinese furniture makers often will prepare stock using one or two jointer size planes, with the first set up much like a jack plane (albeit with a more subtle blade curvature) for rapid stock removal. A second plane, a jointer, is set up and used in a manner similar to a Western-style jointer plane. These first planes are usually about 18" (457mm) to 20" (508mm) long with blades often only about 1¾" (44mm) wide, in response to the difficulty and hard work of planing the tropical hardwoods traditionally used in the furniture.

The blade of the plane is set at a lower angle (55°—maybe less) than that of the next plane to be used, which is around 14" (356mm) long. This second plane is more of a preliminary smoother (what I would call a panel plane), though it is the length of a jack plane. In my experience, tropical hardwoods do not respond well to gouging cuts such as a traditional Western jack would make; the cut is arduous and has disastrous results.

The wood has to be trued and smoothed in gentler, less severe steps. For this reason, all of the Chinese planes have much less blade curvature than their Western counterparts. The angle of their "jack" (panel) plane, which follows the jointer, is 55° to 60° or higher, with the throat or chipbreaker set up according to the artisan's requirements.

PICKING A JOINTER PLANE

What you want in your jointer depends on its planned use. The majority of woodworkers today will use the jointer only for shooting an edge, and for this, stability and low maintenance are priorities. For this reason, the Stanley-type plane has been the first choice among woodworkers for several generations. If you do a lot of surface prep with a jointer, however, you ought to consider a wood-body jointer.

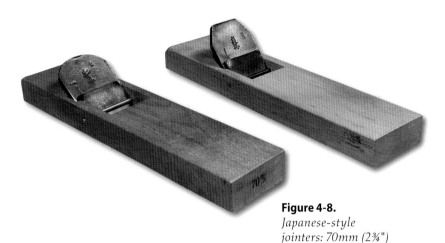

Figure 4-8.
Japanese-style jointers: 70mm (2¾") blade with 40° pitch (left); 70 mm (2¾") blade with 47½° pitch (right), both 16" (457mm) long.

Although the plane is only marginally lighter, a wood sole offers less resistance than an iron one, which is particularly noticeable when making the repeated cuts required to surface a board. In addition, you can sometimes find these with higher blade angles than the Stanley, for use in the harder woods; or you can make a plane to your preference. (See "Making Traditional Wood-Body Planes" on page 258.)

When working with the tropical hardwoods you may encounter considerable difficulty with tearout because of the lower blade angles found on most jointers. If you are working a lot with these woods, you may want to use a Chinese-style jointer.

A carbon or light alloy blade such as an A2 blade is a good choice unless you are using the Chinese plane; then, chrome vanadium or tungsten vanadium blade is a good choice.

IS A JOINTER PLANE NEEDED?

You probably can work without a jointer plane, but for the best quality work, only good tools, well maintained and properly operated, will accomplish something comparable. And even then you have to evaluate the quality of the surface made by these machines. Glue-line ripping saws and well-maintained and accurate power jointers (large enough for the work) are adequate for high quality (and quantity) work. But for work we expect to outlive us, the fineness of the glued edge must be attended to.

Under a microscope, the ripped or sawn edge looks torn. Even with the best blades, there is some scoring, some small irregularities. Most glues bond best when the fibers are cleanly sheared and the surfaces closely mated. A sawn surface compromises both qualities. However, most modern glues are gap filling to the extent necessary between two well sawn surfaces and provide strength in excess of the wood itself.

I believe the true longevity of this joint is in question. Edge-glued planks are under tremendous stress over the years and have no mechanical advantage (such as a mortise-and-tenon joint does) to resist stress. They depend solely on the glue's strength. If the cupping of the planks has not opened the joints, then moisture from the seasons or central heating has opened the joints at the ends.

We place great faith in modern glues, and they appear to be miracle workers. Hide and other protein glues have been around since before the pharaohs' time, so we know how they react. However, our modern glues are only one or two generations old, and while testing assures us they are durable, testing only mimics our best guesses and cannot possibly include all the variables.

As woodworkers, we need to understand wood movement, consider the reaction of the wood during gluing and afterward, and give the glue the best conditions under which to function. We can design the piece and select the wood for optimal structural functionality (as well as grain appearance), making sure the wood is dry and has reached equilibrium with its environment. We can prepare the joint, finessing it for gluing. Tradition recommends the mating edges be planed to a slight concavity over their length, so that clamping them together produces slightly increased pressure at the ends.

As glue dries and gives off moisture at the joint ends first, pressure equalizes and joints at the ends will not open. Finessing increases the joint's longevity because seasonal changes in temperature and humidity affect the open pores of the end grain first, while the rest of the plank lags behind.

This differential movement over the length of the plank also stresses the glue joint. The slight pressure created by planing a bit of concavity along the length of the joint helps keep the joint together. A machine cannot do the subtle shaping. It is done by skilled hands with a jointer plane.

I believe the slight concavity across the *width* of the joint resulting from the blade being sharpened to a curve contributes to the joint longevity. The resulting surfaces puts slightly more pressure at the outside edges, combating the initial stress of the glue drying from the outside in and the differential movement of the outside of the board responding faster to seasonal changes. This is only a conjecture, and would be more difficult to verify than what experience over the years has shown to be true about planing a bit of curve over the length of the board.

Smoothing Planes

The smoothing plane (Figure 4-9) has the widest variety of sizes of any of the planes. Length may vary anywhere from 4" or 5" to about 12" (102mm or 127mm to about 305mm). Blade width may be from 1¼" (32mm) to 2¾" (70mm), or even greater.

Planes outside of that range tend to be called something else, though they may be used for smoothing. Generally, the ratio of plane length to blade width tends to be 4 or 5 to 1, sometimes even less. Selecting the right plane depends on the size of the work and the difficulty of the grain. The general rule is small plans for small work, wider planes for wider work, and longer or larger planes for longer work. The craftsman makes the choice based on his experience.

The blade sharpens either to a shallow curve not exceeding the depth of the blade set (a few thousandths of an inch) or dead straight with the corners slightly rounded off. Both techniques prevent the blade corners from digging in and leaving steps in the work, undesirable because this is the last plane to be used, and the resulting surface must be defect free. The chipbreaker is set right down to the edge, back only as far as the thickest shaving for which the plane will be set (Figure 4-10). Blade angles can be the highest of all the planes of the triumvirate.

Ideally, the smoothing plane should be as wide as possible—as wide or wider than the jointer. This will result in a flatter surface because though perhaps only a few thousandths of an inch deep, the resulting cut

Figure 4-9. Traditional Western Coffin-Sided Smoothing Plane

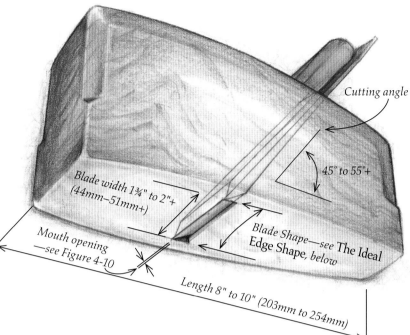

Cutting angle

45° to 55°+

Blade width 1¾" to 2"+ (44mm–51mm+)

Blade Shape—see The Ideal Edge Shape, below

Mouth opening —see Figure 4-10

Length 8" to 10" (203mm to 254mm)

THE IDEAL EDGE SHAPE

Ideally, the edge of a smoothing plane should be straight across, with the ends tapered off to avoid leaving tracks in the work. The taper needs to equal the depth of cut, which may be less than 0.005" (0.13mm). This is most easily achieved by added pressure at each corner when sharpening: five strokes for each corner on the first sharpening stone (in addition to sharpening the main edge), a few more than that on the finishing stone(s) can be enough. The resulting configuration works well, but I could not swear that it looks like the drawing.

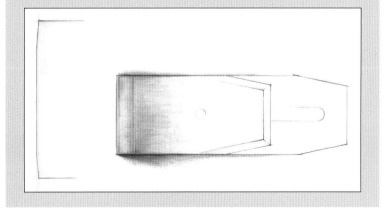

**Figure 4-10.
Smoothing Plane
Mouth Opening**

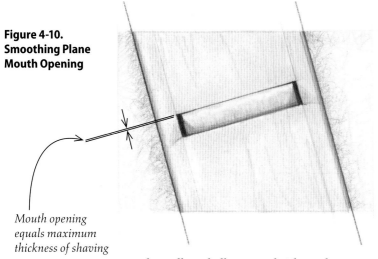

*Mouth opening
equals maximum
thickness of shaving*

is basically a shallow trough. The wider it is in relation to its depth, the less perceptible it will be. There should be, as well, a progression in the blade widths of the planes of the triumvirate, progressing from the jack (the narrowest), to the jointer (wider), and then the smoother (the widest). However, in reality this ideal relationship of the smoothing plane to the jack and jointer is difficult to maintain when working with harder woods.

Because the cutting angle of the smoothing plane is the highest of all the planes and the blade is cutting its full width (unlike the jack, and often the jointer plane, which often are not set to make a cut the full depth of the sweep of their blade), the amount of resistance to the cut is very high.

A wide blade, though making a very shallow cut, will have greater resistance than a narrow blade. On hard woods, this can mean that for all but the lightest cut, smoothing wood will be hard work. For this reason, I believe, European smoothing planes traditionally have blades 1¾" (44mm) to 2" (51mm) wide, even though jointers traditionally are much wider than that, with blades 2⅜" (60mm) to 2¾" (70mm) wide. Because of these factors, generally,

I would tend to limit blade widths on planes with cutting angles of 50° and greater to 2" (51mm) or less.

Short planes can be particularly useful in smoothing difficult woods. Smoothing planes do not have to stick to the common proportions of width to length. The converse of the functional shape of the jointer plane applies: while the length of the jointer trues a surface by bridging the hills and valleys, a very short plane will smooth the surface by following them.

The best way to approach difficult woods, after leveling with a jointer, is to prepare the surface with a smoothing plane finely set to true the surface, followed by an even more finely set smoother, of shorter proportion, that follows the surface and smoothes any remaining roughness.

The procedure is similar to using a *polishing plane*—a small plane about 6" (152mm) to 7" (178mm) long. The difference is the finishing plane is a full-width plane, equal to or greater than the intermediate smoother. The length-to-width proportions of a polishing plane could be as severe as 2-to-1.

CHINESE SMOOTHERS

The Chinese smoother, despite the great hardness of the woods they traditionally have worked, is often as wide or wider than the jointer. Curiously, their smoother is about the same width as the European smoother; they just made their jack and jointer narrower, due to the hard work of preparing such hard woods.

WHAT TO LOOK FOR IN A SMOOTHING PLANE

Blade quality is the most important consideration in selecting a smoothing plane. Other parts of plane anatomy fall in line after this priority. It must be possible to execute tactics finely and precisely. The settings must be easily maintained.

As to the style of the plane, unlike the jointer, where height above the work is advantageous, giving feedback as to the angle of the plane to the work when shooting an edge, I think it is preferable to be low, close to the work when smoothing.

The position gives greater control and more sensitive feedback. Weight is less of an issue than in other planes, as work is less repetitious and physically less vigorous than with, say, a jack plane. Conversely, I do not believe additional weight improves the quality of the cut itself, though perhaps by personal preference it may give you a greater sense of command in use.

A more expensive plane may get you adjustments that are more precise, as well as more dependable maintenance of fine settings, but unless the blade is of the highest quality, and matched to the work, all of that will mean nothing. In the end though, more than any of the other planes, your choice of smoothing plane is personal.

To get the most efficient and effective use of the smoothing plane, use all of the strategies for effective planing. While a nice piece of even-grained wood may be forgiving of sloppiness in the setup of a plane, only precisely set up and fastidiously maintained

planes smooth difficult woods. To effectively plane the most difficultly figured woods, the critical tolerances required of blade shape, sharpness, cutting depth, and sole flatness become difficult to perceive. Maintaining balance between the position of the chipbreaker and throat opening in relation to the blade angle is also difficult.

With practice, you can begin to sense the correct tolerances or what is out of balance in the interplay between particular tactics. This *sense* bears on what we call skill, achieved by striving for excellence through practice. Knowing and understanding the tactics is the first step. More difficult is knowing and perceiving the tolerances involved. That can only be learned through practice.

The smoothing plane is the most commonly available and perhaps most useful plane today. Whereas machines have largely supplanted the plane in dimensioning and truing lumber, the effectiveness of the smoothing plane is hard to cast aside. For some tasks, it is demonstrably faster, more accurate, and more effective than abrasives in producing the highest quality surface. Its main drawback is it takes skill and practice to achieve proficiency; and skill and practice require time and training.

5

THREE MORE PLANES

Strategies for Speeding the Work

While the triumvirate—the jack, jointer, and smoothing planes—form the core of the bench planes, planes that are between or outside them can assist them in their work. I consider these three the most useful of these planes:

- The panel plane, used between the jointer and smoothing plane.

- The scrub plane, used before the jack.

- The block plane, which stands alone, doing a little bit of everything, and, therefore, is arguably indispensable.

The Stanley-style metal block plane is one of the most versatile planes in the tool kit.

Figure 5-1. *At left is a 12"-long razee-style panel plane with a 2¼"-wide blade bedded at 47½°. It works well to prepare the surface for the 8"-long coffin-sided smoother (right), which has a 2"-wide blade bedded at 50°.*

The Panel Plane

The origin of the term panel plane is unclear. One source speculates it originated in a Spiers or Norris catalog, describing a plane 14" to 18" (356mm to 457mm) long with a 2½" (64mm)-wide cutter. While this is the general size of a jack plane, the panel plane, because of its fine, unadjustable throat and great weight, was obviously meant for smoothing, not taking down rough timber.

The implication of the terminology in the catalog is that preparing larger pieces, such as panel boards, is the reason for its name, though it was probably set up and used variously, depending on the needs of its owner. Whatever its origins, it is an extremely valuable type of plane, and its use can both speed and improve results in the woodshop (Figure 5-1).

If you do a lot of handplaning, you will find it faster to use more than one plane for smoothing. Surfaces straight from the jointer plane or the power planer can have many surface irregularities. The jointer plane, with its scalloped cut, leaves a slightly

textured surface. Lumber from the planer often will be surprisingly uneven, usually with some snipe at the ends from before and after it leaves the bed rollers, and often other irregularities, or tearout.

When working the surface with a finely set and maintained smoothing plane, irregularities show up as the plane skips over them initially, leaving large areas untouched. Your first reaction is to set the plane for a deeper cut, to avoid wasting effort cutting air. This may necessitate setting the blade deeper and, depending on the plane, opening the mouth a little (if it is adjustable) and possibly backing off the chipbreaker.

If you have a screwed-on chipbreaker, you will have to disassemble the plane before you can readjust. On a surface prone to tearout, you will have to use all the usual planing strategies to get good results. This means once you have the surface leveled, you will have to close the mouth down and reset the chipbreaker and blade.

If the surface is particularly difficult, the blade should be fresh from the sharpening stone. If you have already used the blade to prepare the board, you will probably need to re-sharpen it. Getting the proper setting for a fine tearout-free cut takes a bit of finessing, so adjusting it back and forth from one type of cut to another takes additional time.

To avoid adjusting, readjusting, and re-sharpening, it is faster to use two, and sometimes three, planes for smoothing. When preparing parts for a project, I often work through the majority of the pieces with only one plane, experiencing no problems, especially when some of the surfaces are hidden. Prominent surfaces, or ones prone to tearout, may require more care. For these, after smoothing away the milling marks with the first plane, I go over the surfaces with a second, more finely set plane.

Sometimes on tougher surfaces, I resort to a third plane. Each plane in the sequence has an increasingly finer set of the blade, as well as chipbreaker and throat settings, and the blades themselves are of increasing quality. The last plane I use has my best blade and is so finely set that it cuts only dead flat surfaces. This plane cuts an extremely fine slice, with shavings like gossamer, leaving a tearout-free surface. However, if the work is not prepared to a sufficient tolerance of flat, it just skips over the low spots.

Initially, I used another smoothing plane the same size as the final smoother for this panel plane—and often still do—and this works well (Figure 5-2). However, I found that using a plane larger than my final smoothing plane is often even more effective in achieving the required flat surface.

The extra length, with a sole prepared as a truing plane, really levels the surface, and the use of a wide blade (2¼" to 2¾", or 57mm to 70mm, depending on the type and size of the wood to be planed) sharpened straight with just the corners honed off as in a finely set up smoother, yields a flatter surface as well (Figure 5-3). This panel plane is finely set up, so that it cannot make a deep cut. If the surface is too rough coming off the machines, I will use a more coarsely set plane to initially level, and then prepare, the surface with the panel plane.

Figure 5-2. *This is one of my favorite combinations: The 70mm (2¾") plane, bottom, with a blade bedded at 40° is one of my most used planes. I often follow it with the plane in the center, which has a 70mm (2¾") blade at 43°. If the surface still needs work, I may use the plane at top, which has a nice 70mm (2¾") blade at 45°.*

The panel plane is my workhorse. Often, it is the only plane I use. Because the sole is set up as a truing plane, I know the surface it leaves will be true. Because the throat, chipbreaker, and blade are set up as a fine smoother, it can plane all but the most difficult surfaces. If I have to use a finer plane, I know the surface the panel plane leaves will be flat enough that I will not have to spend a lot of time planing off the high spots.

THE OLD STANLEY 5½

I believe the old Stanley 5½ (no longer made)—the 2⅜" (60mm)-wide jack plane—was often setup and used as a panel plane by earlier craftsmen, and was probably offered for this reason.

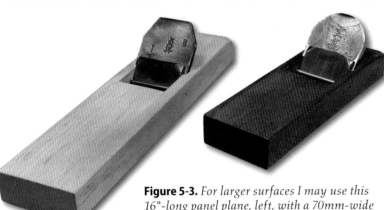

Figure 5-3. *For larger surfaces I may use this 16"-long panel plane, left, with a 70mm-wide blade bedded at 47½°. I may follow it with the 11" smoother with a 70mm blade at 47½°, right, or one of the coffin-sided smoothers.*

The panel plane should be 12" to 16" (305mm to 406mm) long; it depends on the length of your smoothing planes. If your smoothing planes are 8" or 9" (203mm or 229mm) long, then 12" (305mm) should be long enough. If your smoothing planes are 10" or 11" (254mm or 279mm) long, then a 14" or 16" (362mm or 406mm) long panel plane will be good.

Likewise, width depends on your smoothing plane's blade width. If your smoothing planes are 1¾" to 1⅞" (44mm to 48mm) wide, for instance, a 2" (51mm)-wide blade on the panel plane would be good; a 2¼" or 2⅜" (57mm or 60mm)-wide blade would be even better. If your smoothing planes are Japanese with 55mm to 70 mm (2⅛" to 2¾") blades, I would lean toward a 70mm (2¾") blade.

Blade angle on a panel plane should be the same or lower than the plane you finish with. For hardwoods, I believe a blade angle of 47½° works well. Your smoothing planes can be the same or steeper, depending on the wood and your preference. If you have to use more than one plane to get a surface smooth, use a progressively steeper blade angle as you advance from one plane to another.

There are also some hardwoods, such as cherry, that work well in the lower blade angle range. For these, I often use a 43° or 45° plane to finish, with a 40° panel plane to prepare the surface. For softwoods, a panel plane with a blade angle of 40° is useful. I have found no advantage to increasing the blade angle on softwoods. Smoothing planes for softwoods can all be 40°. If you encounter difficult grain, set aside one of your best planes, carefully sharpened and finely set, to be used for the final few strokes (Figure 5-4).

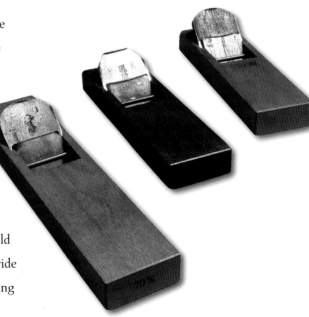

Figure 5-4. *These three planes all have 70mm (2¾") blades set at 40°. The 16" (406mm)-long plane I use as a panel plane to prepare the surface for the plane next to it. If the wood is particularly difficult, I may finish with the plane at the right, which has a high-quality blade.*

The Scrub Plane

The scrub plane (Figure 5-5) has a radiused blade, ideal for removing a lot of wood. It is usually about 9" (229mm) long with a 1⅛" to 1¼" (29mm to 32mm)-wide blade. The edge has nearly ⅛" (3mm) of curvature. It is used before the jack plane, usually to flatten badly warped lumber in preparation for being trued up.

Its anatomy is instructive, as all its features are so exaggerated. The throat is wide, often nearly ¼" (6mm), to clear the heavy chips that it produces. The blade is bedded as low as 40° in order to reduce the resistance to the cut. The blade is radiused not only so the corners will not dig in but to produce the deepest cut with a minimum of resistance. As tearout is not an issue at this stage of the work, it does not have a chipbreaker, although when used diagonally along the grain, it does not tear out as much as you might think, not when you consider how much wood it removes.

The scrub plane can be useful. I would find it hard to insist that it is a necessity today, but it is nice to know it is available.

If you work on a variety of projects, eventually you will run into the board that is too wide to be trued on the power jointer. There are several options:

- buy wider equipment;
- truck the piece over to a woodworker who has a big jointer. You would be surprised how scarce they are, and especially one owned by someone willing to subject it to unknown hazards—such as potential grit embedded when boards are laid on the ground in a lumberyard; or
- do it by hand.

Figure 5-5.
With its blade sharpened to a pronounced radius, the scrub plane is the first plane to use on uneven or warped stock, because it removes so much wood so quickly.

Wide power jointers are expensive, but if you find yourself faced with the problem repeatedly, you might want to consider owning one. Taking it to another shop—if one is available—is time consuming, but again, if it happens only rarely, and especially if you have a number of pieces to do at once, this may work out.

However, for that occasional wide piece, just perfect for what you have in mind, jointing the face by hand need not be slow or physically daunting—if you use the right technique. If your board is really out of flat, the proper technique includes using the scrub plane. The technique is even more useful if the work will fit your planer. While face-jointing and thicknessing a board is a bit of work, straightening a board's face with a scrub and jack plane to make it flat enough to go through the planer is comparatively easy.

All you need do to the board is straighten it enough for it to sit flat on the bed of your planer without rocking or flexing. It does not have to be smooth; the planer will take care of that once the second side is flat enough to be flipped over. Then, the board can be run through to smooth the first side, flipped, and run through again to produce two smooth, parallel surfaces. I use the scrub plane only occasionally, and although the jack plane can be used for the same thing, the scrub plane really speeds things up.

While the scrub plane is not fussy in its setup, you will want to pay particular attention to the ergonomics, as you will be removing a lot of wood while holding on to it. I prefer a Western-style plane as opposed to the Japanese-style plane for this operation. While pulling a plane gives greater control in a smoothing cut, pushing a plane to make a deep cut is easier than pulling. The hands are naturally cupped to grip in pushing and one does not have to rely on finger strength, as you do in pulling, to hold on against the greater resistance to the cut this plane has.

Another consideration is the weight. Because the resulting width of cut is less than ¾" (19mm), many passes with the plane must be made. For this reason, a light plane is advantageous, and I prefer wood to iron.

Besides its weight, iron's surface friction is higher, creating greater stroke resistance. The wear on the throat and sole of a wood scrub plane is not enough to compromise its function or outweigh iron's disadvantages.

I find the most comfortable handles for heavy work to be those on the classic German (wood) horned plane. I find the ball and tote handles on the iron planes rapidly blistering. Horned planes from the factory may need some rounding in places, according to how you like the grip, but they are the style most comfortable for this type of work.

The Block Plane

Strictly speaking, this plane is not really a block plane (Figure 5-6). Why it is called a block plane is a mystery to me. A true block plane is a simple block of wood, sometimes rounded off, with a blade mounted in it for planing. These tend to be small, so perhaps when wooden planes were forsaken for their iron descendants, the name carried through. I usually call them block planes, and probably will continue to do so off and on throughout.

Properly, they are the Stanley #60½ (12° blade bed) and #09½ (20° blade bed) and their various up-market competitors' models. Though I am not a big fan of metal planes, I find this one to be so useful, I am tempted to say it is a necessity. It certainly should be one of the first planes you buy. Its big advantage is its versatility, which is a result of its adjustable throat and having the blade set with its bevel up and the iron body. It is small and so, for the beginner, it is easier to handle and set up, and its features are instructive in understanding how a plane works.

This plane's most important feature is its adjustable throat. It allows the plane to be used both for removing large amounts of wood and for very fine tearout-free planing. The fact the throat is adjustable allows you to experiment and learn the relationship between cutting depth and throat opening.

Once you get the hang of it, you will find yourself adjusting it often for different tasks around the shop. At first you can leave the throat set ¹⁄₁₆" to ⅛" (1mm to 3mm) open and forget it. As your skill grows and you become more demanding of your tool's performance, you can refine the setup, tightening the throat further for fine work. Eventually, when the plane is fully tuned, you will discover that a throat opening of a few thousandths of an inch will produce tearout-free work in almost any wood.

The fact that the blade is mounted bevel-up also lends the plane versatility, allowing you to adjust the blade angle at the grinder or on a honing stone. This is because changing the bevel angle (or adding a microbevel) essentially changes the angle of the cut. Some would argue this feature is even more important than the adjustable throat. I do not often make use of it, as I have found it faster, if I need a different blade pitch, to use a different plane. (See "The Panel Plane" on page 72.)

If you want to try it, it is simple enough to hone a steeper angle as a microbevel to accommodate hardwood that is more difficult. Alternatively, grind a lower angle on the blade to plane end grain or softwoods. The blade is small (and unless you have upgraded your blade, pretty soft in the mass-market planes), and so it is quick to grind and hone.

The fact that the block-plane body is iron has its advantages and disadvantages. In the shop, I find it increases its versatility. Knocking an edge off a piece, usually chamfering it but sometimes shaping it more elaborately, is a frequent task. Doing this with a wooden plane immediately scores the sole of the plane, quickly wearing the plane,

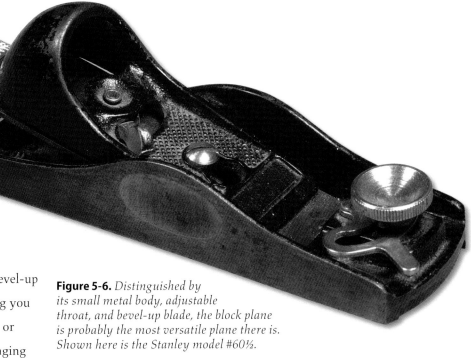

Figure 5-6. *Distinguished by its small metal body, adjustable throat, and bevel-up blade, the block plane is probably the most versatile plane there is. Shown here is the Stanley model #60½.*

MARKET BLOCK PLANES

Record and Lie-Nielsen have adopted Stanley's numbers for their block plane models; Veritas calls their models the low-angle and standard block planes. Whereas Stanley's low-angle block plane has a blade 1⅜" (35mm) wide and the standard block plane has a 1⅝" (41mm)-wide blade, both of Lie-Nielsen's models have 1⅜" (35mm)-wide blades, and both Record and Veritas' models all have 1⅝" (41mm)-wide blades. (Check the catalogs before you buy.)

Both the Veritas and the Stanley low-angle block planes have an adjustable mouth. But the Stanley (right) includes a cam lever that controls the travel of the throat plate, making it easier to adjust and less likely to slip if bumped.

Figure 5-7. *The Record #60½, on the left, with its up-market cousins, the Veritas low-angle block plane (center) and the Lie Nielsen #60½ (right).*

especially at the throat, its most critical area. Rather than chew up one of my good wood planes to chamfer an edge, I use the block plane. If the wood is difficult, I can reset the throat to make a polished cut after I have removed the majority of the wood with a coarser setting. Because the plane is resistant to wear, it is also ideal for use with a shooting board or bench hook (see Chapter 13).

The main disadvantage to the metal plane is, if you drop it, it is very liable to crack. For that reason, I do not take this plane on the job. While this is by far the most popular plane for carpenters because of its versatility, it is particularly susceptible to damage (though the new, higher-end models often use malleable iron for the body, which is touted as being unbreakable—though it seems to rust quicker).

A personal quirk many will disagree with me on is, I find using it freehand to remove the large quantities of wood often required on site is tiring to both hand and arm. Outside the shop, one does not often have the luxury of a bench, requiring you to hold the piece you are shaping with one hand while planing it with the other. I find my planing

hand cramps quickly. It is difficult to apply sufficient pressure up front with the single forward finger, and as you compensate by positioning your hand farther forward, it tends to slip off the plane.

I do not find it easy to pull with one hand, either, when making a heavy cut holding the work with the other hand—also commonly required on-site. As well, the edge on the standard blades of the mass-market planes does not last long, usually not even to the

ADJUSTING THE THROAT

You adjust the throat by holding the plane up to the light, looking down into the top so that the light shines through the throat. A fine but properly adjusted mouth opening will show a barely perceptible—but uniform—opening. It will be the same width all the way across, not tapering. If it touches in one or more spots, the mouth or the blade is not straight or they are not parallel. Both the mouth and the blade must be square to the length of the plane when the cutting edge is parallel to the sole.

morning break, and sharpening is another awkward task outside the shop.

For these reasons, I have for years used a Japanese plane on the job site. It is lighter, the blade stays sharp all day, and it is much more resistant to damage if dropped. The smaller ones (45mm—1¾"—or so blade width) are surprisingly easy to push (do not tell any one) for taking off large amounts of wood, and of course, they can be pulled with one or two hands. However, in the more controlled conditions of the shop, I have a newfound respect for the block plane.

I prefer the low-angle #60½. I feel the low (12°) angle is inherently more versatile, as with a 25° bevel angle you get a 37° cutting angle (Figure 5-7). The lowest cutting angle you will get with the #09½, with its 20° bedding angle and a 25° bevel angle is 45°. If you find yourself working with many difficult or tropical hardwoods, though, you might want to get the #09½ instead of, or in addition to, the #60½.

Do not get a block plane without an adjustable throat. Many of the cheapest and most expensive versions of this plane come without an adjustable throat. Such an acquisition would be pointless, as an adjustable throat is what gives this plane its great versatility. With it, you can have both the power stroke of a heavy farm tractor and the finesse of a fine sports car. Without it, you have just one or the other.

With the mass-market planes such as Record or Stanley, I would seriously consider upgrading the blade to a good quality alloy or laminated blade—an alloy blade if the

ADJUSTABLE THROAT PLATES

The adjustable throat plate on the Veritas does not project in front of the plane where it is vulnerable to being banged and possibly pushed back into the blade. Nevertheless, I have managed to bang it on things and push it back into the blade. I do not remember this happening with my Stanley and I think it is because the cam lever on the Stanley that adjusts the throat plate back and forth also prevents the throat plate from accidentally moving when banged. The lever also makes it easier to adjust the plate. Other than this, I think the Veritas is a far better plane and good value.

majority of your work is shaping (mine usually is), a laminated blade if you are doing more smoothing. I have had good luck with all the laminated blades I have tried and can highly recommend the good quality ones, even for rough work.

On the other hand, I have a Veritas block plane now, which came with an A2 blade. This has proven to be durable and performs well, even when smoothing gnarly woods. The blade that comes with the Stanley (the only other one I have direct experience with) is good if you plan to be planing around nails and will have to regrind frequently. However, as always, let your experience and skill dictate.

If the blade you have is performing satisfactorily, do not change it. If, however, you find the blade dulling quicker than you like, or you are unable, despite tuning, to get the results of which you believe the plane is capable, then upgrade the blade.

6
STYLES OF PLANES
A Wealth of Traditions

Woodworkers of all cultures have used the triumvirate—jack, jointer, and smoothing planes—in much the same manner, utilizing the same anatomical tactics for optimal quality and efficiency with only minor variations. Yet, over time and in various cultures, differences have developed for how the plane meets the hand, the manner in which it is used, and how to hold and adjust the blade. Many of the planes available are the result of hundreds of years of tradition—forms refined by the hands of craftsmen over many centuries. Some newer planes, though evolved from traditional forms, developed in response to the changing nature of woodworking. Some styles work better than others overall, and some work better for just a few of the tasks of the jack, jointer, or smoother. It is important to understand the strengths and weaknesses of a design in order to make intelligent decisions as to which style of plane to choose for a specific task.

Japanese Plane

Bailey Pattern Plane

Chinese Plane

European Horned Plane

Wood Block Plane

Which style of plane suits you and the work you do?

The Bailey Plane

The modern American and English Bailey-type iron hand plane (Figure 6-1) is a perfect example of a woodworking tool that has evolved as a logical response to the changing nature of woodworking. Leonard Bailey patented this plane in 1867. It is a design, I believe, that reflects the changes industrialization brought to woodworking.

The increased availability of woodworking machinery meant handplanes were being used more for fine-tuning the power-milled product than for the milling itself. Toolmakers now had the ability to produce a tool that would have been economically unfeasible 100 years earlier. Stanley Works bought the patent from Bailey in 1896 and has been producing it since. The company made a number of minor improvements over the years, but except for those refinements, the tool has remained unchanged since 1910.

The Bailey-style plane is a standard, continuing to fulfill the needs of most modern woodworkers. That says more about the type of woodworking most of us do than the capabilities of the plane, though. It is only mediocre at many of the demanding tasks planes traditionally handle. The proliferation of alternatives to the Bailey-style plane in recent years also suggests that the market is changing and it may no longer meet the needs of a new group of woodworkers.

The Bailey iron plane (a wood-body version of this plane was also made) has several attractions. It can sit on the shelf for months, be taken down as it was last adjusted,

Figure 6-1. Bailey-Style Plane

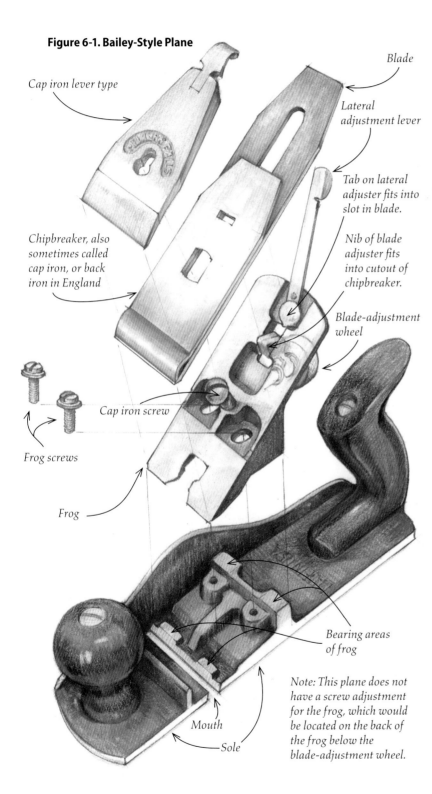

Cap iron lever type

Blade

Lateral adjustment lever

Tab on lateral adjuster fits into slot in blade.

Chipbreaker, also sometimes called cap iron, or back iron in England

Nib of blade adjuster fits into cutout of chipbreaker.

Blade-adjustment wheel

Cap iron screw

Frog screws

Frog

Bearing areas of frog

Mouth

Sole

Note: This plane does not have a screw adjustment for the frog, which would be located on the back of the frog below the blade-adjustment wheel.

and used again without further adjustment. It needs little maintenance once it is set up because it is unaffected by heat or humidity, and the sole is not prone to wearing.

Ergonomically, it works well for precise, single strokes such as shooting an edge or smoothing a board end. Its (usually) alloyed blade will take more rough treatment and impact before dulling and chipping than will a common carbon-steel blade. Its weight (greater than wood-bodied planes) often helps with control on those single-stroke uses.

The Bailey plane's 45° blade angle works well enough for maybe two-thirds of the woods commonly encountered, including most softwoods. All of this fits perfectly with how the majority of American woodworkers

Figure 6-2. *The screw adjusts the frog forward or backward. It is a useless addition to the non-Bedrock plane, because not only do you have to have the blade and chipbreaker removed to loosen the screws that allow it to work (unlike the Bedrock), but without accurately milled ways to run on, you can't count on the frog maintaining a parallel position when adjusted. There is also considerable slop in the adjuster so you also cannot count on the frog returning to its exact position once it has been loosened. Finally, there is little room for your hand and no room at all for a full-size screwdriver to get in to use it (using a screwdriver with a long shank to clear the handle is your best bet). On the Bedrock-style plane, the blade does not have to be removed in order to adjust the frog; however, moving the frog forward to close the mouth requires repeatedly re-loosening the set-screws as well as readjusting the blade—not something that can be done quickly or frequently.*

ANATOMY OF THE BAILEY-STYLE PLANE

The blade angle of a Bailey-style plane is 45°. Unless you have a Lie-Nielsen plane and buy the optional 50° or 55° frog, you have no other choice.

The blade/chipbreaker assembly is fixed with a lever cap, which, on the Record plane, no longer has a lever, but a screw. The chipbreaker is soft steel with a rounded, almost bulbous shape that can get in the way of a narrow mouth opening. It will nevertheless work and is required, as it has the notch that the blade adjuster engages.

The blade adjusts by turning a wheel mounted under the blade at the back of the frog. While the adjustment mechanism has some play, even on the best made versions, once you have the adjustment close to where you want it, you can fine-tune the blade position with your first finger tweaking the wheel without setting down the plane. Lateral adjustment is accomplished with a lever mounted under the blade that engages the same slot used to screw the chipbreaker to the blade. Push the end of the lever left or right to lower one corner of the blade or the other (I have

yet to memorize which is which) to make the blade edge parallel to the sole. This works satisfactorily but tends to change the blade depth when moved.

Mouth adjustment is accomplished by moving the frog forward, which on the basic version of the plane cantilevers the blade precariously. Milling of the blade seat and the mating surfaces of the frog and main casting have become increasingly minimal over the years. Some areas that should be milled are now covered with japanning (or paint on the cheaper models). This makes using the frog to close the mouth a dubious endeavor. The *Bedrock* frog is a better solution, and planes using this design tend to be better made over all.

Of note, especially when comparing the different styles of planes, is that on all the Bailey-style planes the blade edge is located back from the front of the plane about one-third the length of the sole. This is mainly to allow placement of the tote. On the shorter planes, this leaves an awkwardly small amount of sole to rest on the board when starting a cut.

today use planes: occasionally and for a variety of specific tasks.

If your tasks go outside these parameters, you will find the iron plane lacks proficiency. Its main failings are its difficulties in planing a lot of wood and in planing difficult woods. The form that is so ergonomic for the occasional precise stroke soon blisters the hands when significant planing is needed. The weight that enhanced control now becomes fatiguing, and the iron sole presents greater resistance than a wood sole. For planing woods with difficult grain, it is complicated (on some versions of the plane, impossible) to close the mouth to reduce tearout (Figure 6-2).

While the frog adjusts to move the blade forward to close the mouth, on some planes it does not move forward enough, usually leaving the blade cantilevered, unsupported for nearly ¼" (6mm).

Because the standard blade is now about ⁵⁄₆₄" (2mm) thick, the blade in this position is prone to uncontrollable chatter. Though the Bedrock version of the Stanley/Bailey plane does have a frog design that supports the blade better, moving the frog requires re-adjusting the blade depth and fiddling back and forth. This type of frog is the exception rather than the norm. Once produced in limited quantities, the survivors have become rare antiques, and only recently available as expensive reproductions.

The blade-adjustment mechanism is inherently sloppy, requiring at least a third of a turn of the adjustment knob—often more than a full turn, depending on the quality of the tool—before it engages the blade. This makes adjustment tedious because you never know when the spinning is going to move the blade. Once moved (probably too far), it takes an indeterminable amount of spinning back and forth to get the adjustment right. This may be fine for most users today, who set the blade infrequently, but if you are moving through a variety of tasks, or you need to change the setting as you progress in the planing of a piece, it can be a major irritant.

A corrugated sole, available on some planes, debatably reduces the noticeable resistance of the metal sole in use, but the corrugations can catch on a narrow edge. With either sole, frequent light lubrication is a big help.

Manufacturers have addressed many quality issues of the standard Bailey plane in the more recent expensive versions of this plane:

- tighter tolerances on the adjuster,
- a way to close the mouth that works,
- a chipbreaker design and better quality blade that are more successful in dealing with tearout than those of the standard model, and
- optional 50° and 55° frogs to change the blade angle.

More expensive models still retain many of the inherent drawbacks of the design: the plane is still too heavy to be used to remove much stock. (The improved models are heavier than the standard models.) The sole resistance is high—considerably greater than that of a wood plane. While the rear tote is more generous and (usually) better designed, the front knob is not meant for use in hard and heavy work. For some woods, you are better off with a different blade angle than you can get on these planes.

THE BAILEY-STYLE JACK, JOINTER, AND SMOOTHER

For use as a jack plane to remove a lot of wood, the iron (or bronze) Bailey-type plane, with its greater weight, higher coefficient of friction in use, and often blistering handles, is at a distinct disadvantage. Additionally, all but the best made Bailey-style adjustment mechanism has too much slop to be adjusted back and forth repeatedly without frustration, as working with a jack requires.

However, if you need to do things that would quickly gouge the sole of a wood plane—smooth narrow stock, shape sharp edges, clean glue joints—then this can be a useful plane. And the low-blade pitch (45°) is suitable for the kind of stock removal for which a jack plane is used.

Jointing an edge, one of the commissions of a jointer plane, is the one job where I believe the Bailey-style jointer plane can excel: a precise task requiring a lot of control. The thin metal sole sets the handles and the hands down low to the work, giving greater stability. If it is advantageous, the thumb and first finger can grip the thin front of the sole, with the second or third fingers serving as a fence to help gain greater control.

For such tasks, the slop in the blade-adjustment mechanism is less of a deficit (though still irritating), as the blade does not need to be adjusted very often. In fact, once set it can usually be left indefinitely, to be picked up again days or weeks later and used. However, if you find yourself having to do a

lot of surfacing, the metal planes' drawbacks quickly become apparent. In this case, you may want to consider buying (or making) a wooden jointer to make this job easier (see the following sections for descriptions of wooden jointers). Additionally, this could give you the option of a higher blade pitch, which might be advantageous for some woods.

The standard grade of the Bailey-style plane can provide serviceable results when smoothing, but will take some attention to detail when setting up and adjusting. Getting outstanding results is more difficult. The geometry of the mouth and the chipbreaker will have to be reworked to get either to fully function, and the blade will most probably have to be upgraded. Getting a fine setting on the depth of cut is even more frustrating with the smoothing plane than it is on the other models used for dimensioning and jointing.

In addition, the friction of the sole is most noticeable when smoothing, great enough that it often interferes with the feedback you are getting from the cutting action of the blade and requiring frequent lubrication.

The premium grades of these planes do give quite good results nearly right out of the box, though of course, you will have to hone the blade, and it is always a good idea to check the bottom to see if it is as flat as it should be. Blade pitch is still limited to 45° (except for Lie-Nielsen's 50° and 55° optional frogs), so planing harder woods may be less successful.

Figure 6-3. Wood Block Plane

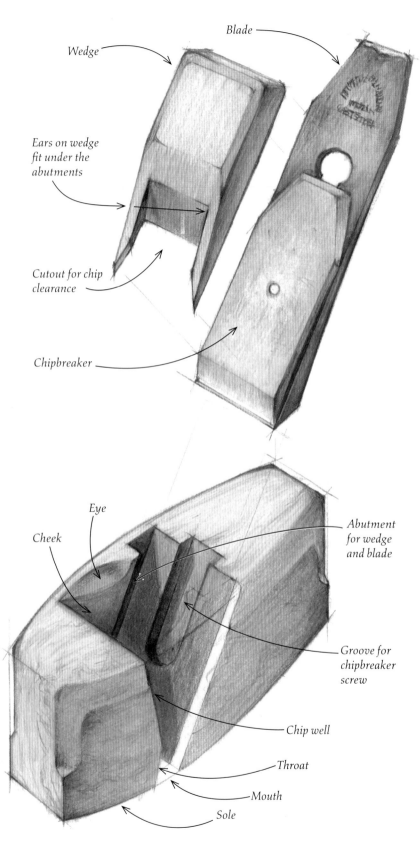

Wedge

Blade

*Ears on wedge
fit under the
abutments*

*Cutout for chip
clearance*

Chipbreaker

Eye

Cheek

*Abutment
for wedge
and blade*

*Groove for
chipbreaker
screw*

Chip well

Throat

Mouth

Sole

Wood Block Planes

The wood block plane (Figure 6-3) from which the Bailey plane evolved has several drawbacks (many of which were improved upon by the Bailey plane), but these planes can still be of great use in today's shop. Old wooden planes are still rather plentiful (if they don't all get bought up by collectors to put on their mantles) and cheap. The blades, either tapered or parallel, are often laminated—do not bother with a plane that does not have a laminated blade—and will generally out-perform any off-the-shelf blade. The wooden bodies can be easily reshaped for use on curved surfaces.

In addition, it is easy to refurbish the plane by installing an insert to close down the mouth opening. They are lighter than metal planes, so they can be less fatiguing for extended planing, or for planing in awkward positions, such as in boat work.

The planes were developed back when everything was done by hand, involving many hours a day working with the tool, and so the handles or grips are effective and comfortable for long periods. Moreover, because they are wood, they can easily be custom-shaped. Often you can find these planes with cutting angles higher than the metal planes' standard 45°, which makes them more suited to producing tear-out-free surfaces in the woods most encountered in North America and Europe.

On the negative side, wood-body planes can be difficult to adjust, at least until you get used to them. The soles can wear fast if mistreated, and they can warp or, if not properly maintained, split. (See "Setting-Up Wood Body Planes" on page 163.

Wooden planes are subject to a singular abuse that has led to their bad reputation among modern woodworkers. Wooden planes are criticized for rapid sole wear—they do wear faster than metal soles. Unfortunately, one of the few jobs for which modern woodworkers consistently use their planes is chamfering and planing narrow edges.

Chamfering a sharp edge will score the sole of a wooden plane on the first stroke; repeated strokes will cause deep damage. Using the plane to smooth or shape thin edges, especially of plywood or other glue-laden man-made sheet good, will do much the same or worse. Less than two minutes of this kind of work will require that the plane's bottom be reflattened before any fine work can be done. Do not abuse your wooden planes; use your metal-bottom planes for chamfering and other harsh work.

THE TRADITIONAL WOOD JACK, JOINTER, AND SMOOTHER

The traditional English pattern wood jack, or the razee jack with a decent tote, is pretty easy on the hands and body, and considerably lighter than its iron cousin. It is a good choice to remove a lot of wood. While the traditional wooden wedge is not really made to have the depth of cut adjusted back and forth a lot, which I believe is a drawback to using this style of plane for the jack, it does adjust faster than you might think, once you get used to it, and is serviceable. If this is a plane you use

ANATOMY OF THE WOOD BLOCK PLANE

The wood block plane has been made in a variety of blade angles or *pitches* over the years. While 45° is by far the most common, 43°, 47½°, and 50° pitches can be found relatively easily; others exist but are harder to find.

The mouth opening is fixed and on any used plane, it will be large. Occasionally, I have seen an old plane with a metal mouthpiece fitted to close down the mouth for fine work, or a hardwood piece inserted as a repair. Wooden planes today often have a tight mouth, but check with the manufacturer. Close down any mouth on a wooden plane by adding a fixed or moveable mouthpiece.

Chipbreakers (as well as blades) are heavy and tend to be well formed (at least originally). Blades are most often laminated (hard steel for the edge, forge-welded to a softer steel) and are tapered. Parallel (untapered) blades and *uncut* blades (without the slot to attach the chipbreaker) also can be found.

The blade is fixed with a wedge, which must be fit to the curve of the chipbreaker assembly. Adjust the blade depth by tapping the blade or the body with a wooden mallet or small hammer. Blade adjustment takes some getting used to; proficiency at it requires practice. It is not a good system for making major adjustments back and forth, but despite how primitive it seems, precise adjustments are possible.

Like the Bailey-style planes that succeeded it, the blade placement is pretty far forward, the edge emerging from the sole about one-third back from the front.

infrequently, refurbishing an old jack plane could be an economical alternative, because they can often be inexpensively purchased.

There are, of course, modern versions of the wood jack and one of the most useful is the English-pattern Primus jack. The Primus combines the advantages of the wood plane for use as a jack with a quick, accurate adjustment mechanism. (See "Horned Planes" on page 91 for a description of this adjuster).

PARALLEL AND TAPERED BLADES

At the time most old wood planes were made, there were two types of blades. The first, and most common, was the *tapered blade*, which is just that: a blade that tapers in thickness from its bevel to its opposite end. These were so much the norm, in fact, that they were also known as *common blades*. *Parallel blades*, a blade that is constant in its thickness, was the other available type. This was used less frequently, and usually on premium planes, because no matter how often the blade was ground and sharpened, the mouth opening remained constant and did not enlarge. Both tapered and parallel blades came cut—with a slot for the chipbreaker screw—and *uncut*. Parallel blades are the most common blades today and are found on almost all modern planes; these are the blades we are all familiar with. For more on tapered blades, see "Tapered Blades" on page 164.

Use of the traditional wood jointer plane is pretty much a personal choice, as the plane has both drawbacks and advantages to consider according to how you like to work. The wooden jointer moves over time, often warping slightly, and requires periodic maintenance. You cannot leave the blade under pressure for more than the day's work.

If you find yourself doing a lot of surfacing, you may want to buy (or make) a wooden jointer. Used ones can often be purchased for a fraction of the cost of a new metal one.

While the weight advantage over most models of the Bailey-style plane is marginal, the improvement in ergonomics and the reduction in friction from the sole is immediately apparent. Using a wood jointer can also give you the advantage of a blade pitch different from the standard 45°. Some antique jointers have different pitches while, of course, if you make one, you can make it with any pitch you want.

The traditional European wood jointer with the tote set 3" (76mm) or so above the work (as opposed to being about ⅛" (3mm) above the work in the Stanley-style plane), while initially awkward to use, can with practice give much better feedback as to the angle of the plane to the edge of the work. This is because the greater distance of the hand from the work makes the angle easier to feel. Apprentices graduated to the full-bodied jointer after being trained on the (initially) easier to use (because its tote is positioned lower) razee-style.

The wood-smoothing plane has the same advantages and disadvantages of the wood jack and jointer: light in weight, lower in friction, tricky to adjust, and higher in maintenance.

There are additional considerations when contemplating a wood-body smoother. If you can find an antique smoother in decent condition, the blade will usually be laminated and of good quality. The plane and blade often can be purchased for less than the price of a good-quality aftermarket plane blade alone.

Old wood planes can often be found in higher blade pitches than most planes made today. There are some premium versions of the traditional smoothers being made, saving you the trouble of refurbishing a plane, and having to close the mouth down (something that almost always has to be done on an old plane). If you make your own wood-body plane, customize it to your requirements.

The Norris Plane

Though often considered the epitome of the plane-maker's art, the Norris-style plane (Figure 6-4) is more properly a transitional plane set between the wooden block plane and the metal Bailey plane. Where the Bailey plane was initially an iron frog and adjustment mechanism mounted to a large wood block for the sole, the Norris-patterned plane had a metal sole with a wood infill and was for nearly 70 years adjusted with a mallet, much like a wooden plane.

The Norris Plane was developed by Spiers of Ayr, Scotland, around 1845 and was later made by manufacturers including Alex Mathieson & Sons of Glasgow and Edinburg, and Thomas Norris of London. Later, Norris planes used Norris' patented adjuster (Figure 6-5), which is quite effective and could well be the reason his planes continued to be made until 1940, unlike most of his competitors.

The basic form of the plane consisted of a cast-iron or gun metal—and later also a rolled-steel—channel filled with rosewood, or beech in the economy model.

The most elaborate method of making the channel used double-through dovetails to fix the sole to metal sides. This joint in wood is impossible to do, but can be done in malleable metal. It is accomplished by laboriously fitting and then peening the corners of each tail into the dovetail-shaped voids filed into the face of the mating pins.

Constructing Norris-style planes is described in detail in *Making and Modifying Woodworking Tools* by Jim Kingshott (Guild of Master Craftsman Publications, 1992).

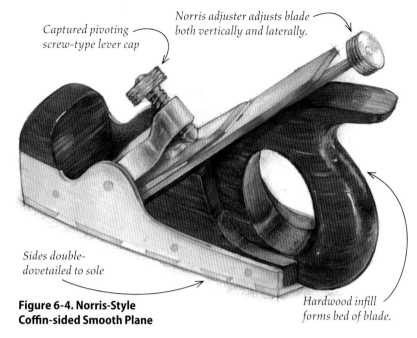

Captured pivoting screw-type lever cap

Norris adjuster adjusts blade both vertically and laterally.

Sides double-dovetailed to sole

Hardwood infill forms bed of blade.

Figure 6-4. Norris-Style Coffin-sided Smooth Plane

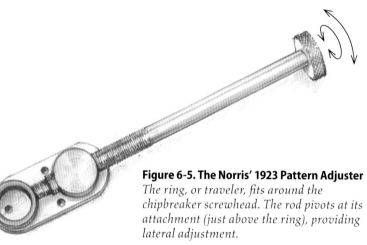

Figure 6-5. The Norris' 1923 Pattern Adjuster
The ring, or traveler, fits around the chipbreaker screwhead. The rod pivots at its attachment (just above the ring), providing lateral adjustment.

Unlike casting, the construction purports to provide a sole with no built-in stresses.

I cannot verify if it eliminates stress, but I believe it allowed the manufacturers to make the plane to higher tolerances, because the metal was not going to continue to move.

The plane is heavy, which is considered one of its qualities. While weight may aid in control when working some woods, it does not improve the quality of the cut, which is dependent solely on the blade quality and long-term setup and maintenance. I have not had the pleasure of owning a Norris plane, so I cannot vouch for its performance. They are beautiful and—an elegant example of beauty

ANATOMY OF THE NORRIS-STYLE PLANE

Norris usually pitched his blades at 47½°, though I would not say this was always the case. If you have a particular plane you are considering, you should check. That pitch is a serviceable angle, especially for hardwoods. The blades are heavy, ⁵⁄₃₂" (4mm) thick, parallel, not tapered.

In early Norris-pattern planes, the chipbreaker/blade assembly was held in place with a wedge, and depth was adjusted by tapping the blade, as with a wooden plane. In 1913, Norris patented his adjuster, modifying it in 1923 and again in the 1930s. This single mechanism regulated both the depth and lateral adjustment of the blade. Along with this development came a pivoting screw-down lever cap, to hold the chipbreaker/blade assembly in place. This type of adjuster is one of the most effective; with careful manufacturing, it greatly eliminates backlash (see Figure 6-5 on previous page.)

There is no way, however, to adjust the mouth opening (though usually the Norris came with a pretty small mouth). If you do not like the mouth opening, you are stuck. It is not possible to adjust or repair it

in service to utility—and an inspiration to have around. The adjusters are brilliant, though sometimes a bit sticky and not without a bit of slop. The blades are of good quality, and can be exchanged.

The planes were expensive, costing about a week's income. Collectors have kept the prices high. Are they that much better? No. You can purchase comparable planes for less. However, with this plane, that is not the issue.

And this raises a disturbing consideration. Many have speculated—not just with woodworking tools, but with many cultural objects—that as an object becomes obsolete it is embellished and elevated to an icon. The elevation to icon status signals the demise of that object's usefulness.

This can be clearly seen at the end of the nineteenth century, when elaborate plough planes, of ivory, rosewood, boxwood, and silver—and indeed the Norris plane itself, of gun metal and rosewood—were made. Their use, and handwork in general, was already diminishing. With Norris reproductions, and the variety of other high-end tools made of materials valued more for their looks than for their practicality, I hope we are not witnessing the demise of handwork and craft itself, as it devolves into a curious hobby.

THE NORRIS SMOOTHER

This is not the plane to use for roughing down lumber, despite the fact that Norris-style planes were made in jack-plane sizes. Most of these were called panel planes and filled the gap between jointer and smoothing plane, and should be used as such.

Jointers were made, and are occasionally made today, but, I believe this plane, more than any of the others, was made to be looked at rather than to be used, given that it weighs in the neighborhood of 10 to 12 pounds.

The smoothing planes work well. However, the collector's market has distorted pricing. If it looks as if you are getting a bargain on an old plane, then it probably has significant problems. Besides all of the problems that can beset both used metal and wood planes, the interface between the metal and wood infill is often a source of problems.

The Norris adjuster has another problem. The blade usually cannot be adjusted with the cap iron fully tightened, requiring a loosen/adjust/tighten process every time you want to make the least adjustment. Because of this, many old Norris planes have the adjuster stripped out by woodworkers who tightened the cap iron down too much.

The new planes are wonderful tools, perform well, are available in pitches suitable for hardwoods, but they can be used only for fine finish-planing because of the fine mouth setting (not necessarily a drawback). Most of the makers use a high-quality high-carbon steel blade ideally suited to the type of work this plane is intended to do.

Figure 6-6. Lignum Vitae or Hornbeam Sole

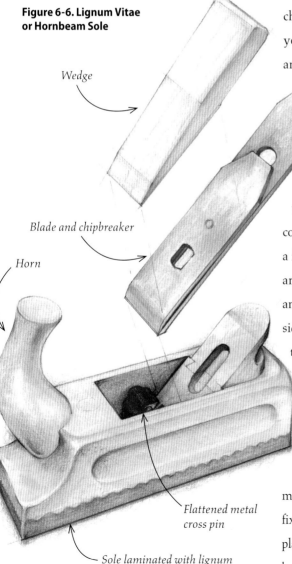

Wedge

Blade and chipbreaker

Horn

Flattened metal cross pin

Sole laminated with lignum vitae or hornbeam

Horned Planes

The horned plane (Figure 6-6) favored by the Germans and Scandinavians is a workhorse. It is comfortable to use for extended periods, for numerous deep and heavy cuts in hardwood. In addition, with its current refinements, it can be made to produce exceptionally fine work. The bodies are wood, so they are lighter than their metal counterpart.

For longer wear, the soles are often made of a harder wood than the body. One commonly available option is lignum vitae, which is hard and self-lubricating—a perfect choice for a plane sole. Overall, that means you are pushing less (reduced friction) and you are lifting less (reduced weight) throughout the day.

Several blade-adjustment mechanisms are available, all improvements over the original designs. One style is the old-fashioned wedge, which is better than its ancient counterpart because it is long and fits under a flattened cross pin (Figure 6-7). This arrangement allows the wedge to be loosened and removed by pushing or tapping it sideways, rather than by repeated tapping on the body, thus speeding blade removal. The design allows for use of a parallel, rather than a tapered, blade, which speeds and eases initial blade adjustment. It also seems easier to adjust.

Another type of blade-adjustment mechanism uses a screwed down lever cap to fix the blade (Figure 6-8). This, at least on my plane, is less successful. The blade is adjusted by tapping it with a mallet much like a wedge blade. The blade will not move under full pressure, so the lever cap cannot be tightened down fully until the blade is adjusted. Because of the thinness of modern blades and the chipbreaker's curve, when the chipbreaker is screwed to the blade, the blade flexes to an arc.

Tapping the blade to what appears to be its final position and then tightening down the lever cap straightens the blade/chipbreaker assembly, usually pushing the blade out of the throat slightly, and changing the adjustment. You must loosen the lever cap again, back the blade off, and second-guess how much the blade will move when the lever cap is tightened back down. This makes fine or frequent adjustments tedious. A thicker blade and/or a different chipbreaker might remedy the situation.

The Primus blade-adjustment mechanism, a third alternative, is one of the quickest and most precise available. It is particularly useful on a jack plane, where frequent readjustment can be required. I particularly like using my Primus jack plane after the scrub plane to level a board because of the plane's ergonomics, and because I can quickly and accurately back the blade off as the board levels.

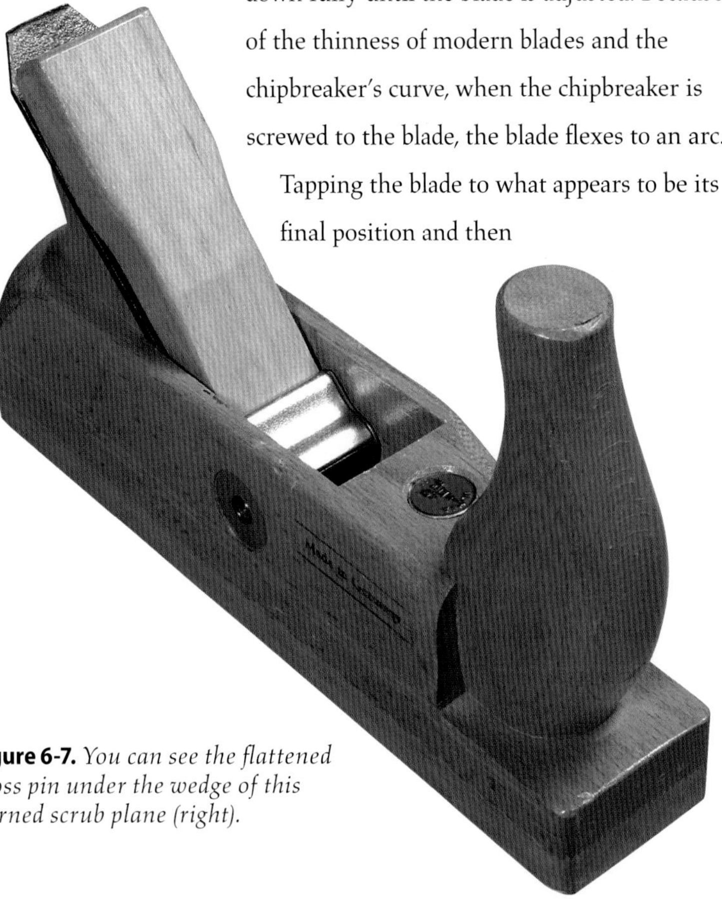

Figure 6-7. *You can see the flattened cross pin under the wedge of this horned scrub plane (right).*

ANATOMY OF THE HORNED PLANE

Horned planes commonly come with 45° or 50° blade angles. I believe they were also made with 43° and 47.5° blade angles. Prep planes such as scrub planes sometimes have a 40° pitch; some finish planes have a pitch above 50°. A toothing plane is made with a 70° pitch. Check with the distributor if you are looking at new planes; or take a protractor to the flea market.

On premium models, the mouth opening adjusts with a moveable mouthpiece (the *reform* plane). Chipbreakers are substantial and well made, though some may require some refinement to function with a finely set mouth.

Primus planes use a traditional approach to bedding the blade by having it contact the bed at just its bottom and top. To do it, they have installed two metal buttons at the top of the blade bed to suspend the blade so it contacts the bed only at these points and at the bottom. This guarantees the blade is supported at the heel of the blade bevel, the most critical area for eliminating chatter. Though the blade and chipbreaker assembly bridges this distance, this assembly, further dampened by the tension rod which holds this assembly and is part of the adjustment system, is thick enough that the blade does not chatter.

The blade placement is a little more central than Bailey-style planes, the blade edge being back from the leading edge of the plane about 40% of the length of the sole. This slightly more central position makes it a little easier to begin and complete a planing stroke.

The horn is available in both right- and left-handed versions.

Its main drawback is its complexity. Removing and replacing the blade for sharpening is time consuming, so frequent re-sharpening is pure drudgery.

To remove the blade, first the blade-tensioning mechanism and blade adjustment must be backed off almost completely. Withdrawing the blade requires pushing the blade-tensioning mechanism back in and twisting, and then pulling the tension rod out.

Because the blade is loose, it flops around as you try to twist the T-bar on the end of the tension rod, because the T-bar gets wedged on the chipbreaker and must be worked off. Once the blade is out, two tight-fitting screws must be loosened to remove the chipbreaker (Figure 6-9).

After sharpening the blade, the chipbreaker must be repositioned and tightened by trial and error. A Sta-Set-type chipbreaker is not an option because the blade-tensioning device and lateral-adjustment mechanism are part of the chipbreaker. Then the T-bar on the end of the blade-tensioning screw is threaded through the hole in the chipbreaker, rotated, pushed forward, re-rotated, and pulled back to its seat on the chipbreaker.

This whole process of removing and reinstalling the blade can take 5 to 10 minutes. Doing it a lot can be irritating. Luckily, with its chrome-vanadium blade, if you are rough planing, you will not have to do it often. Indeed, with its rapid blade adjustment, comfortable feel, and alloyed blade more resistant to impact and the heat of heavy work,

Figure 6-8. A Horned Reform Smooth Plane with a Screw-Down Lever Cap
The body is pear with a lignum vitae sole. The body has had some extra rounding to accommodate the user's hand.

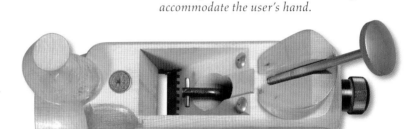

Figure 6-9. The Interior of a Primus Jack Plane
In the well of the plane you can see the two buttons that support the blade assembly at the top, and below that the T-rod that engages the chipbreaker and holds the blade assembly in the plane. The lateral adjustment is mounted to the chipbreaker. Two screws mount the chipbreaker to the blade.

the Primus jack plane is ideal for removing a lot of material quickly. While its blade might not get as sharp as a finely wrought carbon-steel blade, it will hold its edge for quite a long time under such rough work.

A less-common version of the screw adjuster is a setup with the screw (a worm gear, actually) directly engaging threads on the chipbreaker. This version does not use a tension rod. Because the tension rod eliminates backlash or play in the adjustment mechanism, this version without it does have some play, but it is a serviceable adjuster.

Additionally, some depth adjusters have a cam located in the slot in the blade used to mount the chipbreaker. Turning the cam moves the blade back and forth providing lateral adjustment.

Another feature often found on German horned planes—the so-called *reform* planes—is the adjustable throat. An adjustable throat alleviates problems in the frog-adjustment mechanism found on Bailey planes, and simplifies its construction.

The throat-adjustment feature may not perform satisfactorily unless the plane is altered. If you find the chip repeatedly clogs the throat when it is set for a fine opening, then the throat-relief angle must be increased. Possibly the angle on the edge of the chipbreaker may have to be reduced.

THE HORNED JACK, JOINTER, AND SMOOTHER

If you have a lot of heavy planing to do, nothing beats the ergonomics of the horned plane, especially with the body rounded off to suit. The horned scrub and jack planes are well suited to their task. The Primus horned jack plane with its accurate adjustment mechanism is better, allowing quick readjustments as you work. My only hesitation with this plane is its length—only about 10" (254mm). Because of its short length, the horned plane is not very useful for preparing an edge before using the jointer, one of the classic jobs of a jack. It also requires more care than a longer jack requires

to get a surface flat enough to transition to the jointer when prepping stock. (Primus does make a 14"—356mm—English pattern jack with its adjustment mechanism that is a good alternative.) The blades are alloyed—chrome vanadium or tungsten vanadium—good for hard and heavy work in hardwoods.

The manufacturers of horned planes also make jointer planes. Similar to English and American traditional jointers, these are constructed the same way as horned planes, with hornbeam or lignum vitae laminated to the bottom for wear resistance and the same choice of blade-adjustment mechanism as on their other planes.

Horned planes make fine smoothing planes, particularly suitable for work in hardwoods, especially because they are available with a 50° pitch. The geometry of the throat opening and chipbreaker clearance may have to be adjusted to get the most out of the planes. You may want to switch out the blade, because the high-alloy content does not give the keenest edge. The stock blade appears to be geared to heavy work. Be aware, though, when switching blades that not only is the blade width correct, but also that the slot for attaching the chipbreaker works with the fixing and adjustment mechanism of your particular plane.

Japanese Planes

In stark contrast to the elaborateness of the Primus plane is the simplicity of the Japanese plane (Figure 6-10). Its conceptual simplicity, however, belies its great sophistication and structural refinement. The blade itself is wedge shaped and fits into a precisely cut escapement in a block of wood. Only two components constitute a complete plane.

Contrary to a popular misconception, except in the occasional specialty plane and some new, modern variations, the chipbreaker is not traditionally used to wedge the blade into position. However, many nuances to the shape of the blade and details of the block that are not readily apparent must be attended to when setting up the plane. Besides the blade being wedge-shaped, the back of the blade (the side opposite the bevel) is hollow ground.

Much of this hollow is formed at the forge, so not much steel is removed when the blacksmith finishes it on the grinder. The hollow makes flattening the back of the blade easier, something that all blades (not just Japanese blades) must have done to them when they are first sharpened. I am always thankful the hollow is there because the steel of the laminated blade is so hard. (See "Carbon Steel" on page 21 for more on laminated blades.)

The bevel side of the blade, the face bedded to the block, is concave across its width. This probably helps keep the blade from shifting position after being adjusted. The blade seat must be shaped to fit this curve, and not made flat.

ANATOMY OF THE JAPANESE PLANE

When Japanese planes were first imported, they universally had a blade angle of 40°, which is still the most common pitch. While a Japanese craftsman would not hesitate to make his own planes with whatever blade angle he felt he needed, Japanese tool suppliers seem to resist supplying planes with higher blade angles. Under pressure from American distributors, planes now can be found with a 47½° blade angle, and, occasionally, others are available. Because the Japanese believe in a thin, sharp edge, all of the blades, no matter what pitch they are bedded at, will have a 22° bevel angle. For the higher pitches, this is too small and will chatter and/or chip in use and must be reground to a larger bevel angle.

Chipbreakers are hardened (often as hard as Western plane blades) or laminated like the blade. The main bevel is around 25°, and a microbevel is sharpened to as much as 60° on the lower-angle planes.

Except on the roughing planes, the throat is always small, though not as tight as a high-angle single-bladed hardwood plane. Double-iron planes generally rely on the chipbreaker for reducing tearout, supplemented by the throat opening.

Figure 6-10. Japanese-Style Smooth Plane

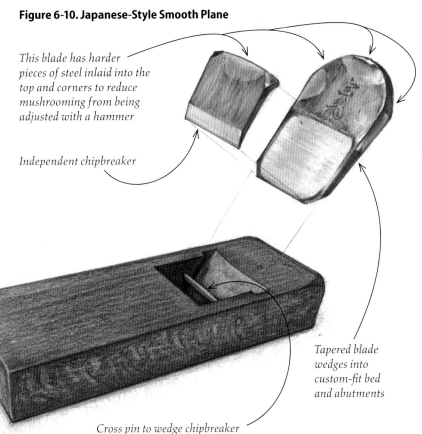

This blade has harder pieces of steel inlaid into the top and corners to reduce mushrooming from being adjusted with a hammer

Independent chipbreaker

Tapered blade wedges into custom-fit bed and abutments

Cross pin to wedge chipbreaker

Figure 6-11. Fine Japanese Blade and Chipbreaker by Blacksmith Miyamoto Masao
If you look closely at the edge of the chipbreaker, you can see the color difference that distinguishes the edge steel from the backing steel.

The best chipbreakers are laminated, like the blades (Figure 6-11). In all but the very cheapest planes, the chipbreaker is at least hardened and tempered. All the chipbreakers are easy to make sharp and crisp and to set down to the blade edge without wearing out or leaving gaps that catch chips. The chipbreaker has two ears on the top end that are bent or straightened slightly to give the right amount of wedging action against the cross pin so it contacts the blade tightly and securely.

The plane is meant to be pulled rather than pushed, and the Japanese apparently are virtually the only woodworking culture where this is true.

Many woodworking traditions have a few pulled tools, but not even their Asian neighbors, from whence their tools were derived, have major planes that are pulled. This may have evolved because the majority of Japanese craftsmen sit while they work, the cabinetmakers and furniture makers use an inclined planing board set on the floor. The board has a stop on the near end and slopes toward the user, allowing an efficient, ergonomic movement. On a wide piece, the

work is shifted along the stop with the foot in between strokes of the plane.

There is another major difference between Western and Japanese planes. In contrast to a Western plane, where the cost of the body is fifteen to twenty times the cost of the blade, a Japanese blade may be ten times the cost of the body, and sometimes much more.

Traditionally, the Japanese blade is laminated and hand-forged. That is something you will not find on a modern Western plane of any quality, though antique planes have laminated blades. Just recently, Clifton has begun offering premium Bailey-style planes with hand-forged blades.

The hand-forged blade is the heart of the Japanese plane. Its production is the result of nearly 1,000 years of metallurgical tradition. Much of the Japanese plane's ability to cut cleanly comes from the blade's ability to shear without tearing. The blade, at an appropriate angle and combined with a fine throat and/or a well-set chipbreaker, will smooth the most difficult woods.

All this comes at a price. Setup and maintenance must be precise, requiring great care, which is true of any plane from which you expect good results. However, because all Japanese blades and chipbreakers must be custom fitted, this part of setting the plane up does require much more time and care than most other planes. Getting half-decent instruction in how to do this, however, greatly speeds things. I find the plane, despite its reputation in some circles, to be surprisingly reliable, and once set up it will perform consistently with only some attention to detail. Storing the plane in a cabinet or drawer with the blade loose when not in use reduces the amount of tuning-up of the *dai* you may have to do because of temperature and humidity swings.

Japanese planes also can be highly effective for shaping work, because they can be easily modified or fabricated in an hour or two for same-day use. They are easy to adjust precisely. Because the chipbreaker is not attached to the blade, it can be easily adjusted up or down to accommodate a variety of work, or even left off if need be.

The blade removes quickly for re-sharpening and re-installation. If the blade is not particularly dull, I can knock it out, sharpen, reinstall, and adjust to use in 3 to 4 minutes. Taking the blade out, putting it back in, and adjusting it to use—without sharpening it—takes about 45 seconds.

THE JAPANESE JACK, JOINTER, AND SMOOTHER

Despite no outward accommodation to the human body, the plane fits comfortably in the hands and does not blister. Heavy planing does take some hand strength, but I find my body gets tired before my hands.

However, the Japanese planes are not my first choice if I have much wood to remove. I find pushing a plane with a comfortable hand grip accompanied by the proper stance, work height, and shift in weight as the stroke is completed to be an efficient way of moving when having to take off a heavy shaving.

The difficult-to-find Japanese jack plane can

STORING JAPANESE PLANES

When you are done using the plane, or at the end of the day, whichever comes first, always fully loosen the blade and then gently tap it and the chipbreaker back in just enough to keep them from falling out when you pick the plane up. Store it in a drawer or cabinet closed off to reduce temperature and humidity swings. (It is always a good idea to keep your shop at a consistent humidity as best you can year round, anyway.) Traditional houses and workshops in Japan were wide open to the air with only a hibachi for heat. Without central heating, and both summers and winters being humid, wide swings in humidity were unknown. (For that matter, the same was true in Europe, and especially England, until barely thirty years ago.)

be handy for use on softwood, with its low blade pitch, but less effective than its Western counterpart when used on hardwoods.

I find the Japanese jointer awkward for shooting an edge, either with the board edge up in a vise or with the piece laid on its face and planed as on a shooting board, which is the more traditional Japanese way. This may be more because I am less familiar with this technique, or because my jointer is too wide to get a comfortable grip.

Having access to other styles of planes, I still prefer Japanese planes for most of my finishing and prepping before finishing. I find the pull stroke and low profile of the plane give a lot of control and feel for the work.

Even before Westerners were introduced to the Japanese plane, many Western woodworkers occasionally pulled their own planes when smoothing because of a shift in grain direction or for greater control.

With its exceptional blade and feel for the work, the Japanese-style plane is an excellent choice for finish planing.

Chinese Planes

The planes used by Chinese cabinetmakers and furniture makers functionally are very similar to early European wood block planes (Figure 6-12). However, there are differences, and both these and the similarities are worth noting. The blade-wedging techniques for the two is exactly the same: a wooden wedge holds the blade, itself held in place in a wedge-shaped slot cut in either side of the blade opening in the body.

The same methods control tearout: the setup of the chipbreaker, mouth opening, and the primary means, the blade angle. I think

Figure 6-13. The Sole of a Chinese-Style Plane
You can see the brass mouthpiece dovetailed into the sole that is used to form a tight mouth and reduce wear.

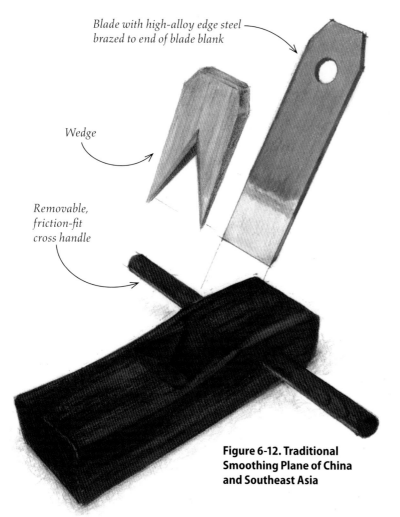

Blade with high-alloy edge steel brazed to end of blade blank

Wedge

Removable, friction-fit cross handle

Figure 6-12. Traditional Smoothing Plane of China and Southeast Asia

this is a result of having to plane hard tropical woods—a high-angle scraping cut seems to be more reliable.

The smoothing plane has a blade angle of 65°+, no chipbreaker, and a mouth opening of only several thousandths of an inch—barely enough to see light through when the blade is set. Often a brass piece is dovetailed into the throat to control wear (Figure 6-13).

The plane is pushed using a slightly oval-shaped handle that is inserted through a hole in the plane body behind the blade. The palms of the hands straddle the plane and handle. The fingers are on top of the plane in front of the blade and the thumbs are behind it. This is a comfortable position, allowing good body mechanics when planing. The handle is friction-fit and removes for storage or transport, or to accommodate those who prefer not to use it.

The traditional blade is often laminated and parallel. The smoothing plane I bought had a piece of steel about an inch long braised onto the end of a longer, softer piece that formed that main body of the blade and projected from the plane. The piece of edge steel is extremely hard, and appears to be high in alloys, because it does not sharpen easily. I have never seen a blade constructed like it (Figure 6-14).

The main consideration is being able to source a plane that can plane tropical hardwoods. Conversely, if you never, or only rarely, use these woods, you will probably be able to get by without them. The planes, with the correct pitch, work exceptionally well, and the ergonomics are easy for the Westerner to adapt to.

Figure 6-14. *The blade on this Chinese plane has a hard piece of edge steel, about an inch long, brazed to a longer piece of soft steel to form the blade.*

ANATOMY OF A CHINESE PLANE

It was not long ago that even seeing, let alone buying, a Chinese plane was a rare thing. Now, not only is the classic style used throughout China and Southeast Asia available, but the market includes high-end Australian-made versions, as well as a number of regional styles.

The classic style of cabinetmakers plane was typically used to plane tropical hardwoods and so has a high blade angle. A set of prep, true, and finish planes would have angles of 55°, 60°, and 65°, respectively. Because of the high-pitch angles, the plane usually relies on a tight mouth opening for controlling tearout, though sometimes a token chipbreaker would be supplied. The mouth opening usually was faced with a brass piece to reduce wear.

Some regional models have the cross handle let into the top and screwed to the body, rather than having a hole in the body. Another regional difference is a lower, wider proportion, reminiscent of Japanese planes, but with sweeping ergonomic curves to the body. The blade assemblies on many of these look like Japanese blade assemblies, with a wedge-shaped metal chipbreaker under a metal cross pin. However, the chipbreaker in the Chinese plane really wedges the blade in place, as the blade itself is not wedged into the body the way a Japanese plane blade is.

I have not worked with these, so I do not know if the result is a compromise in the ability to adjust the position of the chipbreaker or in the effectiveness of the wedge to hold the blade in position. If this design is successful at both of these (I'm not sure if this is a traditional design or a new hybrid), then it is a stroke of genius. One of the advantages of the Japanese plane is the ability to easily adjust the chipbreaker. This can be done because the blade is wedged independently of the chipbreaker. In the Chinese plane, the blade adjustment is dependent on the chipbreaker's position, and adjusting the chipbreaker too far one way may affect whether the blade will hold its position.

In classic Chinese-style planes, the blade edge is positioned near the center of the length of the sole, making entering and exiting the stroke about as balanced as it can be.

The main reason I use Chinese-style planes is their high blade angle and the effectiveness of that angle on tropical hardwoods. The central placement of the cutting edge is a bonus. Many regional styles of Chinese planes are sold with 45° blade angles and an alloy-steel blade cut from stock. They have no real advantage over most other planes, other than perhaps price, and preferable ergonomics.

7

JOINERY PLANES
Tools & Techniques for Making & Fitting Joints

While power tools have largely replaced planes for making joints, certain planes can still be extremely useful for smoothing, trimming, correcting, or finessing joints made by a machine. They can also, in some situations, be the preferred method for producing the joint.

By the beginning of the twentieth century, scores of specialty planes were being produced, each with scores of variations. It is really a testament to the inventiveness of the nineteenth-century mind how prolifically solutions to woodworking problems were produced and how well the elaborate, often ornate, style of the time was incorporated into the functionality of the tool. Only a few of these tools remain in production today, and that is because they remain useful. The ones I find most valuable are the rabbet plane, the router plane, side-rabbet plane, the dovetail plane, and the mortise plane.

A Router Plane levels the bottom of the dado of a tapered sliding dovetail joint.

Rabbet Planes

A rabbet plane is any plane whose blade projects to the edge of the sole on one or both sides of the plane. This allows it to cut right into the corner of a stepped cut—called a rabbet (also, a rebate)—something a bench plane cannot do. There are a number of rabbet plane variations, and though similar, each does a different job. Besides the basic rabbet plane (which does not have a fence), there is also:

- the fillister plane (a rabbet plane with a fixed fence),
- the moving-fillister plane (a rabbet plane with an adjustable fence),
- the shoulder plane (a differently proportioned rabbet plane with a low blade angle), and
- the bull-nose and chisel planes.

THE BASIC RABBET PLANE

The basic rabbet plane (Figure 7-1) has the blade bedded with the bevel down (usually), at any of the angles you might find in the bench planes—from 40° to 70° and above—though 45°, 48°, and 60° are most common. It may or may not have a chipbreaker. It has no fence. The blade may be mounted square to the length of the plane or it may be skewed, in which case the plane is often open only on one side and thus comes in right- and left-handed versions.

Taking the blade to the full width of the sole is done in different ways. The most common is to have a T-shape or spade-shaped blade—called a shouldered blade—the blade wide at the sole and narrowing above to pass through and be captured by the body of the plane (Figure 7-2). This style is used in both iron- and wood-body planes.

Alternatively, the blade can be full width for its entire length, with the body flaring on one or both sides of the plane a distance above the sole of the plane. This is common on older wooden body planes as well as contemporary German wood-body planes

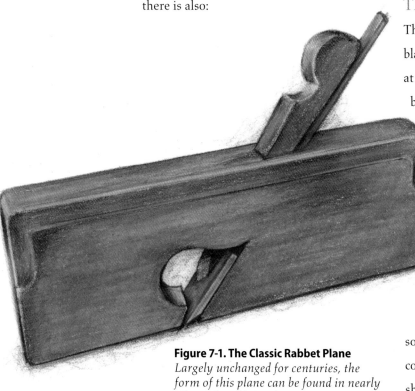

Figure 7-1. The Classic Rabbet Plane
Largely unchanged for centuries, the form of this plane can be found in nearly all woodworking cultures.

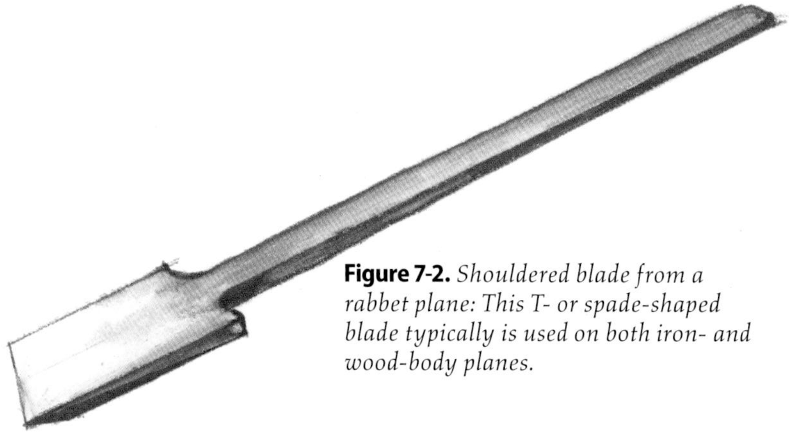

Figure 7-2. *Shouldered blade from a rabbet plane: This T- or spade-shaped blade typically is used on both iron- and wood-body planes.*

and many iron planes as well. This may limit the depth of the cut on deep rabbets, as the body eventually gets in the way.

The sizes of rabbet planes range from less than 6" (152mm) long to more than 12" (305m) (though the Chinese will often use a rabbet plane 16"+ (406mm), long), and from about ½" (13mm) wide or less, to more than 2⅛" (54mm). I have a Japanese rabbet plane that is 2¾" (70mm) wide (Figure 7-3).

Figure 7-3. *An uncommon Japanese rabbet plane with a full width 2¾" (70mm) blade. This plane is unusual because, in this case, the chipbreaker is also the wedge that tightens the blade. The plane is narrow on top to give hand clearance when working.*

USING THE RABBET PLANE

The rabbet plane is versatile and nearly every woodworker should have one. It was my second professional plane after my block plane. I first discovered how necessary a tool it can be while working as a trim carpenter retrofitting elaborate Victorian door trim to large out-of-plumb openings. The tapers on each piece were different and often tapered in two directions. There is no way to do this by machine—at least not without elaborate jigging. The rabbet plane was a necessity here. No other tool could do this task.

In addition, any exposed rabbet or step in the work is going to have to be dressed. Cutting the rabbet on the table saw leaves saw marks that must be smoothed, and using a router leaves fine scallops, if not the occasional burn mark or even dip, where the router was accidentally tilted ever so slightly.

The basic rabbet plane has no fence, which can make it quicker to trim a variety of rabbets, tenon cheeks, tongues, and other adjacent stepped faces that have been made by machine. Compared to a fillister or moving-fillister plane, it is also faster for forming tapered rabbets because you do not have to adjust the fence back and forth, or remove it altogether because it is in the way.

If you are using a rabbet plane to form a rabbet from scratch, generally you will need to clamp a straight edge to the work at the cut line, if the rabbet is parallel to the grain. If the rabbet is perpendicular to the grain, you will have to use a knife to score the fibers along the straight edge to begin, and usually score again several times as the work progresses. You can also form a with-the-grain rabbet using the plane itself to establish the edge of the cut. Tilt the plane 45° on its corner and, short of the final marked line, cut an initial V-groove (you can't do this as easily with a skew-bladed rabbet plane, unfortunately). You can then plane the rabbet down adjacent to the V-groove, using your fingers below the plane along the edge of the board as a fence,

PLANING V-GROOVES AND RABBETS

When establishing the cut, it is often easiest to begin just a few inches from the far end of the board (if you are using a push plane), and extend the cut a few inches on each pass, rather than trying to establish the cut for the entire length in one pass. (If you are using a pull plane, you will have to begin the cut nearest to you, and extend the cut away from you on each pass.) This works for both the V-groove and the rabbeting cut. As the V-groove gets deeper, you may need to flip the plane occasionally to plane the other face of the groove.

Figure 7-4. *In the foreground are a right- and left-hand skew-blade Japanese rabbet planes. These planes are open only on their respective sides; that is, the blades do not cut the full width of the sole. In the background, a typical Western-style skew-blade rabbet plane with a full-width blade, open on both sides.*

if necessary, until you reach the desired depth (best to mark this on the board's edge). (See "Planing V-grooves and Rabbets" at left.)

Once you reach that depth, you can turn the plane on its side and finish planing the vertical shoulder of the rabbet back to the marked line. This technique is a virtual necessity if your rabbet has a compound taper or if this joint is made more complicated by the two faces being greater than 90°. If they are less than 90° the faces of the rabbet will have to be finished to the required angle using a side-rabbet plane.

CHOOSING A RABBET PLANE

I generally find the larger sizes of rabbet planes to be more useful, as the rabbet is by definition one sided, so it does not make any difference how much the plane hangs out beyond the rabbet, and a larger size gives you more range.

The other side of this coin is that either the rabbet to be cut is so small as to make the larger plane awkward to use, or there is some space restriction, or you are actually trimming a dado (groove) and not a rabbet, in which case you should use a shoulder plane or router plane.

I also prefer the skew-bladed rabbet planes because I think they are more versatile, though you will have to buy two planes, a right and left (Figure 7-4). A rabbet plane is often used across the grain—to pare the thickness of a tenon or a tongue, for instance.

A skewed blade works at an angle to

the grain, rather than perpendicular to it, resulting in a much smoother cut. It also can be used to form or to smooth the field on a door panel (two of the four fielding cuts on a panel are cross grain), a cut that will show and must be smooth.

A blade cutting directly perpendicular to the grain will only tear the surface. The skewed blade also can hog off more wood with or across the grain, with less resistance, than a blade bedded perpendicular. The drawback is that these planes rarely come with cutters wider than around 1¼" (32mm). If you consistently do larger work, then accuracy in trimming is strained by having to make repeated overlapping passes.

Another difficulty can be encountered if you work with tropical hardwoods, as the efficacy of a skewed blade is lost on these woods when cutting with the grain, though it still cuts superbly across the grain.

To get good results in the tropical hardwoods you may have to use a rabbet plane with a cutting angle around 60°, the blade bedded perpendicular, not skewed. (For setting up and tuning the rabbet plane, see "Rabbet Plane Setup" on page 188.)

Fillister Planes

Four hundred years ago, an English craftsman was as concerned with making a living as anyone today is. To increase his profit, he standardized his product and minimized his tool investment. He might have one rabbet plane he used for everything, or one rabbet plane with a fence integral to the body, because he cut only one size of rabbet in his work.

The craftsman faced with making the occasional new or customized product would take his unfenced rabbet plane and tack a small strip of scrap wood, called a fillet, to the bottom of his rabbet plane to make a fence. This was not uncommon even into the twentieth century.

About 300 years ago, toolmakers started offering a rabbet plane with an adjustable fence (moving fillister) that could cut any size rabbet without having to put nail holes all over the plane.

The fillister rabbet plane (Figure 7-5) is a joint-forming more than a joint-trimming

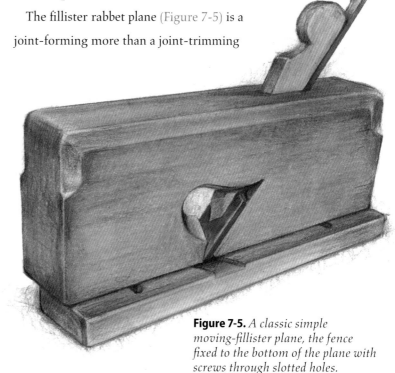

Figure 7-5. *A classic simple moving-fillister plane, the fence fixed to the bottom of the plane with screws through slotted holes.*

USING THE FILLISTER PLANE

When using this plane, the blade is adjusted ⅟₆₄" (0.4mm)—or slightly less—beyond the side of the plane, even though this appears to put it beyond the edge of the spur (see illustration at right). Surprisingly, this usually works. If the cut is tearing up beyond the score line, then the blade is protruding too much and must be backed off. If the plane steps away from the score line as the cut proceeds, then the blade needs to protrude more. Experiment with your setups before proceeding to the work so you know how your plane is behaving.

Measure the width of the rabbet from the spur—which essentially is the side of the plane (not the edge of the blade). Measure at each fixing point of the fence to ensure the fence is parallel to the sole. If your fence has only one fixing point, be aware you can probably flex the fence if you bear down on it, causing inconsistent results.

When making a cross-grain rabbet with a fillister plane, draw the plane backward at least once to get a clean score line that completely cuts the top fibers. Make sure the fence is in solid contact with the work when you do this, because it is easy to tilt the plane, score a line beyond the rabbet, and mar the work.

If you find your rabbet has stepped out after you have cut it, you have a couple options. If you are not too far along, you can readjust the blade to where it should have been (projecting ≤ ⅟₆₄", or 0.4mm), and then, keeping the fence tightly on the work, take repeated light cuts. The point of the blade will just cut into the work removing what it should have the first time. It is a bit frustrating, but often most accurate if you can keep the fence on the work. Also, check the alignment of the fence. If it is not parallel to the sole, it can hold the plane off the line. Measure at both fixing points and reset as necessary. If your plane has only a single rod and fixing point (such as the Stanley has) check that the fence is parallel to the sole. If it is not, you probably will not be able to make it parallel. You can add a wooden face to the factory fence, and make it parallel.

Alternatively, you can correct a stepped-out rabbet by turning the plane on its side and squaring up the shoulder of the rabbet. You can reset the fence so it does not exceed the score line or just eyeball it to the score line. If you did not reset the blade before you started this, however, the blade will step out in the other direction, resulting in a mess remaining in the corner. Then you will have to use the first technique—even more difficult when you get to this point. On occasion, it may be easier to clean up the shoulder with a side-rabbet plane, but make sure the point does not set below the bottom of the plane or you will repeatedly score the rabbet, and the plane will resist cutting sideways.

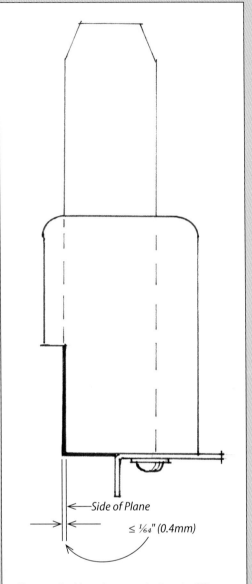

← Side of Plane

≤ ⅟₆₄" (0.4mm)

All types of rabbet planes, including the fillister, should have the blade adjusted to project slightly beyond the side of the plane when in use.

plane, and as such will find fewer uses in most modern shops than the unfenced rabbet plane. However, the fence and depth stop (if provided) can be removed and reinstalled when needed, allowing the plane to be used more easily for a variety of paring jobs.

I do not use my moving fillister plane as much as my rabbet planes. Sometimes the piece to be rabbeted is too big or awkward to put on the table saw, or because of balance, access, or size, it is too risky to use the router. Sometimes assembly precludes cutting a rabbet until after the piece is installed. If you do woodworking for any length of time, you will need a moving-fillister plane.

Besides the fence, which by definition all moving fillister planes have, they often come with a depth stop and a cutting spur. The depth stop is useful but not necessary. It is often hard to depend on. Depth stops tend to be small, so if the plane is tilted out of parallel with the stop's bearing surface, you will get a misreading—usually stopping short of the rabbet's full depth but occasionally cutting slightly deeper.

The depth stop is best used as a reference, checking the rabbet's depth when the stop first appears to bottom out. On some planes you can retrofit a larger full-length stop. A full-length stop is more accurate but harder to set up because it must be parallel to the sole.

More important is having a cutting spur or scoring knife. This speeds the work, because you do not have to score the wood for a cross-grain rabbet and then try to get your fence exactly adjusted to the score line. Spurs

have a couple different configurations: one is some form of knife, and the other is more literally a spur—or *nicker*—a small scoring blade that can be rotated when one side gets dull. I prefer the knife form because the spur does get dull and sometimes rather quickly.

I believe a skew-bladed fillister plane with a chipbreaker or adjustable mouth is preferable to a straight-bladed fillister for the same reasons a rabbet plane is: the skew blade can hog wood more easily, but with a chipbreaker or adjustable mouth it can do fine smoothing; and it's more effective on cross-grain work.

I prefer wood-body fillisters. They glide more smoothly on the work. The Record and Stanley fillister iron planes, present a lot of resistance. I have not had experience with the bronze planes, but the brass wear plate on my Japanese fillister seems to generate very little friction (Figure 7-6).

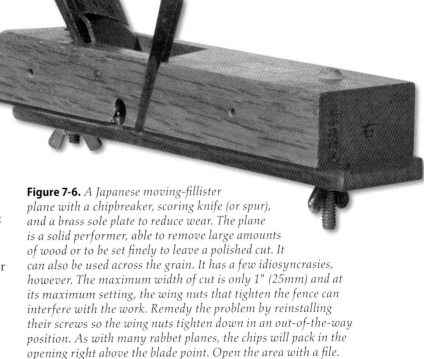

Figure 7-6. *A Japanese moving-fillister plane with a chipbreaker, scoring knife (or spur), and a brass sole plate to reduce wear. The plane is a solid performer, able to remove large amounts of wood or to be set finely to leave a polished cut. It can also be used across the grain. It has a few idiosyncrasies, however. The maximum width of cut is only 1" (25mm) and at its maximum setting, the wing nuts that tighten the fence can interfere with the work. Remedy the problem by reinstalling their screws so the wing nuts tighten down in an out-of-the-way position. As with many rabbet planes, the chips will pack in the opening right above the blade point. Open the area with a file.*

The Dovetail Plane

The dovetail plane (Figure 7-7) cuts the male portion of a sliding dovetail, either cross grain or along the grain. It is a moving-fillister plane with its sole angled to its side so that it cuts a 73° or 80° rabbet (a dovetail) rather than a 90° rabbet.

The blade is usually skewed, with the leading point on the offside of the cut, unlike the skew-bladed rabbet plane where the leading point is toward the work. This allows the blade to slice with the grain of the rising dovetail V-groove on the cross grain dovetail that you might find on the end of a board, used to join a shelf to its standard, for instance. It has, by necessity, a fence and, for cross-grain work,

a scoring knife. It does not usually have a depth stop because you do not usually need to use one when cutting the male dovetail. The planes come in at least a couple different angles (10° and 17° usually).

The sliding-dovetail joint is an excellent solution to mounting cross-grain battens used to stiffen and keep straight panels and doors. It is a common technique throughout the world. I have seen 500-year-old Chinese tabletops kept nearly dead flat by the use of a dovetailed batten underneath. Japanese shoji makers use the dovetailed batten to keep the wood panels in doors flat.

It is a more effective and definitely more elegant solution than a batten attached with screws through slotted holes. But, if you have ever tried to cut and fit a long sliding dovetail you know how difficult it can be to get a fit both sufficiently tight and yet accurate enough that you can still drive the batten all the way home.

The friction on even a well-cut sliding dovetail is tremendous. One way to make the joint both tighter and faster is to use a tapered, rather than a straight, sliding dovetail. The joint goes together easily, cinching up tight at the last tap. The dovetail plane excels at this joint. You can cut and fit tapered dovetails on a number of battens

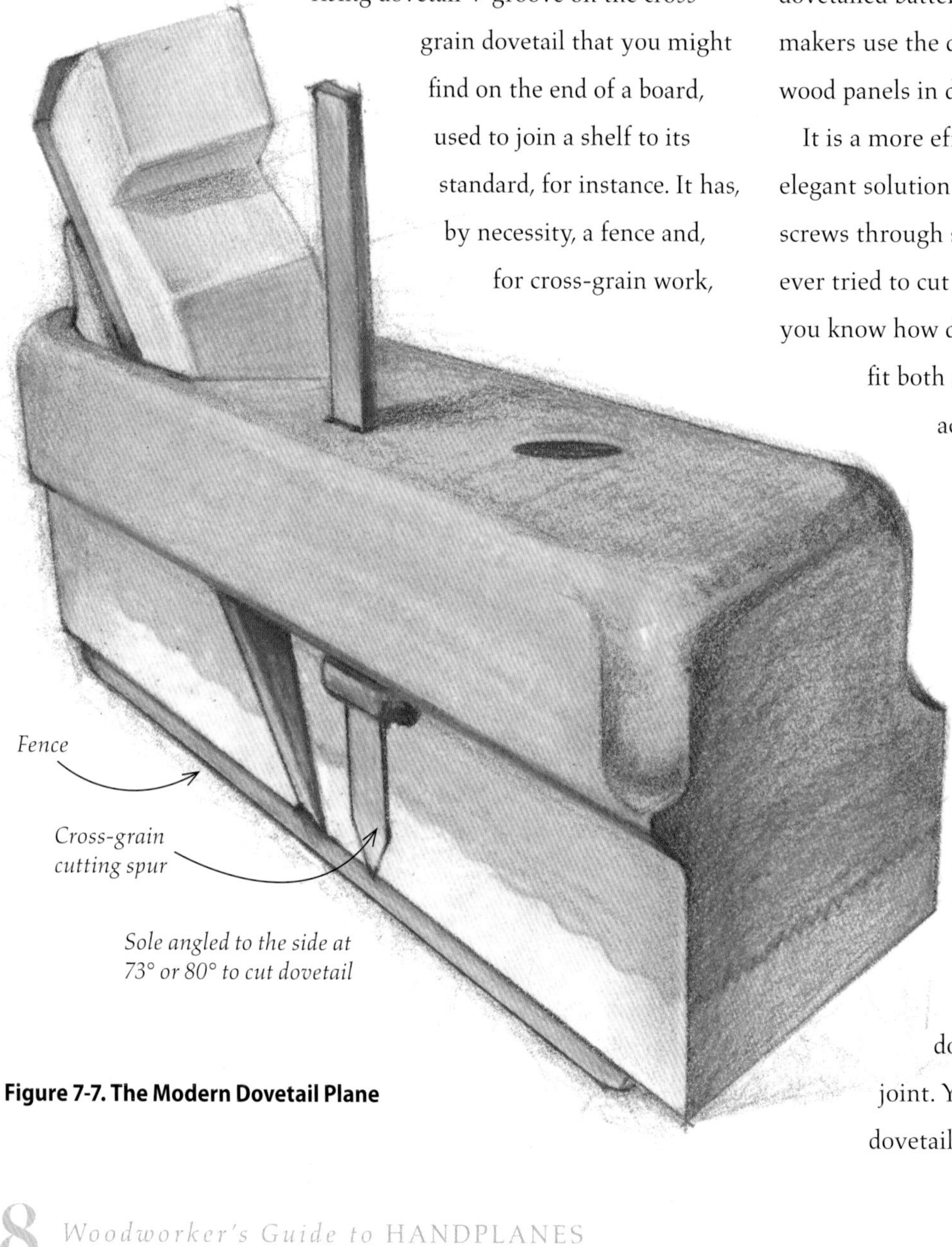

Fence

Cross-grain cutting spur

Sole angled to the side at 73° or 80° to cut dovetail

Figure 7-7. The Modern Dovetail Plane

Figure 7-8. *Use the dovetail plane to form the male portion of a sliding dovetail on the edge of a batten that is to be inserted into a matching groove.*

in the time it would take you to make the complicated jig to rout them. In addition, sometimes the pieces to be dovetailed are too long to easily machine.

For instance, the tapered sliding dovetail is an excellent joint for locking the ends of shelves into a carcass. Such shelves, however, can often be too long to accurately and consistently balance on a router table, and the shelf ends too narrow to cut effectively with a router. If you have a bunch of joints to do, you can rout the dovetail groove using a jig and router and then cut the end of the shelf or batten (the more difficult part to machine) using the dovetail plane (Figure 7-8). The technique for cutting both the groove and batten joint by hand is detailed in "Making a Shooting Board" on page 238. Setting up and maintaining the dovetail plane is the same as for the moving-fillister plane.

SLIDING DOVETAIL

The reason it is so difficult to get a sliding dovetail to fit tight is pure geometry. With a 10° dovetail, for instance, removing material perpendicular to the face of the dovetail results in a gap equaling more than five times that amount in a direction perpendicular to the face of the housing. Therefore, if you shaved 0.01" (0.25mm)—off the face of the dovetail, you would end up with a gap close to 1⁄16" (2mm) in the direction that would normally wedge the dovetail tight. This is even more dramatic along the length of a tapered dovetail batten. Because the taper may be only a couple of degrees (or less), a single pass with a dovetail plane may remove enough material to advance the batten a ½" (13mm) or more.

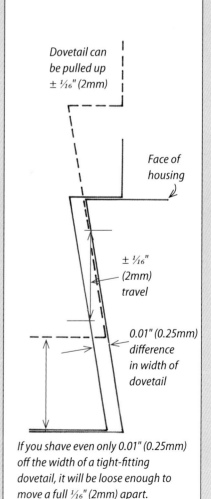

Dovetail can be pulled up ± 1⁄16" (2mm)

Face of housing

± 1⁄16" (2mm) travel

0.01" (0.25mm) difference in width of dovetail

If you shave even only 0.01" (0.25mm) off the width of a tight-fitting dovetail, it will be loose enough to move a full 1⁄16" (2mm) apart.

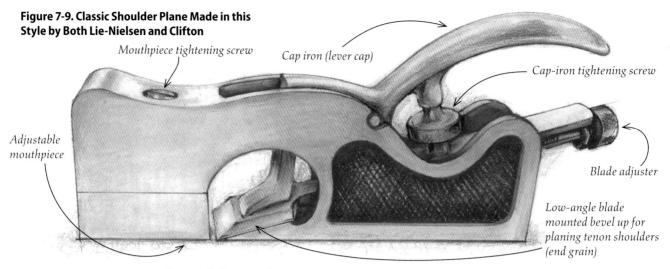

Figure 7-9. Classic Shoulder Plane Made in this Style by Both Lie-Nielsen and Clifton

Mouthpiece tightening screw

Cap iron (lever cap)

Cap-iron tightening screw

Adjustable mouthpiece

Blade adjuster

Low-angle blade mounted bevel up for planing tenon shoulders (end grain)

Shoulder Planes

A variant of the rabbet plane, often called and used as such, the shoulder plane (Figure 7-9) is distinguished from the basic rabbet plane in that its blade is bedded at a low angle with the bevel up. This setup makes it easier to plane end grain—of the shoulder of a tenon, for instance—its original task. (See "Cutting End Grain" on page 36.)

The shoulder plane's body is tall in proportion to its width for both visual as well as physical reference to the work. (In trimming a tenon shoulder, the shoulder plane is put tight to the tenon to keep the shoulder square to the tenon face (Figure 7-10). The plane can be flipped to trim the adjacent tenon face, with the plane's proportional height giving good visual reference for squareness. It has no scoring knife or fence.

Just a few years ago, these planes had almost disappeared; trimming tenon shoulders had evidently dropped far down the woodworker's to-do list. However, more recently, woodworkers have begun to realize how versatile and useful they can be, and now we have a good selection of well-made and thought-out models. I would not have said this a few years ago, but now I believe that if you were to get only one rabbet plane, consider one of these, probably one slightly narrower than ¾" (19mm), so you can also use it in a ¾" (19mm) dado as well as to clean up and adjust rabbets.

Traditionally, woodworkers used rabbet planes on tenon shoulders (end grain), and other planes for other rabbet-related tasks. The traditional shoulder plane did not have an adjustable mouth. Clifton's shoulder planes—beautiful copies of traditional forms that have been in production for a long time—do not have an adjustable mouth.

Newer planes, however, such as from Lie-Nielsen and Veritas, are designed for greater versatility and all have an adjustable mouth. Stanley still makes the #92 and #93, which is a very old pattern, and both have adjustable mouths. I find this feature desirable, though not critical. It allows you to quickly and easily reduce tearout, should you need to make a finishing cut. Though a plane might have an adjustable mouth, you should check a few things, if you can, before you buy:

- Can the mouth be closed down an effective amount?
- Is the mouth crisp and well formed?
- Does the plane go out of alignment when the mouth is re-adjusted?

Generally, blade projection beyond the side of these newer planes is less than suggested for rabbet cutting, but I will go with the manufacturers on this one. If your plane should step when cutting a rabbet, or is unable to reach the inside corner, you can adjust the blade to that one side a little more. However, the blade, blade's sides, and plane body are square and parallel to one another, and doing so throws the blade edge out of parallel to the sole.

If the blade cannot be made parallel to the sole with an equal amount projecting on either side (assuming the blade edge is honed square and the plane's sole is square to its

sides), and the plane steps out in the cut, I would return it because there is not enough blade width. On the other hand, with a new plane, there should be no need to grind down excessive blade width. (Setting up a shoulder plane follows many of the same procedures as a rabbet plane, page 188.)

Another thing I do not suggest you attempt is straightening or squaring the sole and sides of these planes. If your plane is out of square, you need to get a new plane.

During use, most of these planes, being iron, develop a lot of friction and benefit from frequent light lubrication. Also, on all of these planes, the throat, which is open on the sides rather than the top, captures the shaving, and after about 5' of rabbet, the chipwell loads tight; so, clear the shavings frequently. Beware: It is easy to crank the blade-clamping screw down too tight.

Figure 7-10. *When trimming a tenon shoulder, using a bench hook to back up the cut can speed the work and improve accuracy. A board ripped to the thickness of the bench hook can be used to support longer stock.*

Bull-nose/Chisel Planes

The most common versions of the bull-nose and chisel planes are variations of the shoulder rabbet plane. In some cases, the variations actually are a shoulder rabbet plane that disassembles into a bull-nose or chisel plane (Figure 7-11).

A bull-nose plane has a short nose, that is, minimal area in front of the blade, usually about ¼" (6mm), so it can work in close to inside corners and other restricted areas. A chisel plane has no nose—the blade projects unobstructed for working right into corners. These are not necessary tools. Wait until you need one before buying.

These planes have limited use outside the tasks for which they were designed. The bull-nose plane works okay for general planing of rabbets, but its short nose makes it harder to start, and, with the plane's short length, reduces its stability. It is more difficult to use than a regular rabbet plane. And, the chisel plane is nearly impossible to use. Removing the sole in front of the blade removes the bearing area that resists the tendency to dive into the cut.

If you need to adjust or smooth a stop rabbet, you will have to use the bull-nose and chisel plane in combination to work into the corner. Plane the majority of the rabbet with a standard rabbet plane (probably faster) or the bull-nose, as far into the corner as the front of either plane will allow, switching to the bull-nose (if you've used the standard rabbet) to get within ¼" (6mm) of the corner.

You will be able to do only two or three strokes before the plane stops cutting because the front of the sole rides up on the uncut portion. Switch to the chisel plane to finish into the corner, and then go back and repeat the process. Alternatively, you can start with the chisel plane and work back out from the corner with the bull-nose and rabbet planes. The process is the same either way.

You will have a better time of it if you can match the bull-nose and chisel planes stroke for stroke so you do not end up cutting the depth of two or three shavings at one pass with the chisel plane—it is difficult enough to use for single shavings. Few of us can justify having both a bull-nose and a chisel plane and must assemble and disassemble our combination bull-nose/chisel plane to accomplish this task. If you have a lot of wood to remove, it is often faster to chisel down close to the depth you want to achieve in the corner for at least the length of the nose on the plane, so the bull-nose plane can work to the corner, and finish into the corner with just a shaving or two using the chisel plane or a paring chisel.

Figure 7-11. *The Clifton 3-in-1 plane disassembled: chisel plane, bull-nose piece, and rabbet-plane nosepiece.*

The Router Plane

Say you have just cut a dado on the table saw across a somewhat large panel and upon trial assembly you discover the depth is not consistent because of the difficulty of keeping a large panel down tight to the saw table. If you put it back on the table saw, you risk coming off the fence. Even if you don't, cutting a dado a second time usually widens it, ruining the fit. If you have cut the dado with a router, re-cutting it risks widening that, too. The safest and most expedient solution is the router plane (Figure 7-12). Its small base, about the size of a router, will follow the surface of the panel closely, resulting in an accurate depth without risk of cutting the sides of the dado.

Before power tools, the router plane was the go-to tool to make a recess such as a stopped dado in a cabinet side for shelves or the recess for stair treads. While the router plane remains useful for making joints, its main use is in fine-tuning them.

The plane is made in both wood and metal. The traditional wood version, pretty much unchanged for centuries, is available, and despite its simplicity (which is probably its strength), it remains an effective, if limited, tool. It is not a subtle tool, however, having no screw adjustment or accessories such as a depth stop. The wood version's main virtue is the ease with which wood can be removed, especially compared to its metal cousin.

Stanley discontinued its model #71 router plane, though I believe the small #271 (Figure 7-13) is still sold. They can be found easily, earlier versions are available,

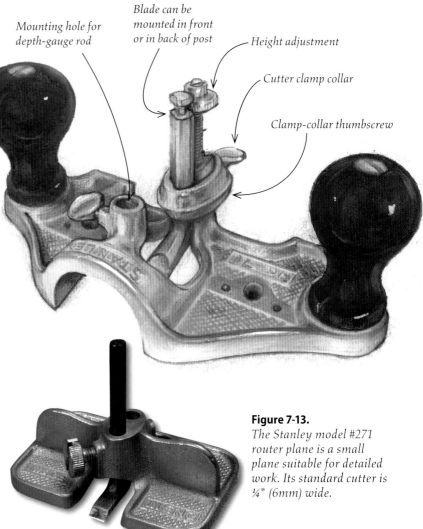

Figure 7-12. Stanley #71 Router Plane

Mounting hole for depth-gauge rod

Blade can be mounted in front or in back of post

Height adjustment

Cutter clamp collar

Clamp-collar thumbscrew

Figure 7-13.
The Stanley model #271 router plane is a small plane suitable for detailed work. Its standard cutter is ¼" (6mm) wide.

and they are priced affordably because few people know what to do with them. They are all, including the last version by Stanley, studies in Victorian design concepts, with function generating flowing lines and edges, and different motifs and textures accenting screws, holes, and housings.

The Stanley #71 included accessories developed because the tool was used for many different tasks. A rod that sits in front of the usual position of the blade (Figure 7-14) can be lowered to slightly less than the blade depth so the blade will take off only this amount on each pass—until the sole bottoms out on the work (the cutter having reached its set depth), stopping any further cutting.

This speeds work because the blade does not have to be repositioned after each pass, and the cutter can be left at its setting for a series of dados. This feature works for grooves and dados, but for something like relieving the background of a carving, it soon gets hung up on the rough surface. The rod hits the borders of the work before the blade, making it difficult to cut to the edge.

This same rod also receives a shoe, a sole plate in front of the blade. The shoe can be set flush with the sole to give support on narrow pieces. The sole plate is needed because the large arch where the depth stop attaches leaves a gap in the sole. Why the arch is there, I am not sure. I suppose it is for increased visibility, chip

USING A BRIDGE BOARD

Many carvers prefer the router plane for relieving the background of a carving, as switching back and forth from power tools to hand carving can be disruptive. In addition, relieving the work by hand gives the carver a feel for the piece of wood being worked. For large areas, you can attach a board to the sole to span the distance.

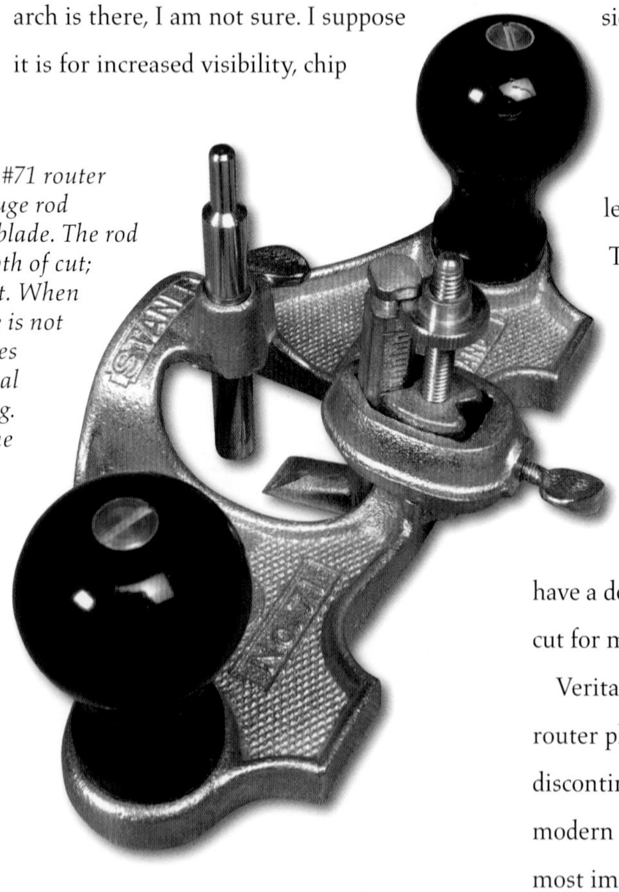

clearance, and to mount the depth-gauge rod. The Stanley #71½ does not have the arch, so it is easier to use on narrow pieces.

Still, I do not like using this plane on narrow edges—to cut a gain for a hinge, for instance, or for the occasional rabbet. The balance is bad because the handles are so far out to the side, making control and consistent cuts difficult. In addition, on short hinge gains, the L-shaped cutter will not cut a gain much shorter than twice its length.

The plane came with a fence for use on straight or curved work. It is not deep, and if the final depth of cut is greater than the fence, you will not be able to use the depth-gauge rod, and will have to repeatedly reset the blade. Because the plane does not have a depth stop, achieving the same depth of cut for multiple grooves is difficult.

Veritas and Lie-Nielsen both make a router plane to fill the void left by the discontinuation of Stanley's model, and the modern lines reveal the tool's redesign. The most important improvement is an effective

Figure 7-14. *The Stanley #71 router plane with the depth-gauge rod mounted in front of the blade. The rod does not set the final depth of cut; the blade depth does that. When the rod is used, the blade is not readjusted between passes but rather is set to its final depth from the beginning. Functioning more like the infeed table of a power jointer, the rod limits only the amount the blade can shave off with each pass.*

depth stop that holds its adjustment.

Unlike the depth-gauge rod of the Stanley that limits how much wood is removed during each pass while the blade stays fixed, this depth stop allows the blade to be adjusted up and down, stopping at a fixed depth determined by the stop. This is helpful when you have to back off the depth of cut, perhaps to work on a set of multiple grooves simultaneously, and then needing to finalize them all to an accurate and consistent depth.

I have discovered how to use the depth-gauge rod and believe having both would make the ideal plane. However, the plane is used more for trimming grooves than forming them, so the depth stop is more useful.

The Veritas also has a longer and deeper fence than the Stanley, though using the fence is more precautionary than necessary. Because any recess the router plane is used to level must first have its boundaries cut with a chisel or saw, the fence functions more as a rough guide restricting movement. With two widely spaced handles, it is easy to torque the plane to the fence causing a misregistration and damage to the sides of the cut.

When setting up the plane you should not have to do much more than sharpen the blades. However, check the blade seat, especially on the Stanley, to see that it supports the blade post and does not flex when cutting. On my Stanley, the blade post groove was milled badly resulting in a cut of inconsistent depth. The blade flexed into the wood on a heavy cut, cutting deeper than it was set. Take a file and carefully flatten the post seat area enough to get a good bearing for

USING THE ROUTER PLANE

When sharpening the blade, it is hard to keep the sharpened edge square to the blade; and if the blade edge is not square, it will not be parallel to the sole of the plane (assuming the plane is manufactured accurately—a real question with the Stanley). This is not that critical, because if you consistently pass the blade over all areas of the cut, the low side of the blade will set the depth and the result will be generally consistent. Some minor surface irregularities will remain, depending on how far out of square the edge is. Because most of the surfaces you cut with this plane are hidden, it will not be a problem. Unfortunately, the router plane does not leave a surface ready for finish. Smooth exposed surfaces further with a scraper, and sand as required.

When using the router plane, try not to be too aggressive in setting the depth of cut. You will have a better time of it if you can just shave off a consistent shaving, rather than banging the plane against the cut and taking off the wood in chunks. The Stanley's adjuster has a lot of slop and it tends to bind, so it is hard to advance the cutter consistently, resulting in a cut that is too deep or not deep enough—very often every time you reset the blade. If you have to advance the blade a lot at one time, the locking collar will bind on the Stanley, so you will have to fiddle with that as well. (When you have to use one of the recently made tools, you realize how far quality control had slid before they discontinued production all together.)

SUPPLEMENTAL SOLE

It is not a bad idea on any of the router planes to attach a thin wood sole to the metal sole to reduce burnishing of the work by the metal sole. The Stanley in particular, even with the sole sanded smooth, still tends to leave marks. Some marring, however, is from minute chips and shavings that get under the sole when using the plane and is unavoidable.

the post. On the Stanley, you will likely have to smooth the sole (the later ones were sanded, not milled, and then nickel plated), or add a wood sole to reduce burnishing the project. An additional sole, however, will reduce the maximum cutting depth of the plane.

Figure 7-15. *Stanley #79 and two versions of Japanese-style side-rabbet planes, used to trim the side of a rabbet.*

Side-Rabbet Planes

These rather unusual looking planes (you might not recognize them as planes at first) are for widening the sides of grooves. They are useful for the same reason the router plane can be useful; sometimes it is just too difficult or risky to return to the work with a power tool. A couple of passes with one of these can solve the problem of a too-tight groove. In addition, like a number of tools in this chapter, no other tool does this job as well.

Three forms of this plane remain: two Stanley models (though one is now made by Lie-Nielsen) and the Japanese side-rabbet plane, whose solution to the problem is different from Stanley's (Figure 7-15).

The Stanley #79 side-rabbet plane was for a while the only Western-style rabbet plane being made. It is an awkward little plane to use and to adjust. It does work, though, and it has some accessories that indicate it has

been given some thought over the years. In addition, it is affordable.

The blades are hard to adjust, but once you get them set, you probably will not have to readjust them again soon (you may use this plane so rarely you seldom ever have to re-sharpen the blades). More than likely, there will not be enough room in the blade escapement to align the blades so the edges are both parallel to the bearing surface (the side) and do not project below the bottom of the plane.

If the blade projects below the bottom of the plane and you cannot adjust it up any further, you should grind off the point of the blade to make sure that it can be made flush to or only very slightly projecting from the bottom of the plane. Otherwise, the plane tends to hang up by the projecting point, making planing the side more difficult.

This plane also has a bull-nose feature, but you will have to remove the depth stop to access the screw that holds the nosepiece. The plane has many sharp, unfriendly areas, and the grip is awkward (at least to me, so far). In addition, the short nosepiece makes it difficult to start a cut.

The #98 and #99 that Lie-Nielsen now make are pretty much the same plane as the #79, except made into two planes (a right and left) that are far better constructed and offer a more ergonomic design.

I have to trim the sides of rabbets so infrequently I have not been able to justify the investment in these tools, so I cannot really comment on their efficacy. Mainly, I use my Japanese side-rabbet plane if I have to do any trimming, and I use my #79 if the groove is too narrow for the Japanese plane to fit. The #79 is nice and narrow, so it fits into many tight places. Sometimes you can find the #98 and #99 in the original Stanley versions at a slightly better price than the new ones.

The Japanese side-rabbet plane comes in a few different sizes. The smallest ones have the blade self-wedge into the side of the plane. The plane I have has a chipbreaker that, unlike many other Japanese planes, doubles as the wedge that holds the blade in position. This means the chipbreaker must be tapped down close to its final position before you can begin adjusting the blade.

If the chipbreaker is not tapped into position, the blade is liable to come flying out at the first disturbance, injuring you, or the blade, or both. Despite this, I like this

USING THE #79

When using the #79, (and the #98 and #99 for that matter), because the short nose piece does not give you a stable area to start the cut, you are often better off starting the cut in from the end (so you can bear more of the side of the plane on the side of the groove). You continue, running the cut to the far side. And you finish by coming back the other way, cutting the first uncut portion with the other blade (or in the case of the complementary planes, the other plane). This technique works fine in dadoes with the grain (technically called a plough). However, if you are trimming a cross-grain dado, you will be forced to come in from the ends to avoid splintering, and will then have to attempt to get the cut started balancing on that short nose piece. Also, because of the #79's low profile and awkward ergonomics, it can be difficult to tell if the cut is vertical.

tool. It is easy to hold, easy to use and adjust, has a high-quality laminated blade with a chipbreaker (sometimes tearout on the side of a groove is not acceptable), and it can be modified. I angled the adjacent face of mine to the angle of the dovetail plane I have.

The angle allows the plane to fit right to the bottom corner of the dovetail grove, and gives me a decent reference face to assist in holding the plane at the correct angle. As with the other side-rabbet planes, if you are not going to take the time to back up the wood when the plane exits a cross-grain cut, you really need a right- and left-hand model. Otherwise, you risk splitting out the wood.

Figure 7-16. Traditional Wood Mortise Plane

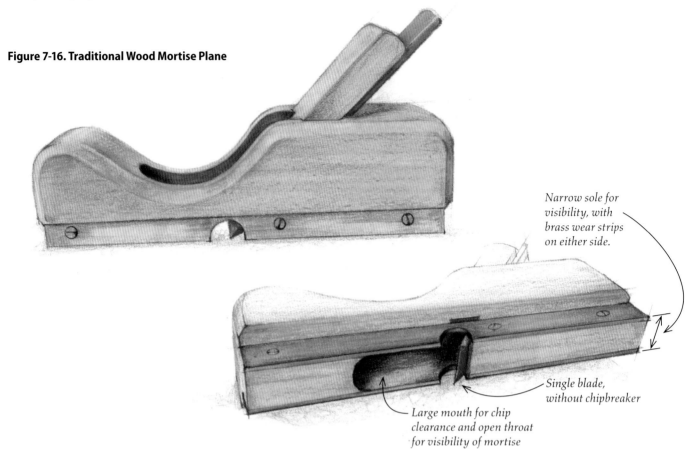

Narrow sole for visibility, with brass wear strips on either side.

Single blade, without chipbreaker

Large mouth for chip clearance and open throat for visibility of mortise

The Mortise Plane

The mortise plane (Figure 7-16) is not a *must-have*. I got mine out of the clearance bin about twenty years ago for $10 and thought, for that price, I will give it a try. It has been very useful. I got my money's worth. I think it is helpful to woodworkers to know what this plane is and how to use it.

This plane is not used to make most mortises, but rather what is called a *gain*, that is, a shallow mortise or recess for mounting a butt hinge and the plates of other hardware. The gain is first outlined and scored to the depth of the thickness of the leaf of the hinge with a chisel; then, the plane clears the chips and shapes the mortise. In order to clear the chips, the mortise plane has a mouth more than an inch wide. The plane is narrow and

sits comfortably on the edge of a door, unlike a router plane, which is hard to balance on a narrow edge.

I often use my mortise plane when I have only a few gains to cut and making a router template would take too long. Often I can have the gains cut in the time it would take to make up the template. I also sometimes use the plane to finesse or correct the gain when the cut from a router template is a little off. To get a good fit on a door, I check the width of the gains (from the front of the door to the back) with a cutting gauge and mark any that are narrower so they are all exactly the same width. After a stop cut with a chisel, I then lift the sliver out using the mortise plane.

1 Mark the length of the hinge leaf precisely with a knife or scribe, using a square to scribe the end cut.

2 Scribe the width of the leaf using a cutting gauge, so that all the hinge gains will be the same and the face of the door and frame will be flush.

3 Chisel a stop cut at both ends and then a V-cut at each end of the gain to a depth equal to the thickness of the hinge leaf. If you feel insecure about judging this, you can mark the thickness of the leaf on the face of the door. The V-cuts and all successive chisel cuts do not have to be to the exact depth but rather to just less than the exact depth.

Cutting a Mortise for a Hinge Using a Mortise Plane *(continued)*

4 Cut a series of successive cuts 1⁄16" to 1⁄8" (2mm to 3mm) apart and just shy of the final depth of the gain from one end to the other. If you rest your hand on the edge holding the chisel in the same position just above the surface, you can make these cuts in very rapid succession with only one or two taps of the hammer each cut.

5 Set the blade of the mortise plane to where the aris formed by the buffing of the hardware stops. If the door is to be painted, set the depth a paper's thickness less than that.

6 Break away any loose chips with your finger.

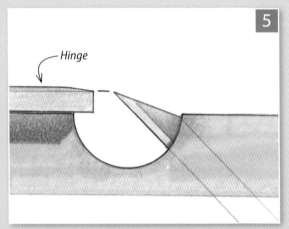

Hinge

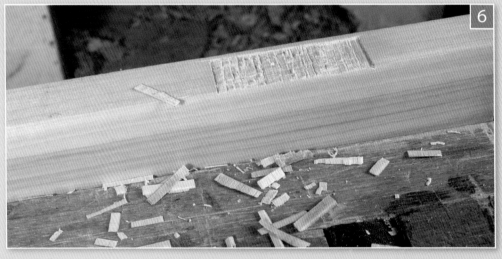

7 Run the plane over the gain, cutting away the remaining chips. It is often best to cut the full depth of the mortise in two passes: the first removing the majority of the chips cut by the chisel, not bearing down with the plane but maintaining light contact with the edge of the door; the second, after clearing away all the chips, by making full contact with the edge of the door so that the blade cuts the full depth. Cut to one end of the mortise.

8 Then, reverse the plane, cleaning the mortise to the other end.

9 Make sure you work completely to the end, all corners, and the edge.

10 Check the fit.

8
PLANES FOR SHAPING WOOD
Specialty Planes that Form and Refine

You need to make two legs—maybe the front legs of a cabinet stand or chest of drawers with beautiful flowing curves. After you have band sawn them, how do you remove the unevenness of the cut and fair the curve? Make a jig? For only two legs, it is probably not worth it. Besides, you would still have to fair the curve of the jig, which is almost like fairing one leg. A spindle sander can take the saw marks off, but it is difficult to get a long even curve with it because the diameter of the spindle is so much smaller than the curve of the work. There are probably other solutions, but by the time you have figured them out you could have the curves cleaned up and faired with a gently curving compass plane.

A Japanese-style compass plane, its sole shaped to a gentle curve, smoothes the sweep of a bench seat.

Perhaps you have a piece of wood 8' (2,438mm) long and ¾" (19mm) square that you want to ease the edge of, maybe to a ¹⁄₁₆" (2mm)-radius round-over or a chamfer. The piece flexes and is hard to hold down to the router table. A handheld router does no better. In addition, you will have to clean up the cut. You can probably get your edges eased with a chamfer plane before changing the router bit, doing a couple of trial cuts, and figuring out how to hold the piece.

Through the end of the nineteenth century, woodworkers relied on a galaxy of planes to cut curves—not to mention innumerable molding planes beyond the hollowing and rounding planes discussed here. Some trades had their own special planes with curved soles or curved blades.

Carriage makers, for instance, had a fascinating collection of planes to cut all types of shapes in all sorts of positions, and a large portion of these seem to be rabbet-type planes. Into the twentieth century, patternmaking was essential to manufacturing, and sets of planes with interchangeable soles and blades for different curves, as well as an adjustable circular plane, able to smooth a range of radii, enabled the development of new designs. And the skilled craftsman made or modified planes as needed.

Figure 8-1. A Collection of Japanese-Style Compass Planes in Different Sweeps

Compass Planes

The sole of a compass plane (Figure 8-1) curves along its length, either convex or (less commonly) concave. While jigs make sense for production runs, if you have only a few pieces to do or a shape to test out or a prototype to make, nothing gives faster, more satisfactory results than fairing a curve with a compass plane. Even if you are doing a production run, the compass plane is best for fairing the necessary jigs.

Few compass planes are manufactured today. If your needs extend beyond those available, you can check out the market in antique planes. Likely, you will have to make or modify a plane to your specifications. I have modified small Japanese-style planes into convex-soled compass planes, and that is my recommendation. I prefer the Japanese-style plane for this because I find pulling the plane and its low position gives me a lot of control. Alternatively, you can reshape most wood-body planes into a compass plane.

Compass planes are most useful when the work is concave. The plane should match the radius of the piece being worked, but in reality, the radius of the plane (on concave work) need be only no larger than that of the work. Nevertheless, the closer the two match, the easier it is to get good results.

A convex curve can be worked with a straight (bench) plane—the plane does not have to be curved at all. I have no planes with soles that are concave in length. Yet, the more closely the curve of the sole matches that of the work, the better the results. I now have a plane with a nosepiece that adjusts up and down that has given satisfactory results on a variety of work (Figure 8-2).

USING A COMPASS PLANE

When fairing a curve along the length of a somewhat narrow piece, whether convex or concave, use the compass plane to remove the obvious high spots first to get a relatively smooth-flowing curve. Then concentrate on the beginning of the stroke and the finish. These are the areas of greatest difficulty.

The most common mistake is to dip the plane on entry and exit from the stroke causing unevenness at one or both ends. It is more difficult because the curve of your plane will almost never be exactly that of your piece. You have to rock the plane slightly until you find the position where the blade contacts the work and begins to cut, and maintain this position through the whole cut.

THE CORRECT SOLE CONFIGURATION

For best results if the piece is concave, the radius of the plane should be equal to, or slightly smaller than, that of the piece; if the piece is convex, the radius of the plane should be equal to or slightly larger. However, even a straight-soled plane can shape a convex curve.

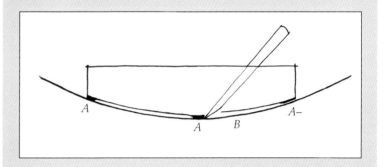

Figure 8-2. *The adjustable nose on this Japanese plane enables it to perform like a compass plane for a limited range of convex surfaces.*

Figure 8-3. *To fair a concave curve along the length of a wide piece, I often work cross-grain first with a large-radius hollowing plane (the sole being convex in width) to take out the high spots and begin evening the curve.*

Figure 8-4. *Then I will work with the grain with the compass plane, sometimes first using a plane of a slightly smaller radius to knock down the ridges left by the cross-grain planing.*

Figure 8-5. *Because the radius of the compass plane is often slightly less than the radius of the piece being worked (it must be no larger than that of the work), you may have to lift the front of the plane slightly to get a good start. Otherwise, the plane will start cutting after you have begun the stroke, not from the very beginning, resulting in an uneven curve at the end.*

Maintaining the position is easy once you find it. The problem is you often do not find it until after you have begun the cut, and you just as often lose it before finishing the cut, resulting in the ends being uneven. Concentrate and find the position at the start, before beginning the cut, and maintain it as you exit the piece. This requires putting pressure on the front of the plane when starting the cut, and shifting the pressure to the back of the plane when finishing.

To fair a concave curve along the length of a wide piece, I often work cross grain first with a large-radius hollowing plane (the sole being convex in width) to even up the curve, taking out the high spots (Figure 8-3). Then I work along the grain with the compass plane, sometimes using a plane of a slightly smaller radius to first knock down the ridges left by the cross-grain planing (Figure 8-4). The start and finish of the long stroke on a wide piece presents the same problem (and solution) here as on a narrow piece (Figure 8-5).

If the piece is a wide convex, I begin with a bench plane, usually a coarsely set smooth plane, to take the high spots out. I skew the plane to the downhill side to get more of a shearing cut so there is less tearing, rather than using it perpendicular. Once the overall curve is even, I begin smoothing the curve with the compass plane (Figure 8-6).

Next to the start and finish in fairing a curve, the point where the grain changes direction on the curve of the piece is the most difficult, whether the piece is convex or concave. After establishing a satisfactory curve, re-sharpen if necessary, back the blade off to make the thinnest of cuts, and adjust the chipbreaker down tight to the blade edge. Work just to where the grain changes, and then come back from the other direction, overlapping slightly so you end up with a smooth continuous curve (Figure 8-7).

Hopefully, your adjustments will reduce the tear-out to a tolerable level. Finish with a scraper shave, if you have one, and a card scraper until the tear-out is removed. Even out any remaining irregularities by using a sanding block made from a scrap band sawn to the curve of the piece. I always save these sanding blocks for any similar curves I encounter in the future.

Figures 8-6. *If the piece is convex, I begin with a bench plane, usually a coarsely set smooth plane, to take off the high spots. Then I use a compass plane, in this case a straight-soled plane with an adjustable nose, to smooth the curve.*

Figure 8-7. *To avoid a hump in a curve where the grain changes, work with a re-sharpened blade set for a thin cut and with the chipbreaker set tight to the edge. Overlap the grain change slightly.*

WESTERN VERSUS JAPANESE PLANES FOR CURVES

Getting a good reference on the plane when starting and finishing a stroke is important.

Therefore, it is difficult to shape a curve with most Western planes. Their small nose (sole in front of the blade) is typically only one-third of the overall length of the plane. This is one of the reasons I prefer the Japanese-style planes for curves. Their blade position, about three-fifths of the overall length from the front, makes it a little easier to start. If you make a compass plane from scratch, proportion it so the blade is closer to the center of the length of the sole. That method provides good reference coming on and going off the piece.

Hollows & Rounds

Sets of *hollows and rounds* (Figure 8-8)—planes that make hollows (rounded grooves) and round edges—were the nineteenth-century woodworker's router bits. Because almost all of the moldings he encountered were combinations of hollows and rounds (think about it), with a full set of these, supplemented with perhaps a syma- (S-) curve plane to blend adjacent shapes and a thin side-rabbet plane to round where the others could not reach, he could make up almost any molding he needed. The same is true today.

A router bit cannot always reach where you need it—say, to the center of a deep, wide molding—and is certainly limited in overall size. Sometimes the run (or schedule) is just too short to justify the time and expense of a custom shaper bit, or perhaps the piece is too small or awkward to put through the shaper. And neither a router bit nor a shaper can undercut a molding. With a combination of planes and router or shaper bits, you have versatility in the profiles you can produce.

Sets of hollows and rounds originally included eighteen planes from ⅛" to 1½" (3mm to 38mm) wide in 1⁄16" (2mm) increments. Half-sets were also available, in either odd or even sizes. I am not a big fan of sets. There always seem to be some (usually too many) you never use. Setting up eighteen planes, or even nine, is a lot of work, though you can wait until you need a size and set up one at a time as you go.

Then again, if the set is a bargain and it is at least possible you will use most of them, a set is the way to go. Because there are plenty of individual planes from broken sets available, I buy one or a few at a time as needed. My first hollows and rounds were Japanese-style with a chipbreaker and 40° cutting angle (Figure 8-9). These perform well, but on some projects a higher pitch works better and I have since added a few hollows and rounds at a 55° pitch.

In addition to the traditional sets of hollows and rounds that range only to 1½" (38mm) wide, wider planes with more subtly curved blades used for smoothing

**Figure 8-8.
A pair of Western-Style Matching Hollow and Round Planes**

HOLLOWS & ROUNDS

There is some confusion in the nomenclature of *hollows and rounds*, probably arising out of colloquial traditions, or perhaps due to the near interchangeability of the terms *hollow* and *hollowing*, and *round* and *rounding*. Often the terms *hollow* and *round* will refer to the shape of the planes themselves, rather than the shapes they cut. Thus, a *round plane* will make a hollowing cut, and a *hollow plane* will make a rounding cut. Generally, I use *hollowing plane* to mean a plane that cuts a hollow, having a convex blade; a *rounding plane* is a plane that rounds a piece over and has a concave blade. I hope that clears that up!

the inside and outside of coopered doors and such should be included in this group. These are very scarce and will probably have to be custom made, either new or from a modified wood bench plane.

Using the planes is relatively straightforward. The hollowing plane is easiest to start in a machine-made hollow, at least a rough concavity. If starting a hollow from scratch, you can clamp a fence to the plane, but oftentimes it is just as easy to use your fingers as a fence.

After a few strokes, the hollow is self-jigging (though you can pop out of it if you don't pay attention). For hollows wider than the blade, you tilt the plane to work the side of the hollow, changing the tilt after each stroke as you work your way across. Chances are the blade radius will not match that of the hollow, so you will have to follow up with a curved scraper to fair out blade marks.

With a rounding plane, it is best to form most of the round with a steel-bottom plane or spokeshave, to save wear and tear on the wood-soled rounding plane. You can also set the bench plane or spokeshave for a deeper cut to speed the work and finish with light cuts of the rounding plane.

Again, chances are the radius of the blade will not exactly match that of the work, so you can fair the blade marks with a thin flexible scraper or a scraper ground to the curve. (For setting up hollows and rounds, see "Setting up Hollows and Rounds" on page 194.)

Other Shaping Planes

There are some more useful planes, though your use of them will depend on the type and style of work you like to do.

Consider the kind of treatment you give the edges of your pieces: the treatment can affect the look and feel of the piece—perhaps soft, with a rounded chamfer, or maybe hard, with the extra shadow line of a beveled chamfer making the piece appear lighter or thinner. The way you approach this feature can become a signature. Chamfer planes can be useful and efficient for forming the edges.

Woodworkers involved in more sculptural shaping of wood—one-of-a-kind furniture-makers, chair makers, reproduction furniture makers, woodcarvers, instrument makers, and the woodworker making prototypes for pieces to be put into production—will find the compass planes and *chibi-kanna* indispensable for successfully forming and smoothing sweeping shapes.

Figure 8-9. *An unmatched set of hollows and rounds in the Japanese style, which I purchased as needed.*

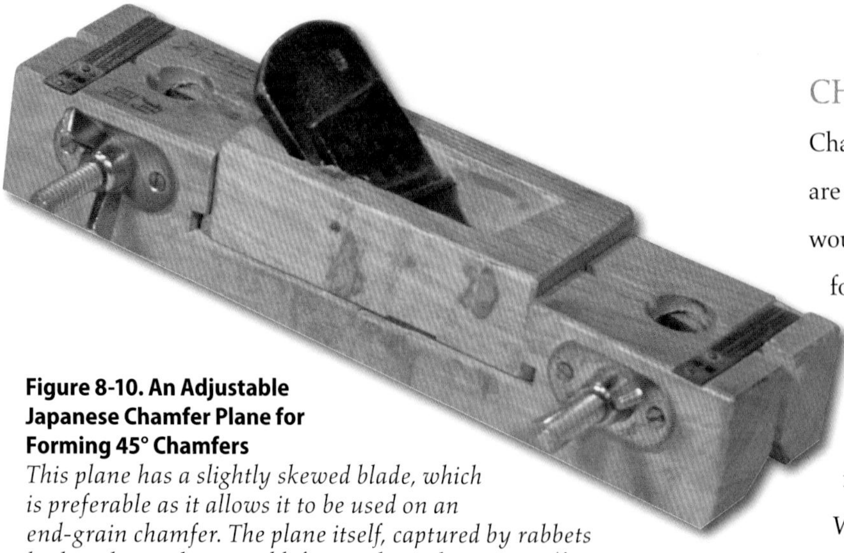

Figure 8-10. An Adjustable Japanese Chamfer Plane for Forming 45° Chamfers

This plane has a slightly skewed blade, which is preferable as it allows it to be used on an end-grain chamfer. The plane itself, captured by rabbets both ends, can be moved left or right in the carriage/fence assembly to extend the wear from narrow chamfers across the full width of the blade; and the plane has a brass piece let into the sole at the mouth to reduce wear. These are also available in 60°/30° chamfer configurations.

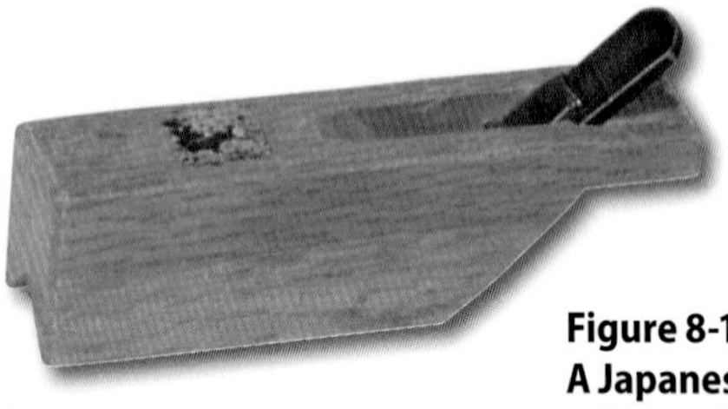

Figure 8-11. A Japanese Chamfer Plane for Forming ⅛" (3mm) Diameter Roundovers

The back underside has been cut away to allow greater access to inside corners.

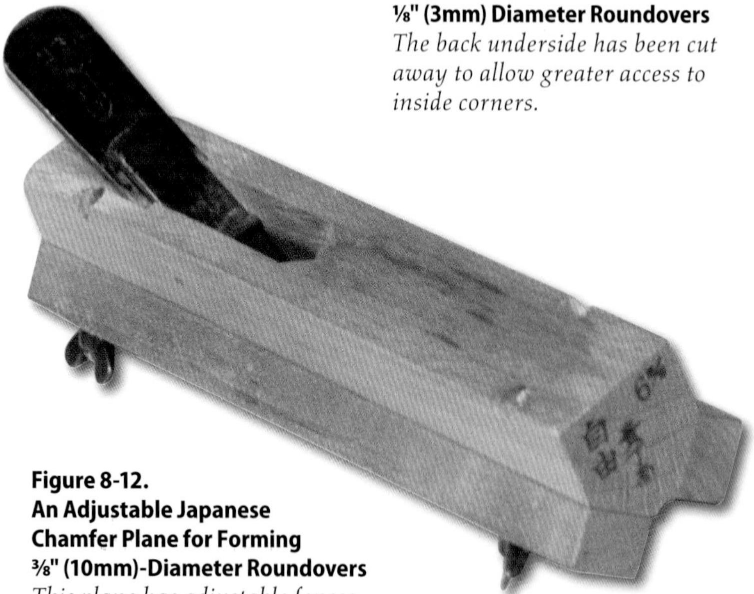

Figure 8-12. An Adjustable Japanese Chamfer Plane for Forming ⅜" (10mm)-Diameter Roundovers

This plane has adjustable fences on either side, allowing three types of cut: a simple roundover, a roundover with a single shoulder or bead, and a roundover with a shoulder on either side.

CHAMFER PLANES

Chamfer planes (Figures 8-10, 8-11, and 8-12) are a useful addition to most tool kits. When it would take too much time to set up the router for a short run, or the work is too awkward or difficult to access, these are the tools to use to finish an edge. They have the added advantage of leaving a surface that may need little or no further smoothing.

While you can use a block plane or a rounding plane to chamfer an edge, the advantage of a chamfer plane is that its fences give quicker, more accurate, and repeatable results. However, chamfer planes are getting harder to find. With the exception of a few odd tools that give inconsistent results, and some antiques, chamfer planes seem to come largely from Japanese makers, and even most of what was available a few years ago is difficult to find now. Looking at some of these can be instructive, should you wish to try them or need to fabricate your own (Figure 8-13).

Figure 8-13. A Homemade Japanese-Style Chamfer Plane

Small rabbets were cut on each end of a purchased plane to capture it in the carriage/fence assembly. The width of the chamfer is fixed by tightening wedges on the cross dowels.

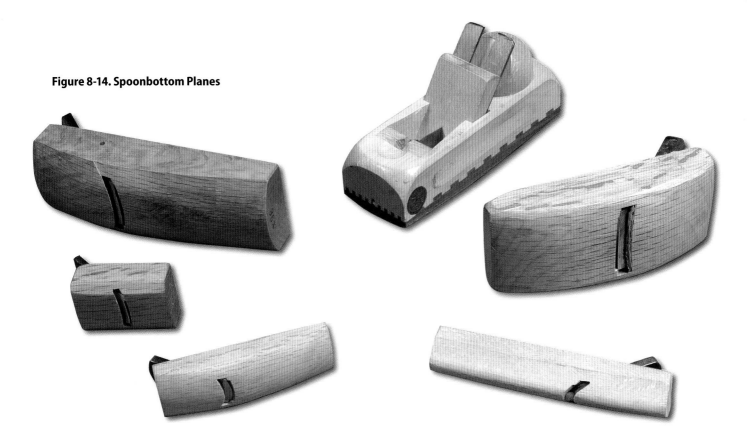

Figure 8-14. Spoonbottom Planes

SPOONBOTTOM PLANES

A spoonbottom plane (Figure 8-14) curves both along and across its sole, giving it a shape somewhat like, well, a spoon's bottom. Most often, they are used for the shaping stage of work rather than final smoothing because of the difficulty of matching the blade and plane curvature rather exactly to the work, especially when the radius is constantly changing, such as in a chair seat.

A number of these are needed if they are to be used for smoothing and transitioning complex curves. Since there are a limited number of radii available, you will probably have to make these yourself. (See "Hollowing, Rounding, and Spoonbottom Planes" on page 301.)

There are a number of types of metal spoonbottom planes and variant tools produced. Frankly, I have not used most of them, but I can offer observations that might be helpful. A plane with a metal sole can be useful, because the sole can take a beating. The trade-off is a metal sole also has iron's high coefficient of friction resisting the stroke, and requires frequent lubrication.

The *squirrel tail* version of the plane is an old form and should have good ergonomics, but it is not intended for heavy, repeated work. For one thing, it is a one-handed tool, made to fit in the palm of the hand, and you are really going to need to use both hands if

BLOCK PLANE, THEN CHAMFER

To speed the work, you can use a coarsely set block plane to rough down a chamfer, especially if it is a big one, and then finish up with a finely set chamfer plane for a smooth edge. This process is usually not only faster but saves wear and tear on the chamfer or roundover plane, which may have a wooden sole.

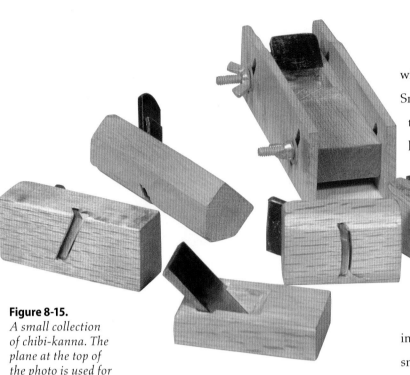

Figure 8-15.
A small collection of chibi-kanna. The plane at the top of the photo is used for planing small strips to the same thickness.

You must be able to push or pull the plane without struggling to keep the blade engaged. Smallish planes (around 4" (102mm) long) that can be used with two hands are the least fatiguing and most effective for heavy work. Smaller planes, such as the *chibi-kanna* are effective for fairing out curves. I have used mostly Japanese-style spoonbottom planes, and had good results.

In use, the spoonbottom plane is an intermediate step in the production of a smooth form. Traditionally, a shape such as a chair seat would first be roughed out with an adze. In some cases, this might be followed by the spoonbottom plane, but more likely the form would be further refined with an inshave and then a travisher, which is a wood spokeshave with a curved blade.

you are removing a lot of material. A quick look at the trades involved in forming shapes in three dimensions, such as chair makers, or *coopers*, show all of the tools to be robust two-handed tools.

Also, be aware that repeated focused pounding of the palm of the hand by a tool handle can cause nerve damage there, as well as *trigger finger*—the involuntary locking closed of one or more fingers of the hand—an occupational hazard of carvers who have the bad habit of pounding their carving tools with the palm of their hand.

Among the things to look for in a spoonbottom plane: a good blade—you may be removing a lot of wood with this plane. Moreover, that being the case, a low-blade angle is helpful as well. The blade should be easy to adjust, but it is also important that the ergonomics be good.

Much like spoonbottom planes, these come in a variety of curvatures to fair out the changing curves. Inshaves and travishers are prone to tearout, used across the grain as well as with it, and leave a rough surface. This is cleaned up with the spoonbottom plane. Having a number of these with different radii is helpful to get into all the areas and not only ease the transitions, but smooth the surface. Remove the light rippling left by the curve of the blade with a series of curved-edge and flexible scrapers.

LITTLE PLANES: *CHIBI-KANNA*

These are little Japanese-style planes usually no longer than 2" (51mm). Used to shape wood, they are made by each woodworker to whatever blade shape and sole configuration he might need.

Many Japanese woodworkers will have a box of them, made over the years for specific projects. They are what the Westerner might call finger planes, or instrument-maker planes, and I have found them to be very useful. They are quick to make and highly effective for getting into all sorts of areas to shape, fair, or smooth some of the more sculptural aspects of a design. Any woodworker whose projects involve curving surfaces of any kind should have a number of these.

Traditionally, the blade stock for the *chibi-kanna* (Figure 8-15) comes in about 4" (102mm)-wide sections (the blade length is about 2" (51mm)). This is a laminated piece of steel, like the material out of which the bigger blades are made and is available in different grades (Figure 8-16). To make a blade, you cut its required width off this 4" (102mm) blank. (See "Making Chibi-Kanna" on page 295.)

Making a blade this way gives the craftsman flexibility in the width and shape of blade he can have. This blade stock is hard to find now (it never was easy to come by), but precut blades of different widths are still available, making the fabrication of these small planes a viable option.

Figure 8-16. *A piece of the blade stock for making* chibi-kanna, *a bit smaller than it was as purchased, because a couple of blades have been made from it; and a couple of pieces of Japanese white oak for making the dai saved from the cut-off of a larger plane block.*

Fabricating these small planes is the same as for the larger ones, but since the blades are usually only ½" to 1" (13mm to 25mm) wide and are not usually fitted with a chipbreaker (which takes extra time), they can be made quickly. In addition, since you do not have to wait for any glue to dry, you can use them right away. I usually make the blade angle 43° (9 in 10) unless I am working some particularly hard woods, in which case I increase the pitch.

9

CHOOSING YOUR FIRST PLANES

A Guide to a Suitable Toolkit

I often ruminate: If I were starting out now from scratch, what would I choose for my first plane? My second? How would I build an effective set of planes that would serve my style of working? Students have asked the question and I have tossed it around for a long time. I certainly do not have the definitive answer, but I can give my opinions and the reasons for them, and you can decide for yourself. If you end up with a plane you just never use, well there is always a woodworker somewhere who can probably use it.

Low angle bevel-up bench planes are more versatile than their bevel down cousins, and can be a good choice for a multi-task plane. Shown here are the Veritas Bevel-up Smoother, and on the right, their Bevel-up Jack Plane.

Figure 9-1.
The Stanley #60½ block plane is a good first plane. With a blade upgrade, you may never feel the need to replace this plane.

The number and type of planes you will eventually need depends upon the type of work you do. If you do a variety of projects, you will end up needing a variety of planes. If your range of work is narrow, you can probably get by with just a few select planes.

Buy planes—and tools in general—only as you need them. Be reluctant to buy sets unless you are sure you will be able to use all of the pieces in the set.

First Things First

If you are just starting out, I would recommend getting a Stanley block plane, such as the #60½, (Figure 9-1) or one of its competitors—the Record or perhaps the Veritas. The Lie-Neilson is an excellent tool, but because of its price, I hesitate to suggest it as a first plane.

I would recommend upgrading to it later (Figure 9-2). Make sure the block plane you choose has an adjustable mouth and the low (12°) blade angle. These planes are versatile and readily accessible to the beginner, at the same time providing good service to the more demanding, experienced professional.

A good block plane will teach you a lot about the dynamics of planing and how the different strategies work and interact. It is forgiving of mistreatment (except being dropped) and its small blade is easy to re-sharpen or grind if need be. Open the block plane's adjustable mouth and use it to remove a lot of wood for shaping. Close the mouth and it polishes difficult, figured woods. The low blade angle allows easy variations in cutting angle (by honing or re-grinding the bevel angle).

Some woodworkers will never have need for another plane, though I think once you experience the full effectiveness of the block plane, you will begin to see where planes of other sizes and configurations can advance your work.

Figure 9-2. *These up-market block planes, the Veritas and the even more expensive Lie-Nielsen, can be the next step up from the Stanley #60½: better blades, more precise machining, and adjustability.*

YOUR SECOND PLANE

Your next plane? There are a number of choices. I would suggest the Lie-Nielsen low-angle jack plane (Figure 9-3) (based on the Stanley #62) or its Veritas counterpart.

The jack plane has all of the features of the block plane—adjustable mouth, low-angle blade—but in a bigger size, making it efficient in planing larger surfaces, though without the experience acquired in the setup and use of the block plane, this jack plane could be frustrating for someone just starting out. I would not make the jack plane my first plane.

With the addition of a couple of extra blades, it could be used as:

- a jack for rough-shaping surfaces (using a blade ground and sharpened to a suitable curve);
- smooth planing or panel planing (using a blade shaped with the corners honed back); or
- shooting on the shooting board, or miscellaneous other precise tasks (with the blade honed straight).

You can have blades ground to different bevel angles for planing, for instance, tropical hardwoods. The downside is that this can make the bevel angle pretty blunt, thus increasing the amount of effort required to push the plane, possibly reducing the quality of the cut (depends on the wood), and usually dulling the blade quicker. This is a cheaper solution, however, than buying or making a new plane (though if I found myself doing this a lot, I would probably consider getting a dedicated plane).

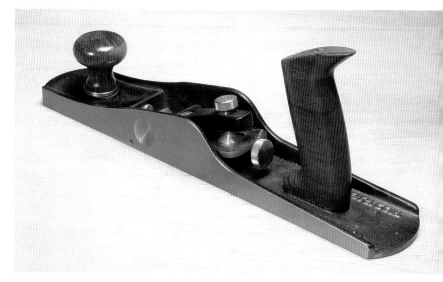

Figure 9-3. *The Lie Nielson and (above) the Veritas low-angle jack are versatile planes suitable for many of the tasks around the shop.*

Figure 9-4.
Refurbishing an old plane like this Bailey-style #05 jack made by Millers Falls, above, can be a viable alternative to purchasing a new plane.

Alternatively, I would consider getting a Stanley #05 jack plane (Figure 9-4), or the Lie-Nielsen #05. The Veritas #5¼W, though slightly smaller would also be a consideration, but I do not think it is as versatile as the low-angle plane (Figure 9-5). Having a blade with the bevel down means changing the cutting angle is not possible unless you grind a back bevel on the top of the edge.

Moving the frog forward to close the mouth down is slower and more cumbersome than adjusting the mouth on the low-angle planes. On Bedrock-type models, moving the frog forward changes the depth setting of the blade. The chipbreaker on the #05 requires disassembly for adjustment, so it is also not an option for frequent readjustment.

You could consider getting the short version of what Lie-Nielsen calls its Low Angle Smoothing Plane, but I do not believe it is quite as versatile as the longer jack. Because of its length, the longer jack produces more accurate surfaces that can be used to shoot or otherwise prepare edges for gluing, or for general smoothing of surfaces.

JOINT-MAKING PLANES

While it is worthwhile getting a plane for adjusting rabbets, dadoes, and other joints, I do not believe there is any need to go right out and buy one on the first day. The first time you need to adjust a joint will be soon enough. (This may come the second day.) I think one of the most useful tools for these kinds of adjustment is the shoulder rabbet plane. This can be used to work in dadoes to adjust the depth, smooth the machine marks left from cutting a rabbet, or taper a rabbet, adjust tenons and tenon shoulders, and a multitude of other uses that are difficult to do any other way.

The Veritas and Lie-Nielsen medium shoulder planes are good choices here. I might have to give the edge to Veritas, as their plane is only ¹¹⁄₁₆" (17mm) wide, which will fit into a dado cut exactly wide enough to take a piece of plywood (about ²³⁄₆₄" or 9mm); a ¾" (19mm)-wide plane will not.

Another important tool is the side-rabbet plane. You may be able to work around not having the side-rabbet plane your entire career in woodworking, but that might be because you did not know it existed. Use a side-rabbet plane to widen a groove, dado, or rabbet for a nice tight fit (as opposed to not fitting at all). Nothing is as fast and accurate in doing this as the side-rabbet plane.

Figure 9-5. *The Veritas shoulder plane, doing what it was originally designed to do: trim the shoulder of a tenon.*

Figure 9-6. *Your first smoothing plane might well be like one of these 48mm Japanese planes at different blade angles. The plane at left, over 30 years old, has a 40° pitch, and I regularly use it on the jobsite. Next to that is my first shopmade plane, about 25 years old, with a 43° pitch and no chipbreaker. The remaining three on the right are a 43°-pitch plane with a chipbreaker, shopmade with a canarywood dai; a commercial plane with a 47½° pitch and a red oak dai; and a 55° shopmade plane, single-bladed with a canarywood dai.*

SMOOTHING IS NEXT

After these planes, I believe the woodworker should consider getting a plane dedicated to smoothing, because one common task today is removing marks from machining, and preparing pieces for finishing. The best candidate for this, in my opinion, is a Japanese plane, with a 48mm- to 55mm- (1⅞"- to 2⅛"-) wide blade and a 40° blade angle (Figure 9-6).

If you are not familiar with setting up and using a Japanese plane, the width of this plane is not too daunting. The challenges increase dramatically with a 65mm or 70mm (2½" or 2¾") plane. The 45mm or 55mm (1¾" or 2⅛") size feels good in the hand, is reasonably easy to set up and maintain, is similar in blade width to Western smoothing planes, and serves as a good introduction to Japanese planes and smooth planes in general.

With its low-friction bottom and low-effort, clean-shearing cut, it represents a benchmark to judge other planes' performance. While it does not have an adjustable mouth or frog, the chipbreaker is easy to adjust and readjust as required for different cuts, which can be invaluable in

learning this important tactic.

As an alternative to the Japanese plane, consider a Krenov-style plane, though from scratch, it may be a bit of work for those without experience. Kits are available, however, for those who do not want to tackle one from scratch. These are comfortable to use for smoothing and can be shaped to the user's preference.

A 45° blade angle is good for a first plane of this type, and I would recommend considering fitting a moveable mouth plate into the sole to increase the plane's versatility and ease maintenance of the mouth opening. My only real complaint with this plane is that, in my experience, even the best blade upgrades are not of a quality approaching good quality Japanese blades.

While I really like the sweet action of wood on wood and a super-sharp blade, and I encourage woodworkers to try the wood planes, most people reading this will be much more comfortable trying the Bailey-style bench planes. In the past, I have been reluctant to recommend the Bailey-style plane because I felt there were better planes available for doing many of the tasks around the shop. And while I still feel that way, I can say that for the earlier stages of your career in woodworking, if I can't talk you into a wood plane, you should consider a Bailey #04-size plane.

The problem is the variety of quality in this style of plane; it takes some experience to tell which ones are going to work well, even though they all look pretty much the same. The instructions in Chapter 10 on setting up planes should help you avoid many problems, however. Lie-Nielsen and Clifton each make a beautiful version, which works well pretty much out of the box. However, I hesitate to recommend them if you are just starting out, because of the price.

It would be better to learn to set up and maintain on a cheaper plane; otherwise, after a few years of experience you will look at that plane and believe you have to apologize to it for all you put it through. As your skills increase and you look back on those first planes, you will realize how much damage you did to them learning how to set them up, tune, and maintain them. For that reason, I suggest not starting out with a $500 plane. Get a solid-quality tool suited to your skill level—one you can learn on and make mistakes with. You can upgrade as your skills progress.

Beyond the Basics

After this stage, you should make or acquire planes as needed for specific projects, especially if you expect to do something again in that wood or on that scale. These at first will probably be additional smooth planes with different blade angles (to deal with different types of wood), or perhaps smaller or larger versions of what you have.

Eventually you may find it useful to use a preparatory smoothing plane—what I call a panel plane—to speed up the work. Acquire as needed: one with a blade angle of 40° or 45° for softwoods and softer hardwoods; one with a blade angle of 47½° or 50° for hardwoods; and one with the blade at 60° for tropical hardwoods (Figures 9-7, 9-8, 9-9, and 9-10).

Matching smooth planes would be of the same angle or about 3° to 5° more than the panel plane. You can fill these in if and when you need them. (See "The Panel Plane" on page 72.)

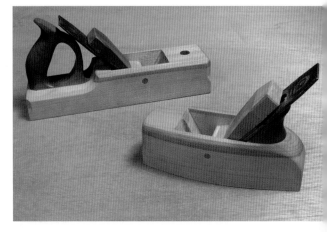

Figure 9-7. *At top is a 12" (305mm)-long razee-style panel plane with a 2¼" (57mm)-wide blade bedded at 47½°. It works well to prepare the surface for the 8" (203mm)-long coffin-sided smoother next to it, which has a 2" (51mm)-wide blade bedded at 50°.*

Figure 9-9. *For larger surfaces I may use this 16"-long panel plane, left, with a 70mm (2¾")-wide blade bedded at 47½°. I may follow it with the 11" smother with a 70mm blade at 47½°, right, or one of the coffin-sided smoothers.*

Figure 9-8. *This is one of my favorite combinations. The 70mm (2¾") plane, bottom, has a blade bedded at 40° and is one of my most used planes. I often follow it with the plane in the center, which has a 70mm (2¾") blade at 43°. If the surface still needs work, I may use the plane at top, which has a very nice 70mm (2¾") blade at 45°.*

When I was starting out, I would purchase a plane for smoothing and set it up as best I could. My skills and understanding progressed, and I would realize my setup was not adequate for the performance I expected. Perhaps the quality of the plane, but definitely, what I did to set it up, limited the performance of that plane. I would therefore upgrade, turning that previous plane into a preparatory plane or panel plane, and use the new plane for fine smoothing.

Not too far into your career, you will need a jointer plane. The best quality work requires edges be prepared for gluing with a jointer plane, and some pieces can be properly prepared only using this plane. If the majority of your work with this plane

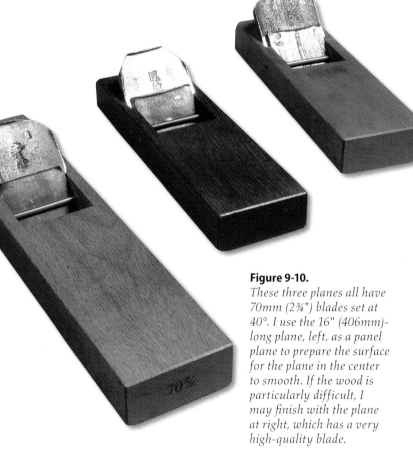

Figure 9-10.
These three planes all have 70mm (2¾") blades set at 40°. I use the 16" (406mm)-long plane, left, as a panel plane to prepare the surface for the plane in the center to smooth. If the wood is particularly difficult, I may finish with the plane at right, which has a very high-quality blade.

is shooting edges and ends and some minor flattening, the Stanley #07 (or the #08, if you can find one) is a good plane (Figure 9-11). If occasional flattening of stock is included in your jointer's job description, you might want to consider getting a wood jointer plane for the improved ergonomics and reduced friction of its sole. (See Chapter 6 for a discussion of jointer planes.)

Eventually your work might grow in volume, scale, quality, and complexity.

When I first started out, I had neither power tools nor access to them. That was educational. I learned the majority of handplanes available were not intended for or capable of substantial work.

Figure 9-11.
This pre-1922 Stanley #08 with rosewood handles is no longer manufactured. Refurbished, it performs quite well, has a blade that takes and holds an excellent edge, and was a fraction of the cost of a new one.

Because I knew our woodworking predecessors were intelligent and developed planes and techniques that worked, I began researching techniques, testing them, and the variety of planes available, over many years.

After learning about traditional tools and techniques for preparing lumber, I discovered I did not have to be constrained by the size of lumber that fit my machinery.

If you find yourself repeatedly falling in love with magnificent pieces of wood and want to incorporate them into your work, or you just tend to think outside the box (no pun intended), you may find yourself faced with pieces you cannot machine. When it happens, you will be glad you know the traditional methods to use.

For preparing stock, the first plane you acquire should be a jack plane. If you are on a budget, you could probably refurbish an old wooden one (Figure 9-12). Otherwise, the Primus horned or English-pattern jack is worth the investment. If your work continues to bring boards that need considerable hand preparation, a scrub plane is very useful.

Figure 9-12. *This English-pattern jack plane was a gift—it does not get any cheaper than that. Though it is not much to look at with a chip off the top of the tote, it has a decent cast-steel blade with a good chipbreaker, and can be put into service quickly.*

If you like to experiment with shapes, you may find it useful to have a plane or two of a size that matches the scale of your work for rough shaping. These would preferably be of wood so they could be shaped to a contour suitable for the project. I have a couple of small Japanese planes that I use to form long sweeps, for instance (Figure 9-13).

Additionally, I have built up a collection, project by project, of small compass planes in various radii (Figure 9-14). These I shaped from small Japanese planes I bought for the purpose. Any wood-bodied plane would do for this. I have been tempted many times to buy the metal adjustable compass plane, but I have not been able to justify the investment.

While the compass planes I own probably cost in aggregate more than the adjustable model, I added to them one at a time, as I needed them. I have been able to finesse these planes to get good surfaces from them. The adjustable compass plane is more of a roughing-out or shaping tool. If I faced a

variety of curves frequently in my work—such as a stairmaker or patternmaker is—I would be able to justify the purchase.

Bottom line: buy tools as you need them; and buy the best you can afford—and appreciate.

Figure 9-13. *Small Japanese planes can be useful in rough-shaping pieces, as the body can be modified to accommodate the shape being sought. I added an adjustable nosepiece to the plane at left to aid in shaping convex curves.*

Figure 9-14. *This collection of small compass planes I have made or purchased over the years. (See "Compass Planes" on page 124 for more on these.)*

10
PLANE SETUP
And Tuning Your Plane to Work Right

Setup and tuning are similar for planes of all styles and functions. Basic procedures are

performed in a specific order to set the plane up, followed by tweaking of the various tactics—

throat opening, blade shape, bevel angle, etc.—which will determine the plane's function. Each

style of plane does require some specific attention, and that will be covered in turn, but in all

cases the same basic procedures are followed in the same order:

1. Inspect the plane for condition issues.
2. Prepare the blade.
3. Prepare and fit the chipbreaker (if there is one).
4. Bed the blade properly.
5. Configure the sole.
6. Adjust the mouth.
7. Attend to the details of the body and sole.
8. Attend to the details related to the grip and finish.

Three of these procedures have basic steps common to the setup of all the planes: #2, preparing

the blade; #3, preparing and fitting the chipbreaker; and #5, configuring the sole. I will lay these

out here to avoid having to repeat them each time when describing the setup of each plane. You

should refer back to them in their proper order as you proceed with your setup.

The use of a shop-made scraper speeds the conditioning of the sole of a metal plane.

Figure 10-1.
This blade has surface rust with only one bad spot at the corner, which can be worked around.

PREPARING THE BLADE

A new blade, or an old blade that needs to be rejuvenated, is always prepared by flattening the back first. This is done first, no matter what style plane it is (though it is more critical with a Japanese plane). If there are serious nicks in the blade, the bevel may be ground first and then the back prepared.

After the back has been flattened to a mirror polish, hone the bevel. Although honing involves alternately stoning both the bevel and the back to remove the wire edge once the back has been polished, sharpening involves only touching up the back on the final polishing stone and not reworking it with all the stones used in first flattening it.

Before starting, remove the chipbreaker, if attached, and inspect the edge of the blade for damage and the back for rust severe enough to cause pitting that is too deep to be honed out (Figure 10-1). Such pits will leave a track in the finish work.

After inspecting the blade, grind the bevel if necessary to remove any nicks and/or to shape the edge. Flatten the back down to a mirror polish, then go back, and sharpen the edge. (See Chapter 11, "Sharpening Plane Blades.")

PREPARING THE CHIPBREAKER

As indicated in "Chipbreaker" on page 45, though they all function the same, chipbreakers take several forms. Despite the slight variations, the procedures for preparing them are similar.

Inspect the chipbreaker for a damaged or badly formed edge. If the problem is severe, see if you will have enough metal left after removing the damage to have a functioning chipbreaker; if not, replace it. Refine the shape of the top contour so there is a microbevel that meets the blade at an angle of about 50°, or such an angle that the combination of blade angle and chipbreaker angle totals 90° to 100°. If the particular configuration allows enough material to remain, put a large second bevel of about 25° behind the microbevel. (You will not be able to do this on a Stanley-type chipbreaker.) The second bevel improves chip clearance and helps eliminate throat clogging.

Next, hold the chipbreaker and the blade together in their final position, and then up to a light (Figure 10-2). No light should appear between the edge of the chipbreaker and the back of the blade. Correct the edge of the chipbreaker if necessary, maintaining its geometry, by stoning the underside on a perfectly flat stone (Figure 10-3). If the edge is badly off, careful work with a smooth file may speed this step, followed by careful stoning. Back-bevel the underside of the chipbreaker slightly so that it meets the blade at a knife's edge (Figure 10-4).

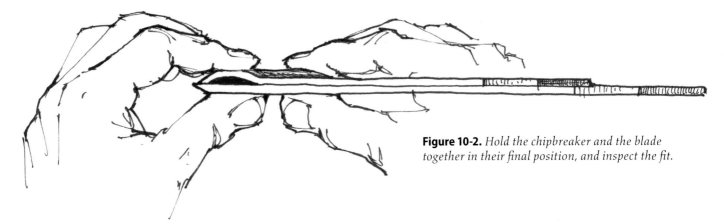

Figure 10-2. *Hold the chipbreaker and the blade together in their final position, and inspect the fit.*

Both the underside and the top microbevel closest the edge should be stoned down to a polish (Figure 10-5). Finish the last strokes of the stoning on the top to ensure that the edge will meet tightly to the blade (Figure 10-6). Hold the chipbreaker and blade up to the light again and check the fit. If the edge appears straight, but is high on one corner and squeezing them together does not close the gap, twist the chipbreaker to straighten it, so the edge fully contacts the blade and no light shows. Make sure the chipbreaker is sprung slightly so that tightening its screw attachment brings the edge of the chipbreaker down tight to

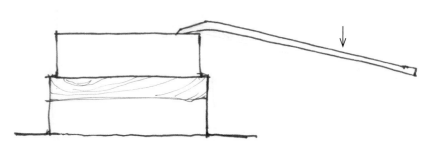

Figure 10-3. *Position the chipbreaker on the stone slightly below horizontal to ensure the edge is slightly back-beveled.*

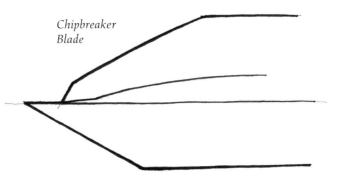

Chipbreaker
Blade

Figure 10-4. *Undercut a degree or so to ensure contact at front edge.*

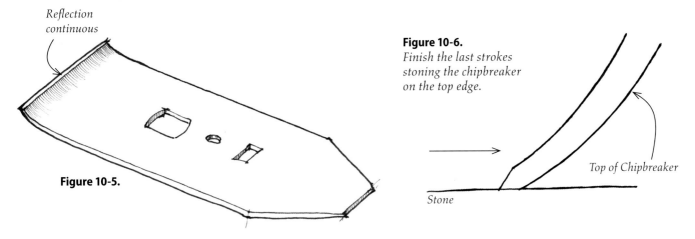

Reflection continuous

Figure 10-5.

Figure 10-6.
Finish the last strokes stoning the chipbreaker on the top edge.

Top of Chipbreaker

Stone

FLATTENING THE BACK OF A PLANE BLADE

There are a number of techniques that can be used to flatten the back of a plane blade. Which technique to best choose in flattening a particular blade is dependent upon how much work must be done to get it flat.

No matter which technique you use, you will have to finish with your sharpening stones, so start by flattening your sharpening stones. (See "Using and Maintaining Waterstones" on page 211.)

Before starting work on the blade, appraise the flatness of the back. Hold the blade up to a large light source, sighting along the blade so you can catch a reflection that goes all the way across the back. Tilt the length of the blade up and down and study the reflection. If the entire back lights up down to the edge, you have a dead flat blade and you will only have to hone it through your usual series of stones. If only a portion of the length of the blade lights up and moves up and down the blade as you tilt it, then the blade has a curve to it. The shorter the reflection the more the curve.

In this case, do not try to flatten the entire length of the blade (from the edge up to about ¼" (6mm) away from the chipbreaker screw slot). Only the lower portion—about ½" (13mm) minimum to maybe 1" (25mm)—needs to be flattened, depending on your blade's curve. Flattening more is tedious, requiring removal of a lot of steel. It is not necessary to get a functioning blade.

Look at the back edge. Tilt the blade until the reflection rolls down to the edge. If you have to tilt the blade more than a little to catch a reflection, or if you can continue tilting the blade and getting a reflection (indicating a rounded edge), use a different strategy. Before flattening the back, grind the main blade bevel back until the rounding or back bevel is eliminated.

Figure 1. *To flatten a severely out-of-flat blade on a kanaban (iron plate), put about one-quarter teaspoon of carborundum in the center of the plate. Add three or four drops of water to the carborundum. In the background is a stick that can be used when holding the blade.*

After appraising the condition of the back of your blade, developing a strategy, and making sure your stones are flat, begin flattening by stroking the blade's back on your coarsest stone. Hold the blade perpendicular to the length of the stone, use the length of the stone, and as much of the full width as possible, back and forth, keeping at least 1" (25mm) or more of the blade on the stone.

Make sure the blade stays flat on the stone. Keep pressure on the blade right behind the edge to keep from gouging the back. After about 30 seconds to a minute, clean and look at the back of the blade. If the new flat is within about ¹⁄₃₂" (0.8mm) of the edge (check the reflection as before), you can continue using waterstones for the process, moving to each individual stone as the polish pattern of each becomes continuous across and down to the entire edge.

If you have to spend more than about four or five minutes of continuous work on a waterstone, you will have to re-flatten it before continuing. If a minute of vigorous work on the coarse stone leaves more than about ¹⁄₃₂" (0.8mm) of edge undone, you are probably better off going instead to a coarse diamond stone to flatten the blade. If not, you can wear your waterstones out of flat, necessitating re-flattening the stones (and probably the back) several times before you are done. After the flat on the back reaches the edge, you can go back and do your normal sharpening sequence on your (flat) stones to polish the back.

If after about a minute on your coarse stone you show the new flat at ¹⁄₁₆" (2mm) or more away, consider more drastic measures (though you can continue to work away on the diamond stone). The cheapest, fastest, and most effective way to flatten a badly out-of-flat plane-blade back is to use the Japanese method of carborundum (silicon-carbide) on an iron plate (*kanaban*). The carborundum particles grip the softer *kanaban* (though it does wear it out—eventually), and abrades the tool steel. The iron-flattening plate, at Japanese tool suppliers, is about $14. An ounce of carborundum is about $3.

The beauty of this method is the grit breaks down as you use it. You can start with coarse 60, 90, or 120 grit, depending on the blade condition. Either breaks down to about 6,000 grit, while increasingly refining the surface. In one step (and about 5 to 10 minutes of vigorous rubbing), you can go from a nasty old blade to a mirror-polished jewel.

To use the flattening plate, put about ¼ teaspoon of carborundum in the center of the plate and add 3 or 4 drops of water to it **(Figure 1)**. Begin rubbing the back of the blade back and forth using the whole length of the plate. Periodically bring the excess carborundum back into the center of the plate **(Figure 2)**. Continue rubbing as the carborundum breaks down into a smooth paste, occasionally adding a drop or two of water if the paste gets too dry to rub. As the paste gets extremely fine, check your progress; you should see a consistent flat at the edge.

Continue rubbing until the back shows a high polish and the paste is transparently fine and

Figure 2. *Rub the back of the blade back and forth using the whole length of the plate. Use of a stick allows you to increase the pressure on the blade at its edge while reducing finger fatigue. The blade and stick are held with the right hand, with the left hand keeping a constant downward pressure. Do not be tempted to rock the blade. The blade must remain flat on the stone at all times. if you lift the right hand even one stroke you will round the edge enough to require 15 or 10 strokes to remove the damage.*

Figure 3. *The carborundum has broken down into a paste and is rubbed until dry.*

rubbed dry **(Figure 3)**. Then add 1 (or maybe 2) drops of water and vigorously rub until the paste is dry again. This will bring up a very high polish. Inspect the blade. Hopefully, the mirror polish of your newly flat back extends to the edge. If not, you will have to do it again, though you can probably start with 120 or 220 grit now. With the final polish, you do not have to follow up with any work on the stones; you can go right to the bevel.

Make sure to keep the carborundum separate from your stones, because it can embed itself and continue to scratch a blade. Wash and rinse the blade and everything else in separate water.

the blade (Figure 10-7). In some cases, the chipbreaker may have to be bent slightly to achieve this.

Attach the chipbreaker to the blade (Figure 10-8), adjust its position according to the work to be done, check again, finally, that no light comes through the meeting of the two at the edge, and tighten the screw down.

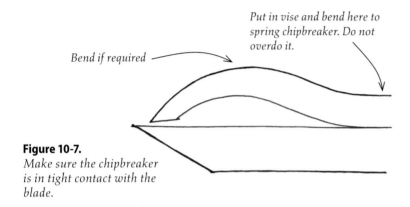

Put in vise and bend here to spring chipbreaker. Do not overdo it.

Bend if required

Figure 10-7.
Make sure the chipbreaker is in tight contact with the blade.

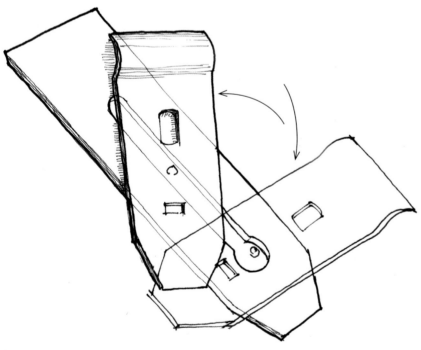

Figure 10-8. *To avoid damaging the edge of the blade, always install the chipbreaker at the top of the blade (no matter which end of the blade the hole for the screw is located) rotating the chipbreaker over the blade and down into position.*

CONFIGURING THE SOLE

(Note: it may be helpful to reread "Length of Plane/Width of Blade" on page 55.)

This is the basic concept for flattening and configuring the sole of a plane that I use. Instead of trying to make the entire sole of the plane flat within a very close tolerance, only a minimum of three narrow parallel areas, the width of the sole, need be in line with one another and contacting the work.

Areas in between these are relieved *slightly* (± 0.002", or 0.05mm) to reduce maintenance. There are always at least two areas in front of the cutting edge, one at the front and one at the mouth of the plane, and form the basic reference area for moving the plane over the work. There is always at least one behind the blade, its location dependent on the task the plane handles—dimension, true, or smooth.

Based on practical experience and the traditional practice of Japanese woodworkers, I suggest a further refinement. Occasionally, relieve the reference area(s) behind the blade a small amount instead of keeping it in the same plane as the two (or more) areas in front of the blade. The actual amount depends on the task the plane is expected to do. My suggestion is, planes used for truing a surface, such as jointers, have all their reference surfaces all in the same line. Smoothing planes should have the reference area behind the blade relieved ever so slightly to facilitate the plane reaching into any very slight low areas of the work that might remain from previous preparation.

Jack planes could, at your discretion, have the reference area behind the blade relieved slightly more than the smoothing plane is relieved, to make it easier to attack areas when initially dimensioning a piece.

Configuring the sole like this, besides facilitating maintenance and the task the plane is expected to do, also helps deal with the continued distortion of the sole that results from the blade-fixing action of the wedge or lever cap tending to push the sole down. This stress is dynamic and changes easily. In order to deal with this variable, I do not have any reference areas right here in my planes, but further back beyond the blade bed area (Figure 10-9).

The main reference area of the sole of the plane is the portion immediately in front of the cutting edge. This area must remain in full contact with the work for as long as it is on the piece being planed. The length of this area in front of the cutting edge varies from one style of plane to another. Western-style planes have the blade pretty far forward, often one-third or less of the way back from the front of the plane.

On a 9" (229mm) Bailey-style plane, the blade is only about 2½" (64mm) from the front. Chinese planes have the blade located about halfway back, and Japanese planes about five-eighths of the way back. Because the size of this reference area and the location of the hands applying downward pressure vary from one style to the other, the sole configuration may need to be different from one style to the other.

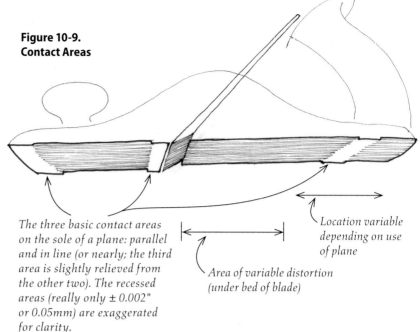

Figure 10-9. Contact Areas

The three basic contact areas on the sole of a plane: parallel and in line (or nearly; the third area is slightly relieved from the other two). The recessed areas (really only ± 0.002" or 0.05mm) are exaggerated for clarity.

Location variable depending on use of plane

Area of variable distortion (under bed of blade)

WHAT REALLY HAPPENS

If you examined what happens when a plane cuts, it might appear the area behind the blade should be exactly in line with the blade edge and project more than the two areas in front—much like how the outfeed table of a power jointer is set up—nearly even with the cutters.

In practice, however, it is often helpful to slightly relieve the third working surface, not only from the blade edge, but often from the other two leading surfaces as well. This is because as the blade edge wears, it withdraws—gets shorter (see "How an Edge Dulls" on page 53)—and a plane bottom that was fixed even with the sharpened edge would soon hold the worn edge off the work.

On longer planes, especially truing planes, there are more than three contact planes. Some recommendations for configuring the sole of different styles of planes are shown within their individual sections. Specifics will be dealt with in the respective sections.

GENERAL TECHNIQUES FOR ADJUSTING THE PLANE BLADE

Adjust the blade by turning the plane over and sighting down the sole from the front of the plane **(Figure 1)**. Hold the plane so that the background or lighting provides contrast between the black line of the blade protruding and the light reflecting off the sole. Using the plane's adjustment mechanism, advance the blade until you can just see it begin to protrude below the sole as a thin black line. Adjust the blade laterally until this line is parallel to the sole. Advance or retreat according to your best guess of the depth of shaving you want. Make a trial and re-adjust as necessary.

Needless to say, sometimes the blade can be hard to see, especially if it is set fine, you are a beginner, or you have aging eyes—or all three. Sometimes you find the black line you thought was the blade was actually the bed of the blade—and you wondered why the blade stubbornly refused to cut. Sometimes on a steeply pitched blade, there is too little contrast between the blade and the sole of the plane. In this case, you are better off sighting down

Figure 1. *Sight down the sole of the plane to see the depth the blade is set at.*

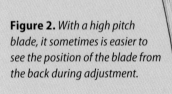

Figure 2. *With a high pitch blade, it sometimes is easier to see the position of the blade from the back during adjustment.*

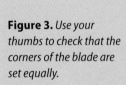

Figure 3. *Use your thumbs to check that the corners of the blade are set equally.*

the sole from the back where the light will shine off the bevel of the blade and contrast with the mouth opening **(Figure 2)**.

Another technique some woodworkers recommend, and one I use to supplement the others, is lightly feeling the protrusion of the corners of the blade with your thumbs **(Figure 3)**. This would seem to risk cutting your thumbs, but the technique is quite common, and I have seen both Westerners and Japanese craftsmen use it. It is a good way to tell if the corners of the blade are protruding evenly, though I have yet to get the hang of using this technique to the exclusion of the others.

Setting Up the Bailey/Stanley Plane

Of all the styles of planes, the ones that look the most alike but have the greatest variation in quality are the Bailey-style planes. Setting aside top-of-the-line models such as Lie-Nielsen, Clifton, and Veritas, whose quality is obvious, the remainders run the gamut.

This style of plane was made by so many manufacturers—Sears, Millers Falls, Sargent, Record—virtually every hardware and big-box store. Even within the Stanley line itself, from the same period, the quality of both materials and manufacturing varied widely.

When purchasing, it is best to stay with the more respected manufacturers and avoid cheaper models. In a higher-quality plane, the milled areas for the blade and the frog will be larger and better designed, resulting in greater cutting reliability and a reduced chance of blade chatter. In addition, the adjuster will be heavier with much less slop, letting you set the blade quicker and more accurately. Buying a better version of the plane also improves your chances of getting a mature casting.

Cast iron needs to rest for about six months as it adjusts to the stresses from the casting process. Better-quality manufacturers will allow the casting to age before milling it despite the cost of allowing material inventory to sit around for six months. If they are milled

THE OILER

For all styles of planes and planing, it is helpful to have a large oiler sitting on the bench. Drag the sole of the plane over it (backward) periodically while working, to keep the sole of the plane—and the blade edge as well—lubricated while working. This allows planing rhythm to be virtually uninterrupted.

The oiler should be around 3" in diameter: a lidded canister, a drilled out block of wood, or, traditionally, a large bamboo knuckle. Rip rags to about 3" or 4" (76mm or 102mm) wide. It will take most or all of a bed sheet. Wrap the rags continuously in a coil until you reach the desired diameter—usually slightly larger than the hole it is to go into. Wrap the end to be inserted with heavy plastic such as a plastic drop cloth or Visqueen, and work the whole roll into the hole. About ½" (13mm) or more of the cloth should protrude from the container; cut the plastic off even with the container. Saturate the cloth with camellia oil (available at Japanese tools suppliers), which provides light, contaminate-free lubrication.

Two oilers, both made from a section of bamboo. The larger one is about 3" (76mm) in diameter and sits on the bench when used. Take the plane to the oiler and stroke its sole over it during planing as part of the rhythm of work. The smaller one is about 1½" (38mm) in diameter and is picked up to be used.

before they have aged, the castings may warp out of true before they reach the end user (you)—or *after* you have purchased, set up, and tuned it. Because of this, parts may not mate well, making the cut unreliable, the use frustrating, and the problems difficult.

STEP 1: INSPECT THE PLANE

When checking out a plane, first, look at the body. On all planes, the quality of the finish may give clues to what you can expect from the plane: is the plane *japanned* (a baked enamel) or just painted? Is it sloppy or well done? Inspect the body of a used plane carefully for cracks, especially around the throat (Figure 10-10).

You may have to try to bend or twist the plane with your hands—do not lock it in a vise and pry on it with another tool!—to get a suspected fault to open up. If the body is cracked at the throat—unless it is a valuable model that might be worth brazing—discard it. Do not bother to tune it up; the crack renders it next to useless.

Figure 10-10. *A small crack a little more than ¼" (6mm) long in the upper corner of the mouth of this plane, parallel to the side, makes this plane unusable.*

And just because the plane is old, do not assume it will perform better. Many planes made for casual users were not high quality. Lower-quality planes are more likely to have been misused and may be damaged in ways not readily apparent. Such planes can also have annoyingly sloppy adjusters, or trouble holding their adjustment.

On the other hand, if you spot an old plane that obviously has been well used, but also well maintained, you might want to give it a second look.

Examine the blade seat. On the cheapest versions of the Bailey plane, the surfaces of the blade seat (and the frog seat on the body of the plane) are not even milled, with the rough casting simply painted over.

As these areas are difficult to correct, if it appears the frog rocks and cannot sit solidly, or if these areas are badly done, painted, or not milled at all, stop here (Figure 10-11). That plane will never make a fine shaving and never give more than basic utility service. Get another plane or save this one for removing paint from used boards.

On all models, check that the adjustment mechanisms will allow you the settings you may require of the plane: heavy cut, very fine cut, fine mouth setting, etc. Sometimes the adjusters run out of adjustment at the extremes. For instance, on some Bedrock-style planes, because the blade descends as the frog is moved forward, the blade depth-adjuster can run out of adjustment when the frog is moved forward to close the mouth down to a very narrow gap.

This particular malady is often a result of a misplaced hole for the depth-adjuster nib on the chipbreaker. Exchanging the chipbreaker to correct this may not be an option, as many of them are specific to their own particular model and will not work in other makes or models of planes. This will limit using the tactic of closing the mouth down, which may be a liability depending on the uses planned for your plane.

In addition, on an old plane, sometimes the chipbreaker has been exchanged and as a result, will not give a satisfactory range of adjustment. This can be remedied by replacing it with the correct chipbreaker for that model—assuming, of course, that it was manufactured correctly the first time.

STEPS 2 & 3: PREPARE THE BLADE AND CHIPBREAKER

After you have inspected your plane and scoped out its condition, begin setting it up by preparing the blade. Go back to the sections on general procedures "Preparing the Blade" and "Preparing the Chipbreaker," and follow the directions there.

STEP 4: BED THE BLADE PROPERLY

On a decent-quality plane, all of the surfaces of the blade seat and the back edge of the mouth opening will be nicely milled and free of enamel, needing at most only cleanup of a little bit of enamel, or a recalcitrant corner or a bit of flash, missed by the milling machine (Figure 10-12). Clean it up carefully with a file. Remove the two screws residing under

Figure 10-11.
The blade seat on a cheap plane: the bed remains unmilled and painted over.

the blade that attach the frog to the body of the plane, and remove the frog. Be certain the frog-adjustment screws do not protrude above the level of the bed when fully tightened, and interfere with the bedding of the blade.

Inspect its bottom and mating surface on the plane for the same problems, and correct minor aberrations with a file or diamond file as before. With the screws replaced but left

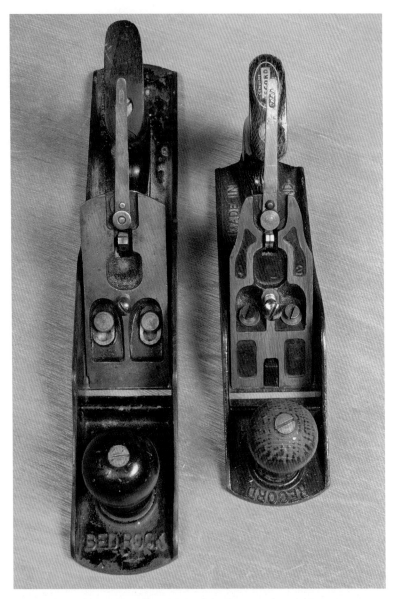

Figure 10-12. *The older plane (on the left in Figure 10-12) has a considerably larger contact area on the blade bed, though it is not clear whether this makes any real difference in the performance of the plane. The contact area for the frog in each plane below is about the same.*

slightly loose, see if it can be rocked on its mating surfaces. Experiment with the screws lightly tightened to verify the frog can be securely and solidly bedded. Reinstall the frog and check that the opening of the mouth at the back (frog side) is square to the length of the plane, and that the frog can be made parallel to it.

The frog and the back of the throat at the body form the seat of the blade (unless you have a Bedrock-type plane, in which case the blade is supported solely by the frog), and the two must be able to form a continuous flat plane (Figures 10-13, 10-14 and 10-15).

Hopefully, the frog can be set back far enough and rotated if necessary to align with this edge. A little bit of filing on the edge of the back of the mouth might be called for if the frog cannot be rotated enough. I would recommend not filing because it can bring about a cascade of problems, and blade adjustment will compensate (within limits) for out of square anyway.

Unless you are doing some exceptionally fine planing, adjust the frog to give the blade its maximum support, that is, aligned with the back edge of the mouth of the body. Insert the blade, making sure it is properly seated, with the hole in the chipbreaker over the blade-adjuster nib, and the slot in the blade over the nib of the lateral-adjustment knob. Adjust the lever cap's screw so there is only enough pressure to keep the blade from shifting under its workload. Too much pressure, and there is danger of damaging the plane.

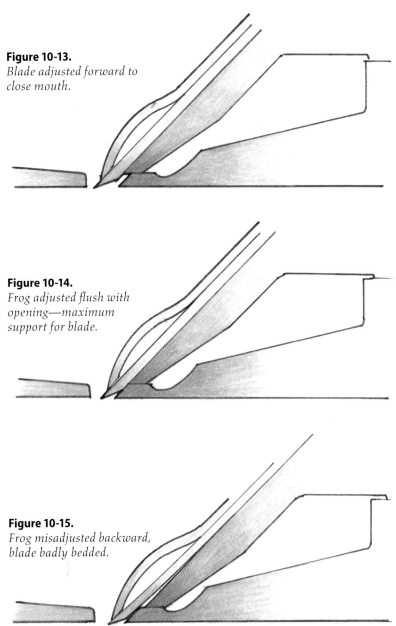

Figure 10-13.
Blade adjusted forward to close mouth.

Figure 10-14.
Frog adjusted flush with opening—maximum support for blade.

Figure 10-15.
Frog misadjusted backward, blade badly bedded.

WORKING AROUND THE BLADE-ADJUSTMENT NIB

Because the blade-adjustment nib protrudes above the blade bed, is pinned, and cannot be removed, any overall flattening of the bed will have to be done piecemeal working around the nib. Working like this will most likely make its condition worse. Leave it alone. Just look for protrusions of enamel or missed milling. If the overall flatness of the bed is bad—get another plane.

STEP 5: CONFIGURE THE SOLE

It is important to have the blade assembly installed under full working pressure: the pressure from the lever cap distorts the sole and this must be corrected during this process. Retract the blade about ¹⁄₁₆" (2mm) from the bottom to avoid contacting the blade edge when working.

Using a good straightedge against the bottom, hold the two up to the light to check for high spots (Figure 10-16). Check all across the bottom, especially the area right in front of the mouth, as well as diagonally, and perpendicular to the length (Figure 10-17).

Check for twist with winding sticks (Figure 10-18). Having appraised the sole's condition, you can choose the most expedient method for flattening the bottom. If badly out of flat (more than ¹⁄₆₄"(0.4mm) at any one place), you might consider using a machinist's scraper to scrape the high spots initially. If the high spots are less than this, a good mill file will be sufficient. Machinist's dye on a platen can be used to spot the high areas, but it will not tell you how much material you need to remove or if you are rocking the plane on the platen and not disclosing any twist or rounding.

Complete final leveling with wet/dry sandpaper or any of the new abrasive papers or films suitable for working metal. I do not recommend you do all the leveling with sandpaper, especially if you have a lot to do. I have found a lot of sanding results in a distorted bottom rather than a flat one. I think the distortion results from the slight repetitive error in weight shift that happens when making hundreds of strokes.

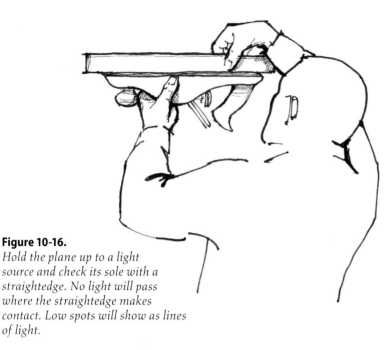

Figure 10-16.
Hold the plane up to a light source and check its sole with a straightedge. No light will pass where the straightedge makes contact. Low spots will show as lines of light.

If you have had some experience in sharpening, you know you can take more material off one part of the blade simply by putting more pressure on that area. Better to carefully remove material indicated by a straightedge, and/or machinist's bluing (or the scratch pattern of sandpaper on a flat surface) with a file and to reserve the sandpaper for polishing out the file marks (Figure 10-19). It is also much less tedious. In fact, after filing, if sanding does not level the sole to the degree required after about three minutes, you should go back to filing before

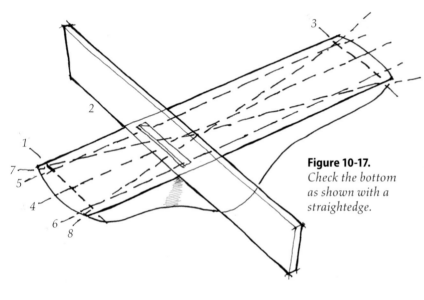

Figure 10-17.
Check the bottom as shown with a straightedge.

A SCRAPER FOR METAL

A serviceable metal scraper can be made by grinding the end of a file to about a 60° bevel, then touching it up a bit with a diamond file. Push the scraper over the work or hold it nearly vertical and pull it with a scraping action.

The end of this old file has been ground to form a scraper for tuning the sole of a metal plane.

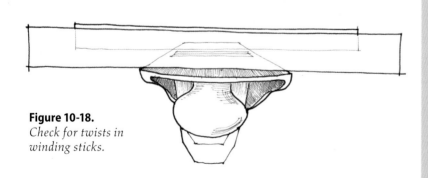

Figure 10-18.
Check for twists in winding sticks.

returning to sanding. Sanding for more than three minutes before checking could distort the bottom.

As discussed earlier in general procedures, "Configure the Sole," on page 150, the entire sole of your plane does not have to be dead flat (unless maybe you're a pattern maker); it needs only to contact the work at three places—six or so with a #07 or #08 plane (Figure 10-20).

The points should be the full width of the sole and parallel (i.e., not twisted) to one another. Once three (or more) points

Figure 10-19. *The scratch pattern after about one minute rubbing on sandpaper on a granite platen. The bright areas have been sanded. Notice the darker area, in front of the mouth; this area is slightly lower and has not been sanded. This critical area needs to be brought into line. The dark oval top center is a depression resulting from distortion of the casting because of the extra thickness at the handle mount. This area can remain depressed, so long as a flat toward the back of the plane is established.*

GAUGING STRAIGHTNESS

You can use feeler gauges under a straight edge to measure the amount a surface is out of flat, but it is easier to gauge the amount just by sighting under a straight edge: the human eye can see light through a gap of less than 0.001" (0.025mm).

contact a flat surface across the entire width of the sole, you are done with this stage. If you are ambitious, you can level the bottom beyond this point, flattening until the entire bottom has been polished (sometimes you nearly have to anyway). Doing so, however, increases the chance of sanding the bottom out of flat, and of exceeding your own tolerance for tedium.

Start with any high areas between the intended contact surfaces, scraping or filing these until they appear to be slightly lower than the intended contact surfaces. Check frequently when using the scraper so that you do not remove too much. Then move to the contact surfaces.

Try to lay the file simultaneously across two of the contact surfaces at any one time, keeping the file flat at all times and the pressure evenly distributed (Figure 10-21). Usually the file will be oriented along the length of the plane.

Occasionally, if you have a particular high spot, you can work across the width of the sole to concentrate on that spot and then turn the file along the length again to even up the surface. A good rule to follow is to have as much of the file in contact with the bottom of the plane as possible. Periodically vary the alignment of the file to avoid repetitive error.

As you file, bringing the contact surfaces

Figure 10-20. Schematic of Contact Areas of the Sole of Bailey-Style Planes

Contact areas extend the full width of the plane, are parallel, and are on a line with one another except where they have been relieved slightly as suggested in the illustration.

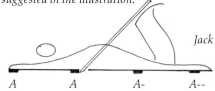

Jack

A   A   A-   A--

Areas in between contact areas are relieved only a few thousandths of an inch; A to A-: 1 or 2 file strokes; A to A--: 2 to 4 file strokes.

Jointer

A   A   A A--   A   A   A

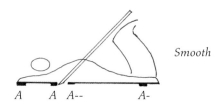

Smooth

A   A A--   A-

FILE MOUTH RELIEF

Before you start, file a little relief either side of the mouth to make sure the area does not contact the work after the sole is generally flattened.

Figure 10-21. Filing

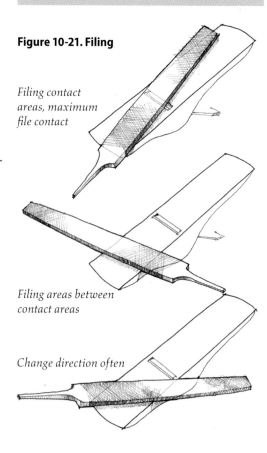

Filing contact areas, maximum file contact

Filing areas between contact areas

Change direction often

into alignment, some areas in between—areas you want to be low, non-contact areas—may show themselves to be high, despite your previous efforts to lower them. You have two choices here: Continue to file, enlarging these areas until the file contacts the reference planes you are trying to bring into line. In such cases, you will have contact areas larger than you anticipated, which is okay. Alternatively, you can go back and put a little extra work on these areas to lower them and then go back to bringing the contact areas into line. This whole process may happen several times before you are done.

Once you have satisfied yourself that the bottom is flat by checking with a straightedge, you can move to sandpaper. Sandpaper will not only smooth the marks from the filing, but the

areas of polishing it leaves will in short order tell you if the bottom is flat, or if you will have to go back to filing.

You can use wet/dry sandpaper, micron-graded plastic-backed abrasives, or adhesive-backed sandpaper. Tape (or adhere) one or two pieces (depending on the length of the plane and the size of abrasive sheet you are using) to a flat surface such as a jointer bed. A granite platen is best but not necessary. Make sure your surface is flat. Just because it is a milled surface such as a table saw, does not mean it is flat. (My table saw is not, unfortunately).

If you do not have a machined surface you can or want to use, a flat worktop will do. Put a piece of ¼" (6mm) plate glass over it to bridge any minor surface irregularities. (If the surface underneath the glass is not flat, the glass will flex under pressure.)

Using water with wet/dry sandpaper will keep the paper from clogging and hold the sandpaper in place on a sheet of plate glass. Wet or dry, but especially wet, sanding will make a mess, so protect the surface you are working on. Start with 80- or 100-grit paper and work through at least 220- or 400-grit max. I am not a glutton for punishment, so I am not tempted to go any further. Besides, cast iron is rather porous and will polish only so much anyway (Figure 10-22).

After leveling with the sandpaper, you may wish to further finesse the sole as described in Figure 10-20. You can carefully stroke these specific contact areas with a file the one to four strokes recommended to complete your configuration of the sole.

Do not do metal work on your bench, as the metal filings will infect your workpieces for years, dulling tools and showing up in the work, sometimes years later, as black dots or splotches, as the filings slowly rust.

Figure 10-22. *Completed sole of a jack plane. The brighter areas have been filed and are slightly lower. The slightly darker areas are the major contact points and have been leveled and aligned by sanding on sandpaper on a granite platen. Completely removing the oval casting depression is not necessary.*

STEP 6: ADJUST THE MOUTH

Having finished the bottom, inspect the mouth. The mouth should be square to the length of the plane, straight, sharp where it meets the sole, and crisply formed (Figure 10-23). Insert the blade and chipbreaker assembly and the cap iron, and adjust the blade to a working position, making sure the edge is parallel to the sole.

The mouth opening should also be parallel to the blade edge—a factor more important than the mouth opening being square to the length of the plane (Figure 10-24). If the mouth opening is not parallel to the blade edge, adjust it with a file. The relief angle of the mouth opening should be 90° or slightly greater.

Carefully touch up the mouth with a file as needed. Go slow with this: you do not want to open up the mouth any more than you have. It is hard to mark a line parallel to the blade and then file to the line dead straight.

MOUTH GOING OUT OF PARALLEL

Taking too much off one side of the sole when flattening it can cause the mouth and back edge of the mouth opening at the frog to go out of parallel. The result is both go out of square with the length of the plane. This is because the relief angle and blade-bed angle are acute angles and not square to the sole, resulting in their diverging rapidly as material is removed from the sole.

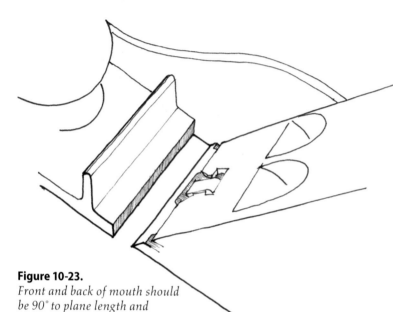

Figure 10-23.
Front and back of mouth should be 90° to plane length and parallel to each other.

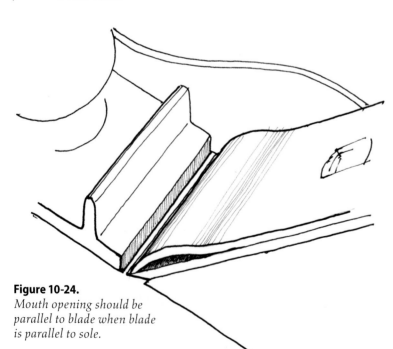

Figure 10-24.
Mouth opening should be parallel to blade when blade is parallel to sole.

STEP 7: ATTEND TO THE DETAILS OF THE BODY AND SOLE

Gently smooth all of the edges around the bottom, making sure there are no sharp edges to mar the work. Give the plane the once-over and check for any other edges that might damage you or the work, and correct them with file or sandpaper.

Check the operation of the blade (depth) and lateral adjusters. See that they operate freely and are not distorted, bent, or broken, and engage the blade and chipbreaker fully. Some woodworkers have suggested twisting the fork that engages the wheel of the blade adjuster decreases the play in the adjustment mechanism. I have not had success doing this, and in some models, it is not possible anyway, as the fork is cast.

Adjust the blade to make a light cut and a trial shaving. If the bottom is truly flat, you should be able to make a shaving as thin as you want. (Do not be misled by a board that is less flat than your plane bottom. The plane will only cut the high spots until the board is sufficiently and incrementally flattened.)

STEP 8: ATTEND TO THE DETAILS OF THE GRIP AND FINISH

I find it helpful to soften the slot of the screw that holds the front knob with a little sandpaper, and soften as well any mismatch of the screw to the front knob. This will reduce wear and tear on your hand. Now, unless you have a used plane with damaged handles, or want to refit the handles to your own specification, this completes setup.

Setting Up Wood-body Planes

Setup for a wooden plane—either the wood block or horned variation—proceeds in the same order as other planes. There are specific things to look for with these planes, however, and some slight differences between the antique planes and the new ones.

STEP 1A: INSPECT THE PLANE: OLD PLANES

Inspect the body of the plane. Look for rot, or worse, and more common, beetle or wormholes. Avoid these. I once bought a transitional Bailey plane with a few beetle holes—the inside was nearly hollow. Beetle holes appear as tiny pinholes. However, do not mistake holes made from brads used to hold temporary fences nailed on by a previous owner for beetle holes. Holes from brads are acceptable, though sometimes hard to distinguish from the beetle holes.

Often a body will shrink over time, especially if the plane was made on the East Coast or Europe and was moved to the West or Southwest, or was made in Japan, China, or Southeast Asia and was imported to anywhere in the United States. The body will dry out and shrink around the blade causing the body to crack or, at the very least, warp badly around the blade.

If this is not too severe, the opening for the blade in the body can be carefully pared to give the blade more room (once you get the blade out). If it is too severe, you may have to remove too much wood, weakening the body, especially if it is a traditional Western plane,

ADJUSTING THE BAILEY-STYLE PLANE

Sighting down the sole of the plane, turn the wheel of the depth adjuster until the blade protrudes your best guess of the intended amount. Push the lever of the lateral adjuster to make the blade parallel. (Honestly, I can never remember which direction gives which result, so I usually end up doing it the wrong way.) This usually changes the depth of the blade, so it must be re-adjusted.

This is where it can get a bit aggravating, as it will take some spinning of the wheel to change direction. However, once you have about got it and take a trial stroke, you can fine-tune the blade depth in motion by turning the wheel in between strokes with your first finger without having to turn the plane over or change your grip **(Figure 1)**.

Day to day, there is no need to back the blade off or loosen the lever cap. You can return to the plane time after time at the same setting. However, if you put the plane into storage or do not use it for a long time, it is a good idea to loosen the lever cap and/or take the blade out, as the prolonged pressure of the lever cap eventually distorts the sole of the plane slightly, necessitating tuning up the sole. This has to be done periodically anyway (though it can usually go a long time between tune-ups), but the less often you will have to do this, the happier you will be.

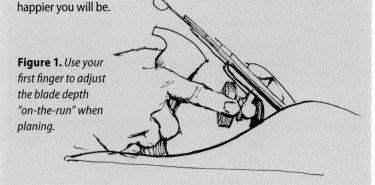

Figure 1. *Use your first finger to adjust the blade depth "on-the-run" when planing.*

TAPERED BLADES

Old wood-body planes usually have tapered blades, thicker where the cutting edge is and thinning toward the opposite end. Why? The tapered blade is handmade. I believe that besides being easier to make by hand than a parallel blade (whose dimensions can be guaranteed only by a mill machine), its shape conveniently solved a number of issues around the setup and reliability of the plane. The natural wedging action of a tapered blade resists being pushed back under the load of cutting wood, and makes it easier to remove, because you can tap the blade down and it will release quite quickly (often too quickly).

I believe these traits are (questionable) side benefits of the method of manufacturing the blade. As we all know now—and they probably did then—parallel blades stay put just fine under the wedge. They are also easier to adjust because they do not lock in so tightly. You can move them down further than a fraction of an inch and not have to worry about them unexpectedly flying out of the mouth of the plane.

Here is my theory for the taper. When making a laminated blade by hand, you have the extra thickness of the edge steel added to the backing steel blade blank, the two of which must be forge-welded together. Then you have to hammer the assembly until the backing steel flushes with the edge steel on the top of the blade. If you do not hammer out the blade at the edge end as well—it is easier not to—then you have begun giving the blade a taper. From there, you continue the taper just making sure the back of the blade is slightly concave. This guarantees the blade will bed properly at the heel despite any irregularities along its length, or irregularities in the hand-cut bed. This means you can reduce the amount of grinding on the back. I have blades that still have the hammer marks on the back **(Figure 1).** A parallel blade must be accurately ground on both faces, which cannot easily be done freehand. An added benefit is you have maximized the thickness of the blade near the edge, further reducing the chances of chattering in use, especially if a substantial chipbreaker is added.

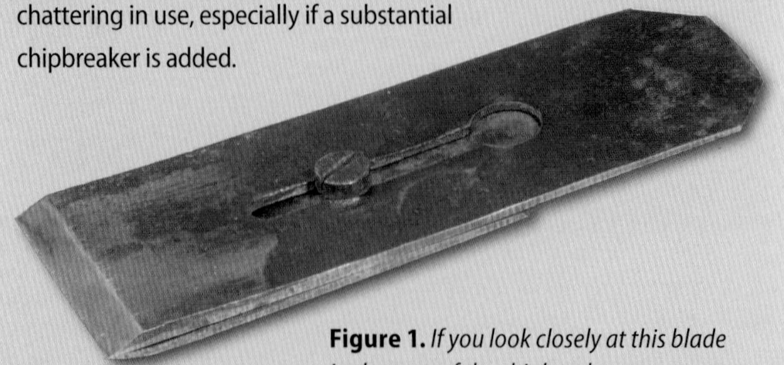

Figure 1. *If you look closely at this blade in the area of the chipbreaker screw, you can see the semicircular edges of the impressions left by the forging hammer.*

which leaves very little material on either side of the blade.

In this case, the blade may have to be ground down a bit to make it narrower. If the body is cracked at the cheek that holds the wedge, the plane is probably useless, as this area is under a lot of stress, and re-gluing may not hold (Figure 10-25). Minor checks can often be tolerated; cracks around the throat, if not bad, can be injected with glue and clamped, or fitted with wood wedges that are then glued in. (You can see this being done on a rabbet plane in Figure 10-54 and Figure 10-57 on page 189 and 191.)

Handles can of course be refitted. Twists can be planed out, but if the distortion is too severe, squaring up the body to the flattened sole may remove too much wood at the wedge area either side of the blade, weakening the plane and leaving it unstable.

Usually the mouth wears open on an old plane. If the plane is to be used for smoothing, a piece can be inlaid into the bottom to close it up. In some cases, install an adjustable throat. This gives the plane some added versatility, plus the throat piece is removable for maintenance or replacement.

Check the condition of the blade and its chipbreaker (see general procedures on "Preparing the Blade" and "Preparing the Chipbreaker" on page 146). Also, check the amount of usable steel left in the blade. Most old blades are laminated cast steel. With careful examination, the lamination lines can be discerned. Often times, the steel will have been sharpened away, or nearly so, leaving little usable steel edge in front of the slot. Finally, check the hard, brittle-edged steel for cracks and other signs of abuse. Check to see that the chipbreaker does actually work with the blade; sometimes these have been switched.

STEP 1B: INSPECT THE PLANE: NEW PLANES

Manufacturers are producing few new traditional block-style planes. Those produced tend to be high-end well-made planes. The new horned-style planes I have seen are also of excellent quality. Both styles of planes should require only tuning up of the sole rather than a major makeover as is often required of an old, used plane.

With a new wood plane, it is always a good idea to pull the blade/chipbreaker assembly out and let the plane sit for a few months and allow it to acclimate to your shop.

If your shop is drier than where the plane was made, this will save you the agony of trying to withdraw a blade seized by a shrunken body and the coincident possible damage to the plane.

Waiting for the plane to acclimate before fine-turning it saves time in the end. After the plane has acclimated, check the body for twist and check that the blade has enough room either side for lateral adjustment.

If the plane body has twisted, the blade bed may have some twist as well. Check the fit of the wedge to the body and chipbreaker and check the mouth opening. Accept no checking or cracking (unless it is cracked around the blade because you failed to remove the blade). While checking or cracking might be tolerated

Figure 10-25.
This cheek crack (on the left) is precarious, but so far has held.

on an old plane, there is no need to deal with it on a new plane—it will only get worse.

After you have inspected your plane, either old or new, and have assessed the issues that have to be dealt with, you can begin to set up the plane.

STEPS 2 & 3: PREPARE THE BLADE AND CHIPBREAKER

If you have an old blade, whether tapered or parallel, you probably have some work ahead of you. See the general procedures on "Preparing the Blade" and "Preparing the Chipbreaker" on page 146 and "Flattening the Back of a Plane Blade" on page 148.

STEP 4: BED THE BLADE PROPERLY

If your plane block has shrunk, you may first have to widen the escapement where the blade and chipbreaker fit. You will also need a little additional room (± ⅟₃₂", or 0.8") to allow for lateral adjustment. If you have to remove a lot of wood here, and you are afraid it might weaken the plane, you may have to grind the width of the blade and chipbreaker down. (Remember, if the plane is twisted as well, you will be removing some material later from both sides.)

Determine that the notch for the chipbreaker screw is big enough, correcting as necessary by careful paring with a sharp chisel.

Check the blade seat for flatness and lack of twist by sighting down the ramp or blade bed (Figure 10-26). Carefully pare this with a chisel (or you can use a float if you have one) to take out the twist. Once you have the twist out, as best as can be visually determined, begin seating the blade. Screw the blade and chipbreaker together with the chipbreaker in its final position.

If you have a tapered blade, check to see that its back (underside) is arched along its length (see Figure 3-30 on page 47). If it is, you will have to pay particular attention to the bed down near the sole and at the top of the plane, as that is where the blade will contact it.

If your blade is parallel and not arched (some will arch with the chipbreaker attached), make sure the blade is contacting the bed at least at the bottom and top, similar to the tapered blade, and that it is not sitting on a high spot in between.

With both blades, you can check the flatness of the bed top to bottom with a small straightedge, and correct as necessary. After that, you will have to use one or a combination of techniques to finalize the fit.

First, set the blade/chipbreaker assembly onto its bed in its approximate final position and hold it down in the center with one finger. With a finger of the other hand tap the four corners one by one (Figure 10-27). They should make little or no noise when tapped. If you hear a clicking or tapping sound on one or opposite corners, that (those) corners are low.

Pare the high corners until all the corners are silent when repeating the test. In addition, you can use the Japanese technique of rubbing pencil lead on the back of the blade and then rubbing the blade assembly in its position on its bed. Where the lead has

CHECKING FOR A CUSTOM FIT

In some rare cases, the wedge or blade seat, or both, may have been custom-fitted to the hand-wrought blade assembly and will appear to be twisted or out of parallel. Check the blade assembly for matching eccentricities, and then put the blade into position and operating tightness.

Inspect the fit, checking especially that the blade beds solidly, especially at the heel, and the wedge is tight all around. Check visually, tapping and pushing, looking (and listening) for deflection. If it appears contact is good, and the blade does not chatter in use, then you are all set. If it chatters, see "Troubleshooting" on page 197.

rubbed off are the high spots. Pare these away with a chisel, and repeat the process until you get solid bearing across the bed at least at the bottom and the top. This last technique is particularly good for fine-tuning the fit.

Once you are confident the blade/chipbreaker assembly is well bedded, check the fit of the wedge to the assembly. Chipbreakers often have a singular curve and the wedge must fit well. They can sometimes be carelessly switched. Adjust the fit as necessary.

The wedge must also fit its abutment on the body. The angle must be correct so it is in continuous contact with its abutment, and both sides must be equally tight. You can check for equal tightness by tapping the

Figure 10-26. Blade bed

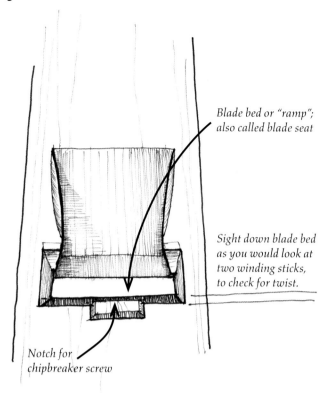

Blade bed or "ramp"; also called blade seat

Sight down blade bed as you would look at two winding sticks, to check for twist.

Notch for chipbreaker screw

wedge lightly into position (with the blade in) and pulling from side to side. Both sides should have equal resistance to withdrawal.

If one side pulls free more easily than the other, that side is not as tight. Remove a *very thin* shaving off the top of the tighter side of the wedge until, when tested, the resistance is equal. Check the fit one shaving at a time; and do not distort the angle of the taper.

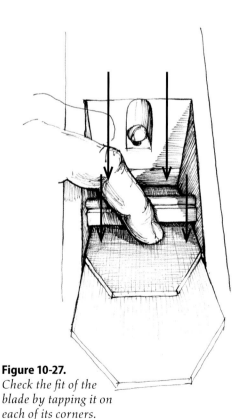

Figure 10-27.
Check the fit of the blade by tapping it on each of its corners.

STEP 5: CONFIGURE THE SOLE

A wood plane bottom is flattened differently than a metal plane bottom. First, it is never sanded. I know this goes counter to most of what you will read, but there are good reasons for it. Sanding embeds grit into the bottom of the plane and it is released gradually during use of the plane. (For the same reason, you should never plane a surface that has been previously sanded, as the grit left in the surface will also rapidly dull a plane blade.) Anyway, sanding is too slow and tedious if any amount has to be taken off, and too indefinite in its results.

If you are setting up an antique or used plane, it may require a fair amount of work. With the blade wedged down to working pressure (this is important!), but retracted from the bottom about ¹⁄₁₆" (2mm), put a straight-edge across the area immediately in front of the mouth and check to see if this is straight (Figure 10-28). On an old plane, chances are you will find a worn hollow. The whole of the plane's sole will have to be brought down to this level until this area is straight and crisp at the mouth. Check the body for twist with winding sticks, and then check along its length.

If the plane must be corrected ¹⁄₁₆" (2mm) or more, then you will want to run it over the power jointer, or plane it carefully with another plane (Figure 10-29). (When running a plane over the power jointer, always remove the blade assembly. There is too much danger that the blade will loosen under the vibration of the cut or more material will be removed than anticipated, or the blade will contact the power jointer's cutters, an extremely dangerous occurrence. After the work with the power jointer, the blade assembly can be reinstalled to finish preparing the bottom.)

With either the power jointer or another plane, remove as little material as possible. The first cut with either should remove just a whisper of a shaving. Better to remove too little than misjudge and remove too much. The best technique will be a series of light passes, each cut being as productive and removing as little material as possible.

After planing flattens the sole—there generally will be no areas of the old wood color left where critical reference areas will be—check to see that the sides of the plane are square to the sole. Make corrections by setting the corrected sole against the power jointer's fence or by using a jointer plane.

With either method, check your progress frequently with a square. Also, carefully watch the areas at either side of the blade. You do not want these to get too thin. (See illustration at left.) In some cases, the best you may be able to do is establish a basic reference area that is

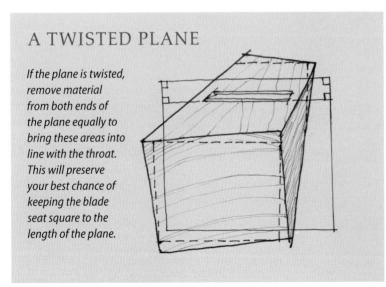

A TWISTED PLANE

If the plane is twisted, remove material from both ends of the plane equally to bring these areas into line with the throat. This will preserve your best chance of keeping the blade seat square to the length of the plane.

square to the sole, and you will have to stop short of surfacing the whole side.

Reinstall the blade assembly (again with the edge withdrawn from the sole about ¹⁄₁₆", or 2mm) and check the sole with a straightedge. There should be only a couple hundredths of an inch variance. If more, carefully plane the high spots with a finely set plane or a handled cabinet scraper, just until the three critical areas of the sole contact, or nearly contact, the straightedge. Refine the sole further, if necessary, with judicious scraping.

I do not recommend the Stanley #80 for the task because the blade-adjustment mechanism flexes the scraper blade into an arc, resulting in a concave cut. You want a flat cut, so a handled scraper with a flat bottom and a straight blade is the best tool.

A Japanese scraper plane, made for tuning up the soles of wooden planes, is a good choice, though it is made for work across the grain and the commonly available smaller ones are a little less efficient in truing up large areas. Many Japanese craftsmen make their own scraper planes in larger sizes, often with 70mm (2¾") blades, in order to more effectively flatten the soles of their larger planes.

Once the sole is flat within a couple of hundredths of an inch, begin refining it. If the plane is for rough work, it might actually be flat enough, but for any other type of plane, it must be further refined. Check with a straightedge again that the area in front of the mouth was flattened by your work so far and is not still worn hollow. Straighten it

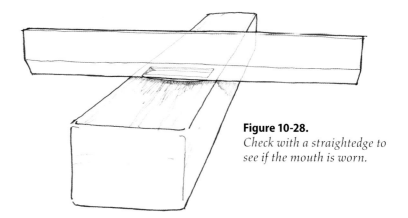

Figure 10-28.
Check with a straightedge to see if the mouth is worn.

Figure 10-29.
This jointer plane is badly twisted, so areas are being handplaned first to give good registry on the power jointer.

out if it is, re-leveling as required. Hopefully your earlier work removed all of this. I usually use a Japanese scraper plane.

Using a card scraper is an option, but is more difficult. Check the length for high spots and the three critical areas with winding sticks again for twist.

With a scraper or scraper plane, lower areas between the critical areas until the barest bit of light shows against the straightedge (Figure 10-30); then bring the critical areas into line (Figure 10-31). This may require the non-critical areas be lowered again, and going back and forth until the critical areas are all in a plane, and the areas in between are slightly lower.

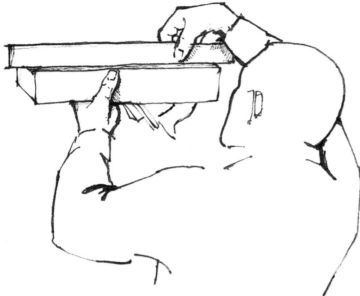

Figure 10-30. *Check the configuration of the sole by putting a straightedge against it and holding it to the light. Light will shine through where the straightedge does not contact the sole.*

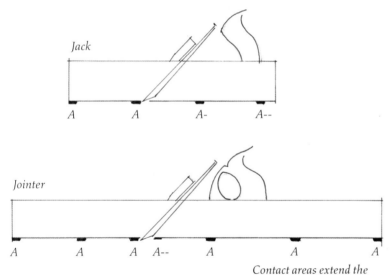

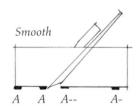

Figure 10-31. Schematic of Contact Areas of the Sole of the Western-Style Wood Plane

Contact areas extend the full width of the plane, are parallel, and are on a line with one another except where they have been relieved slightly as suggested here. Areas between contact areas are relieved only a few thousandths of an inch. A to A-: 1 or 2 passes with a card scraper; A to A--: 2 to 4 passes with a scraper.

The relieved areas are only several thousandths of an inch lower than the contact areas, perhaps slightly more so on a roughing plane, less on a fine smoother. I usually smooth the roughness left by the Japanese scraper with a card scraper, being careful to enhance and not destroy the geometry I have constructed. The whole strategy of relieving non-critical areas simplifies maintenance of the sole as you are only maintaining the relatively small contact areas in a plane, rather than the entire sole.

STEP 6: ADJUST THE MOUTH

On an old plane, the mouth likely will be worn open and will have to be closed down by inlaying a new piece into the sole in front of the blade. New wooden planes have a mouth sized for its intended use, or an adjustable mouthpiece. The material used should be hard, such as ironwood (ipé) or *lignum vitae*. The inlaid piece should be about ⅜" (10mm) thick or thicker, depending on the throat configuration. It can be a solid piece to match the plane, or a sandwich with harder surfacing material about ⅛" (3mm)-thick either side.

Making the core material of the sandwich piece out of the same wood as the body of the plane will help reduce the chance it will shrink at a different rate and separate from or crack the body (see "Fitting a Sole Plate at the Mouth of a Plane" on page 306). If you expect the plane to perform a lot of fine smoothing work for which it will depend heavily on the condition of the mouth, you might want to inlay a ¼" (6mm)-thick piece

ADJUSTING WEDGED, TAPERED BLADES

Set the plane down on a clean wooden bench and carefully insert the blade until it just touches the bench. Hold the blade down tight to the bed with a finger and insert the wedge without moving the blade's position **(Figure 1)**. Push the wedge tight with your hand so the blade will not move (or fall out). Tap the wedge gently with the mallet to lightly set it. Turn the plane over and sight down the sole to see how deeply the blade is set.

Holding the plane upside down with one hand with a finger (or fingers) and putting pressure on the blade to keep it from falling out (just in case), lock the elbow of your other arm to your side (to increase accuracy) and tap the top of the blade to set it deeper. Tap the back top of the plane body (or the striking knob) to back the blade off. Tap the side of the blade to adjust it laterally.

Each time you move the blade with a tap, tap the wedge to snug it up (do not over tighten, however). The blade is wedge shaped, so every time you set it deeper, it loosens. Remove the blade by tapping it deeper (to loosen it), then tapping to back it off to loosen the wedge. Keep a grip on the blade with your non-striking hand at all times **(Figure 2)**.

Adjust a wedged parallel blade similarly, except the blade will not loosen as it adjusts down. It may loosen when adjusting the blade back and forth, so give the wedge a *light* tap with every two or three adjustment taps of the blade to keep the wedge from loosening unexpectedly.

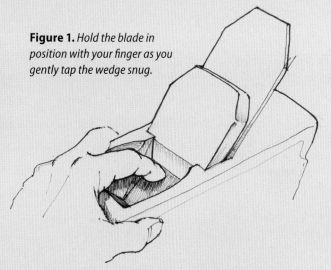

Figure 1. *Hold the blade in position with your finger as you gently tap the wedge snug.*

On planes with a tension rod holding the blade assembly, such as the Primus, adjusting the blade down will tighten the tension rod. If you are not careful, you can over-tighten the rod and damage the plane. Usually you have to adjust the tension as you go if you are making significant blade adjustments.

Always store the plane, even if overnight, with the wedge and blade loose—with only enough pressure to keep the blade from falling out when the plane is picked up. If storing the plane for a long time, remove the blade and wrap it in a lightly oiled cloth.

Figure 2. Sight Down the Sole

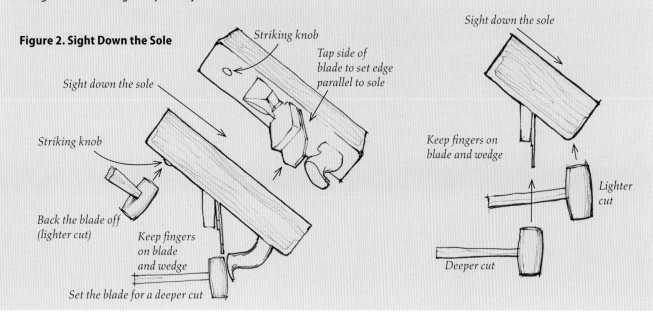

Sight down the sole

Striking knob

Tap side of blade to set edge parallel to sole

Sight down the sole

Striking knob

Back the blade off (lighter cut)

Keep fingers on blade and wedge

Set the blade for a deeper cut

Keep fingers on blade and wedge

Deeper cut

Lighter cut

of brass (Figure 10-32). It will wear better than wood, wood, it is not difficult to work or install, and it need not be so big that the amount of friction noticeably increases and it becomes difficult to work or install.

You might want to consider inlaying a moveable mouth, similar to those on the Reform planes. The process is very similar to inlaying a fixed sole plate, but it adds versatility, allowing the plane to be used for coarser or finer work, as desired. (See "Fitting a Moveable Sole Plate" on page 309.)

In some respects, inlaying a moveable mouth is easier to do because you create a tight-fitting mouth by loosening a screw and moving the piece closer to the blade, rather than by delicate paring. Also, it can last longer because as the sole wears and is repeatedly flattened, gradually opening the mouth over time, the moveable sole plate can be moved closer to the blade to compensate, rather than having to replace a fixed piece.

After you have finished fitting the sole plate, you will have to go back and touch up the level of the plate to make sure it is in the plane of the other contact areas. Have a contact area about ¼" (6mm) long by the width of the sole right at the mouth and relieve the rest of the sole plate to make sure the leading edge of the plate does not catch the work.

Test what you have done: tap the blade out to a working position, to take a light cut, and make a trial shaving. Because the blade is sharp, if it will not cut, the sole is not flat. Make sure the board you are planing is flat. Back the blade off just enough to clear the bottom, and check for flat.

A wood body is more flexible than an iron body, and the dynamics of the sole configuration may change slightly when the blade is finally adjusted to its working depth. Touch up the bottom, and try another cut; the degree of flatness determines how fine a cut you can make. Continue the process until the plane makes the cut you want.

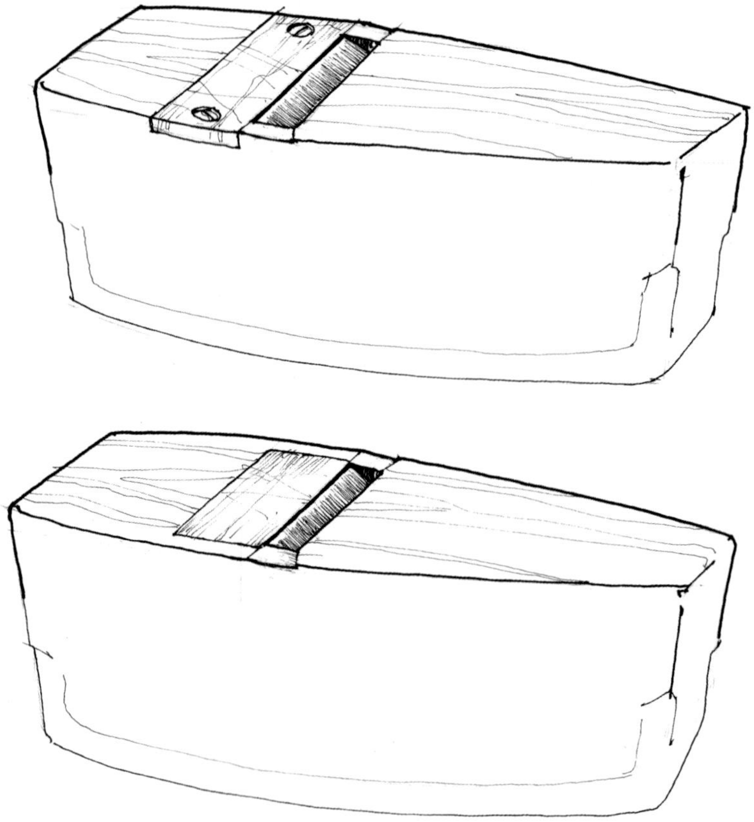

Figure 10-32. *Tighten the mouth of an old plane by installing a brass plate, as shown in the drawing at top. I have also seen iron plates used in old repairs. Another option is inlaying a hardwood piece, as shown at the bottom.*

STEP 7: ATTEND TO THE DETAILS OF THE BODY AND SOLE

After flattening the sole, I like to relieve the long edges on either side of the sole with a chamfer of a few degrees just to the edge of the blade opening. This reduces the area of the sole that must be maintained, simplifying future maintenance. I also like to make a relief cut either side of the blade opening to make sure this area is not high—it is easy to miss when conditioning the sole—and to help eject chips that tend to collect at the corners of the blade.

This is similar to what is shown for Japanese planes in Figure 10-50 on page 184. It is a personal preference of mine, and is at your option. The leading edge of the sole should be crisp to prevent shavings from sliding under the plane while working; so do not round this edge.

STEP 8: ATTEND TO THE DETAILS OF THE GRIP AND FINISH

If flattening and straightening removed some of the planes original chamfers, you can reinstate them if you want, or make new ones to suit your hands. Totes can be repaired, remade, or reshaped as per your requirements. If you have a horned plane, it is helpful to round off the back of the plane to engage the hollow of your hand, and to relieve the little ridge alongside the horn so it doesn't cut into your hand (Figure 10-33).

Figure 10-33.
Round off the back of a horned plane and relieve the little ridge alongside the horn to fit more comfortably in your hands.

Setting Up Chinese Planes

The blade-holding mechanism on a Chinese-style plane is similar to the old European wood planes, so much of what was said about setting up a wooden plane applies here to the Chinese plane.

STEP 1: INSPECT THE PLANE

The Chinese planes are wood bodied planes and as such are susceptible to the same problems discussed in "Setting up Wood-Body Planes" on page 163, so you can use that as a guide when inspecting your plane. However, there are a few extra things to note. The traditional high-pitch Chinese smoothing plane depends almost entirely on a restricted mouth opening to reduce tearout.

For this reason, there is usually a narrow brass piece dovetailed across the width of the mouth to reduce wear (Figure 10-34). Inspect carefully to see that the plane block has not

Figure 10-34.
Chinese planes rely on a small, crisp mouth opening to help break the chip. The narrow brass piece dovetailed into the sole at the mouth of this Chinese plane is typical.

shrunk across its width causing it to split around the brass piece.

If it has, and is only a hairline crack, you may be able to tap the sides of the plane with a small hammer gently at the area of the sharp point of the dovetail and cut a few wood fibers, reducing the stress on the block. Any more than the slightest crack and you will have to tap the brass piece down and out from the top and carefully remove the slightest bit of wood to make the inlaid piece fit. Then tap the mouthpiece back in place, flush with the bottom of the plane.

As with any wooden plane, it is best to remove the blade when you first get it and set the plane aside for a few months to acclimate before setting it up. After that period check the fit of the brass insert again and, if needed, adjust the lateral clearance of the blade.

STEP 5: CONFIGURE THE SOLE

After performing the set-up procedures presented earlier in general terms for Steps 2 and 3 ("Preparing the Blade" and "Preparing the Chipbreaker," on page 146), and the procedures for step 4 as described for setting up a wood-body plane ("Bed the Blade Properly," on page 166), follow the same procedures used for configuring the sole of a wood-body plane (Figure 10-35).

If your plane has a piece of brass inlaid at the mouth, you will not be able to use a power jointer or a handplane to level the sole. However, the brass is soft enough to be worked with many woodworking tools and can be leveled with a quality cabinet scraper.

Figure 10-35. Schematic of Contact Areas of the Sole of Chinese-Style Plane

Traditionally, a woodworker could have two jointer-length planes: one set up and used as a jack plane, the other set up and used for truing.

Contact areas extend the full width of the plane, are parallel, and are on a line with one another except where they have been relieved slightly as suggested in the illustration.

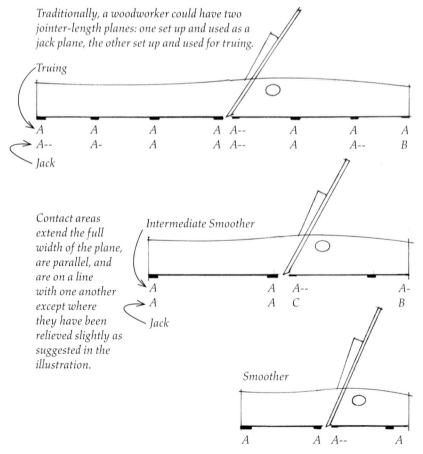

STEP 6: ADJUST THE MOUTH

Because the mouth is reinforced with brass and is not wood, adjust it using procedures similar to those used for Bailey-style planes (page 153). File the mouth opening back to a line marked parallel to the blade edge when the blade edge is set parallel to the sole.

The mouth opening on all of the planes should be tight—just large enough to let a fine shaving through. With tropical hardwood, you are not going to be removing a thick shaving anyway. But a smoothing plane should show only the very slightest bit of light when the blade is positioned to cut and the plane is held up to the light (Figure 10-36). If the gap is too large, the blade can be shimmed with a piece of paper, moving it forward and closing the gap, but be careful: if the gap is small to begin with, a common sheet of typing paper may be too thick.

CHECK THE BRASS MOUTHPIECE

When first putting the plane up to acclimate, check the brass insert at the mouth. If it shows signs of cracking, drive it out and store it along with the blade. Refit it after the plane has acclimated. If it initially seems okay, you can leave it in, but check it frequently.

STEP 7: ATTEND TO THE DETAILS OF THE BODY AND SOLE

After the sole has been flattened, as I do on my other wood planes, I often like to relieve the long edges on either side of the sole with a chamfer of just a few degrees just to the edge of the blade opening. Doing so reduces the area of the sole that must be maintained, simplifying future maintenance.

I also make a relief cut either side of the blade opening to make sure the area is not high—it's easy to miss when conditioning the sole—and to help eject chips that collect at the corners of the blade. This detail is optional, similar to what is done on Japanese planes (Figure 10-50). The leading edge of the sole should be crisp, to prevent shavings from sliding under the plane while working, so do not round or chamfer this edge.

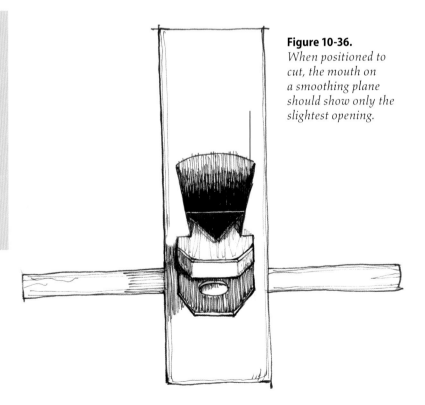

Figure 10-36.
When positioned to cut, the mouth on a smoothing plane should show only the slightest opening.

STEP 8: ATTEND TO THE DETAILS OF THE GRIP AND FINISH

Most planes available now come with the body of the plane shaped, smoothed, and ready to go, with the possible exception of the cross handle, which may need some shaping and smoothing to fit through the hole in the body. This cross handle is meant to be pressure fitted and is left unglued so it can be tapped out of its oval hole for storage. Another form of cross handle is permanently attached to the top in a similar position right behind the blade. In China, this is often shaped to an ox-bow curve to accommodate the hands.

Sometimes you can get unfinished planes from China or Southeast Asia. I got several once—a jointer, jack, and small block plane—through a friend of a friend from Thailand (Figure 10-37). The planes had the profile band sawn and the escapement cut for the blade and wedge, though the wedge was unfitted, as was the blade. On some of

them, the chipbreaker was drilled but not sharpened, badly shaped, and of such mild steel, that it was usable.

However, the blade, a little roughly finished, was laminated steel—a fact not immediately apparent until I sharpened it. I almost threw it away. It has turned out to be a decent blade. On the jack plane, I threw away the useless chipbreaker and set a brass piece in the mouth to close down the opening.

I also had to finish fitting the cross handle and smooth off the shape from the rough band sawing. It has turned out to be a dependable performer. A few years earlier, I had picked up a very nice smoothing plane, which was set up and ready to go, and this gave me the model to finish setting up these others.

Figure 10-37. *Both these planes came unfinished with only the shape band sawn, the chipwell and abutments cut, but not fit, and the hole drilled for the cross handle. The plane at top is in its original state, with its accompanying (unfinished and unfitted) parts. The plane at bottom has been completed, tuned, shaped, and smoothed.*

ADJUSTING A CHINESE PLANE

Adjust Chinese-style planes in much the same way as a Western wood-body plane that uses a wedge. After initially setting the blade, because of the high angles of traditional planes, it's helpful to sight down the sole from the back to see the contrast between blade and sole. Once you have established the blade protrudes, sight down the front to establish how much. The blade is not tapered and the body is hard, so it takes more pressure on the wedge to keep the blade locked in position.

As with any wood-body plane, store the blade loose, either completely separate or wedged just tight enough that it will not fall out when you pick it up.

Setting Up Japanese Planes

Nearly everything about the Japanese plane is different from what you know about Western planes. The tactics of the anatomy are the same, but solutions to the mechanics are different and highly refined.

STEP 1: INSPECT THE PLANE

The idea of setting aside any wooden plane for a few months before working with it is particularly important with regard to Japanese planes, as the climate is very humid in Japan, and the *dai* (block) requires considerable acclimation when moved to the (almost always) drier climate of the West. Withdraw the blade by tapping the top back edge of the *dai* with a very small (approximately 4-oz.) hammer or small mallet. Turn the plane upside down to allow gravity to assist, but it is best if you grip the body with the thumb and second finger and keep the first finger on the top of the blade to keep the chipbreaker from flying out (Figure 10-38).

Actually, this is the general procedure always for removing the blade and chipbreaker. Sometimes the *dai* will shrink around the blade after it has been imported to our drier climate. This can be so severe that the *dai* cracks, or, more usually, deforms, clamping down on the blade so hard it

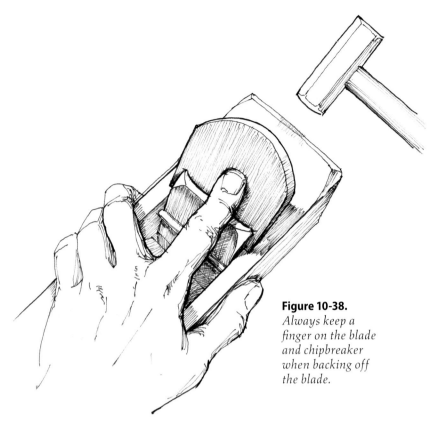

Figure 10-38.
Always keep a finger on the blade and chipbreaker when backing off the blade.

becomes nearly impossible to remove it. Inspect for this and avoid it, if you can, when buying your plane. If you end up with a plane to which this has happened, if the warp is not too severe and the *dai* is not cracked, you may be able to straighten it out by clamping it down with an equal reverse bend for several days. In the long run, this will probably compromise getting top-notch performance out of the plane. The few times I have observed this malady, it was in cheaper planes. In any case, remove the blade and chipbreaker and set the plane aside to let it adjust to our drier climate and stop moving.

TAPPING OUT A JAPANESE BLADE

Eventually, after many sharpenings, you will lose the *ura*, or flat, on the back of the blade at the edge (**Figure 1**). The *ura* must be re-established if the blade is to be useable. Traditionally, the easiest way to do this is to tap out the blade. Not only does this save you from having to flatten the entire back but also cold-working the steel this way may add some toughness to the edge.

You will need a small anvil with a rounded corner on the top (the horn of an anvil is ok), and a small 4-ounce square or octagonal hammer. Traditionally the Japanese used what looks like a section of railroad track for an anvil. This has a chamfered edge along one side for setting saws, and one or two rounded corners on one end for tapping out the blades.

Figure 1.
This hollow-ground blade has nearly lost its flat at the edge.

Figure 2. The Strike Zone

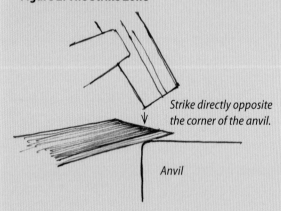

Strike directly opposite the corner of the anvil.

Anvil

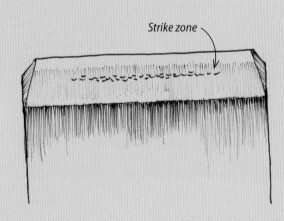

Strike zone

Body position is important. Be in a stable standing or sitting position where you cannot sway. Lock the hammer arm to the side so the wrist forms an unchanging pivot point. This allows the hammer to fall of its own weight with repeat accuracy.

The corner of the hammer strikes the blade bevel **on the soft backing steel,** slightly closer to the edge than about midway in the width of the bevel, in a line across the width of the blade (**Figure 2**). This will force the edge steel out a few ten-thousandths of an inch, which can be then flattened on the stones into a new *ura* (**Figure 3**).

Here is the secret: support the blade on the anvil's corner exactly opposite the hammer strike. If you do not, *you can crack the edge steel.* You can tell if it is properly supported if the hammer strike results in a dull thud. If the strike causes a ringing sound, then the anvil is not directly under the hammer. Do a light trial tap to check for the sound and adjust your position. Then strike the soft steel with slightly more than the weight of the hammer once or twice leaving a distinct mark. Work your way across the center two-thirds of the blade, doing trial taps with each re-adjustment before striking (**Figure 4**).

After working across the blade, you can flatten the back, usually on waterstones, rather than using one of the more intensive methods (see "Flattening the Back of a Blade" on page 148). If a new *ura* does not quickly appear when honing, go back and repeat the process (**Figure 5**).

Figure 3. *Swinging it from the wrist, the hammer must fall of its own weight on the bevel, slightly closer than midway to the edge. The corner of the anvil must support the blade directly under the corner of the hammer.*

Figure 4. *Tapping leaves a series of dimples across the soft backing-steel portion of the bevel. These do not interfere with the function of the blade and are soon honed out.*

Figure 5. *The blade with its new flat after being tapped out and honed.*

STEP 2: PREPARE THE BLADE

Because the blade is wedged into the body, preparing the blade before proceeding with any of the other steps becomes particularly important. First, flatten the back as usual, but notice its hollow grind. If you have flattened other plane blades, you will especially appreciate the refinement—even more when you realize the blade steel is much harder than most blade steels. The hollow saves a lot of tedious work. The edge must be flattened across the width of the blade, and at least as far back as where the hollow grind begins.

While the blade is laid on the stone for most of its cutting length—it must be moved back and forth gradually across the width of the stone as you work, or it will wear the stone unevenly—only the last bit of blade at the edge really has to be flat. Some craftsmen recommend tapping out the blade as part of the initial preparation, believing the cold work aligns the crystalline structure and toughens the blade. I cannot verify that.

The most common reason to do this is to speed up flattening the back, when the flat has been sharpened away over time. Tapping out a new blade pushes even more blade steel out to be flattened. If you have not yet lost the edge back into the hollow grind, you are just making more work. Anyway, I suggest you familiarize yourself with Japanese blades before attempting to tap one out. The time it takes to sharpen the blade back into the hollow will be soon enough.

Check that the cutting edge is only as wide as the mouth opening (Figure 10-39). Grind the blade's corners back as required to narrow the edge to this width. You probably will not have to do this on a new blade, but you will as the blade wears. Otherwise, the blade will cut a shaving in the area where it is captured by the *dai*, which then jams with chips. Be careful: it is easy to burn the blade. Try to replicate the angle it was originally ground to. Lap the burr off the back on your finish stone.

Sharpen the bevel, and then stone the outside edges off the top (hollow-ground side) of the blade. Dull these slightly so they are not sharp.

Figure 10-39. Grinding Corners.

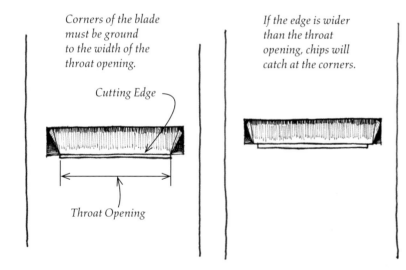

Corners of the blade must be ground to the width of the throat opening.

If the edge is wider than the throat opening, chips will catch at the corners.

Cutting Edge

Throat Opening

STEP 3: PREPARE AND FIT THE CHIPBREAKER

Begin by placing the chipbreaker on the blade in what will be its final position. Pinch the two together tightly and hold them up to the light (Figure 10-40). The blade should be flat (because you just flattened it).

If there is any light coming between the two, then the chipbreaker needs to be flattened. (Do not worry if the chipbreaker does not sit flat overall on the blade at this time; that is the next step after this.) The chipbreakers on the best planes are laminated steel, similar to the blade itself. On lesser quality planes, the chipbreaker is tempered but not laminated.

Occasionally, on smaller, cheaper, usually specialty planes, I have seen some poorly formed chipbreakers that appear to be made of mild steel. You can get these to work, but they will not take much demanding service. With the better quality and laminated chipbreakers you will have to flatten them using your sharpening stones, as they are too hard to be filed.

Make sure your stones are perfectly flat, and if you have to work the chipbreaker a lot, periodically re-flatten them or use a diamond stone to straighten them. The bevel edge is stoned as well down to the fine finish stone, to a polish like the blade. Do not get overzealous and enlarge the microbevel at the edge of the chipbreaker; you want to keep this as small as it was originally made. On a 40° plane this microbevel is about 60° (see "Chipbreaker" on page 45).

Once the edge of the chipbreaker is fitted, the overall fit to the blade can be completed. Set the blade down on the bench with its chipbreaker on top in its position. Hold the edge of the chipbreaker tight at its edge and alternately tap the top two corners (Figure 10-41). There will be no sound at the corners that fit tight to the blade.

If a corner is high, it will make a metallic tapping sound when tapped. Take this corner to an anvil, and, holding the chipbreaker on the edge of the anvil, aligned with the crease at the corner ear, tap the ear with a small hammer to bend it over (Figure 10-42). If you bend it too much, place the chipbreaker on top of the anvil, spanning the point of the ear and another point about equally distant into the body of the chipbreaker, and tap the bend to flatten the ear back out.

Repeat this until you can hold the blade and chipbreaker tight at their cutting edges and tap both upper corners without making a sound. Later, after you have fitted the blade to the *dai*, you may have to do this again if the location of the cross pin is badly off, or you need more or less room under it to make the chipbreaker hold its adjustment.

I've had to do this on planes where I have drilled and installed the cross pin, but I can't ever remember having to do it on a plane I bought, except perhaps one of the cheaper specialty planes with the mild steel chipbreaker.

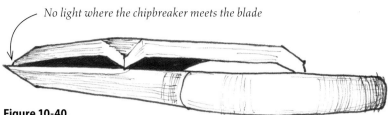

No light where the chipbreaker meets the blade

Figure 10-40.
No light passes through where the chipbreaker edge meets the blade.

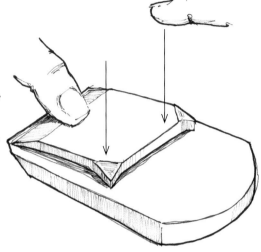

Figure 10-41.
Check the fit of the chipbreaker to its blade by holding the chipbreaker down to the blade with one finger and tapping alternate corners: there should be no sound.

Figure 10-42. Proper Placement on an Anvil.

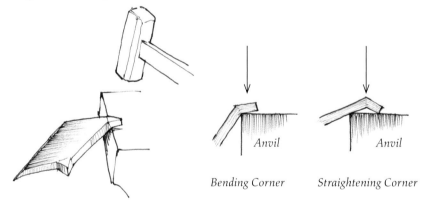

Anvil *Anvil*

Bending Corner *Straightening Corner*

4: BED THE BLADE PROPERLY

Before beginning to fit the blade to the *dai*, check again the width of the blade escapement (Figure 10-43). The opening in the *dai* should be perhaps ⅓₂" (0.8mm) wider on either side of the blade, enough for the blade to slip in unimpeded by the sides.

Once the blade is fitted, there must be enough space so the blade can be tapped left or right to adjust for parallel to the sole. Take a small chisel and pare a slight amount, as required, from both sides until the opening is wide enough. Also, check that the opening is wide enough for the chipbreaker. If it is not, then the cross pin must be driven back out, and the chipwell pared slightly wider.

Once the width of the blade opening has been checked and the blade and chipbreaker prepared, begin final fitting of the blade. The blade is fit independently of the chipbreaker, and does not require any wedging action from it. The chipbreaker, in fact, should be a gentle fit, no tighter than is required to maintain its setting. Set the chipbreaker aside, and put the blade into the plane, pushing it in by hand as far as you can (Figure 10-44).

When the blade is finally fit, you should be able to push it in to within about ⅛" (3mm)

Figure 10-43. Bed the Blade Properly

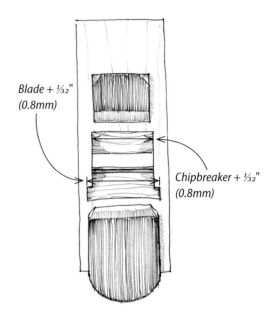

Blade + ⅟₃₂"
(0.8mm)

Chipbreaker + ⅟₃₂"
(0.8mm)

of its final position. (This depends some on the nature of the piece of wood used for the *dai*: you should be able to push it in by hand a little more if the block has some give, a little less if it is more resistant.) Chances are the blade will go in far short of its final position.

The underside of the blade is concave across its width (Figure 10-45). This means the blade bed is convex, and a close look at the area confirms it (Figure 10-46).

Often the bed is a little too convex. You want to fit this curve to the blade along its entire captured length so the blade makes solid contact with the bed at all points, and especially at the outside edges at the side groove. The upper edges of the side groove are not worked, because they are the reference surfaces that position the blade.

Withdraw the blade by tapping the top back edge of the *dai* with a small hammer or mallet while holding the blade with two fingers and the *dai* with the rest of the hand.

Figure 10-44.
When first fitting the blade, put the blade into the plane, pushing it in by hand as far as you can. The further in you can push it, the less material you will have to remove to fit it.

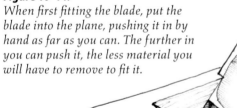

Figure 10-45.
The underside of a traditional Japanese blade is not flat, but concave across its width.

Coat the blade's back with graphite (rub it with a pencil), ink, or (strangely enough) Vaseline, which is how I was shown. Push the blade in and tap it in a little deeper with three or four taps of the hammer. Then tap the back of the *dai* again and remove the blade.

The pencil (ink, Vaseline) will have marked the high spots on the blade bed of the *dai*. With a freshly sharpened chisel, carefully pare away the stains left by the marking (Figure 10-47), only enough to remove the mark. Reinsert the blade as before and remove. Pare again.

Continue until the blade goes to within hammer-tapping distance of a working position. You will have to recoat the back of the blade periodically. Do not get impatient and pare away any more than the finest shaving, slightly more than dust. This whole procedure takes at least five passes—maybe as many as 30—but not usually that many.

The blade should fit tightly in its escapement, particularly at its outer edges, where it is captured. Do not neglect to coat the back of the blade all the way to its outer edges, and to carefully check the corresponding part of the *dai* when fitting the blade, as it hard to see into the slot and thus easy to neglect.

If you pare away too much and the blade slides in too far, finish fitting the blade, making sure it is solidly bedded, even though it may protrude too far. Then you can glue a piece of paper to the blade bed to shim the blade tighter. Try a piece of onionskin paper first because it does not take much to tighten up the fit of the blade;

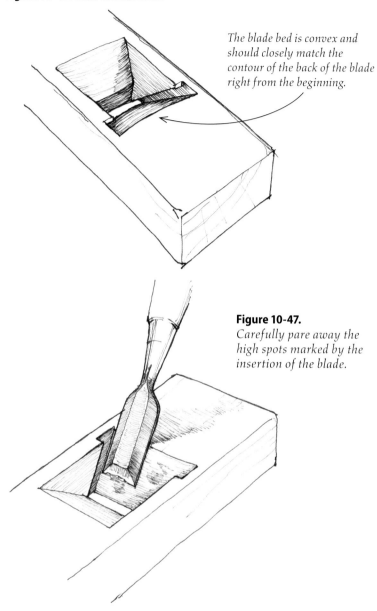

Figure 10-46. Convex Blade Bed

The blade bed is convex and should closely match the contour of the back of the blade right from the beginning.

Figure 10-47.
Carefully pare away the high spots marked by the insertion of the blade.

often a piece of 20-lb. typing paper will be too much (Figure 10-48). If it is very loose, a piece of brown Kraft paper (like from a paper bag) can be used. Eventually, you will probably have to shim the blade because it loosens with time and use.

Once the blade is fitted, tap the blade to its working position and check again that it has enough room on either side for lateral adjustment. If not, remove the blade and pare away the sides of the blade slot as required

Figure 10-48. *After several years, the self-wedging blade on a Japanese plane can become too loose to hold its adjustment. Remedy the problem by gluing a piece of paper to the bed. Here, a piece of very lightweight tracing paper was sufficient to correct the fit.*

STEP 5: CONFIGURE THE SOLE

Install the blade and chipbreaker and tap them to within about ¹⁄₁₆" (2mm) of the bottom, maybe a little closer, but make sure the blade is back from the bottom (you will be removing material from the bottom so pay attention) and the chipbreaker is set within working distance of the blade edge. Now the sole of the plane can be prepared.

Before you begin conditioning the sole, you can plane a slight chamfer of just a few degrees down both sides of the plane's sole, just to the width of the blade opening. I actually like to chamfer the edges all the way to the cutting edge (Figure 10-50). Not every Japanese craftsman approves of this option. It reduces the area of the sole, which must be conditioned to the width of the blade. This is not so much a laborsaving device, but one that helps eliminate trouble spots later.

(Figure 10-49). Reinstall the blade and tap the chipbreaker into working position. Do not force it: if it is too tight, flatten the ears out a bit as described earlier. If it is too loose, bend the ears over a bit. Make sure the chipbreaker still sits flat on the blade by tapping the ears as described.

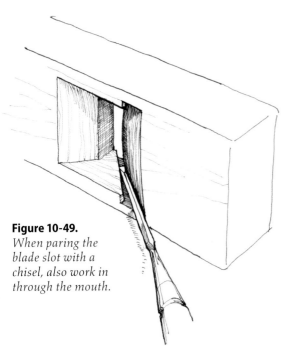

Figure 10-49.
When paring the blade slot with a chisel, also work in through the mouth.

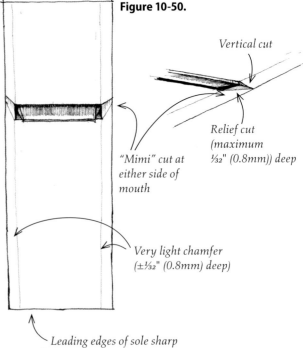

Figure 10-50.

Vertical cut

Relief cut (maximum ¹⁄₃₂" (0.8mm)) deep

"Mimi" cut at either side of mouth

Very light chamfer (±¹⁄₃₂" (0.8mm) deep)

Leading edges of sole sharp

Often the plane's sole will contact the work in an area outside the blade path. Some of these areas are easy to miss when checking the sole for flatness, especially at either side of the blade, and will prevent the plane from cutting because they are high and contact the work, or will leave an annoying burnished spot making the texture of the finished surface inconsistent.

On a truing plane, you may not want to have a chamfer quite that wide because you may want as much reference area as possible contacting the work in order to have the flattest resulting surface.

Choose the configuration of the bottom by the type of plane you have or function you wish it to perform: roughing, truing, smoothing or variations of these (Figure 10-51). Put a straightedge on the bottom, and check the length for contact points at both sides and the center. Check across the width for straight, and check all the contact spots across the width for parallel by using winding sticks.

Also, check diagonally (Figure 10-52). If the sole is badly out of flat, you may have to use another plane, finely set, which you know is accurate, to initially level the bottom. (I have never had to use a power jointer to level the bottom.) A scraper plane with a longish sole and a straight blade (not the Stanley #80) can be used.

Generally, the Japanese scraper, made for this purpose, is the tool of choice for shaping the bottom of the plane. They come in different sizes for different size planes, and craftsmen will make different sizes,

Figure 10-51. Schematic of Contact Areas of the Sole of Japanese-Style Planes

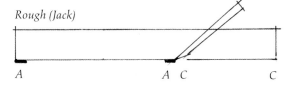

Rough (Jack)

A   A C   C

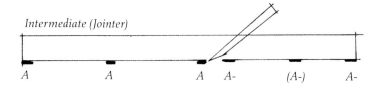

Intermediate (Jointer)

A   A   A   A-   (A-)   A-

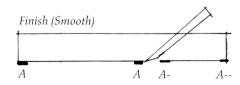

Finish (Smooth)

A   A   A-   A--

Contact areas extend the full width of the plane, are parallel, and are on a line with one another except where they have been relieved slightly as suggested in the illustration. Areas between contact areas are relieved only a few thousandths of an inch. A to C <¹⁄₆₄" (0.4mm); A to A-: 1 or 2 passes with a card scraper; A to A--: 2 to 4

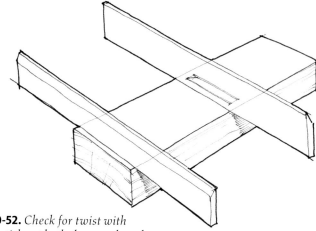

Figure 10-52. *Check for twist with winding sticks at both the mouth and the ends. Also, check with a straight edge across the width of the plane as well as diagonally.*

often from a miscellaneous plane blade they have around, for specific tasks. Except for the widest ones, which are for general leveling, Japanese scrapers are used to attack specific high spots, first lowering the non-contact areas below the contact areas, and then bringing the contact areas into line as required by the desired bottom configuration.

The Japanese scraper plane is used mostly across the grain; sometimes a bit diagonally to even things up if required. Because it is scraping across the grain, I find the cut it makes can be a bit rough. Sometimes, after the bottom geometry has been established, I go over areas I think need attention with a card scraper.

Every day you use your planes, you should check their sole configuration before starting work, like warming up before doing exercise, and touch them up as required. This is especially true of fine finish planes, which take a very fine cut. In fact, if they are not giving the service you expect, you may have to check and tune them during the day as you work with them.

Generally, though, once the plane has acclimated, and if your shop does not go through big temperature and humidity swings, you will find the planes rather stable, and except perhaps for achieving the very demanding, smoothing cut, will not require that much maintenance. Remember at the end of every day, and when you are not using them, to loosen the blade, just to where they will not fall out when you pick them up.

STEP 6: ADJUST THE MOUTH

Most often on a new manufactured plane I do not do any fitting of a sole plate or a *kuchi-ire* (on page 42), relying instead on the quality of the blade and the effectiveness of the chipbreaker. I find the mouth opening on new planes is usually accurately formed.

As to used planes, unfortunately, not many in serviceable condition reach our shores. I have seen many that are a day short of being wore out, with badly worn *kuchi-ire* repairs that are themselves old, with the *dais* worn down to a third of their original thickness and blades with ¼" (6mm) or less of serviceable edge steel left. Sadly, these cannot be reconditioned, but they look as if they have served their original masters well.

ADJUSTING A JAPANESE PLANE

Put the blade into the plane first, pushing it in and then tapping it a few times to make it fit snuggly, and then insert the chipbreaker. Tap the chipbreaker down gently to make it snug, but be careful you do not push it down further than the blade edge. Grab the plane with your non-hammer hand. Keep your first or second finger on the blade/chipbreaker to keep them from falling out and turn the plane over. Sighting down the sole, with your elbow locked to your side for stability, tap the blade until you can just see it protrude **(Figure 1)**.

Turn the plane back over, and sighting from the top, adjust the chipbreaker down until it is in close proximity to the blade (but not its final position). Turn the plane over again, and sighting down the bottom, adjust the blade to its final position. Adjust the blade laterally by tapping one side of the blade or the other.

Turn the plane over again and tap the chipbreaker to its final position, adjusting it parallel to the blade edge by tapping down one corner or the other. Besides tapping the sides of the blade for lateral adjustment, you can fine-tune the blade position by tapping the top of the blade (as opposed to the side) on one corner or the other. Likewise, you tap the back corners of the *dai* on one side or the other to gently back that side of the blade off.

To withdraw the blade, you can turn it over so gravity assists—though it is not necessary and I often do this without turning it over. With a finger or two of one hand (probably the left) on the blade/chipbreaker, tap the back top edge of the *dai* with the hammer/mallet until the blade loosens.

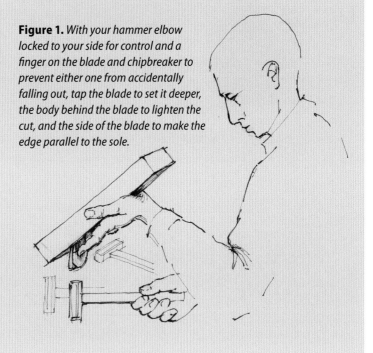

Figure 1. *With your hammer elbow locked to your side for control and a finger on the blade and chipbreaker to prevent either one from accidentally falling out, tap the blade to set it deeper, the body behind the blade to lighten the cut, and the side of the blade to make the edge parallel to the sole.*

STEP 7: ATTEND TO THE DETAILS OF THE BODY AND SOLE

Now you can finish detailing the *dai*. It is good practice to make sure the sides of the *dai* are square to the sole. It is mandatory if the plane is to be used on its side to joint boards. If you did not add the slight chamfers at the edges of the sole when first configuring the sole, as described in that section, you can do that now if you wish.

Besides the chamfer, you should also make a couple of relief cuts (*mimi*—Figure 10-50 on page 184) on either side of the blade to allow chips, which tend to get caught at the outside edges of the blade where the *dai* wedges the blade, to escape, and to aid in conditioning the sole. The leading edges of the bottom are left sharp. This is to prevent errant shavings from sliding under the plane and causing it to ride up.

STEP 8: ATTEND TO THE DETAILS OF THE GRIP AND FINISH

Generally, outside edges are gently rounded to be easy on the hand, however. The top edge behind the blade is rounded more, as are the corners of that edge, to reduce damage from the adjusting hammer (Figure 10-53).

A final optional step is to saturate the *dai* with camellia oil. The few times I have done this, I am not sure I have been happy with the results. A full description of the process can be found in "Making a Japanese-style Plane" on page 286.

Tap the blade and chipbreaker down to a working position, making a light cut, and take a trial shaving. Because you know the blade is sharp, if it will not cut, the sole is not flat. Back the blade off just enough to clear the bottom, and check for flat. It is easy to misread the straightedges or to miss an area. Touch up the bottom, and try a cut again. The degree of flatness will determine how fine a cut you can make. Continue this process until the plane makes the cut you want.

Figure 10-53. Round Edges

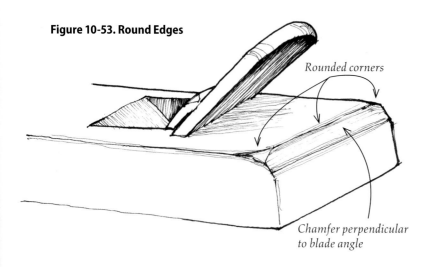

Rounded corners

Chamfer perpendicular to blade angle

Setting Up Rabbet Planes

The same procedures, in the same order, are followed when setting up the rabbet plane as when setting up a bench plane, so check the procedures for your particular style of plane in the corresponding section of this chapter. Some things, however, are done a little differently, as follows.

STEP 1: INSPECT THE PLANE

Large portions of a rabbet-plane body are often cut away to provide chip clearance or to allow the blade to do its job. Check for cracks at all narrowed portions of the plane, especially if there is pressure associated with them (such as from the lever cap or wedge). Cracks in a metal plane will render it useless; many cracks in wood planes can be repaired if not too deep (Figures 10-54).

Wood rabbet planes often suffer from the same malady as the bench planes with a blade that has had the wood body shrink around it tight. Once the blade is removed, though, the escapement for the blade can be widened. On a metal rabbet plane, check that the sole and two adjacent sides are square to each other. Reject any metal plane that is not square.

The most important thing to know about a rabbet plane is the blade must be able to protrude on its cutting side(s) about 1/64" (0.4mm) or maybe a little less. This seems counter-intuitive, but unless the blade protrudes slightly, the plane will step away from the cut line as the cut deepens, resulting in an out-of-square shoulder and a generally narrower rabbet. Check, when you first get

Gouge marks
from expanding
one side of
opening

Figure 10-54. *Repairing a crack: First, the crack in the sole behind the blade will be cleaned by cutting into it with a thin-kerf saw blade (left). The tapered sliver sitting on the vise will be glued in (above). Notice how the previous owner opened up the chipwell with a gouge. You are now ready to prepare the sole.*

the plane, that the blade is slightly wider than the plane body. (The check is not necessary on a one-sided rabbet plane.)

If for some reason the blade exceeds 1/64" (0.4mm) on both cutting sides (unlikely on a metal plane, but an old wood-body plane can have shrunk or been worn away by at least that much), then the blade can be carefully ground narrower. If the blade is too narrow on a metal-body plane, you will have to get a new blade or a new plane.

While the blade can sometimes be pushed to the working side to accommodate a too-narrow blade, there is no reason to have to deal with it on a new plane. And if the blade cannot be pushed to the side, tilting the blade toward that side is not a satisfactory solution. Both the blade and the plane are ground square and tilting the blade puts the edge out of parallel with the sole. On a wood-body plane, the body can be planed down to achieve the required protrusion.

JAPANESE SKEW-BLADED RABBET PLANE

Setting up a Japanese-style skew-bladed rabbet plane involves some additional steps. First, prepare the blade and chipbreaker, and fit the blade to its bed. Check that the blade slot that captures the blade allows enough lateral adjustment so the blade can be adjusted both parallel to the sole as well as about 1/64" (0.4mm) proud of the side. If not, carefully pare the side of the slot with a narrow chisel to increase lateral adjustability.

All rabbet planes have an inherent problem with chip clearance, and this plane is no exception. Its chip-clearance problem happens right at the point of the blade. Using a small round file, flare the inside of the hole on the side of the plane above the point—just a little. You do not want to weaken the plane. Proceed a little at a time, alternately using the plane and flaring the hole, until it stops jamming.

Most often, the plane will have a brass wear plate the length of the sole and the width of the cut. This can be configured using the same methods used for metal planes: files and scrapers for the initial leveling followed by sandpaper for the finishing touch. As with all planes, remember to install the blade and chipbreaker up to tension (but retracted from the opening) when configuring the sole.

STEP 2: PREPARE THE BLADE

After inspecting your plane—and establishing that you have the correct width blade—begin setting it up by sharpening the blade. As described in the general procedure "Prepare the Blade" on page 179, flatten the back first (Figure 10-55). The bevel must then be sharpened straight across, no curvature, and must be square enough to its length so it can be made parallel to the sole within the plane's range of adjustment (usually not very much). With a skewed-blade rabbet plane, you will have to establish (or maintain) the correct angle of the blade to accomplish the same parallel relation to the sole. You will not be able to check it with a square, so, if you have lost the correct angle, it may take some putting it in and out of the plane to get it right.

Figure 10-55.

Restoration of a Japanese-style rabbet plane: blade and chipbreaker before (Figure 10-55) and after (Figure 10-56). When I got the plane the blades were nearly rusted together, and firmly stuck in the plane. However, the blade and chipbreaker were not pitted and cleaned up nicely.

Figure 10-56.

STEP 3: PREPARE AND FIT THE CHIPBREAKER

If there is a chipbreaker, fitting it is pretty much the same as with the bench plane. You can refer to the general procedures "Prepare and Fit the Chipbreaker" on page 180 and to the setup section specific to your style of plane (Figure 10-56).

STEP 4: BED THE BLADE PROPERLY

Inspect the blade bed for flaws. I strongly suggest you do not touch this area on a metal plane, because it is difficult to access and easy to mess up. If you have a flaw, return the plane and get another. The bed on a wood plane is prepared as described in the setup section specific to your style of plane.

STEP 5: CONFIGURE THE SOLE

I usually do not attempt to condition the sole of a metal rabbet plane for two reasons. First, the bottom does not need to be as flat as that of a fine smooth plane, because this plane is for shaping rather than smoothing wood. Second, it is easy to lose square between the sides and the sole in trying to flatten either. If the sides are not square to the sole, I suggest you return the plane.

I have fewer reservations about straightening and squaring up a wooden rabbet plane, as the wood is much easier to work, and thus correct, and it will probably need it periodically anyway. In addition to flattening the sole, make sure both sides are straight (they tend to get pushed out of line around the blade) as well as square to the sole (Figure 10-57).

Remember, when flattening the sole to put the blade in place at full operating pressure, about ¹⁄₁₆" (2mm) shy of the sole. On the traditional wood rabbet planes open on both sides, the blade bed is supported only by the bulk of wood behind it and pushes the sole down behind the blade a greater amount than on many other planes.

After planing the sole flat with a jointer plane, I remove a little extra from the area behind the blade with a scraper (± 0.01", or 0.25mm) to compensate for the extra flex. After planing the sole flat, you can place your jointer's blade at the mouth of the rabbet plane and take one or two light strokes off the area behind the blade to lower it.

Sometimes, the traditional wood rabbet plane is badly twisted, with the area in front and behind the blade badly misaligned. Straightening this up with a plane might remove too much wood. You can remedy this by cutting a portion of the sole off and re-gluing a continuous piece back on. After the glue has set, the blade bed and mouth opening can be cut back in. This gives you the chance to cut a tighter mouth opening.

STEP 6: ADJUST THE MOUTH

On a metal rabbet plane with a fixed mouth, you are stuck with what you get. Correcting a badly formed or abused mouth will be unproductive, and closing it down, impractical. On a plane with an adjustable mouth, you can, of course, adjust the mouth tighter. Just make sure the parts stay in alignment when they are moved (though this is going to be tough to correct if these parts are not milled right).

On a wooden rabbet plane without an adjustable mouth, you can repair it as described above for fixing a twisted sole—or you can live with it. If you find you need a plane that can make a more finished cut, you will have to upgrade to a plane with a tighter mouth, an adjustable mouth, a chipbreaker, or two of these three.

Figure 10-57.
Preparing the sole of a wood rabbet plane. Besides the split that had to be repaired, this plane had a broken nail embedded in its sole that had to be set below the surface before it could be planed.

Figure 10-58.
The Finished Plane
It hurt me to remove some of the beautiful patina that the plane had acquired, but now it works beautifully.

STEP 7: ATTEND TO THE DETAILS OF THE BODY AND SOLE

Rabbet planes have a strong tendency to jam with chips (the bench- and block-plane styles are mercifully free of this problem).

The solution can be as simple as frequently pushing the shaving out the exit hole—sometimes as often as every stroke of the plane. This can become annoying, but if you forget to do it, the consequence is worse: the shavings become tightly jammed, and clearing them entails a prolonged struggle. And it becomes even more frustrating when you have to do this repeatedly.

On a metal plane, you do not have much recourse, but on a wood one you can open the chip spillway. This is best accomplished by opening one side more than the other in

kind of a funnel shape so that the shaving has a tendency to spiral out the side when it hits the chip opening, rather than getting captured and bunching up. (Figure 10-54 on page 189 shows the gouge marks left from where the previous owner opened this up.) You can use a gouge for the initial opening, followed by a small half-round rasp and files. You may not be able to get it to actually spiral out the side, but at least it will make the plane easier to clean out. Just do not remove too much wood and weaken the plane (Figure 10-58).

The rest of the procedures are similar to the bench planes.

Setting Up Fillister and Moving-Fillister Planes

All the procedures for rabbet planes apply here. Additionally, you must prepare the fence, scoring knife, and depth stop.

The fence must be straight, square to the sole, able to be made parallel to the side of the plane, and securely fixed. The fence should not flex under normal use. Cast-metal fences are usually tolerably straight, but it does not hurt to check and spend a few minutes sanding yours smooth. If it is not straight, square, or parallel, you will have to file and then sand it, similar to the instructions given for preparing the soles of Bailey-type planes, using scrapers, files, and straightedges.

Whether you need to tune it up or not, the fence should at least be smoothed to 220 or 320 grit and the edges filed and sanded smooth to avoid marring the work. I say avoid, but it is difficult to keep a metal fence from marring the work. You will have better luck screwing a wood face to the metal fence.

Besides being less likely to mar a project, a wooden face has other advantages. You can use it to correct an out-of-whack fence because wood is easier to shape (though the best procedure is to do the fence itself). You can make the fence bigger, often improving accuracy and stability in use, though a larger fence will also often get hung up on the work, in which case you may want to have several faces of different sizes available.

The stamped metal fence and depth stop of the German planes must be looked to as well; sometimes it is bent, and you may have to tap a bit with a hammer to straighten it before sanding. Check to see the fence is square to the sole. It is not very deep and part of its depth has a radius, so it is hard to tell. The same is true of the depth stop.

On the German moving-fillister planes, be careful when adjusting the blade. If it descends too far, it will contact the metal fence and nick the blade. The underside of the fence is relieved, but only slightly, so you do not have much play.

Depth-stop designs vary. Make sure its contact surface can be made parallel to the sole and locks securely.

The nicker (or spur) or scoring knife should be flush with the side of the plane. If not, shim it with paper to bring it flush. If it protrudes too far, on a wooden rabbet plane carefully pare a little wood away from under the scoring knife. On a metal plane, you will have to hone some off the back of the knife. Sharpen the scoring knife, but do not hone the back any more than you have to, as taking away metal here affects the alignment with the side of the plane.

When using the plane, the blade should be set anywhere from flush to a slight projection beyond the nicker. If wood beyond the rabbet tears, the blade is set too far beyond the side of the nicker. If the plane steps out in the cut, the blade is set too far in. If the blade cannot be reset satisfactorily, the nicker may have to be shimmed slightly proud of the side of the plane (a paper thickness or less).

Setting Up Hollows & Rounds

The construction of hollowing and rounding planes is the same as for their flatter cousins: in their construction, Western-style planes are similar to rabbet planes. Japanese-style planes are similar to smoothing planes. Because there are still a fair number of the Western-style planes around, in blade pitches from 45° to 64°, and for that matter the Japanese-style can be found as well, I suggest if you can find a width that will work for you, tune-up an old plane, or modify it if the blade curvature does not suit your needs.

The shape of the blade of a Japanese-style and other wood-block plane can be altered only slightly, or you will destroy the geometry of the mouth opening. The old Western-style hollowing and rounding planes are more suitable for alteration, but are limited as well.

The procedures for setting up hollows and rounds are followed in the same order as with other planes, beginning with the inspection of the plane itself. Look for all of the problems discussed under wood planes. Normally, the first step is to sharpen the blade.

If you alter the curve the plane cuts, or feel the curvature of the blade is not correct, save this step until later, as noted below. Sharpen and fit the chipbreaker as described in the general procedures "Prepare and Fit the Chipbreaker" on page 146, and then prepare the blade seat as described in "Step 4: Bed the Blade Properly" for woodbody planes on page 166. Prepare the sole as described later.

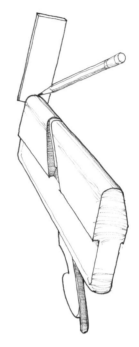

Figure 10-59.
Make a template of the original curvature before beginning to condition the sole.

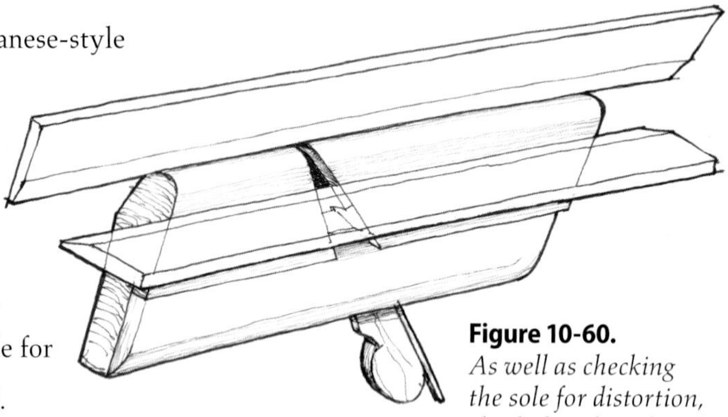

Figure 10-60.
As well as checking the sole for distortion, check that the sides of the plane are in line.

If you are setting up hollows and rounds, start with the hollowing plane first, as its convex sole can be shaped with a bench plane or block plane. You can then use the hollowing plane to shape the concave sole of the rounding plane.

Before starting, make a template of the curve of the bottom. You can then use this to check your accuracy (Figure 10-59). Because of their construction, these planes often warp along their length as well as having the sole distorted by the wedge. Check this (Figure 10-60) and straighten the plane as required with another plane. Have the blade wedged under tension, but withdrawn so you do not run into it (be careful on the side also).

Hopefully, some of the original curve will be preserved; if not, this is why you made the template. Plane with a very slight set on the blade so that it takes a very narrow shaving until the sole is in line and the same shape as the remaining original profile (Figure 10-61). If you have had to take more than that off, use the template to check the profile. Use a straightedge held to the light to check for straightness. When the sole and the sides are straight and the profile is correct, you can fair and smooth the sole with a fine file. Use a light touch—you do not want to destroy the profile.

Check the blade and see if its profile matches the profile of the sole. If it does not, you will have to grind the blade to match. Usually the blade is only slightly off, so trial and error in grinding, frequently checking your progress by putting the blade into the plane, is as efficient a method as any. If the discrepancy is significant, then marking the blade can be helpful. Though pencil is hard to read, it does not vaporize under the heat of the grinding the way a felt tip does.

After grinding, use your sharpening stones similar to how you would for your other blades. Orient the blade to the stone in the usual manner, but use a rocking motion that rotates the edge through its entire length on each stroke. It is helpful to have a separate set of stones for this, as the convex blades will soon wear a hollow in the stone. I often take some of my old worn-out, or even broken

Figure 10-61.
Use a block plane for the initial preparation of the sole of this hollowing plane.

stones, and dedicate them to curved plane blades and carving tools. Alternatively, you can use the edge of your sharpening stones, saving the face for your straight blades. Flatten the back as with other blades. You can use a hard buffing wheel to sharpen the edge, but use stones for the back. Do not be tempted to use the buffing wheel.

Shape the blade to a slightly different radius than the sole so that the blade tapers out to zero at the edges (Figure 10-62). This will keep the blade from leaving tracks or steps in the work.

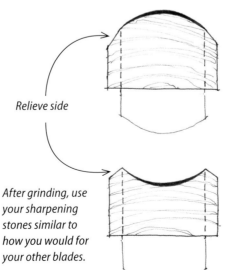

Relieve side

After grinding, use your sharpening stones similar to how you would for your other blades.

Figure 10-62.
The areas along the sole either side of the blade may have to be cut back at a greater angle in order to be able to fully access the hollow or round form you are shaping.

For tuning up a rounding plane, with its concave blade and sole, after straightening the sole and sides, you can use a hollowing plane to reform the sole (Figure 10-63) and round files to smooth it (Figure 10-64). Grinding a concave blade takes a grinder that can access the curve. In a pinch, you can carefully use the corner of a grinding wheel, but it is hard to do a good job. Ideally, you would use a narrow grinding wheel or one shaped with a diamond dresser to an appropriate curve.

Alternatively, you can use a sanding drum on a drill press. Hone the blade; a diamond cone is ideal for the first stages of taking out the grinding marks because it will not wear and change shape as you work the edge. Slipstones then finish the edge. Scraps of broken Japanese waterstones or slipstones of the same material can be ground on a standard grinding wheel (the waterstones are quite soft) to shapes required.

On block-plane-style hollowing planes with unshouldered blades (including Japanese-style planes), the sides of the sole must continue at least in the radius of the blade. Often they will have to be planed off at an even greater angle in order to access the cut on particular projects (Figure 10-62). On rounding planes, the sides of the sole may also have to be planed off at an acute angle to access work.

Figure 10-63. *A completed hollowing plane is used to prepare the sole of this rounding plane.*

Figure 10-64. *The completed planes. The shopmade scraper in the lower left is helpful for fairing the curve of the sole.*

Troubleshooting

Using a handplane can be rewarding, but it is not without its frustrations. Sometimes it seems you have done everything right but your results are still disappointing or inconsistent. I cannot answer all questions you will ask yourself while you work, but a review of this book should answer most of them. I will try to answer some basic questions here I hope will tie information together and send you in the right direction when analyzing a problem.

1. Problem: The blade leaves a series of parallel marks on the work, perpendicular to the stroke of the plane.

This is called blade chatter and happens because the blade or its edge is flexing under pressure of the cut. The edge digs deeper into the wood until the blade's resistance to bending exceeds the resistance of the wood, and the blade springs back up. The blade then re-engages the wood, flexes, and the process repeats. Blade chatter happens because the blade is not fully supported at the heel of the bevel, or because the bevel angle is too small. There are a number of things to check, in the following order:

A. Check that the blade is bedded properly. The things to look for here depend somewhat on the type of blade you have: parallel, tapered, or Japanese.

Bailey-style planes: Check that nothing is between the blade and the frog: sometimes when you re-install a blade after sharpening,

for instance, an errant piece of shaving is trapped under the blade. Make sure every time you replace the blade after sharpening that the frog is clean. It is possible the frog was badly machined and the blade cannot seat properly. Check for any irregularities. Be certain the frog is securely screwed down and unable to be rocked.

It's possible the frog is adjusted incorrectly. If it is too far back, the blade will ride up off the frog and be part on the body casting and part on the frog. If it is too far forward, the blade will not be supported at the heel of the bevel. Or, if it is not parallel to the main body casting, the blade will be lifted up on one corner (Figures 10-13, 10-14, and 10-15 on pages 156 and 157).

Be certain the blade is properly set on the adjuster nib; otherwise, the blade will be prevented from bedding properly. You can usually tell because the cam lever on the cap iron (lever cap) will be noticeably more difficult, or impossible, to engage. If your cap iron tightens with a screw, you will not be able to tell without physically checking.

Wood-body planes (with parallel blades): Check that the blade bed is both flat, or maybe even ever so slightly concave, and that it is not twisted. Use a straightedge to check the bed for flat, and sight down the blade bed to check that the top and bottom edges are parallel and the bed is not twisted.

If the chipbreaker is screwed on, make sure the slot for the screw head is deep enough and that it is not riding up on a slot that is too shallow. Check that the wedge fits the chipbreaker—the chipbreaker is not necessarily flat, and the wedge should closely match its contour. Go through the bedding procedure described in the next section.

Planes with tapered blades: Because these usually are used on wood planes, go back to the section on setting up old wood planes and recheck your setup of the blade, chipbreaker, and blade bed. If everything checks out, check further, using a technique similar to fitting a Japanese blade. Rub soft pencil lead over the back of the blade, put it into working position, and secure it with the wedge. Adjust it up and down about ¼" (6mm) a few times and remove the blade.

Inspect the blade bed: You should at least have graphite marking at the bottom of the bed where the heel of the bevel would be and at the top of the bed. If you don't have satisfactory contact, pare away areas marked with graphite, and recheck until you have full contact in critical areas.

Also, check the fit of the wedge to the contour of the chipbreaker again. Check that *both* sides are tightly wedged. If only one side is wedging down, you can tell by pulling the tightened wedge sideways. The wedge should

give equal resistance in each direction. Check that the wedge is bearing over its full length.

Check for gaps visually and by pressing down on the blade and wedge in different areas, trying to detect some motion or flex. Verify any suspicions with feeler gauges and using the graphite marking technique. You should not be able to put a feeler gauge of any thickness anywhere along the wedge. Correct the fit as required.

Japanese planes: With a Japanese plane, I check the bevel angle first, because the blades usually come with a 22° bevel, which is often too small.

If the bevel angle seems appropriate, check the fit of the blade using plane setup techniques. Check the bed, particularly at the sides of the blade under and near the abutment. You should have a good fit here.

B. The second most probable cause of blade chatter, and the primary suspect on a well set up plane, is the bevel angle.

If the bevel angle is too small, the bevel flexes and causes chatter. "Too small," however, is relative. The bevel angle must be appropriate for the depth of cut, the blade (cutting) angle, and the type of wood. A bevel angle may be sufficient for a certain depth of cut, but may begin to chatter if set deeper, or if used to plane a harder wood.

Another important factor related to the bevel angle is sharpness: When a blade dulls, it encounters greater resistance to the cut, causing the edge to flex down and begin to chatter. You may notice it in the midst

MARKING

Because the surface of the blade bed on an old wooden plane may be darkened with age and dirt, pencil lead may not read very well marking high spots for shaving. Try a China marker (wax pencil); crayon in red, blue, or white; machinist's bluing; or, surprisingly, Vaseline, which will leave a glossy mark in contrast to the dull, darkened surface. Because the bearing area may be rather small, sometimes you may have to recoat and reinsert the blade several times to get a reading.

of working. The same plane that has been cutting well on the same piece of wood starts chattering and the only thing that has changed is the sharpness of your edge.

This means your bevel angle on this blade is at its performance limit. You will have to keep the blade sharp, or increase the bevel angle. If you suspect the bevel angle is incorrect, adjust your bevel angles (see "Bevel Angle" and "The Correct Bevel Angle" on page 52).

C. Poor design and manufacture can cause blade chatter.

This is a problem largely inherent in Bailey/Stanley planes. See "Chipbreaker" on page 45 for more.

A thin modern blade, however, is not necessarily condemned to chatter. The blades often perform without problems. But a thin blade, a thin chipbreaker that forces the blade into an arch, lifting most of it off the bed, and a cap iron that does not set the blade assembly fully to the blade bed, constitute a setup prone to problems. Add a chipbreaker set to the edge, a frog adjusted forward to restrict the mouth opening, a deep cut— or any of these in combination—and the potential for chatter is high.

If you believe the blade bed is satisfactory and bevel angle appropriate, but are still getting chatter, it may be the thin, arched blade assembly. You may want to upgrade to a thicker blade and possibly a better chipbreaker. A more substantial blade assembly will likely remain flat and fully bedded. If there is insufficient room at the mouth to use a thicker blade, then you can only upgrade the chipbreaker.

2. Problem: I cannot cut as fine a shaving as I want. The plane goes from a cut slightly too deep to no cut at all.

Either your plane or the work is not flat. Check the plane first—you probably have missed some area on the sole when you tuned-up the plane. The other factor is the work. If the work is not flat enough, you may have to set the blade deeper than you want to get the plane to cut even intermittent areas of the surface. If your plane cuts a fine shaving here and there, or even at one small place, the problem probably is in the preparation of the work.

3. Problem: I get tearout.

Using this book, you should be able to see markedly improved results in the performance of your planes. With practice, I hope you find yourself planing and getting results you had not thought possible—and knowing when to put down the plane and head for the scrapers and sandpaper.

Plane setup is critical for effective planing. Technique adds to effectiveness, but does not compensate for bad setup.

To reduce tearout, first sharpen the blade. Match the blade steel to the work and make it—*sharp*. Use an appropriate blade pitch, adjust the chipbreaker and mouth opening to restrain the shaving, and use as light a cut as is appropriate for the stage of the work.

If your plane and the surface of the work are well prepared, you can usually get good, reliable, tearout-free results on the final surfacing in most woods. Still, there will be those pieces that defy your best efforts.

A WELL-TUNED PLANE

I once watched a small 8-year-old girl take a full-width, full-length see-through-thin shaving off a cedar plank, 6" (152mm) wide by 6 feet (183cm) long, in one single continuous stroke—on her first attempt. The plane was a Japanese temple builder's 8" (203mm)-wide finishing plane that had been setup by a master carpenter. She walked backward pulling the plane with two hands while he walked along following her with a single finger kept lightly on top of the plane behind the blade to keep a consistent pressure on the work and to prevent her from flipping the plane off the plank. Probably the little person's skill was not yet highly tuned—but that plane certainly was.

Avoiding tear-out is a bigger problem when preparing stock because you are removing a lot of wood, which necessitates a deeper cut, with the chipbreaker and mouth opening set back accordingly. The setup diminishes the effectiveness of these two major tactics in eliminating tearout. Gradually adjust the chipbreaker and mouth openings down to restrict shaving and take a lighter cut. At each stage, you want to see tearout reduced, aiming for total elimination by the final smoothing.

Avoiding tearout also entails reading the wood and changing directions as you move across the surface. Curly areas that change direction in the middle of the board may necessitate rotating the plane as you approach that area, to change the angle of attack, and then rotating it back again.

Planing adjacent boards where the grain direction changes at the glue line often requires you to plane along the glue line in each direction without bridging the joint. Holding the plane at a bit of a diagonal localizes the cut and sometimes helps to skirt along the joint.

Tearout hotspots notwithstanding, you should plane the entire surface in overlapping strokes across the width and length of the piece and back again. If you finish scraping and sanding, do not be tempted to give trouble areas extra strokes, as this will distort the surface and be visible after finishing.

A technique both Westerners and Japanese use is to dampen the surface of the wood with a wet rag to soften the wood fibers, allowing them to be sheared cleanly. I have had indifferent results trying this, and I suspect it will not work in all woods.

4. Problem: Chips jam the plane's mouth.

First, take the blade out of the plane and check to see if the chips are jamming in the mouth itself, or at or under the chipbreaker. The chips may appear to be jamming at the mouth when in reality they are jamming

KEEP YOUR EYES ON THE PRIZE

The goal here is to get a beautiful surface suitable for the chosen finish and position of the piece in the work, in the most efficient manner possible. This is not an academic exercise. On the other hand, when you are learning about planes and trying to improve your skills, a little extra effort trying to figure out what is going on before turning to scrapers and sandpaper will be rewarded in the end. Ultimately, you have to decide when handplaning is no longer the most productive solution. Learning to make that decision is also part of the acquisition of skills.

at the chipbreaker and backing up to fill the mouth. The latter is more likely.

If the chips jam between the chipbreaker and blade, and not the mouth, tune the chipbreaker's fit to the blade so it is tight. The underside edge of the chipbreaker, where it meets the blade, must be straight, and slightly undercut (Figure 10-4 on page 147). The chipbreaker also must be formed so it puts sufficient pressure at the interface between it and the blade to keep chips from forcing their way in.

If all of these are tuned up and chips still find their way between the blade and chipbreaker, possibly the edge of the blade is flexing under the pressure of the cut and opening up a gap between it and the chipbreaker. The bevel is flexing because it is too small or the blade is flexing because it is not properly supported.

Sometimes the chipbreaker is rigid enough—and not tight enough—to allow a badly supported blade or too thin edge to flex independently. Check the bevel angle and consider regrinding it to a larger one if it appears questionable. Check the blade seat and make sure the blade is supported. Correct these and verify the chipbreaker has enough pressure on the edge to maintain contact under working conditions (see Figure 10-7 on page 150).

Sometimes if tolerances are close, a blade flexes down into the wood in use and takes a deeper chip than the mouth or throat opening will accept. This is actually blade chatter, but because it happens only once and jams instead of leaving chatter marks, it is hard to diagnose because the blade or its edge flexes.

KEEP THE SURFACE FLAT

Do not get distracted with localized problems. You must plane the entire surface the same amount—difficult areas as well as straightforward—in order to maintain flat. Otherwise, not only will the surface appear irregular but also the plane will begin to bridge the troubled areas by riding on the adjacent, less planed surfaces. These higher areas will then have to be planed down in line with the low areas before you can go any further.

5. Problem: The plane leaves tracks or ridges.

Rotate the work so the light source shines parallel to the work surface. Look closely and see if it is a ridge or a step. If it is a ridge, then you have a nick in the blade. You will have to go back and re-sharpen.

If the track is a step, then one or both corners of the blade are set too deep for the shape of the blade. You need to back the blade off or adjust the lateral adjuster until the blade no longer leaves steps. If it no longer cuts, then you need to either flatten the bottom of the plane some more or prepare the work better as described above. Check the different sections for the appropriate blade shape for the plane you are using.

6. Problem: The plane seems to leave shiny streaks on the work.

These are usually burnishing marks from some slightly higher spot on the sole of the plane. The most likely culprit is the area just to either side of the blade opening, since these are easy to neglect. I relieve these areas on my planes; however, another missed spot on the sole can do this as well. Also, shavings can collect at the mouth (especially at the corners), pack tightly, and cause burnishing.

11

SHARPENING PLANE BLADES

A Basic Skill that Leads to Others

OK, OK. I know anyone who has ever sharpened a plane blade has a firm, perhaps even adamant,

opinion about how it should be done. I say, if it is working for you, you do not need to fix it.

But in the interest of coaxing new growth out of any woodworker who wants to improve his or

her craft, and to give at least a sense of direction to those who are starting out, I throw out the

following for your consideration.

I have two goals when sharpening:

• the acquisition and improvement of skills (sharpening and otherwise); and

• getting back to working wood as quickly as possible—with the most effective blade edge.

The ability to sharpen quickly and well is essential to the craft of woodworking.

SHARPENING FUNDAMENTALS

Sharpening is fundamental to woodworking. Learning to sharpen fast and effectively lays the foundation for the acquisition of nearly all skills required in the craft. It teaches body mechanics and the art of working efficiently. It teaches how to focus your attention and efforts for maximum productivity. It teaches you to see, and what to look for. It teaches you to feel your own rhythms, the material, and the feedback from the tool—less smooth, smoother, smoothest, sharp, and sharper.

In some woodworking traditions, the first real task given to the apprentice was sharpening tools. Only when the apprentice could produce an adequate edge did the master judge his skills and knowledge sufficient to proceed. Acquiring skills begins with sharpening.

Because of the importance of sharpening in teaching body mechanics and the art of working efficiently, I encourage woodworkers to sharpen without a jig. This is where woodworkers learn to make each motion pay off. Through sharpening, woodworkers learn:

- The edge is not scrubbed back and forth across the stone but rather stroked with direct intention each time it is moved.
- There is clear focus of effort, pressure, and attention at the cutting edge, not the bevel.
- While the bevel remains flat, not rocking on the stone, it is the bevel edge being sharpened.

Learning this and how to do it, as well as how to do it each time, makes it easier to understand other tasks, including:

- That sawing is not a tiring repetition of frantic arm motion but a series of individual strokes, each advancing the cut on the shoulder of the scribe line and to the maximum amount the wood and the cut of the saw will allow.
- That clearing waste for a dovetail or mortise with a chisel is a series of distinct, clean, and precise cuts of exactly the same amount, to the line, so waste is cleanly excavated the first time to its final shape (though perhaps not its final size).
- That each stroke of the plane is individual, dependent on the grain of the wood at that particular place, the angle of attack, your speed, your body position, the diminishing sharpness of the blade, and your increasing fatigue.

JIG DRAWBACKS

Use a sharpening jig and your energy is dissipated, half of it going to the roller, half to the bevel, and little going to the edge of the blade, which is where your energy should go. The roller becomes a blindfold, obscuring your interaction with the edge you are sharpening, and keeping you from learning:

- the feel of the bevel sitting flat on the stone as you stroke it;
- to focus your attention at the edge, while keeping the bevel flat to the stone; and
- not to rock or lean, yet produce maximum results at that cutting edge where you want it.

All of this ties into my second goal: getting back to working wood. Because the jig dissipates both your energy and your focus, effort is wasted and time is lost. It is slower and disruptive. Add to that the problem of jigging the blade the exact position in the apparatus—because if it is not exact, you create a new bevel on the blade when you go to sharpen—and your time and tedium increase exponentially.

Learn to sharpen with the attention of the mind and body focused to your fingertips, because in the end, this will be how you will be doing woodworking. Yes, there is a learning curve, but really, woodworking is just one big learning curve. The challenges woodworking offers is one of its appeals. You can take a shortcut, but it will catch up to you later. Time invested here will serve you throughout your further woodworking endeavors.

Bevel Shape

Three bevel configurations can be used on a sharpened blade:

- flat,
- hollow ground, and
- microbevel.

Traditional sources I have seen emphasize the bevel must be flat—for several reasons. First, it gives maximum support to the edge while allowing the thinnest possible bevel. A rounded bevel, usually a result of rocking the blade when sharpening, results in a much thicker bevel angle at the cutting edge, even though the average of the bevel overall may be the intended angle. This results in the blade ceasing to cut at the least bit of dulling,

as the bevel behind the edge begins to rub and suspend the edge from the work.

A hollow-ground blade undercuts the edge leaving little material to support it. It actually undercuts it more than you think because the actual angle is that of the tangent of the hollow just behind the edge. This is much smaller than the angle the blade was ground to, and often results in a support angle behind the edge of much less than the 20° to 22° generally considered to be the absolute minimum practical bevel angle (see Figures 1 and 2 on page 53). This may or may not be a problem.

Telltale signs the blade is a problem are:

- chattering (even though properly bedded, the undercut metal leading to the edge is flexing under load);
- clogging at the mouth or throat of a properly adjusted plane (the blade—not sufficiently supported by the bevel—is flexing down under load, enlarging the mouth, causing it to cut a shaving larger than the opening can accommodate); or
- clogging between the blade and the chipbreaker, even though the chipbreaker is fitted properly (again, the blade's thin edge is flexing under load and opening a gap between it and the chipbreaker).

A flat bevel provides the thinnest possible edge with the greatest support behind that edge. If any of these problems show up with a flat bevel, it is because the bevel is ground at too small an angle, a geometry that is plain to see and easy to deal with. Laminated blades are honed to a flat bevel, as the hard, brittle steel is too vulnerable without the support of the bevel behind it.

Besides its potential functional problems, I have always believed the hollow grind presents maintenance problems as well. A grinding wheel leaves deep scratches, many of which seem to remain even after establishing a brightly honed bevel. To ensure they no longer remain near the edge, I always give the bevel a few extra strokes on the first sharpening stone.

Waterstones, however, cut so fast—much faster than the old oil or Arkansas stones— that this nearly eliminates the hollow, especially on an unlaminated carbon-steel blade. After two or three sharpenings, the hollow has been honed away. I could never understand the point of regrinding the hollow when the waterstones cut so fast.

There are some occasions, however, when I purposely establish a hollow grind, even if an edge does not have to be reshaped (because of a nick, for instance). The primary reason is to take the hump out of a rounded bevel. Sometimes, after a number of honings, I just lose it. The bevel is simply too rounded to easily flatten.

In such cases, I put it on a grinding wheel and hollow-grind the area between the edge and the heel of the bevel. I do not take it all the way out to the edge, both for expediency and to avoid possibly overheating the edge. I grind away just enough that the blade sits flat on the sharpening stone and does not rock. I can then easily hone the blade to a flat, unrounded bevel. At the first honing, however, I do not necessarily take the time to

fully remove the hollow left by the grinder. I just hone until the edge is sharpened. If a bit of the hollow remains, it is not enough to compromise the functioning of the blade, and it will be gone soon enough in the next honing or two, anyway.

MICROBEVELS AND HONING GUIDES

The microbevel is, again, a maintenance issue with me. The microbevel gives a good edge the first time. The next time you sharpen, you have two choices: (1) sharpen only the microbevel, or (2) sharpen the whole bevel and the microbevel.

If you sharpen only the microbevel, after two or three sharpenings you will have a macro bevel. You will have lost the advantage of a microbevel, and you have a main bevel that is rapidly developing a rounded profile. If you hone the main bevel to get the best edge, you must hone it all the way out to the edge, not just to the beginning of the microbevel. Then, putting a microbevel on the blade at this point is just redoing work.

If you hone without a guide (as I recommend), some slight variation in the bevel angle is unavoidable. With proper technique you can make it work for you. By rotating the blade orientation to perpendicular to the length of the sharpening stone on your final stone, rather than using the approximate 45° orientation that gives the most stability when sharpening, you assume higher risk (Figure 11-1). The slight increase in inaccuracy ensures the edge itself is polished and slightly bolstered.

I believe many elaborate systems—hollow-grinding, microbevels, jigs—do not address one of the main issues of sharpening: its frequency. If you are using your planes to their maximum benefit, for periods, at least, you may have to resharpen several times a day—maybe every 15 or 20 minutes at some point in some projects.

Fiddling with contraptions and a variety of angles each time consumes too much time and is distracting. With just a good set of stones and a properly established bevel angle, you can be back to woodworking after 3 or 4 minutes at the stones, which is sometimes less than the amount of time it would take to get a jig attached.

Grinding

I was once told to never grind a Japanese blade. Getting out a nick in a blade without a grinder can be very Zen. I became enlightened when a Japanese chisel maker told me you can grind a Japanese blade on a grinding wheel—with the proper technique. Keep a finger directly behind the bevel, as close to the grinding wheel as possible. When the blade becomes too hot for your finger, it is too hot for the edge, and grinding pauses (Figure 11-2).

NOT JUST JAPANESE BLADES

This brings up an important issue. Not just Japanese blades are sensitive to the stress of grinding. Treat any good blade in the same manner. While a grinding wheel can easily draw the temper of an edge, especially if the wheel is glazed stopping short of changing the

Figure 11-1. Positions of Risk

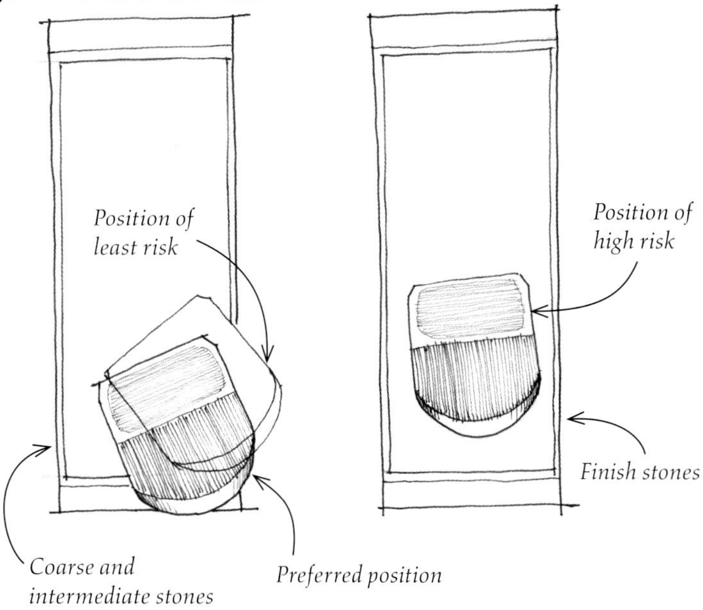

Position of least risk

Position of high risk

Finish stones

Coarse and intermediate stones

Preferred position

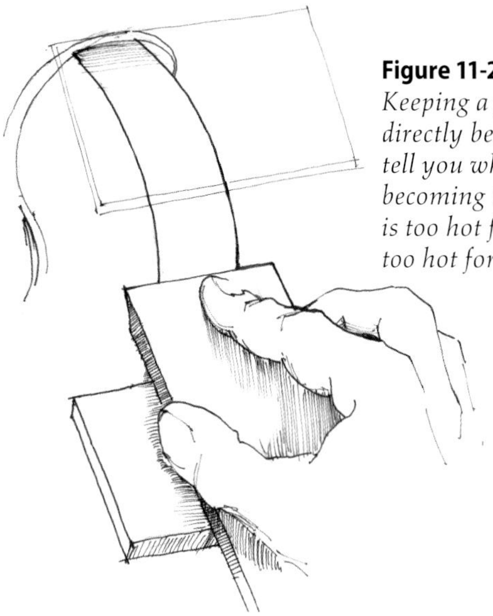

Figure 11-2.
Keeping a finger at the edge directly behind the bevel will tell you when the blade is becoming too hot. If the blade is too hot for your finger, it is too hot for the edge.

color of the edge is still too hot. Aggressively grinding, stopping just short of color change, quenching, and then regrinding, causes noticeable structural change in the edge. Quenching alone may cause microscopic cracking. All of this degrades the edge, reducing the cutting ability and life of the edge.

Alloy steel blades are somewhat more forgiving of this treatment, because the alloys usually added mitigate some of the effects of heat stress. However, a carbon steel blade will not tolerate the temperature extremes.

GRINDING EQUIPMENT

At some point, you will have to reshape a blade edge. For this reason, some sort of grinding device is indispensable. The power-grinding wheel is the most common, and probably, all things considered, the most practical. Get the slow-speed version (1,750rpm or so) and 8" (203mm) wheels for less undercutting of the edge. Keep the wheels trued and clean. Keep your finger behind the bevel, and work patiently.

An alternative to the grinding wheel is the standing stationary belt sander, about 2" (51mm) wide. Knife makers and many metal workers prefer them. They cut aggressively but have less tendency to overheat because the sanding belt carries away much of the heat. (You still can be too aggressive and overheat the blade, but it is much harder).

This machine allows you several options for shaping the bevel. Besides the flat platen that produces a (nearly) flat bevel, usually you can work at one of the end wheels of the belt and achieve a hollow grind. The machine I have has an 8" (203mm) wheel that is usable. In addition, most machines have an arbor at the other side of the motor, which can be fitted with a grinding or buffing wheel.

Water grinding stones guarantee no heating of the edge. They tend to be slower (though not much) than power grinding or sanding, but they leave a great edge with little risk to the blade. They are, in some respects less versatile. You cannot do general reshaping tasks, such as grinding a new blade profile (as for a molding plane).

GRINDING OUT A NICK

Do not remove a nick by grinding the bevel; grind perpendicular to the edge. After removing the nick, grind the bevel until it just reaches the edge. If you grind out the nick by grinding the bevel, you are always working at the thin edge. This thin edge has no mass to help dissipate the heat, and is therefore at greater risk for overheating.

On the other hand, the horizontal water grinder can sharpen power jointer and plane blades, something other grinders cannot easily do. Also, the horizontal wheel leaves a dead-flat bevel, which no other grinding wheel does. It does need more maintenance than the others, though. The stones quickly wear and require frequent truing.

Vertical water grinding wheels have the same advantage as the horizontal water wheels. There is no risk of heat damage to the tool, but they leave a hollow grind. It is a matter of preference as to what shape you want behind your edge. Most of the wheels are much larger than most dry grinding wheels, so edges are less undercut. Some of the systems seem quite elaborate—and expensive—and, considering you will probably have to get another system for the shop's other grinding/shaping tasks, the cost seems downright luxurious.

Sharpening Stones

It was not that long ago that woodworkers did not have many options for honing the edges on blades. Oilstones or Arkansas stones were pretty much it. Oilstones were messy. They still clogged with debris, decreasing their effectiveness, despite all of the oil that was supposed to float away the debris. In addition, flattening them was impossible, and they did not cut very fast. Arkansas stones, a natural stone, were a step up, but the quality of the stones varied widely, and they shared many of the problems of the oilstones.

In the 1970s, manufactured Japanese waterstones became available, and they have revolutionized sharpening. Since then, major strides have been made in the quality and type of product available. American manufacturers now make waterstones, and by reports, their product is equal to, if not better than, some Japanese stones. I cannot keep track of the different stones. I have settled on a number of stones that serve my needs, so I have not experimented widely with the different ones available. I suggest you consult the woodworking magazine reviews for comparisons of products and systems.

Nevertheless, you have to take some of the tests they do with a grain of salt. It is not simply a matter of which is the best sharpening stone, or the best sharpening system, but the best match, blade to stone.

Though I have no verification for this, I suspect the technique used also is a factor in the effectiveness of different sharpening stones. I would not lose sleep at night over matching stone to blade, but some broad categories can be delineated. The clearest distinction can be made between the alloy steels and the carbon steels. Waterstones are much less effective on many of the alloy steels. On some alloys, waterstones do not really cut at all. If your waterstones seem ineffective on your alloy blades, you will have to use diamond stones and/or paste.

After that, determinations become much more subtle. When first imported,

Japanese waterstones reflected the unique characteristics of the Japanese blade. Now they are responding more to the American market. The Japanese craftsmen, intimately familiar with the character of his tools, will prefer different stones for different tools, because he knows that certain matches yield better results.

The common Western carbon-steel blade is not very subtle or complex. A 1200-grit stone followed by a 4000-grit polishing stone often gives you as good a result as more time spent on finer stones. Laminated blades, both Japanese and cast steel, generally respond well to an additional polishing stone, 6000- to 8000-grit, using a 3000-grit stone as an intermediate. If you have a very fine, special Japanese blade you may eventually want to consider getting a good quality natural finish stone, as recommended by a good dealer and as your pocket will allow.

OTHER ABRASIVES

A few other sharpening materials can be useful. I have mentioned diamond stones. These are particularly useful for flattening the back of blades, as you can hone on them almost indefinitely without wearing them out of flat. With a waterstone, if your blade back needs a lot of flattening, the waterstone soon wears out of flat and will have to be flattened again. If you wait too long to do it, the curve of the stone will be honed into the back of the blade, so using a non-wearing "stone" is helpful here (Figure 11-3, 11-4, and 11-5).

DIAMOND STONES

Diamond stones actually cut faster and smoother as they wear. This is because the large points break into many smaller points, creating both a finer cut and more points to more quickly abrade the surface.

If your plane blade back is badly out of flat, it may be faster to use carborundum on an iron plate (*kanaban*) to flatten it. The iron grabs the carborundum and keeps it from grinding the plate (though it will wear out eventually and have to be replaced). (See "Flattening the Back of a Plane Blade" on page 148.)

A hard felt wheel can be useful. It must be hard felt to minimize rounding over of the edge. While I would never use this on my good smoothing-plane blades, it is sometimes helpful to touch up the blade on a jack or scrub plane. Felt wheels often cut faster than you think, so it is easy to distort a subtle, critical edge—or even slightly gouge it.

This slight distortion and rounding that result from using a hard felt wheel is less critical to the blade of a plane used for dimensioning or shaping. Never use a felt wheel on the back of a blade: the back must still be lapped on the finish stone. Eventually buffing will round the bevel of the blade. It must then be hollow ground, at least partially, and stoned to a good edge to keep the blade cutting effectively, before it approaches the buffing wheel again.

Figure 11-3. *Besides using a straight edge to check the stones for flat (which I find difficult when the stones are wet), you can check by using your flattening stone, which in this case is a diamond stone. A few strokes with the flattening stone will reveal the hollow, stained with the iron removed in sharpening.*

Figure 11-4. *Here the stone is almost restored to flat.*

Figure 11-5. *Flat once again.*

USING AND MAINTAINING WATERSTONES

Before use, synthetic waterstones need to be soaked for at least ten minutes, or until air bubbles stop coming out of the stone. If they do not have a wood base, you can store them indefinitely in water. A large lidded plastic tub is good for this. If they have a wooden base, you can still store them in water, but eventually the base will fall off. Synthetic finish stones (#3000 and above) generally do not need to be soaked, but check with the manufacture and/or dealer.

Natural waterstones are never stored in water because doing so causes them to disintegrate. Coarser stones are soaked for 5 or 10 minutes before using and removed after sharpening. The natural finish stones generally do not need to be soaked, but again, check with the seller. Natural stones will often crack, by the way, if allowed to freeze.

The stones will have to be trued before they are used the first time and frequently as they are used. There are a number of ways to do this. My favored approach now is to use a diamond stone rubbed against the waterstone. I have been using the same diamond stone now for more than eight years and it has not worn out yet, so it is cost effective.

Alternatively, you can use sandpaper—220-grit wet/dry on a piece of ¼" (6mm) plate glass laid on a flat surface. However, you will get only about two flattenings before the sandpaper wears out, so costs can add up. In addition, sandpaper tends to glaze some stones (such as the Bester), so it is not always an option. I have also flattened stones on a concrete block, which works fine until the concrete becomes polished and the block wears out of flat. Also, a special stone is sold just for flattening sharpening stones, which works fine, but eventually it too gets glazed and out of flat.

Some stones are harder than others, so the frequency of flattening will vary. Frequency also varies according to the task. A good procedure is to sharpen your finest smoothing plane blade first, right after flattening the stones. Then follow in order with blades of increasing edge curvature, right down to the jack. That way you can actually use the wear of the stones to help shape the blade edges.

In use, coarser stones are periodically washed clean and kept wet by adding a bit of water from the soaking container. The blade is abraded directly against the stone. The finish stones are kept barely wet, but not allowed to dry out; the slurry is allowed to build up, because it is what does the polishing, not the stone. Using a *nagura* stone (a chalk stone available where waterstones are sold) raises the slurry more quickly.

Technique

I learned to sharpen on the floor. It has a number of advantages. You do not need to build a special table and have it take up space in you shop, and sitting, kneeling, or squatting can actually be restful to legs that have been standing all day. However, I do not seriously believe I can convince many people reading this to even try it, though I do highly recommend it.

I learned from using this position that it is of little importance whether you are on the floor, sitting, or standing. What is important is the height of the stone relative to the body, and a solid, centered position that allows both movement and stability. The stone should be about 4" or 5" (102mm or 127mm) below the belly button. Lower than this and you will overextend your arms at the end of the stroke. Any higher and your elbows will be too bent and flailing about. Both positions will cause you to rock the blade on its bevel, rounding it over. Even if you use a jig, this is a good position, because it maximizes the energy of your movement.

Position yourself to maintain good solid balance even at the extremes of each stroke. If standing, have your feet apart, one slightly in front of the other. Feel the bevel lying flat on the stone and learn to recognize the feel and sound when the bevel loses full contact with the stone and rocks. Stop and feel the bevel's position again. Train your body to follow the bevel, to internalize the movement required to keep that bevel flat to the stone, and to maximize the expenditure of energy directly to the cutting edge itself. Have your mind focused on this cutting edge and this bevel in solid contact with the stone, with the body following in total attention and coordination. This is the beginning of skill.

LISTENING

Learn to recognize the sound of the full bevel being stroked on the stone: whenever the blade is rocked or lifted, the pitch of this sound of the blade on the stone will change. It will sound different when just the heel of the bevel is stroked, and different again when just the edge is stroked. In fact, there is a slight bit of difference in sound when pressure is applied more toward the edge than the heel—even though the blade is sitting flat on the stone.

Responding to the feedback that sound gives you is an important lesson that will carry throughout all your work. It can tell you when you a nearing the end of the cut with a handsaw even though you can't see it, when a power tool needs to be turned off—immediately—and investigated for a dangerous problem, and when you have just lifted the blade off its bevel and are starting to cause problems for yourself.

SHARPENING

Years ago, a young man apprenticed to a furniture maker in Japan showed me this sharpening technique. It has served me well. I suspect it will do likewise for you.

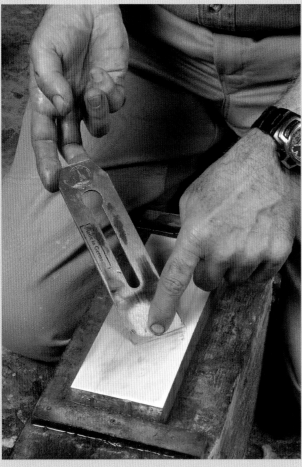

Figure 1. *Before beginning to sharpen, first find the bevel. You do this by putting one or two fingers down on top of the blade directly opposite the bevel, while simultaneously tilting the blade up with a single finger of the other hand underneath. Tilt the blade up and down with this finger while keeping pressure down on the bevel with the other hand until you can feel the blade rest securely on the flat of the bevel. Do this exercise every time before you start sharpening, and several times during.*

Figure 2. *Similar to the exercise, when sharpening, the first one or two fingers of the off hand—the left if you're right handed—finds and maintains a steady pressure down on the bevel. At the same time, the right hand lightly grips the blade with the thumb and second finger, maintaining the angle, with the first finger applying downward pressure on the bevel (along with those of the left hand). The third and fourth fingers are lightly wrapped underneath. The number of fingers in each position may vary as sharpening proceeds, but the basic positions of the first fingers of each hand putting pressure on the bevel, with the rest of the fingers of the right hand maintaining the angle of the blade, remain the same.*

SHARPENING *(continued)*

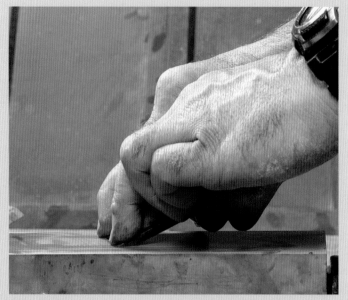

Figures 3 and 4. *When sharpening a shorter Japanese blade, use a variation of this same basic grip (left) for the smaller blades (50mm (2") wide or so). Put the right thumb under the top of the blade, supported by the left thumb (above), and the rest of the fingers in about the same location as described in* **Figure 1.** *While the broad bevel of the thick blade does make it a little easier to keep it flat on the stones, having the thumbs under the blade rather than holding the blade with the right hand, similar to the Western blade grip, is a position of higher risk and I usually use it only on the finish stone.*

When moving the blade back and forth over the stone, the finger(s) of the left hand maintain a constant pressure down on the bevel to make sure it stays in constant contact with the stone. The right hand generally does the moving, assisted by the left hand, though neither hand does only one task: they each assist the other.

Listen to and feel the bevel: when you sense you are no longer holding the bevel in constant contact with the stone—stop, relax your hands, do the exercise of finding the bevel, and start again.

Special Note: *Do not* attempt to steady the blade

by putting fingers on the stone and dragging them along as you sharpen. This will soon cut through your fingertips, though you will not feel it until after it has happened, resulting in a painful, slow-to-heal wound.

Once you have had some practice sharpening and have gotten a better feel for keeping the bevel, you can begin working on an advanced technique. This is to actually put the focus of the sharpening effort right at the edge while still keeping the bevel flat on the stone when sharpening. It took me a while to discover this: after I got proficient at keeping the bevel flat, I noticed that over time the bevel angle on my laminated blades was getting smaller. I finally figured out that because the edge steel is harder than the backing steel, equal pressure across the bevel will wear away the softer steel quicker, eventually making the bevel angle smaller.

To compensate, I concentrated my pressure when sharpening on the edge itself, while still keeping the bevel flat to the stones. Blades suddenly became sharper a lot faster. To do this, the right hand that supports the blade gives a little bit of pressure—focus—on the cutting edge itself by increasing the support it gives underneath the end of the blade while simultaneously concentrating the front fingers on the edge. I could say something like "the right hand lifts the end of

the blade imperceptibly" instead to describe this, but this would give the wrong impression: it is an upward pressure there coupled with focused pressure at the blade's edge (rather than just the bevel). The blade is never actually lifted because this would round the bevel.

The required bit of curvature can be put on a smoothing plane blade by alternately putting pressure on each corner of the blade with the fingers that reside above the bevel. This is done three or four strokes at a time, on each stone. Similarly, pay attention to the distribution of pressure with the fingers. Unequal pressure may result in an unexpected and unwanted blade shape.

 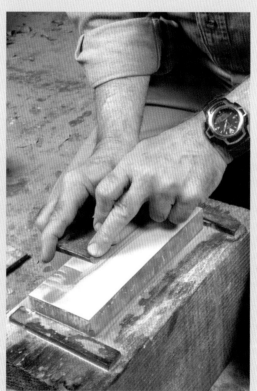

Figures 5 and 6. *The back of the blade, whether Western or Japanese, is lapped with a similar grip and pressure distribution as when doing the bevel: the right hands grips the blade with the thumb and second finger, with the first finger putting pressure on the very edge of the blade (above left). The fingers of* *the left hand also put pressure just at the blade's edge. While the blade is never, ever lifted, the right hand does contribute an upward pressure at the off end of the blade while simultaneously focusing pressure down at the edge (above right). The blade, of course, stays in solid contact with the stone the whole time.*

12

BENCH WORK

Of Slaves, Dogs, and Deadmen

Over many generations, European cabinetmakers developed a very sophisticated bench for

holding work that was to be planed and joined. This bench, especially when used along with

its various accessories, will hold pieces of almost any shape in virtually any of the positions

that might be required to effectively work them: shaping, dimensioning, smoothing, joining,

whatever. If you do a wide variety of work, especially in the traditional styles, you will

eventually have to invest in this classic bench, or one like it.

This large board is held in the front vise and supported on pegs set into the face of the bench's legs while its edge is planed. The ability to hold work securely, and position it quickly, greatly increases productivity.

While there are numerous variations of the European bench, they all have at least one distinguishing feature: a row of dog holes—traditionally square, sometimes round in contemporary versions—into which adjustable height pegs, or *dogs*, are put. Used with a *tail vise* on the end of the bench, the dogs run the length of the bench at regular intervals near the front edge.

The tail vise also has one or more dog holes, allowing the user to clamp a length of board between a dog on the bench and a dog on the end vise when the vise is tightened. This innovation allows a variety of shapes and sizes of boards and panels to be held securely during planing.

The bench also typically has a vise on the front. The front vise has a number of variations depending largely on the type of furniture being made and the bench's region of origin, and each has its advantages and drawbacks. The oldest variation, the leg vise can hold a variety of sizes and a limited amount of shapes, but is cumbersome to readjust.

The shoulder vise form can clamp a variety of straight and tapered pieces, but can get in the way when working with long pieces. The classic woodworking vise can have a quick-adjustment mechanism, making it easy to go back and forth between large and small pieces quickly, but cannot easily hold tapered or odd-shaped pieces. An Emmert-style vise, designed for use by patternmakers, can hold just about anything, in a lot of different positions, though it can require some jigging if, for instance, you want to shoot the edge of a long piece.

The only drawback I find to the classic European bench is it can be a bit cumbersome or slow when you have to plane regularly shaped pieces, especially when you have many of them to do. On medium-to-small size pieces, the time it takes to dog and un-dog a workpiece is roughly equal to the time it takes to plane a side. Thus, using the bench can double your work time.

Our predecessors noticed the problem. Specialty trades, for instance, often used much simpler benches and holding devices where work could be rapidly repositioned, with fresh pieces quickly replacing the finished ones. Craftsmen often worked by the piece, so speed was of the essence. If you did not have to take the time to turn a crank or vise handle to hold a piece and then turn it again to release it, you were saving time and energy, and making more money. Many of the trades were compensated barely above subsistence as it was.

A SIMPLE-STOP BENCH

The vast majority of pieces the woodworker will want to smooth with his plane can be worked against a simple stop fixed to the bench. Although bench dogs and vises of the European bench are useful for holding workpieces while chiseling or shaping as well as planing, it is often not necessary to clamp regular-shaped pieces down to the bench with dogs or other clamping devices just to plane them. A workpiece can have its first side smoothed (if it is small, a side can be smoothed in a pass or two), flipped end for end (to maintain the best grain orientation), planed, then turned onto its side and planed, and then flipped again end for end—all without having to reach for a vise handle. You can smooth a stack of parts quickly this way.

For planing and basic woodwork, you do not need an elaborate bench. A stout plank with a stop fixed to it often is the fastest and most effective way to hold the work. This stop should be as wide as possible, not a single iron or wood peg, in order to handle boards of various widths without the push of the plane causing the board to pivot away from you. The stop should be a strip of wood fitted near the end of the planing board in a tapered dado or sliding dovetail so it can be removed or replaced.

If you use only Japanese-style planes, the planing board, with a stop at the near end to accommodate the pull stroke, might slant down toward the user in the Japanese manner to make it more comfortable throughout the length of the planing stroke. If the board is also used for joinery or Western-style planing, supporting it horizontally, parallel to the floor, turns it into a simple bench. The planing board can be as little as 3' or 4' long, depending on the nature of the work, and as little as only 9" (229mm) wide.

A simple planing board as described above, used with a holdfast and a few vise-type accessories will be quite serviceable, and portable, and will probably serve the woodworker's planing and hand tool work quite well. If you have a European-style bench, however, there are a number of things you can do to speed planing operations.

Figure 12-1.
A board or piece of plywood put into the tail vise can be used as a planing stop for small and medium size pieces.

ADDING VERSATILITY

To avoid having to repeatedly dog and undog boards you want to surface-plane, or having to install a fixed stop to work against on your bench, you can clamp a short board in the tail vise so it projects above the bench top and plane against it. This works best if you are using a pull-plane (Figure 12-1), but can also be used for short pieces when using a push plane. Or you can make up a stop of three pieces of wood or plywood to clamp in the tail vise that will also handle wide boards, again for pull planes (Figure 12-2). A similar device can be made for the front vise to be used with push-planes. This needs to be made of only two pieces (Figure 12-3).

A SIMPLE BENCH

Years ago, in the basement of a house I was renting, I came across a 4x10 (102mm x 254mm) beam in amongst some scrap lumber, abandoned by the previous tenant. It was 8' long, had a series of pairs of ⁵⁄₁₆" (8mm) holes drilled through the broad face down its length, and a ledger screwed along the whole length of one edge. Obviously, someone had intended this to be a workbench, perhaps in the Japanese style. However, as it was, it did not appear that usable to me. Nevertheless, the wood was a nice piece of fir, dry and straight. I used it for years as a portable bench on the worksite supporting it on a pair of workhorses, and gradually became aware of its potential **(Figure 1)**.

I have since installed two removable stops of different heights, one at each end, that slide in on tapered dovetails. They can be removed or moved to opposite ends as needed, with just a tap of the hammer. I need stops at either end because I use both push and pull planes **(Figure 2)**.

I installed a wooden hook near one end above the ledger similar to the hook on the Roubo bench in Scott Landis' The *Workbench Book* (Taunton Press, 1987). This allows me to set a board on edge on the ledger and push the end of the board into the hook to stabilize it while shooting the edge **(Figure 3)**. You can also shoot edges like on a shooting board. Set the board flat on the surface of the bench and run the plane along the ledger.

Into the holes, I inserted ⁵⁄₁₆" (8mm) dowels about an inch longer than the thickness of the bench. As it turned out, most fit snuggly, allowing me to adjust their height by tapping them up or down with a hammer. I generally do not use these as stops because they are rather small, but more for positioning alongside work to keep it from shifting to the side because of either an irregular end or diagonal planing. If I had to do over again I probably would make the holes ¾" (19mm) in

Figure 1. *The planing bench in its simplest incarnation, sitting on a pair of workhorses (Japanese-style, in this case).*

Figure 2. *Full-width stops are fitted into dovetailed grooves near either end, so that they can be easily tapped out and removed or exchanged. Holes have been drilled for holdfasts.*

Figure 3. *This hook captures pieces for edge-planing when set on the ledger.*

Figure 4. *Clamp a handscrew to the bench for use as a versatile vise.*

Figure 5. *A chairmaker's vise can be clamped to the top.*

Figure 7. *I added a tool shelf behind the work surface and a slotted stop against which I can work. To keep the horses from rocking from heavy planing, I pressure-fit a lower shelf on the stretchers of the horses to lock in their placement, pressure-fit the tool shelf, and added diagonal braces. Half-lapped and notched at either end to tightly fit to the top rail and stretchers of the horses, these help make the assembly rigid. Everything disassembles without tools.*

diameter so dowels in them would be stout enough to use as stops, and then the holdfast could be used as well in the holes.

When I use the bench in the field, if I need to hold a piece for shaping or cutting, I clamp a large hand-screw clamp to the top at the end. This works well and, unlike many vises, will hold tapered pieces **(Figure 4)**. For holding pieces to be shaped, a chairmaker's vise (sometimes called a carver's vise) could be clamped to the top through one of the holes drilled through it, allowing a variety of positions along the bench **(Figure 5)**.

For some complex pieces, and operations I still have to resort to my European bench, but for most planing operations I find this simple bench very versatile and much faster.

Figure 6. *The bench has seen adjustments and additions as I have worked with it over time. I placed a couple of stout dowels in the bottom of the bench to fit into holes drilled into the workhorses to keep the bench from scooting around under heavy planing.*

Figure 8. *The planing bench at its home in the shop. When not being used in the field, the bench rests here atop my tool chests.*

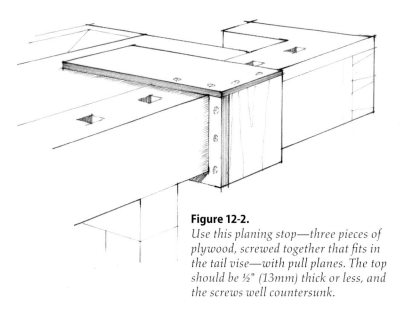

Figure 12-2.
Use this planing stop—three pieces of plywood, screwed together that fits in the tail vise—with pull planes. The top should be ½" (13mm) thick or less, and the screws well countersunk.

Figure 12-3.
For push planes, this simple planing stop clamps in the front vise. The top piece is ½" (13mm) thick or less. The block clamped in the vise is preferably solid wood ¾" (19mm) thick or thicker.

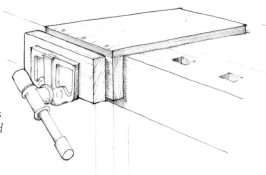

For planing the edges of long, narrow pieces that will flex if not fully supported, I put a 4" (102mm) handscrew clamp in the tail vise (Figure 12-4). On the side of one of the jaws of the clamp, I have glued a strip of veneer (Figure 12-5). The veneer allows the other jaw to be adjusted freely when the clamp is held in the vise. When using the clamp, I first adjust it so the jaw opening matches the work it is holding. I position the clamp in the vise at a height that works with the piece I am planing (so it extends above the bench surface less than the thickness of the board being planed), tighten the tail vise to hold the clamp, and then the clamp to hold the piece.

Figure 12-4. *A handscrew clamp in the tail vise is a versatile clamp for holding work to be planed.*

Figure 12-5. *Glue a piece of veneer to the side of one jaw to provide clearance that enables the other jaw to be moved while the clamp is in the vise.*

DEADMEN AND HELPER BOYS

For planing the edges of long, wide pieces, you can use the front vise to hold pieces up to around 5' long if they are not so narrow to flex when planed. Longer pieces will have to be supported. There are a number of ways to do this. The first is to build a way into the bench. This assumes you are building your own bench or are willing to do some major modifications to an existing bench.

One way to increase the versatility of the European bench is to build the legs flush to the front edge of the bench and drill a series of ¾" (19mm) holes in the front right leg. This allows work up to about 3' wide (such as a door or tabletop) to be supported on edge, on a dowel or holdfast inserted into one of the holes. The left end clamps into the front vise and the right end sets on the dowel or holdfast. You can drill holes in the left leg as well, as shown here, to aid in positioning

Figure 12-6. *This European-style bench has peg holes in the legs and a traveling helper that rides on the top and bottom stretchers to help support long and wide pieces when edge-planing.*

large heavy work before fixing it in the vise, but it is not necessary. This works for pieces long enough to span from leg to leg.

For shorter pieces, some sort of helper (often known as a *deadman, slave,* or *helper boy*) is needed. If you are building your own bench, you can build two stretchers in the front, one low and one high, with runners on them to accommodate a traveling helper, similar to those found on Shaker benches. This is a board 6" to 8" (152mm to 203mm) wide with a series of staggered holes that slides back and forth on the stretchers (Figure 12-6). Some of the holes match the height of those you drilled into the legs. If you do not have the option (or energy) to build or rebuild the legs on your bench, a portable helper can be made, several designs for which exist (Figure 12-7).

Figure 12-7. Bench Slave

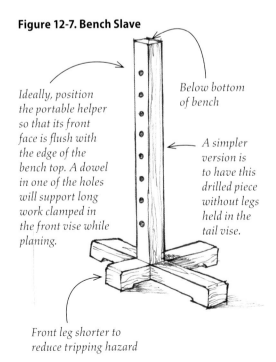

Ideally, position the portable helper so that its front face is flush with the edge of the bench top. A dowel in one of the holes will support long work clamped in the front vise while planing.

Below bottom of bench

A simpler version is to have this drilled piece without legs held in the tail vise.

Front leg shorter to reduce tripping hazard

BENCH DOGS

I have several recommendations for bench dogs. First, get rid of the metal ones that came with the bench. Sooner or later—and probably sooner—your plane blade will find them, often at high speed. Not only does this take enormous chunks out of the edge, but it damages the plane bottom as well.

In addition, this assumes you do not simply set the plane down on one, nicking the blade or dinging the sole. In fact, remove all metal objects from the bench, including other tools, especially when planing, because they tend to knock into one another. Make new dogs out of wood; you can make lots of them and keep one in every hole to save time.

A worthy variation on the bench dog is one that tapers and has a metal point fixed in its face (Figure 12-8). This is particularly useful for shaping or planing stock that must be

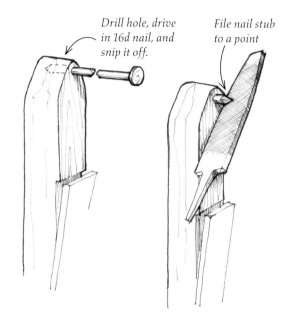

Drill hole, drive in 16d nail, and snip it off.

File nail stub to a point

Figure 12-8. Bench Dog with Tapered Head

rotated as it is worked. The safest variation has a 10d (or bigger) nail bedded in the face of it. Cut the nail off about ¼" (6mm) or so above the surface and file it to a point. If used frequently, the top of the dog will receive wear from the plane. With the metal point bedded only in the face, your plane does not find metal.

A faster way to make this dog is to drive a screw through the back until the point protrudes from the face. If the pieces you are planing are large and you use the dogs infrequently, these will probably serve as well, especially if you use a trim-head screw and countersink the head. I say probably, because, if you end up using the dogs a lot, you can plane the top of the dog down over time and, eventually, nick your blade on the screw head.

Figure 12-9. *Three variations of the shooting board. Left: the sloping ramp extends the wear from cutting thin material over a wider area of the plane blade. Center, the parallel ramp will shoot thicker stock. Both these boards have stops fixed with a sliding dovetail. The shooting board on the right is the down-and-dirty version, with a piece of ¼" (6mm) hardboard creating the ramp and screwed-on stops.*

SHOOTING BOARD

Probably the single most effective accessory for any bench, however, is the shooting board, or its cousin, the bench hook (Figure 12-9). I underestimated the usefulness of this tool for a long time but have gradually become more and more appreciative of its speed and versatility. Its first use is the trimming of ends of pieces, either square (probably most useful) or at a particular angle, such as 45°, done on a shooting board made just for this angle.

Using a shooting board for trimming can greatly increase your accuracy. You can take off the thickness of a shaving, say a few thousandths of an inch with each stroke, giving you incredible accuracy, and because the stop supports the grain at the back of the strip, you do not have to worry about your piece chipping out at the exit side of the cut. (In the next chapter, I detail making and using a shooting board.)

Dimensioning Stock

Before power machinery, this is how woodworkers dimensioned stock nearly every day, sometimes all day. This task was performed this way well into the twentieth century in many parts of the world (and in some parts, I'm sure, still today).

As a notable example, the English Arts and Crafts furniture maker, Edward Barnsley, resisted installing power machines in his shop until the late-1950s, believing machines would change the nature of the work and the craftsman's enjoyment of it, and so continued to surface lumber by hand until that time.

If you have ever done this task before, you will recognize the importance of the variations in the anatomical tactics of the jack, jointer, and smooth planes. Dimensioning stock without the correct setup of these planes is not just difficult—it is nearly impossible. A craftsman certainly could not do this every day, all day, without having developed and understood the required setup for his planes and their sequence of use.

Today, machinery largely spares us the effort of having to bring stock from rough to final dimension by hand. However, sometimes you have to surface boards too large to fit into your machinery. Most often, the jointer is too small.

Using these techniques to flatten one side so it can be put through the planer increases your versatility, allowing you to use lumber you might otherwise have to pass up. Nor does it take as much time and energy as you might first imagine. And then there might come the time when, unable to pass up that certain piece of wood even though it fits in no machine you have, you have no choice but to reveal the beauty of that rough board by the final polishing strokes of your handplane. This is how to do it.

WINDING STICKS

Winding sticks can be any two sticks that are rectangular in section and long enough to lie across the work you are checking. The sticks need to be straight and have the two parallel edges. For checking timber, the sticks do not have to be of great refinement: you can literally grab two sticks out of the scrap pile—they don't even have to be the same width—as long as they are straight and parallel. The longer they are, the greater the accuracy in checking for parallel, as the greater length exaggerates the distortion.

If you want a tool of greater sophistication, you can buy wood or metal ones, or you can make you own. When making your own, the principal is simple enough. Pin two pieces of wood together so they can be separated, plane both edges straight, pull them apart, and check them by holding the edges together up to the light. Any error in straightness doubles. If light shines between the edges at any point, put them back together and plane them until no light is visible when they are held against one another. If the pieces are used in the same orientation as when they are pinned together (make a habit of doing this), it will make no difference, even if a taper has been planed along their length, because the pieces will still be parallel to one another **(Figure 1)**.

To make a set of winding sticks, select two pieces of any stable, well dried wood, preferably quartersawn (mahogany is a good choice, as is white oak), say about 1½" (38mm) wide by ½" (13mm) thick by 18" (457mm) long. Align the two pieces, drill though both near the ends, and insert dowels through both. Glue the dowels to one side only so they can be pulled apart. It is helpful to relieve the inside edges of the ends so you can get your thumbs in to get them apart. Bevel the faces so the reference edges are about ⅛" (3mm) wide, in order to make them easier to read.

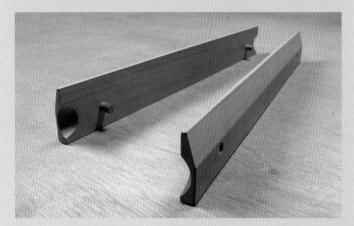

Figure 1. *A matched set of wood winding sticks.*

PREPARING THE FIRST FACE: SCRUB AND JACK PLANES

Before beginning any work, check the piece to be planed for warp, twist, and cupping by sighting down the length and across the width of the board (Figure 12-10). If the distortion is subtle, you may have to use a straight edge and winding sticks to determine where and how much it is warped. You can put notes or marks on the board indicating what needs to be done where, if you want, including scribble marks on the high areas to be planed off. This technique is secondary to the frequent checking of the surface with a straight edge, winding sticks, and the information you will get from the shaving the plane makes.

Figure 12-10. Examine Your Boards

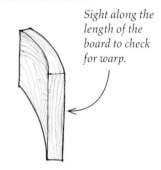

Sight along the length of the board to check for warp.

Sight along the ends of the board to check for cupping.

Sight along the length of the surface of the board to see if the edges of the ends are parallel.

Dog the board onto the bench. Usually, crown-side-up gives better support (you may have to shim one corner) and less chance of splitting out the edges when working. Check for twist and cup with winding sticks (Figure 12-11).

If you do not have a European-style bench with dogs, a work surface with two stops will do: one for the end of the board, and one along side the board to keep the board from shifting sideways when planing diagonally (Figure 12-12). The stops can be tacked, if you do not mind putting tacks in your work surface, or clamped down. Stops must be thinner than the board, and clamps must be well back so you do not hit them when planing. (Wide pieces of plywood clamped from the far side of the bench work well.)

Using a scrub plane, flatten the crown of each end. Work on a slight diagonal, with the grain, to reduce chewing up the wood, as happens when working across the grain (Figure 12-13). Depending on the hardness of the wood and how bad the board is, the scrub plane is set to take a cut about ⅛" (3mm) deep or less.

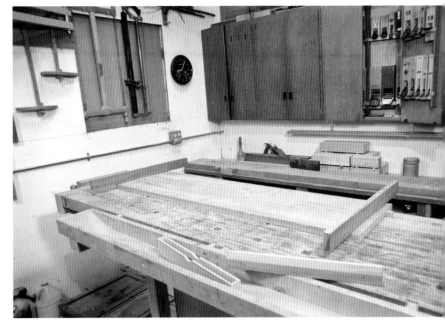

Figure 12-11. *Winding sticks, one at each end of a board to be planed, will help determine twist in the board. Sight from one end of the board, along the tops of the sticks.*

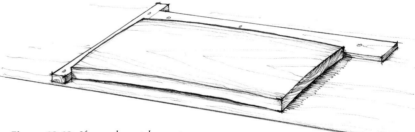

Figure 12-12. *If you do not have stops on your work surface, you can tack or clamp strips of wood or plywood to keep the work from moving around when planing.*

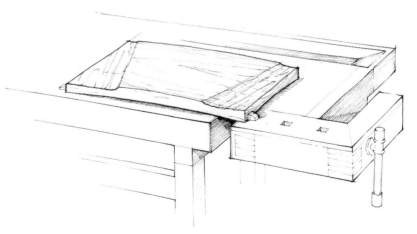

Figure 12-13. *Begin with the scrub plane: Make both ends flat and parallel to one another.*

Figure 12-14. Check for Parallel

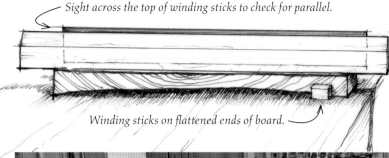

Sight across the top of winding sticks to check for parallel.

Winding sticks on flattened ends of board.

Figure 12-15
Straighten the ends of the boards with the scrub plane and use winding sticks to check that they are parallel.

Place winding sticks on the flats at each end (Figure 12-15) and check for wind (twist), sighting over the tops of the sticks and lowering your line of sight until the top edges are brought nearly together (Figure 12-14). The edges should be parallel. If not, plane the high corners down, keeping the ends flat and straight, until the sticks show parallel.

Once the ends are flat and parallel, the area in between can be lowered to match (Figure 12-16). Starting in the middle (high point of the crown) flatten an area. Repeat, gradually extending the flat area (Figure 12-17). Make consistent, full-width strokes slightly overlapping the same amount each time (Figure 12-18 and 12-19).

Plane across the grain on a diagonal (usually about 45°). This greatly reduces

Figure 12-16. *The area in between the flat and parallel ends can now be leveled to match using the scrub plane.*

Figure 12-17.
Starting at the high point, flatten an area.

Figure 12-18.
Plane the area again, extending it further.

Figure 12-19.
Make repeated passes over the area, each time extending it until it matches the flattened ends of the board.

tearout and splintering of the far side that can happen when removing this much wood. It will also make the planing physically easier. Always work with the grain: for instance, with the board at your right as you stand at the bench ready to plane, start at the left or far end of the board and work toward yourself with each successive stroke stepped further to the right (Figure 12-20). Continue to extend the flat area until it reaches and is even with the leveled ends (Figure 12-21).

Check at several points for flat and wind with winding sticks. Check the length for straight by sighting along it or using a straightedge (Figure 12-22). Correct areas as needed.

Once the board is relatively flat overall,

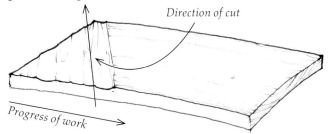

Figure 12-20. Right-Handed Means Start at Left

Direction of cut

Progress of work

Figure 12-21.
Plane the rest of the board down to match the now flat and parallel ends.

Figure 12-22.
Check the progress of the work frequently with a straight edge.

Figure 12-23. *The jack improves the rough texture left by the scrub plane.*

Figure 12-24. *Use a jack plane to remove the ridges left by the scrub plane to further refine the surface.*

Figure 12-25. *The board has been leveled by the jack plane and is ready for the power planer or the jointer plane.*

remove the ridges left by the scrub plane with the jack plane. Work systematically, slightly overlapping each stroke, trying to maintain the flatness left by the scrub plane. Work diagonally as with the scrub plane (Figure 12-23 and 12-24).

Confirm you are done with the jack by checking for wind and straightness. Work any high spots. Once the board tests flat and does not rock when put face down on a flat surface, you can put the board face down into the power planer (Figure 12-25). You are done with the handwork—unless, of course, you do not have a power planer or one big enough to accommodate this board. You will have to change to the jointer plane and continue.

CONTINUING WITH THE JOINTER PLANE

Unlike the jack and scrub planes, the jointer is usually used with the grain (rather than diagonally to it), at least initially. Again, work systematically, carefully overlapping the strokes, starting at one side of the board and working all the way across and back again (Figure 12-26). Try to work all parts of the board equally, planing in the direction of the grain. If you find you have large areas of tearout, reverse the board and see if you get less in that direction.

If you have small areas of tearout, reversing the board probably won't do any good. It's probably a rapid change in direction of the grain and reversing the board will just tear out the other side of the spot where the grain changes direction. If tearout is particularly troublesome, you can back the blade off a bit as the board gets flatter, making a lighter cut (some tearout at this point is acceptable, as the smoother and, if needed, a panel plane will get rid of it).

If tearout is still excessive, once the board is flat, resharpen the blade and go over the surface with a light cut to remove what tearout you can. Periodically check the board for flatness. The fastest way is to use the bottom edge of the jointer against the face of the board, tilting the plane up on its long edge and looking for light between it and the board's surface; these are the low spots (Figure 12-27). Low spots will also manifest as places where the jointer skips cutting. Work the entire surface consistently to bring these into line.

If you have a very wide board or panel, you may have to use the jointer across the grain, until the plane makes a shaving at all areas. High areas may have to be worked diagonally, as with the jack. Finish planing with the jointer by planing with the grain until all areas are cut and the face of the board tests flat.

Figure 12-26. *The jointer removes the texture left by the jack and brings the board to straight and flat.*

Figure 12-27. *You can use the edge of the sole of the jointer as a straight edge to check the work.*

Figure 12-28. *The first of two smoothing planes, here a 70mm (2¾") 40° Japanese plane, is used to smooth the surface left by the jointer on this piece of cherry.*

Figure 12-29. *Final smoothing with a 70mm (2¾") 43° Japanese plane, finely set.*

SMOOTHING THE FIRST FACE

Once the jointer makes a consistent shaving over the entire face and the face tests flat, you can move on to the smoothing plane. My favorite smoothing planes are Japanese, but whatever you have that works for you is fine (Figure 12-28). If using a Japanese-style plane after Western-style planes, as I have shown here, you may have to reverse the board end for end to reduce tearout.

The cut made by the jointer is comparatively coarse, so it may be more expedient to use two smoothing planes, one set coarser to remove the tracks left by the jointer, followed by a fine-set plane to finish (Figure 12-29). Alternatively, you can reset your smoothing plane.

If the surface is prone to tearout, it may be best to use a panel plane—a wide and long smoothing plane with the sole setup as a truing plane—to prepare the surface left by the jointer. (See "The Panel Plane" on page 72.) This will remove much of the tearout left by the jointer while truing the surface even more. The smoothing plane that follows can then be set much finer than it otherwise would be, greatly reducing or eliminating tearout. Sometimes, on difficult pieces, another smoothing or polishing plane may be used after that. This would be your best plane most finely set.

Final smoothing of the first side may be postponed until the second side is ready, to avoid marring the surface of the first while working the second.

PLANING THE EDGES AND SECOND SIDE

Next, either the opposite face or the two edges are done, at your discretion. If the board is being done entirely by hand, often the edges are done next. This reduces the width, leaving less area to surface (that is, less work), and makes it easier to mark the thickness, as the edge is now smooth and not rough-sawn.

If the board is very wide and is to remain close to its rough width, it might be best to surface the second side; the board may have to be cross-planed, and this may splinter out the edges. Do the edges afterward to remove any splintering.

To plane an edge, set the board in the front vise. (If you have a simple planing bench as I have described earlier—see page 220—and have installed a hook on the front for holding boards when shooting, you can use that.) If the edge is badly out of straight, use a jack plane or fore plane to take the high spots off, gradually extending the straight section until it runs the whole length of the board (Figures 12-30 and 12-31).

After the edge has been roughly straightened, shoot the edge with a jointer plane in continuous single passes (Figure 12-32). When the plane makes a continuous full-width shaving, check for square to the flattened face. Correct as necessary.

Once the first edge is done, mark the width with a panel gauge (if you are sawing by hand) and saw the board to width. Cut the width about 1⁄32" (0.8mm) wide if using a table saw, or about 1⁄16" (2mm) wider if sawing by hand,

Figure 12-30.
A fore plane quickly straightens a badly curved edge.

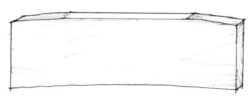

Figure 12-31.
Use a jack or fore plane to initially level a badly curved edge, followed by the jointer to finish.

Figure 12-32.
A jointer plane finesses the edge left by the fore plane.

Figure 12-33.
If you are sawing the width by hand, use a panel gauge to mark the desired width of the board.

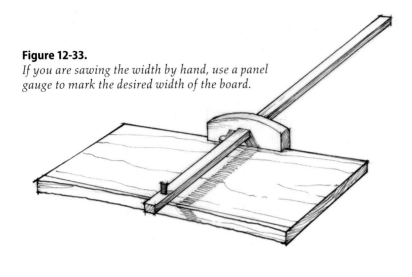

Figure 12-34.
With a marking gauge, mark the desired thickness of the board on all four edges.

Figure 12-35. Completing the Board's Surface

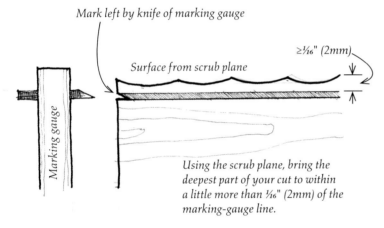

Mark left by knife of marking gauge

Surface from scrub plane

≥¹⁄₁₆" (2mm)

Marking gauge

Using the scrub plane, bring the deepest part of your cut to within a little more than ¹⁄₁₆" (2mm) of the marking-gauge line.

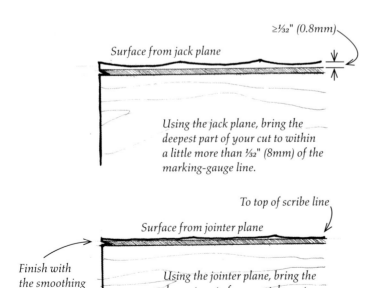

≥¹⁄₃₂" (0.8mm)

Surface from jack plane

Using the jack plane, bring the deepest part of your cut to within a little more than ¹⁄₃₂" (8mm) of the marking-gauge line.

To top of scribe line

Surface from jointer plane

Finish with the smoothing plane right to the point or center of the scribe line.

Using the jointer plane, bring the deepest part of your cut down to the top edge of the scribe line.

depending how good a cut you can make (Figure 12-33). If you've sawn the board by hand, plane the edge down until you are about ¹⁄₃₂" (0.8mm) away from the scribe line. Check for square, correct, and plane to the line. With both edges done, mark the required thickness all around with a marking gauge (Figure 12-34).

Repeat the process used on the first side for the second side, except that the ends do not have to be flattened to test with winding sticks first. Work the entire board, taking extra strokes on the high spots to make the entire second side parallel to the first. Then bring the entire side down to the line (Figure 12-35). This completes the surfacing of the board.

Other Handplane Preparatory Work

Few woodworkers nowadays will be faced with surfacing a board entirely by hand—perhaps only a special board that does not fit in machines. More likely, you will smooth boards prepared by machines, removing snipe and ripples left by the blades. This is usually accomplished by one or two smoothing planes, which can make quick work of machine-made blemishes. Larger pieces would benefit from preparation with a panel plane.

Pieces with difficult grain can be prepared with two planes, the second one set finer than the first to remove any remaining tearout. With tough and hard woods like oak, major imperfections such as snipe can be removed with a plane with a 55° or 60° pitch, followed by a Stanley #80 handled scraper. If imperfections are minor, you can go right to the #80. Follow with a card scraper once over the board. A better plan is to follow the #80 with a scraper plane to take out the slight scallops left by the #80. Once over followed by a light pass with a card scraper usually does it.

Some woods can be planed fast and with little difficulty, and the surface left by the plane is stunning. Others not only are difficult to plane but do not seem to be improved by planing. For these, and for pieces that are less critical, such as shelving, handled scrapers followed by card scrapers, with the plane used here and there to remove a bit of material that might otherwise take too long to remove with a scraper, can be the most efficient approach.

Shooting an Edge

Planing a long edge to straighten it for gluing is called *shooting*. For most people it is one of the most frustrating tasks in woodworking. Having a gentle curve honed into the edge of the blade of the jointer plane can make this task manageable. I like this technique better than any I have tried (see "Techniques for Shooting an Edge," page 236).

To plane an edge straight, focus your attention and energy at the cutting edge. The shaving (eventually) must emerge continuous, full width, unbroken.

At first, most of your energy will be everywhere but at the edge, causing tense muscles, cramped hands and shoulder and back muscles, and quick fatigue. Eventually, your energy will be expended efficiently, with no muscles tensed except for those used to cut the edge, and no motion will be wasted. You will be able to do this all day and feel better at the end of it than you would after sitting at a desk all day.

Practically speaking, the following things must be done:

- The stance must be balanced from the start to the finish of the stroke.
- The work must not be too high or too low. The planed edge at about 34" (86cm) above the ground is good for a person 5' 8" to 5' 10" (1,727mm to 1,778mm) tall; less if you are shorter, more if you are taller.
- The weight on the plane must be on the front at the start of the stroke and the back at the finish, shifting as the stroke progresses.

You can practice holding the front half of the plane at the beginning of the board edge using your left hand only, supporting the weight of the plane cantilevering off the back.

Practice doing the same thing holding the back of the plane with your right hand only, supporting the cantilevered front of the plane off the far end of the board. Practice smoothly shifting your weight while purposely lifting one hand and then the other as the stroke progresses. Every time your plane accidentally dips off the end at the start or the finish of a stroke, practice this weight shift some more.

Techniques for Shooting an Edge

1 One of the main difficulties in shooting an edge occurs when the edge is out of square. With a straight blade, you have to attempt to balance the plane square to the face, literally on the corner of the board, and plane that narrow edge repeatedly at the same angle.

2 You can, as I have seen recommended, clamp two boards together so that even though they are out of square with their faces, they will have the same angle. The boards are then flipped to be joined and their complementary angles zero each other out. There are two big problems with this method:

3 The first problem is that any error in the straightness will be doubled when the boards are joined. To correct the problem, the boards must be unclamped and checked and re-clamped and planed, and unclamped and checked, maybe many more times. The second problem is the boards have to be perfectly re-aligned every time they are re-clamped, or the method will not work at all. This is tedious and time consuming.

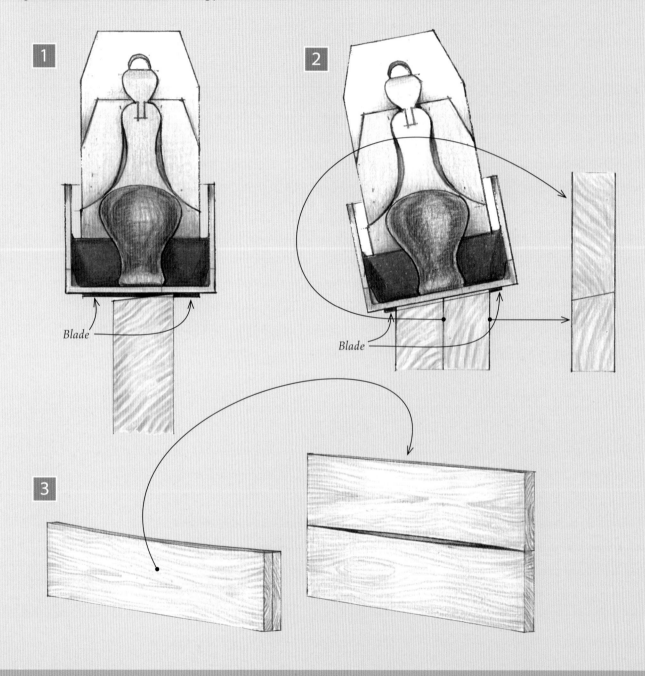

Blade

Blade

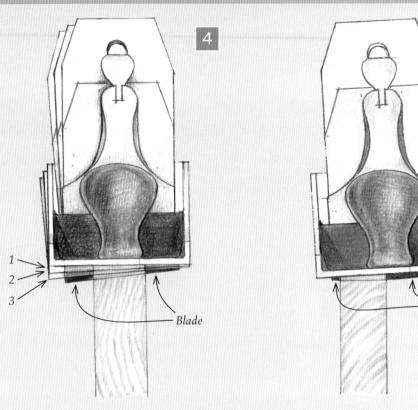

4 5

1
2
3

Blade

Blade

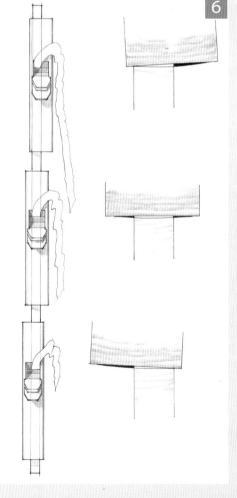

6

4 You can plane one board at a time, marking them to be flipped after planing so the angle of their edges will be complementary when joined, resulting in a flat panel. While you may find you favor one side or another repeatedly, this technique works consistently only when a shooting board is used. Without a shooting board, even if you repeatedly favor one side, this technique has problems. If your plane's straight blade is out of parallel with the sole of the plane, each stroke will increase the error. If you plane one board's edge more than the other, then your angles will not match, and you are back to where we started—correcting the angle on the edge of the board, trying to balance the plane.

5 If you have a bit of a curve to the edge of your 2¾" (70mm)-wide jointer-plane blade, set the sole of the plane flat on the edge. You will not have to balance it and by keeping the plane so that the board is to one side of it or another, you can alter and correct the angle in one or a few strokes. I have been sharpening my blades so they project about ¹⁄₆₄" (0.4mm) over the 2¾" (70mm) width of the blade (which, because of the blade's bedded angle to the sole, is about ¹⁄₃₂", or 0.8mm, of curvature on the blade itself). I find this amount of curve very serviceable.

6 Because using the plane to one side of the board or the other effectively lowers that side, you can even take out a twist in the edge by starting the plane with the board to one side of the plane and finishing with the board on the other. After you have checked for square, make a pass down the board with the plane centered on the edge, repeating until a continuous unbroken full-width shaving emerges, indicating that your edge is now a flat continuous plane.

13

MAKING & USING SHOOTING BOARDS

Invaluable, Often-Overlooked Tools

Did you ever have to trim the length of a piece to fit precisely between two others, such as a panel stop or a frame rail? You carefully make your mark and cut it on the chop saw or table saw, probably a little conservatively. Chances are it is a bit tight. You go back over to the power saw and try to cut that whisker of thickness off. You walk back to the cabinet or frame you are working on and try it. You walk back to the saw again and try to cut another whisker off. You walk back to the work and try it again. You do it repeatedly, with more or less success, over a multitude of pieces. The process is time consuming and frustrating. It is difficult to cut just a few thousandths of an inch off using a power saw to get that exact fit, and on small pieces, it can be dangerous. You ultimately settle for a fit that is not quite as good as you would like.

The stop of this shooting board prevents the end grain of the tenon's shoulder from splitting out as the shoulder plane exits the cut.

Types of Shooting Boards

With the shooting board, you can take the board right to where the work needs to be fit. If the piece to be cut is small, you can mark and cut the piece with a handsaw and clean it up with a plane, right on the shooting board. Take a few thousandths off with a stroke of the plane and check it. Another stroke or three, check, and you are finished.

There is no walking back and forth across the shop, and the piece drops in with an airtight fit. The process is fast and accurate. It works particularly well for fitting drawer parts, where the back, sides, and front can all be sized, to both length and width, exactly to fit the pocket for which they are being made. And, if the bench stop on the underside of the shooting board is cut down to ⅜" (10mm) thick or so, flip it and plane the faces of the drawer parts as well, using that simple stop to plane against, again speeding the work.

A shooting board made at a 45° angle is also useful—indispensable, really—if you are doing miters such as the ends of stops for holding panels or glass within the stiles and rails of a door (Figure 13-1).

Figure 13-1.
A 45° shooting board is indispensable for fine miter work.

A shooting board for 45° trimming was my first shooting board, actually. Years ago, I was trying to fit many stops on several glass doors for a cabinet. Despite setting up consistent jigs for different lengths, quite a number of the stops still needed finessing, resulting in much frustration and lost time.

Later, I mentioned this problem to my uncle, who was a patternmaker, and he sent back a drawing of a shooting board for trimming miters, a device he had used for years. The drawing was enlightening (Figure 13-2). This tool makes trimming pieces to exact length easy and safe, and can be built for trimming at any angle. They are often worth making at that angle if you have many joints to trim.

Another joint that often needs trimming is the face miter—a miter cut across the thickness at the end of a 1x6 or 1x4, for instance, as might be found in a fascia board on a cabinet. This mitered end is too wide for trimming by a plane with the shooting board previously described. Traditionally, variations of a device often called a donkey's ear, miter jack, or miter shooting block were used to help shoot this joint. These always looked to me to be awkward to use, elaborate to make, and expensive to buy—when you could find them.

When using the donkey's ear, because the work is held at an angle to the floor, the length of the piece to be trimmed is limited by the working height off the floor. I developed a simplified version of the traditional shooting board to trim these miters (Figure 13-3).

Because it functions similarly to the classic shooting board, the length of the piece to be trimmed is not limited. Basically, it is a shooting board with the ledge at 45° to the surface upon which the work rests. The edge of this surface and the stop are cut at a complementary 45° to back up the plane cut (Figure 13-4).

You can use any plane on a shooting board, except a rabbet plane, as a rabbet plane will continually cut into the ledge on which it rides. Lower-angle planes—ones with a 45° cutting (blade) angle or less—will work better for cutting end grain. The low-angle Stanley-style block plane is a good candidate, although many woodworkers prefer larger bench planes.

Some planes were made specifically for miter or shooting-board work (called, coincidentally, *miter planes*). And a special wooden plane was sometimes used, fitted with an iron plate at the throat for wear, a skewed blade for a shearing cut, and a handle to hook your hand around mounted at an angle to the work. At one time Stanley made

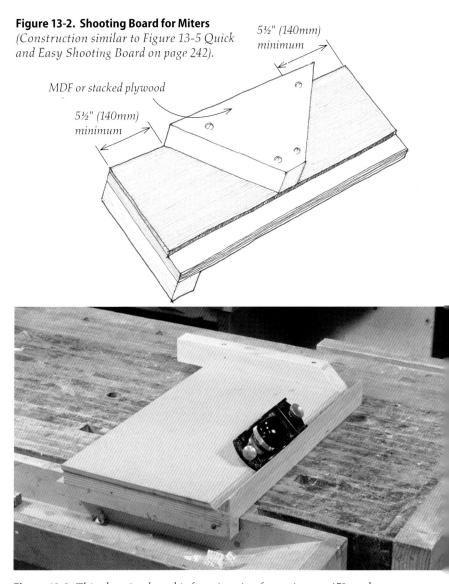

Figure 13-2. Shooting Board for Miters
(Construction similar to Figure 13-5 Quick and Easy Shooting Board on page 242).

5½" (140mm) minimum

MDF or stacked plywood

5½" (140mm) minimum

Figure 13-3. *This shooting board is for trimming face miters: a 45° angle cut across the grain of wide boards.*

Figure 13-4. Shooting Board for Face Miters
(Construction is similar to shooting board (Figure 13-2, above.)

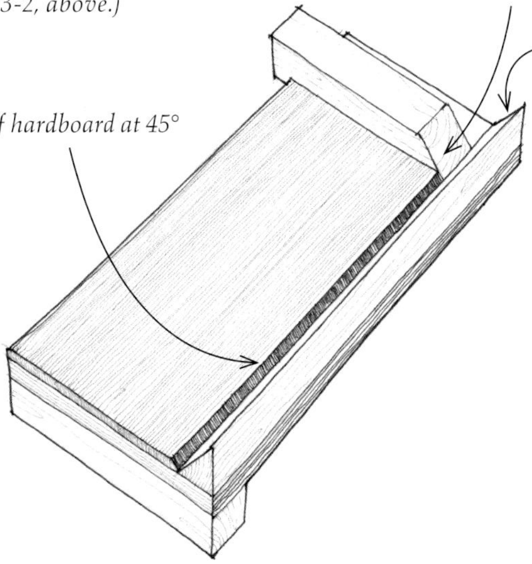

Batten end at 45°

Edge of hardboard at 45°

Rip a strip of hardwood at 45° for the ramp

Figure 13-5.
Quick and Easy Shooting Board

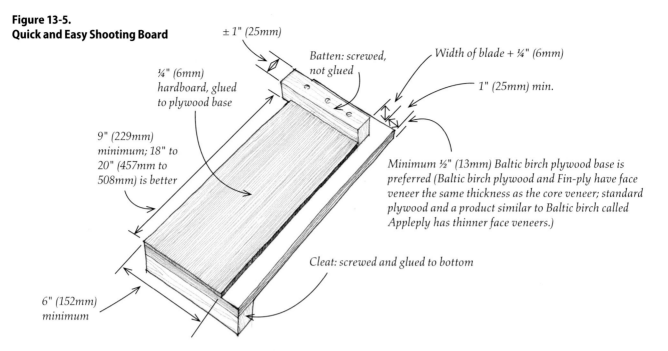

± 1" (25mm)

¼" (6mm)
hardboard, glued
to plywood base

Batten: screwed,
not glued

Width of blade + ¼" (6mm)

1" (25mm) min.

9" (229mm)
minimum; 18" to
20" (457mm to
508mm) is better

Minimum ½" (13mm) Baltic birch plywood base is
preferred (Baltic birch plywood and Fin-ply have face
veneer the same thickness as the core veneer; standard
plywood and a product similar to Baltic birch called
Appleply has thinner face veneers.)

Cleat: screwed and glued to bottom

6" (152mm)
minimum

an iron version of this plane, the #51 that
went with its own iron shooting/miter board.

Heft or extra length is not necessary in a
plane used on the shooting board. The main
requirements are:

- keep the blade sharp—and sharpened
  straight with no curve and adjusted
  parallel to the sole;
- square the sole to the side that runs on
  the ledge; and
- cut lightly with the plane.

In use, the plane touches the workpiece
and the user pushes it the length of the
cut to shear a shaving off. Many first-time
users make the mistake of having the blade
adjusted too far out, causing the plane to stall
in the cut.

The common reaction is to get a running
start with the plane and crash it into the
piece. Do not do this. It is hard on the plane
(and you) and will result in inaccurate work.

Adjust the plane for a light cut. If the plane
doesn't seem to be cutting, make sure the end
of the piece is projecting a fraction past the
stop. The plane may cut only a tiny piece of
the corner at first, but will gradually extend
the cut. You should be able to shear the
shaving off in a smooth push. Admittedly,
however, some cuts will require a bit of
momentum.

On a shooting board, the piece to be planed
is restrained by a stop that also supports the
back edge of the end of the piece, keeping
it from chipping out (Figure 13-5). The end
of this stop can, over time, get worn back,
reducing its chip-restraining ability. Also,
over time, sometimes the stop shifts its
alignment slightly, requiring readjustment.
For these reasons, it is a good idea to make
the stop replaceable.

In order to solve the (rather minor) problem of having to periodically renew the stop, I've fabricated a shooting board using a stop fixed to the board with a tapering, single-sided sliding dovetail friction-fit into place. This piece has extra length so it can be removed, the working end renewed, and the stop tapped back into place.

To extend the wear across more of the blade and the time between sharpenings, and simultaneously reduce blade wear on the one narrow portion of the blade that happens as a result of a running the plane on a parallel ledge, I cut the ledge as along a tapering rabbet, creating a ramp for the plane to ride.

Besides looking better than a piece of hardboard on your bench, it is a good project for learning how to make tapering sliding dovetails. (See "Making a Shooting Board" on page 244.) Tapered sliding dovetail battens are useful in wood construction for keeping wide panels flat. Additionally, the project is a good demonstration of the use of specialty planes.

Figure 13-6. *A shooting board solves all the problems of planing an end-grain edge. You can quickly and easily plane virtually any size board, producing a perfectly straight, square, splinter-free, and consistent-looking edge, not to mention continuous transparent shavings—but only if the plane is properly sharpened and set.*

SHOOTING END GRAIN

No matter what kind of plane you use to smooth the end of a board, you will have to do one of two things to keep the sides from splintering out: you will have to back up the cut when making a stroke the full width of the board, or you will have to plane in from either side.

In the first instance, you can put the board in a vise and clamp a block of wood the same thickness to one side of the board to restrain the grain from splintering. I personally find this tedious and slow going, and oftentimes the board is too long to be stood up in the vise and must be put at some awkward angle. It also does not guarantee the end will be square, either to the sides or to the face.

Planing in from both ends (the second method) tends to leave a slight hump in the middle where the plane strokes meet, though this can be avoided with care. It also leaves a different pattern on the end grain from the two different planing directions, which takes more sanding to remove than when the end grain is planed from a single direction. Again, it does not guarantee the end will be square.

The most expeditious method for smoothing the ends of a board is to use a shooting board. You can plane the end of a board from one direction avoiding irregularities. The stop you plane against keeps the side from splintering out. There is no tedious clamping. You are not limited in the length of board you work on. Your width is limited only by the size of your shooting board. While it does take some user input, the shooting board almost guarantees a square and straight end (Figure 13-6).

Making a Shooting Board

1&2 There are two forms of the standard 90° shooting board. The first **(Figure 1)** has a parallel ramp for the plane, which allows for planing thick pieces of wood. The second **(Figure 2)** has a sloping ramp. While the slope reduces the thickness of the pieces of wood it handles, the blade wear spreads across a wider area.

3 & 4 Prepare stock for your shooting board. For the base, use a piece at least 7" wide by 12" to 24" long (178mm by 305mm to 610mm). The shorter length is a little more convenient to move around and store. The longer length allows you to do wider and longer pieces, such as drawer parts, but puts you working at the far side of the bench because the stop is 20"+ (508mm+) away from you. Do not make the shooting board longer than your bench is wide. Use any species of wood as long as it is dry and has stopped moving, though using rift or quartersawn stock provides the best stability.

For the parallel-ledge version, the board needs to be at least ¾" (19mm) thick. For the sloping ramp version, it should be at least 1" (25mm) thick. Determine the cross-sectional dimensions of the stops, or battens, from the information in **Figures 3** and **4**. Mill these and cut them 2" or 3" (51mm or 76mm) longer than the board is wide. This will give you extra length to correct the fit if needed and to repair the end of the stop as it wears over time. It also does not hurt to make an extra one or two of these.

The shooting boards shown are for right-handers. If you are left-handed, you will probably want the ledge or ramp on the left. If you want to use a pull plane—and are right-handed—you will also want a left-handed ramp, though you will use the shooting board with the ramp on the right, the board hooked over the far side of the bench.

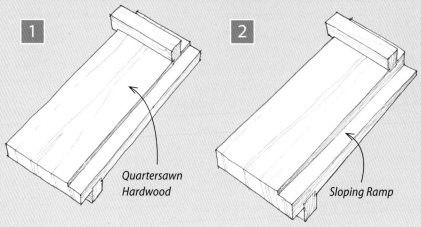

Quartersawn Hardwood

Sloping Ramp

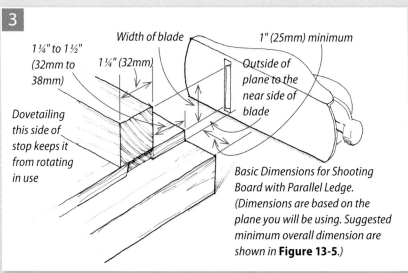

Width of blade

1¼" to 1½" (32mm to 38mm)

1¼" (32mm)

1" (25mm) minimum

Outside of plane to the near side of blade

Dovetailing this side of stop keeps it from rotating in use

*Basic Dimensions for Shooting Board with Parallel Ledge. (Dimensions are based on the plane you will be using. Suggested minimum overall dimension are shown in **Figure 13-5**.)*

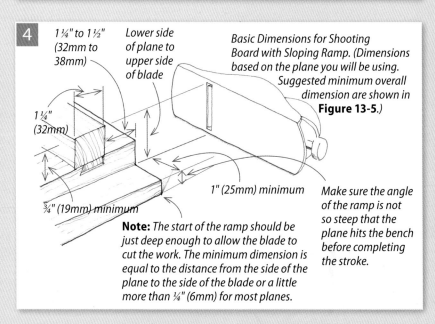

1¼" to 1½" (32mm to 38mm)

Lower side of plane to upper side of blade

*Basic Dimensions for Shooting Board with Sloping Ramp. (Dimensions based on the plane you will be using. Suggested minimum overall dimension are shown in **Figure 13-5**.)*

1¼" (32mm)

1" (25mm) minimum

¾" (19mm) minimum

Note: *The start of the ramp should be just deep enough to allow the blade to cut the work. The minimum dimension is equal to the distance from the side of the plane to the side of the blade or a little more than ¼" (6mm) for most planes.*

Make sure the angle of the ramp is not so steep that the plane hits the bench before completing the stroke.

Notes:

• Always reference off one face and one edge that you are sure are straight, flat, and square to each other. The reference edge should also be the edge upon which the ramp will be formed.

• The narrow end of the tapered dovetail is at the ramp side. The taper allows you to cut off and clean up the end of a stop that has been worn over time and then plane a stroke or two (literally) off the back of the stop to advance it to the correct position when it is tapped back into place.

• In laying out the dovetails, some lines are cut lines, and some lines are layout lines used to derive the cut lines. It is helpful (and more accurate) to use a scribe or marking knife for the cut lines, and pencil for the layout (non-cut) lines. Pencil allows you to erase the layout lines for correction or for clarity.

1. Begin by laying out and cutting the batten that will be the stop against which work is trimmed.

2. Measure and mark the distance of the batten from the end of the board 1½" (38mm).

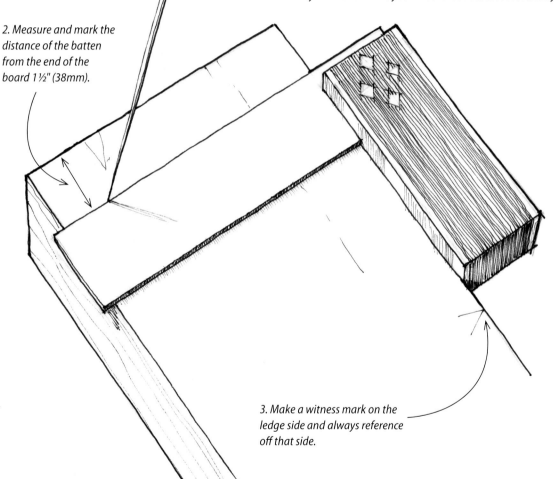

3. Make a witness mark on the ledge side and always reference off that side.

MAKING A SHOOTING BOARD *(continued)*

6 Place the batten on the marked line and carefully mark the width. Err on the side of narrower.

7 Mark the batten width precisely with a sharp pencil.

8 Continue the marks around the edges of the board. They need not extend all the way across the edges. Continue the pencil mark.

9 Mark the depth of the dovetail—about ¼" (6mm), or the same as the step-down of the ledge, if you are making a parallel ledge.

10 Take a bevel gauge and set it to the angle of your dovetail plane.

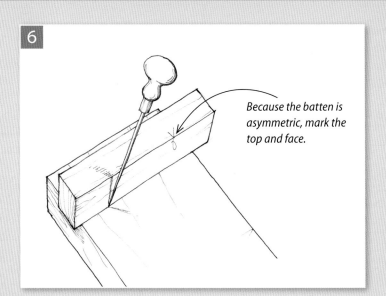

Because the batten is asymmetric, mark the top and face.

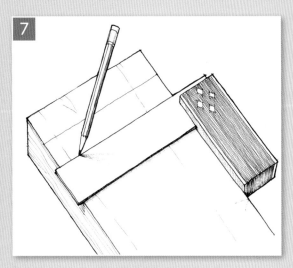

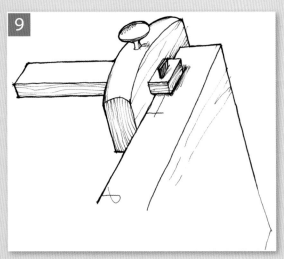

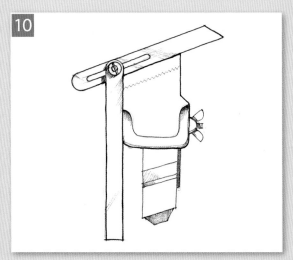

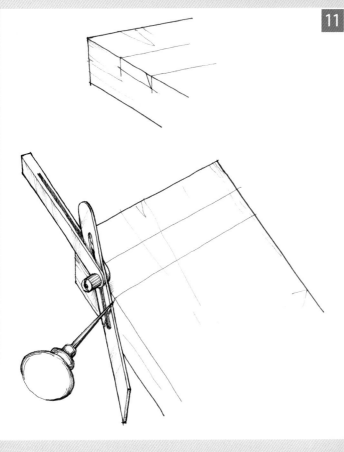

11 Transfer the angle you measured in Figure 10 to the edge of the board at the precise intersection of the mark for the bottom of the dovetail (marking gauge line) and the width of the batten (pencil line). Err on the side of a narrower dovetail.

12 Mark a line (in pencil) square across the face of the board connected to the dovetail angle line.

13 Make a mark on the ramp side ⅛" up from the pencil line. With a straightedge, scribe a line from the dovetail mark on the edge opposite the ramp side to the ⅛" (3mm) mark on the ramp side. This is the taper of the dovetail. (Note: the amount of taper is not critical. However, if you have too much, the batten knocks loose easily. If you have too little, the requirements for matching the angle of the taper exactly, and its width, escalate geometrically.)

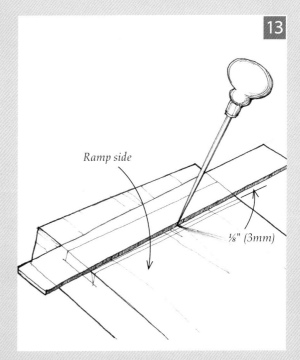

Ramp side

⅛" (3mm)

MAKING A SHOOTING BOARD *(continued)*

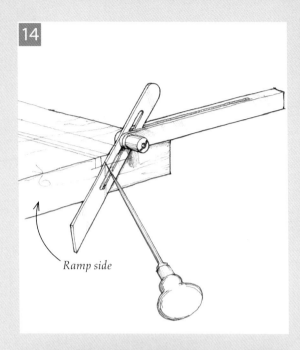

Ramp side

14 Mark the dovetail angle on the edge of the board from the taper line on the face.

15 Make up a guide block at least as long as the width of the board (if you make it longer, you can use it for other projects later), and at least 1" (25mm) thick, with one edge ripped square, the other at the angle of the dovetail (the same angle as your dovetail plane). Clamp the edge of the guide precisely on the scribe line, and to the outside of what will be the dovetail groove, so that you will be cutting into the waste. Use the square edge of the guide on the cut toward the end of the board, because this cut is square.

16 Using a Japanese *ázebiki* (mortise) saw in contact with the guide, make a sawcut the full depth of the groove as marked, square to the surface of the board, and extending the full width of the board. Normally, the crosscut teeth are used, as this cut is across the grain. Sometimes, however, if the teeth load too fast, it may be preferable to use the rip teeth. Stop frequently to clear the gullets of the saw. To improve accuracy, keep a light pressure on the saw against the guide with your other hand. The *ázebiki* saw is ideally suited for this job. You can use a Western back saw that's big enough to clear everything, but I think you will find the shallower teeth of the back saw load quicker; it is harder to keep the full length of the back saw's blade on the guide block. You can use a sliding dovetail saw, also called a stairbuilders saw, but I find it is difficult to be accurate with it, and the results are rough.

17 Reclamp for the second cut, using the dovetail-angle side of the guide. Set the guide precisely on the scribed taper line, with the angle of its edge oriented the same as the marked flair of the dovetail. Cut into the *waste side* of the scribed line, to the full depth of the cut, and extending the full width of the board. Make a clean start (very important) by keeping pressure against the guide board.

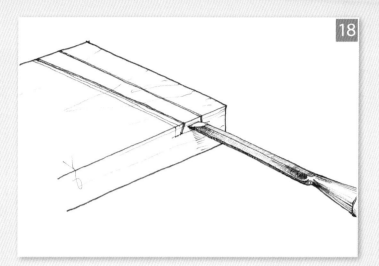

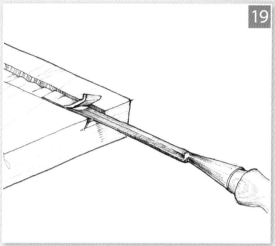

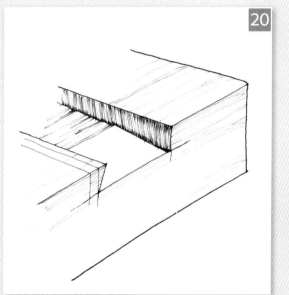

18 Clear most of the waste with a chisel, taking small amounts at a time to avoid breaking out the wood below the scribe line on the edge of the board.

19 Work in from both sides to avoid splitting out at the ends.

20 Clear the waste to within about 1/16" (2mm) of the bottom. Carefully pare in from each end down to the scribed depth line for about 3/4" (19mm) from the edge of the board into the groove.

21 Adjust the router plane to just take the high spots off the remaining waste. Clean the waste, and then lower the blade and shave away more waste. Continue until the bottom of the groove is completely level and at the precise depth of the scribe line.

22 Inspect the groove. Sight down it to see if the sides are straight. Check also that the bottom corners are clean. Clean these up if required.

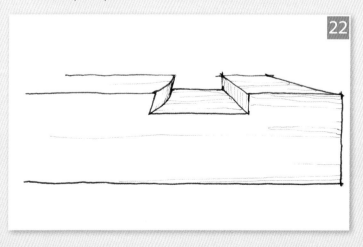

MAKING A SHOOTING BOARD *(continued)*

23

1. Use a side-rabbet plane to straighten up sides that are uneven or curved. While you can use a Japanese-style side rabbet plane as shown here, the Stanley-style side rabbet plane is effective also. (See "Side-Rabbet Planes" on page 116).

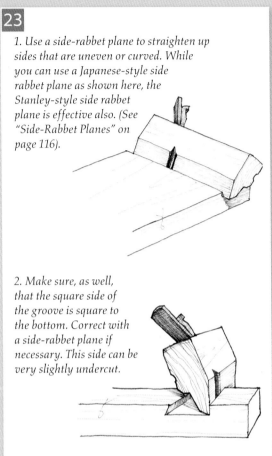

2. Make sure, as well, that the square side of the groove is square to the bottom. Correct with a side-rabbet plane if necessary. This side can be very slightly undercut.

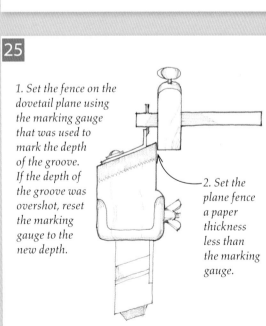

24

2. Then mark the taper, starting at the mark for the board width, tapering toward the ramp end of the batten. This can be marked in pencil.

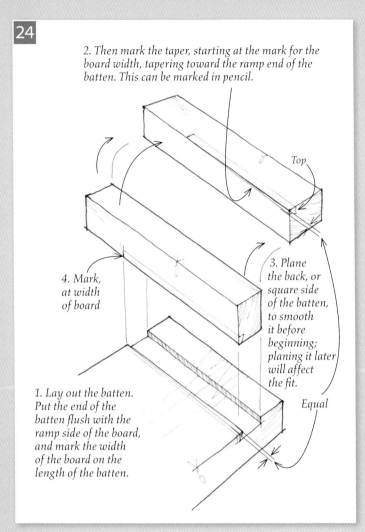

Top

4. Mark, at width of board

3. Plane the back, or square side of the batten, to smooth it before beginning; planing it later will affect the fit.

Equal

1. Lay out the batten. Put the end of the batten flush with the ramp side of the board, and mark the width of the board on the length of the batten.

25

1. Set the fence on the dovetail plane using the marking gauge that was used to mark the depth of the groove. If the depth of the groove was overshot, reset the marking gauge to the new depth.

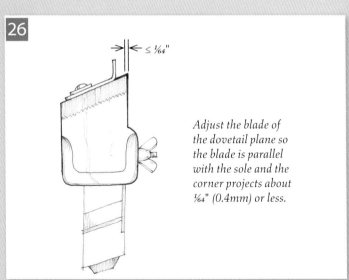

2. Set the plane fence a paper thickness less than the marking gauge.

26

$\leq \frac{1}{64}"$

Adjust the blade of the dovetail plane so the blade is parallel with the sole and the corner projects about $\frac{1}{64}"$ (0.4mm) or less.

27 Clamp the batten in a vise or a handscrew clamp clamped to the bench, so it projects enough for the plane's fence to clear. With the plane held vertical (that is, not tilted) and the fence against the batten, make a short stroke at the narrow end of the tapered dovetail. Make repeated short strokes to establish a cut parallel to the marked taper line.

28 Once the cut is established parallel to the marked taper line, make precise full stokes of the plane to lengthen the cut until it is within about 1/16" (2mm) of the line and parallel to it.

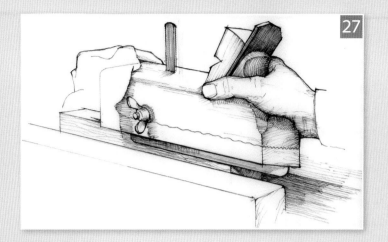

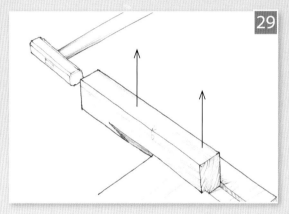

29 Tap the batten in until it stops moving. Pull up at the front and then at the back of the batten. If it lifts at the front, the taper is too narrow there. If it lifts at the back, it is too narrow there. Visually inspect the joint as well. If the joint taps in tight but shows gaps at both ends, either the batten tenon or the groove is curved, or both are. Remove the batten by tapping it back out and sight down the parts to determine what to adjust: Correct a curve in the length of the groove with a side rabbet plane. Correct a curve in the length of the tenon with the dovetail plane. Note: except for correcting for straight, no work is done on the groove when fitting the dovetail of the batten. Do all work on the batten with the dovetail plane.

30 Put the batten back in the vise and plane the dovetail, gradually extending the cut until it runs the full length. Take no more than three or four strokes before checking the fit. If your taper matched that of the groove, take full-length strokes from the batten, trying to maintain parallel.

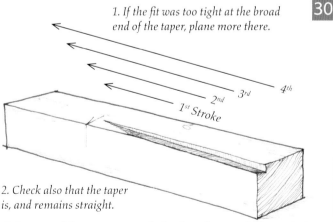

1. If the fit was too tight at the broad end of the taper, plane more there.

4th
3rd
2nd
1st Stroke

2. Check also that the taper is, and remains straight.

3. Because of the geometry, each shaving advances the batten in its slot quite a bit. A heavy shaving could advance the batten almost 1/8" (3mm) or more. So check the fit every 3 or 4 strokes—or less. When you are within about an inch of the end, check every 2 or 3 strokes. Make sure, however, on each trial that the taper is parallel by lifting the ends.

MAKING A SHOOTING BOARD *(continued)*

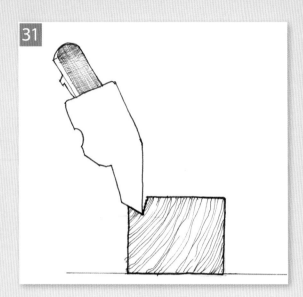

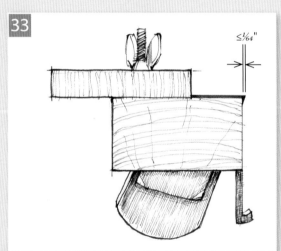

31 If the dovetail plane was miss-set, correct the steps with the side rabbet plane.

32 At each trial fit, use a small hammer or mallet to lightly tap the batten into place. (Remember to keep a strong downward pressure on the batten with your other hand as you tap it in to keep it from riding up). Stop when the batten stops moving. When it is snug just at the far edge of the board, you are done. If you overshoot it—that is why the batten is over long—you can trim it to fit. If, however, you run out of length, you will have to make another batten. Next, flip the board over and fit the other batten. This second batten will be on the underside and will hook against the front edge of the bench or work surface in use, keeping the board from scooting across the bench. It can also be placed in the front vise to hold it even more securely.

33 To cut the ledge upon which the plane will run, set up the fillister-plane fence to an inch or more from the side of the plane. Set the blade parallel to the sole, projecting out the side about ¼" (0.4mm) or less. If you are making a shooting board with a parallel ledge, you can cut the ledge with a table saw or router. It can be cleaned up with the rabbet plane. If you are making a shooting board with a sloping ramp it is surprisingly fast to cut it with a fillister plane, especially when you start trying to figure out the jigging required to make the cut with a power tool—it is safer and quieter, too. It is a bit of vigorous work, but you can make this cut in less than five minutes. I know you have already spent that amount of time trying to figure out how to jig the cut for a power tool.

34 To plane the sloping ramp, remove the battens from the board. Begin at the face-batten end to establish the angle of the ramp. Work back from this end, gradually lengthening the stroke. Try to keep the ramp face, from rabbet edge to board edge, parallel to the face of the board.

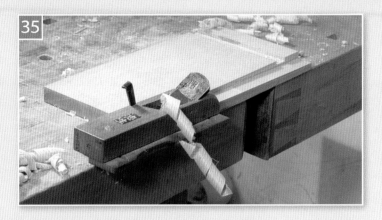

35 Ideally, your plane should be able to cut down the ramp rather than up, as shown here. This should reduce the chance of tearout. However, I have only one fillister plane, and usually experience no problem using it uphill, into the grain, when necessary.

36 The ramp angle completed.

37 When the angle of the ramp is complete, check the surface for parallel to the face of the board by putting a square on each surface and seeing if the blades are parallel. Check every 3" or 4" (76mm or 102mm) along the length. Reset the fillister plane to a finer depth of cut and correct the ramp, section by section, if necessary. End by taking one long finishing stroke with the plane.

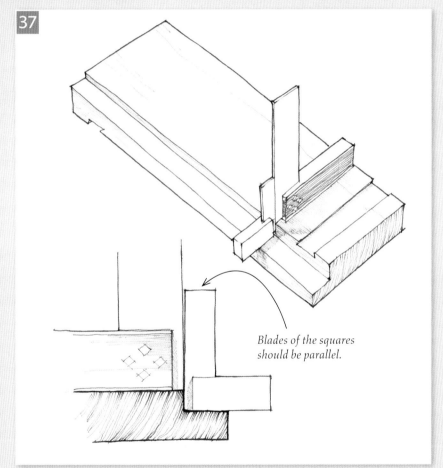

Blades of the squares should be parallel.

MAKING A SHOOTING BOARD *(continued)*

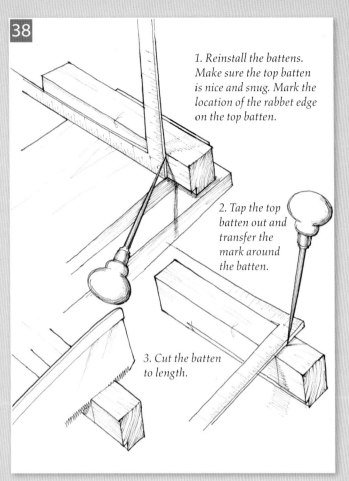

38

1. Reinstall the battens. Make sure the top batten is nice and snug. Mark the location of the rabbet edge on the top batten.

2. Tap the top batten out and transfer the mark around the batten.

3. Cut the batten to length.

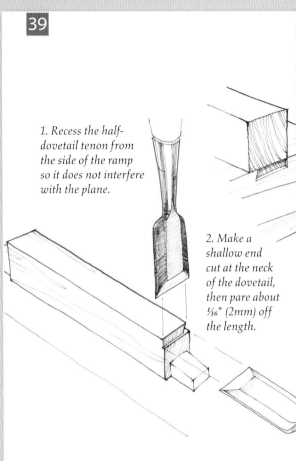

39

1. Recess the half-dovetail tenon from the side of the ramp so it does not interfere with the plane.

2. Make a shallow end cut at the neck of the dovetail, then pare about 1/16" (2mm) off the length.

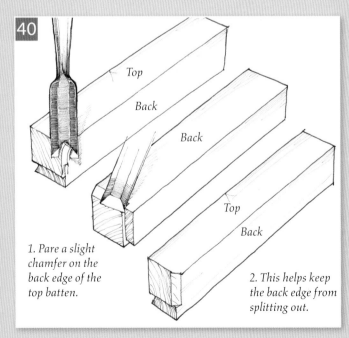

40

Top

Back

Back

Top

Back

1. Pare a slight chamfer on the back edge of the top batten.

2. This helps keep the back edge from splitting out.

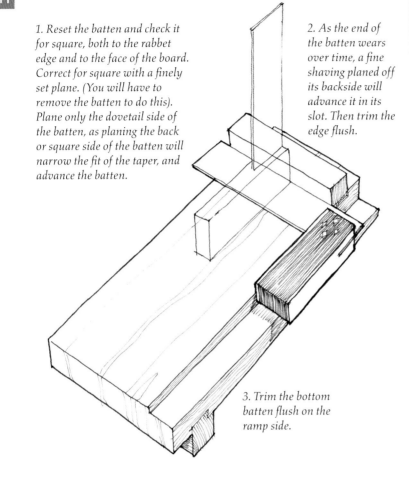

41

1. Reset the batten and check it for square, both to the rabbet edge and to the face of the board. Correct for square with a finely set plane. (You will have to remove the batten to do this). Plane only the dovetail side of the batten, as planing the back or square side of the batten will narrow the fit of the taper, and advance the batten.

2. As the end of the batten wears over time, a fine shaving planed off its backside will advance it in its slot. Then trim the edge flush.

3. Trim the bottom batten flush on the ramp side.

42 The completed shooting board. A shooting board with a tapering ramp spreads the wear on the blade from trimming thin stock over a greater area, extending time between sharpenings.

14

MAKING &
MODIFYING PLANES
Expanding Your Options

A little more than a hundred years ago—and still today in some places—woodworkers were expected to make their own handplanes. For a woodworker today, making your own planes allows you to customize your tools to specific criteria and not be limited by what is available commercially. Your planes can be larger or smaller, with blade angles, widths, and lengths more appropriate to the work you are doing.

This chapter gives you instructions for a full set of wood-body planes in the Western tradition, planes ideally suited for work on the hardwoods we most often encounter. In addition, there are instructions for making Japanese-style planes, which (at least in the smaller sizes) are quicker to make, as well as very effective and versatile. I have included some modifications you can make to planes you may already have that will improve their performance.

Some of the planes made in this chapter. From the left: a fore plane, a jointer plane, a panel plane, a 50° coffin-sided smoothing plane, and a 55° coffin-sided smoothing plane.

Making Traditional Wood-body Planes

Based on traditional wooden planes still found in Europe and North America, the planes in this set are familiar to many. The lengths, blade angles, and blade widths are intended for use on moderately sized work in hardwoods. I have chosen to do a set of planes in this style not only because it is more familiar to the majority of readers, but also because it more clearly demonstrates the relationship of blade angle, width, and shape, to the length and function of the plane.

It also allows the use of full-length blades—avoiding what I consider a shortcoming in the Krenov-style plane and giving you the option of using either antique tapered, parallel, or modern blades. While an entire set of planes is shown here, giving you some economy of manufacture, you do not have to make the whole set. You can make whichever ones you feel are useful to the type of work you do, and, of course, you can modify them as you see fit.

The planes are made using a hollow-chisel mortiser to cut the blade bed and chipwell—either an attachment mounted in a drill press (which is affordable, assuming you have a drill press) or a large floor-model mortiser, which not too long ago was an uncommon tool, but recently has become readily available. A table-mounted mortiser, unfortunately, will probably not have the capacity under the chisel. Larger planes require more clearance, so check the capacity of your machines. A drill-press attachment has more vertical capacity, because you can lower the table. The jigs used for mortising cuts are the same for either machine.

This design uses a cross pin with a bearing plate and wedge, rather than tapered abutments and a wedge, for fixing the blade. The former is a little easier to fit than the latter, and though the chip well is more constricted, it is sufficient. Most varieties of chipbreakers—except the Bailey-style chipbreaker—can be used with this system. The Bailey-style's hump interferes with the wedge. All planes are fitted with a moveable sole plate to simplify long-term maintenance and getting a tight mouth.

The set I am building consists of a jack plane, fore plane, jointer plane, panel plane, and two smoothers. Inclusion of a fore plane, an unusual plane today, makes it easier to prepare large boards. (Boards too large to fit into your power jointer are the only ones you would probably consider doing by hand.)

Its length, 18" (457mm), and blade curvature, about $\frac{1}{32}$" (0.8mm), bridges the gap between the jack and jointer planes, and, as well, allows the curvature of the jointer's blade to be reduced to about $\frac{1}{64}$" (0.4mm) or less for use mainly to prepare edge joints. The jack and fore planes are both in the razee style to reduce weight. The jointer has a full block for better feedback as to its angle on the edge of a board when edge-jointing.

The 12" (305mm) panel plane is included to more speedily prepare and smooth a surface after the 24" (610mm) jointer and before one of the two 8" (203mm) smooth planes. On most jobs, the surface it leaves will be all the planing you will have to do. It may be your most used plane.

The two smooth planes, one at 50°, the other at 55°, handle a range of hardwoods. The blade angles of the other planes step up to that of the smoothers: The jack plane's blade is bedded at 43°; the fore plane's at 45°; the jointer's at 47½°; and the panel plane's at 47½°. The blade width also progresses to facilitate the job each plane has to do.

MATERIALS

Have your blades in-hand before you start, as some antique blades come in sizes not made currently. For instance, I had both a 2¼" (57mm)-wide blade for the panel plane, and 2½" (64mm)-wide blade for the fore plane available. You can also find 2¾" (70mm)-wide antique blades for your jointer plane.

For a set of full size planes as shown here, your choices for blade width could range as follows:

- **jack:** 1¾" (44mm) (commonly available) or 1⅞" (48mm) (German blade size);
- **fore:** 2⅜" (60mm) (modern) or 2½" (64mm) wide (antique);
- **jointer:** 2⅝" (67mm) (modern) or 2¾" (70mm) (antique), though 2⅜" (60mm) is also a possibility;
- **panel:** 2" (51mm) (modern) or 2¼" (57mm) (antique); and
- **smoothing:** 2" (51mm).

In this set, for the:

- **jack plane:** a 1¾" (44mm) wide Hock A2 cryo blade with a Lie-Nielsen chipbreaker.
- **fore plane:** a 2½" (64mm)-wide antique cast-steel blade with chipbreaker.
- **jointer:** a 2⅝" (67mm)-wide Clifton forged blade with a Lie-Nielsen chipbreaker.
- **panel plane and the two smoothers:** antique blades and chipbreakers 2¼" (57mm)-wide, and 2"-(51mm) wide, respectively.

As a general recommendation, you could use good quality antique blades on all the planes. Alternatively, use:

- tungsten-vanadium, chrome vanadium, or A2 blades on the jack;
- A2 blades on the fore plane and jointer; and
- a good carbon-steel forged blade on the panel and smoothers. (Chapters 2 and 4 discuss blade steel at length. Chapter 3 discusses chipbreakers.)

Begin by selecting your stock. Beech has been the preferred wood for this style of plane. Birch was also commonly used in the United States. Thick stock in beech is difficult to find. Birch is far more available. Oak, walnut, cherry, and mahogany are also possibilities. Oak, a tougher wood than the other choices, grips the blade well but is often subject to severe internal cracking from the drying process. I do not recommend maple. Maple is hard and dense but does not grip the blade well. Select the pieces so you can get a true quartersawn blank 2¾" (70mm) thick

Figure 14-1. Jack Plane

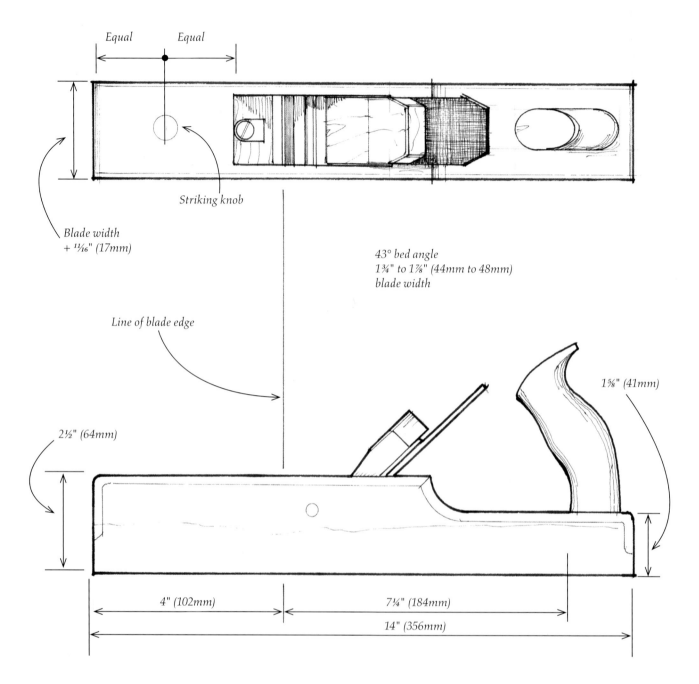

Equal   *Equal*

Striking knob

Blade width + ¹¹⁄₁₆" (17mm)

*43° bed angle
1¾" to 1⅞" (44mm to 48mm)
blade width*

Line of blade edge

1⅝" (41mm)

2½" (64mm)

4" (102mm)   *7¼" (184mm)*

14" (356mm)

Figure 14-2. Jack Plane—Details

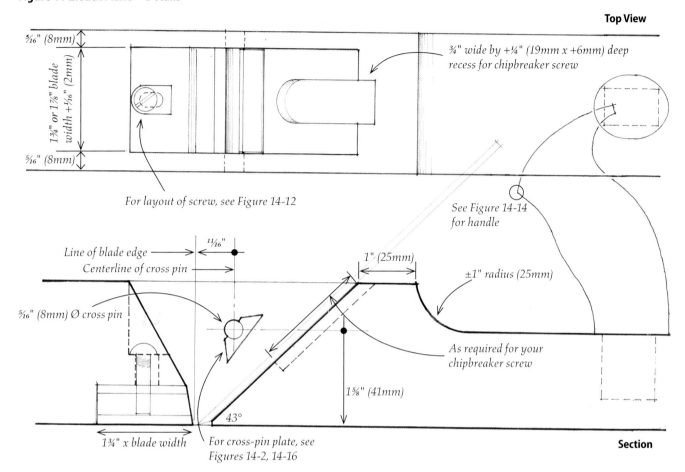

⁵⁄₁₆" (8mm)

1¾" or 1⅞" blade width +¹⁄₁₆" (2mm)

⁵⁄₁₆" (8mm)

¾" wide by +¼" (19mm x +6mm) deep recess for chipbreaker screw

For layout of screw, see Figure 14-12

See Figure 14-14 for handle

Line of blade edge

¹¹⁄₁₆"

Centerline of cross pin

1" (25mm)

±1" radius (25mm)

⁵⁄₁₆" (8mm) Ø cross pin

As required for your chipbreaker screw

1⅝" (41mm)

43°

1¾" x blade width

For cross-pin plate, see Figures 14-2, 14-16

Section

by the width of the blade, plus ¹³⁄₁₆" (21mm). Do a cutlist from the drawings for the planes you are making (Figures 14-1 though 14-16), rough-mill your blanks, and let them settle (stickered) for at least a week, though six months is better (Figure 14-17). Also at this time, mill and glue up the sole-plate blank (see "Fitting a Moveable Sole Plate" on page 309) so the glue will be thoroughly dry by the time you want to use it (three or four days, at least). After the blanks have settled for as long as you can let them, mill them down to within ¹⁄₁₆" (2mm) of their final dimension and let them rest again. Finally, square up the blanks one last time and bring them to ¹⁄₃₂" (0.8mm) or so of their final dimension (Figure 14-18).

Figure 14-3. Fore Plane

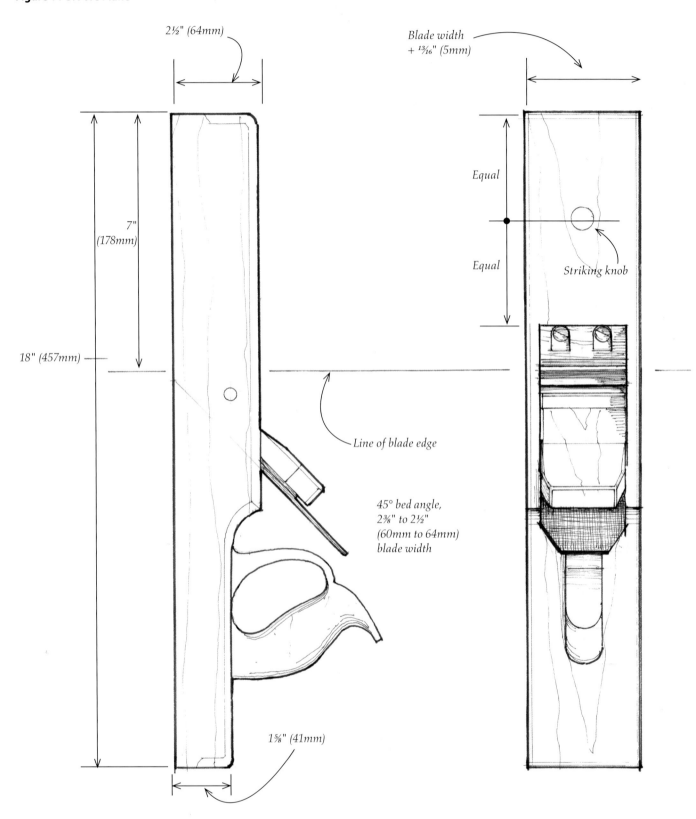

2½" (64mm)

Blade width
+ ¹³⁄₁₆" (5mm)

7"
(178mm)

Equal

Equal

Striking knob

18" (457mm)

Line of blade edge

45° bed angle,
2⅜" to 2½"
(60mm to 64mm)
blade width

1⅝" (41mm)

Figure 14-4. Fore Plane—Details

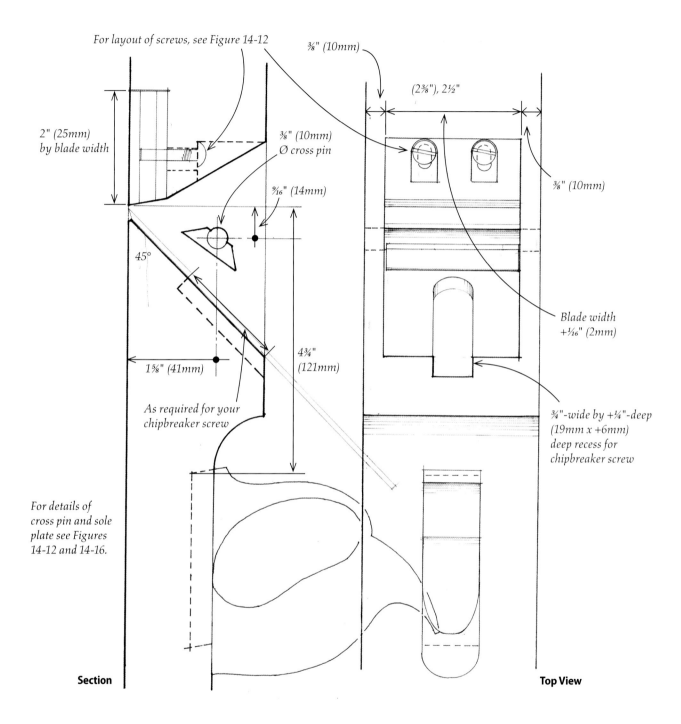

For layout of screws, see Figure 14-12

⅜" (10mm)

(2⅜"), 2½"

2" (25mm) by blade width

⅜" (10mm) Ø cross pin

⁹⁄₁₆" (14mm)

⅜" (10mm)

45°

Blade width +¹⁄₁₆" (2mm)

4¾" (121mm)

1⅝" (41mm)

As required for your chipbreaker screw

¾"-wide by +¼"-deep (19mm x +6mm) deep recess for chipbreaker screw

For details of cross pin and sole plate see Figures 14-12 and 14-16.

Section

Top View

Figure 14-5. Jointer Plane

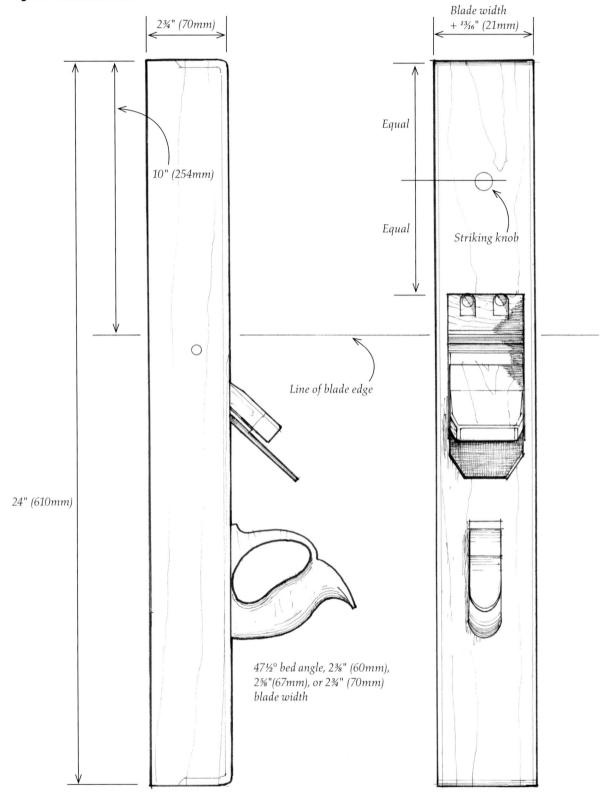

2¾" (70mm)

10" (254mm)

24" (610mm)

Line of blade edge

47½° bed angle, 2⅜" (60mm),
2⅝"(67mm), or 2¾" (70mm)
blade width

Blade width
+ ¹³⁄₁₆" (21mm)

Equal

Equal

Striking knob

Figure 14-6. Jointer Plane—Details

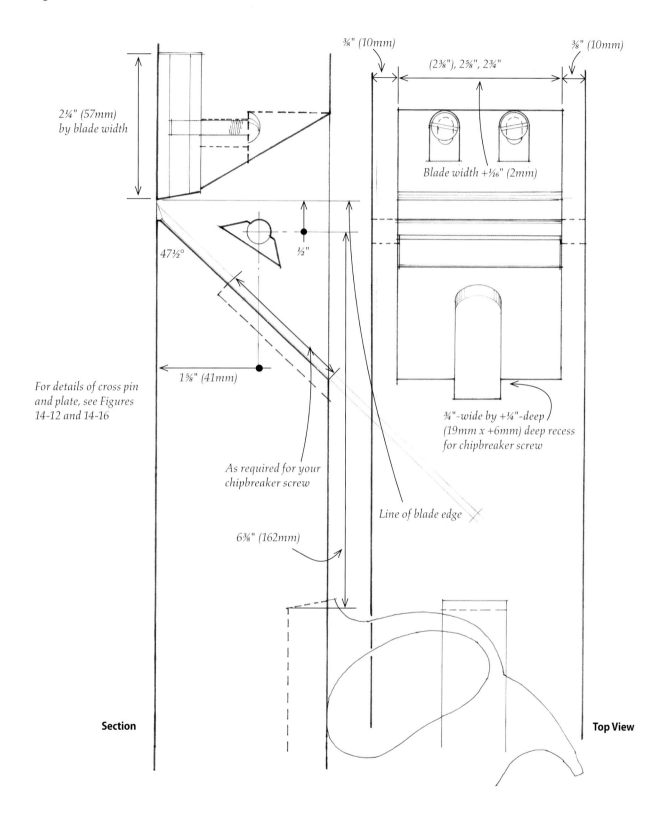

2¼" (57mm)
by blade width

¾" (10mm)

(2⅜"), 2⅝", 2¾"

¾" (10mm)

Blade width +1/16" (2mm)

47½°

½"

For details of cross pin
and plate, see Figures
14-12 and 14-16

1⅝" (41mm)

¾"-wide by +¼"-deep
(19mm x +6mm) deep recess
for chipbreaker screw

As required for your
chipbreaker screw

Line of blade edge

6⅜" (162mm)

Section

Top View

Figure 14-7. Panel Plane

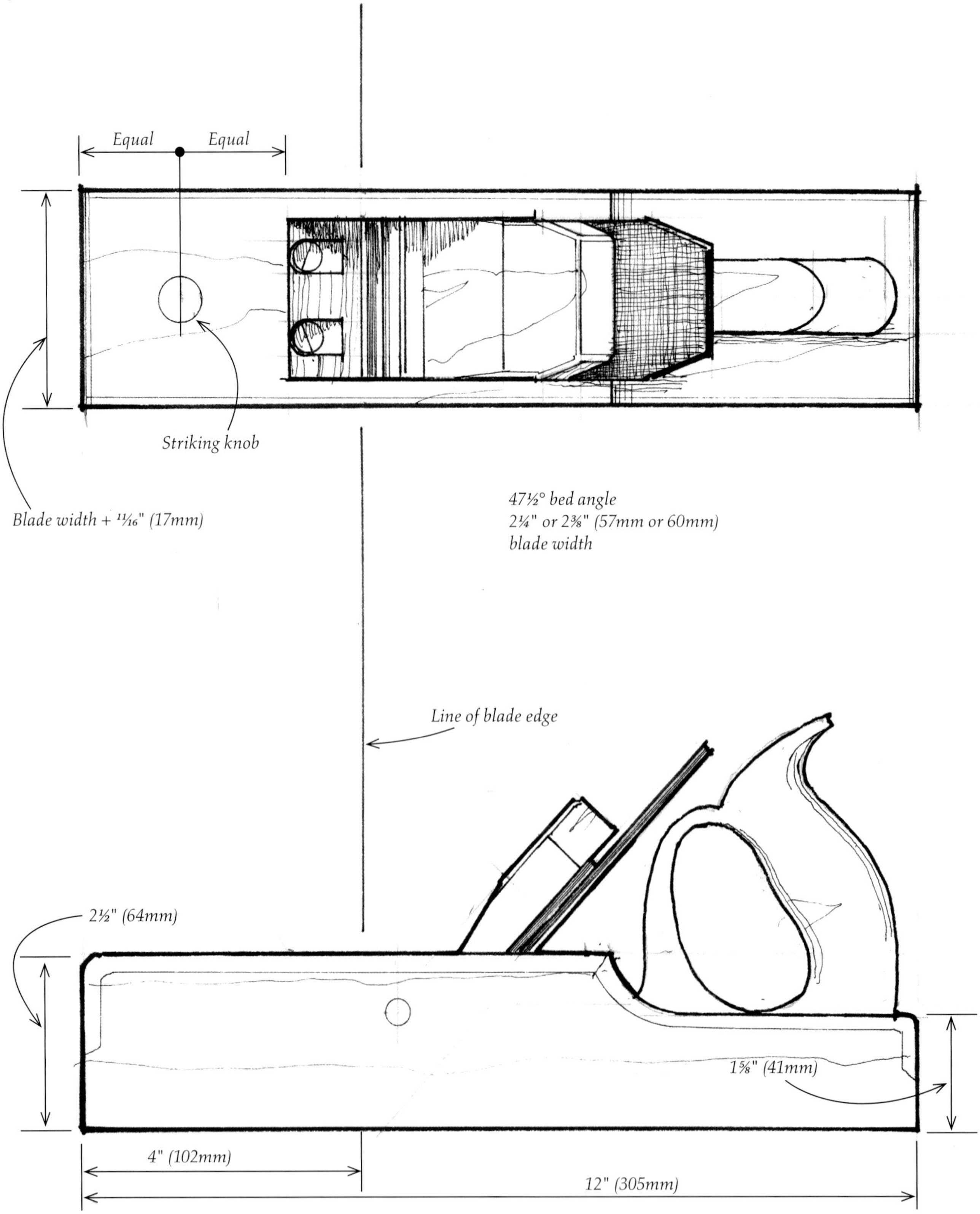

Equal   *Equal*

Striking knob

Blade width + ¹¹⁄₁₆" (17mm)

47½° bed angle
2¼" or 2⅜" (57mm or 60mm)
blade width

Line of blade edge

2½" (64mm)

1⅝" (41mm)

4" (102mm)

12" (305mm)

Figure 14-8. Panel Plane—Details

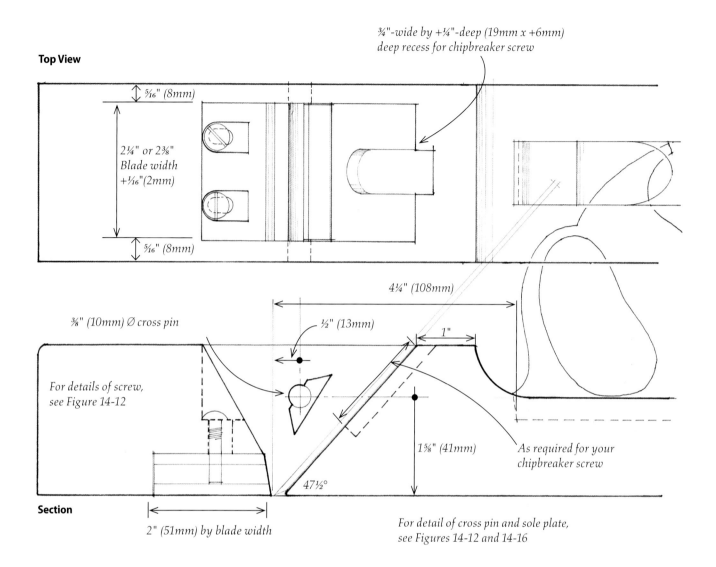

Top View

³⁄₄"-wide by +¹⁄₄"-deep (19mm x +6mm) deep recess for chipbreaker screw

⁵⁄₁₆" (8mm)

2¹⁄₄" or 2³⁄₈" Blade width +¹⁄₁₆"(2mm)

⁵⁄₁₆" (8mm)

4¹⁄₄" (108mm)

³⁄₈" (10mm) Ø cross pin

½" (13mm)

1"

For details of screw, see Figure 14-12

1⁵⁄₈" (41mm)

As required for your chipbreaker screw

47½°

Section

2" (51mm) by blade width

For detail of cross pin and sole plate, see Figures 14-12 and 14-16

Figure 14-9. 50° Smoothing Plane

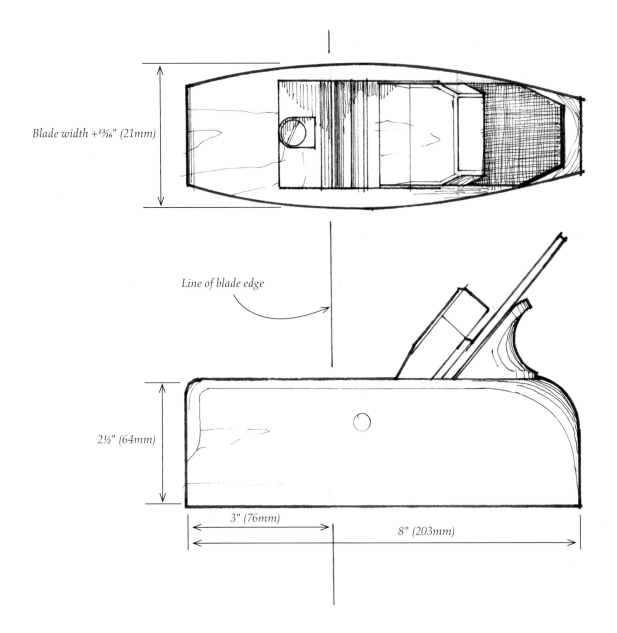

Blade width +¹³⁄₁₆" (21mm)

Line of blade edge

2½" (64mm)

3" (76mm)

8" (203mm)

Figure 14-10.
50° Smoothing Plane—Details

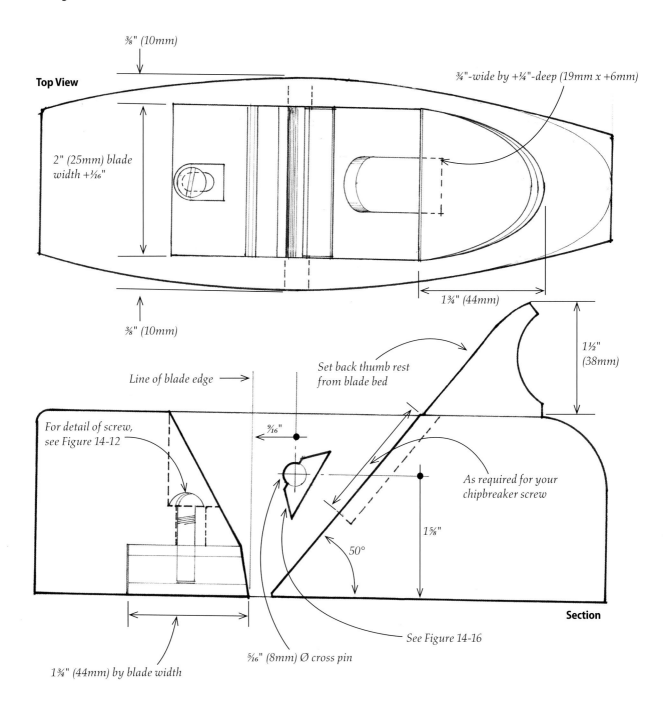

⅜" (10mm)

Top View

¾"-wide by +¼"-deep (19mm x +6mm)

2" (25mm) blade
width +1⁄16"

1¾" (44mm)

⅜" (10mm)

Set back thumb rest
from blade bed

1½"
(38mm)

Line of blade edge

For detail of screw,
see Figure 14-12

9⁄16"

As required for your
chipbreaker screw

1⅝"

50°

Section

See Figure 14-16

5⁄16" (8mm) Ø cross pin

1¾" (44mm) by blade width

Figure 14-9A. 55° Smoothing Plane

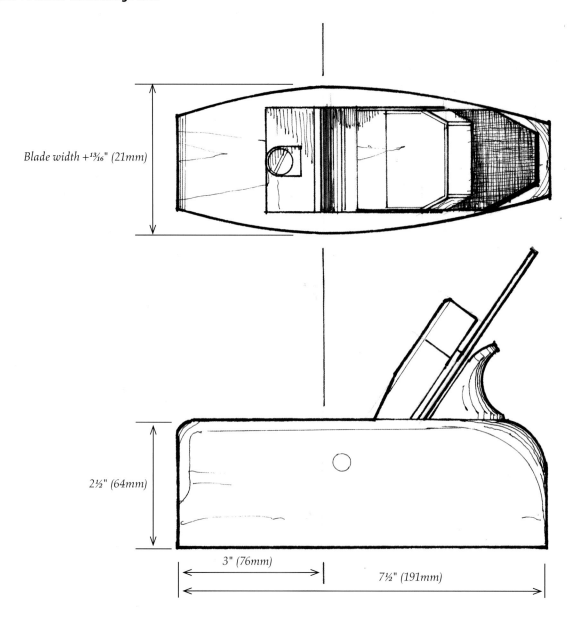

Blade width +¹³⁄₁₆" (21mm)

2½" (64mm)

3" (76mm)

7½" (191mm)

Figure 14-11. 55° Smoothing Plan—Details

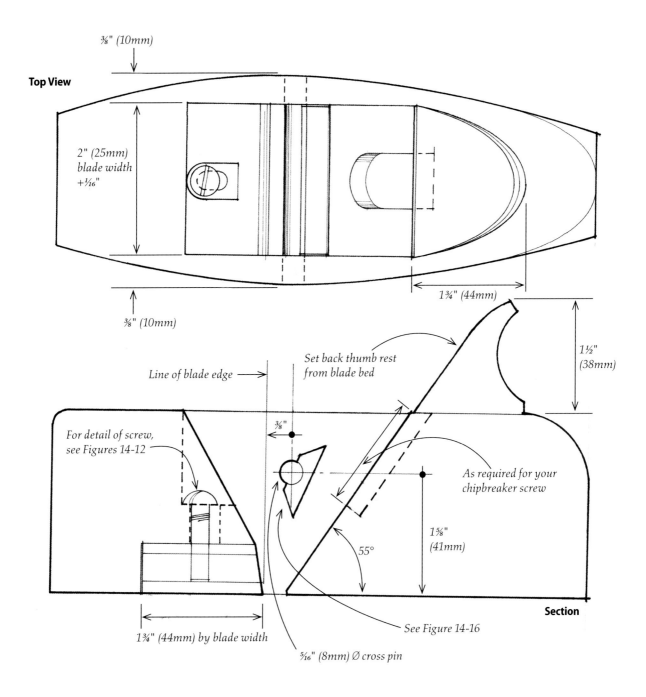

⅜" (10mm)

Top View

2" (25mm)
blade width
+¹⁄₁₆"

⅜" (10mm)

1¾" (44mm)

Line of blade edge →

Set back thumb rest
from blade bed

1½"
(38mm)

For detail of screw,
see Figures 14-12

⅜"

As required for your
chipbreaker screw

1⅝"
(41mm)

55°

Section

1¾" (44mm) by blade width

See Figure 14-16

⁵⁄₁₆" (8mm) Ø cross pin

Figure 14-12. Layout of Slot for the Sole-Plate Fixing Screw

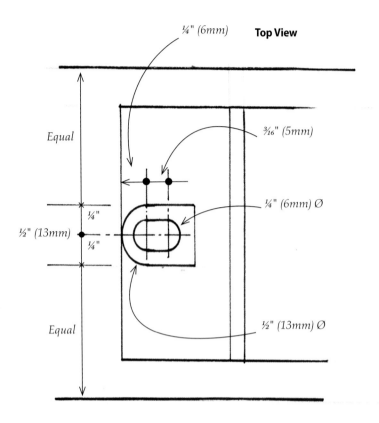

¼" (6mm)   **Top View**

³⁄₁₆" (5mm)

Equal

¼" (6mm) Ø

¼"

½" (13mm)

¼"

Equal

½" (13mm) Ø

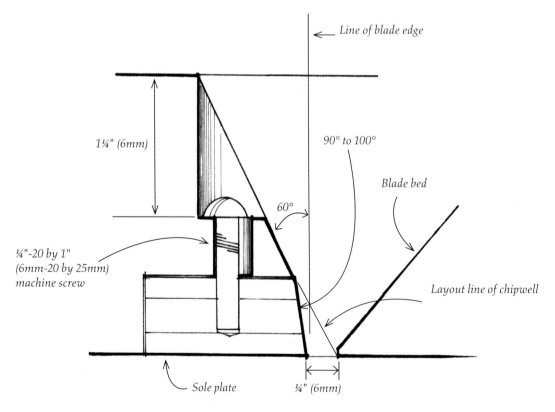

← *Line of blade edge*

1¼" (6mm)

90° to 100°

Blade bed

60°

¼"-20 by 1"
(6mm-20 by 25mm)
machine screw

Layout line of chipwell

Sole plate

¼" (6mm)

Section View

Top View

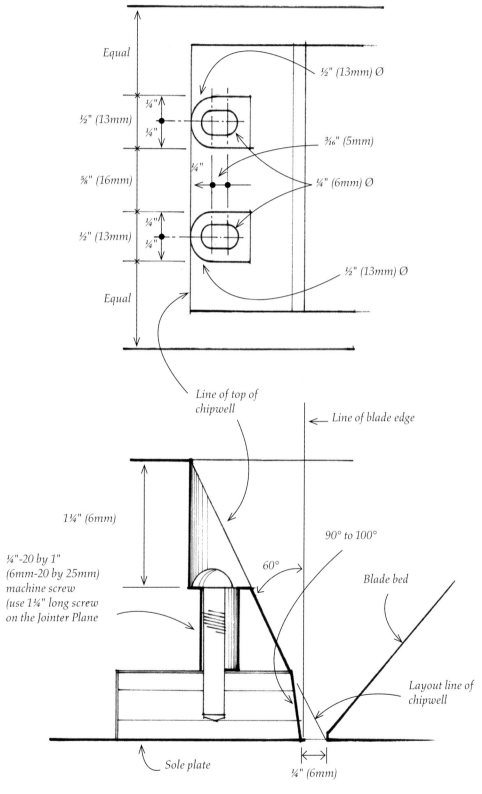

Equal

¼" ½" (13mm) Ø

½" (13mm)

¼"

³⁄₁₆" (5mm)

¼"
⅝" (16mm)

¼" (6mm) Ø

½" (13mm)

¼"
¼"

½" (13mm) Ø

Equal

Line of top of
chipwell

Line of blade edge

1¼" (6mm)

90° to 100°

¼"-20 by 1"
(6mm-20 by 25mm)
machine screw
(use 1¼" long screw
on the Jointer Plane

60°

Blade bed

Layout line of
chipwell

Sole plate

¼" (6mm)

Section View

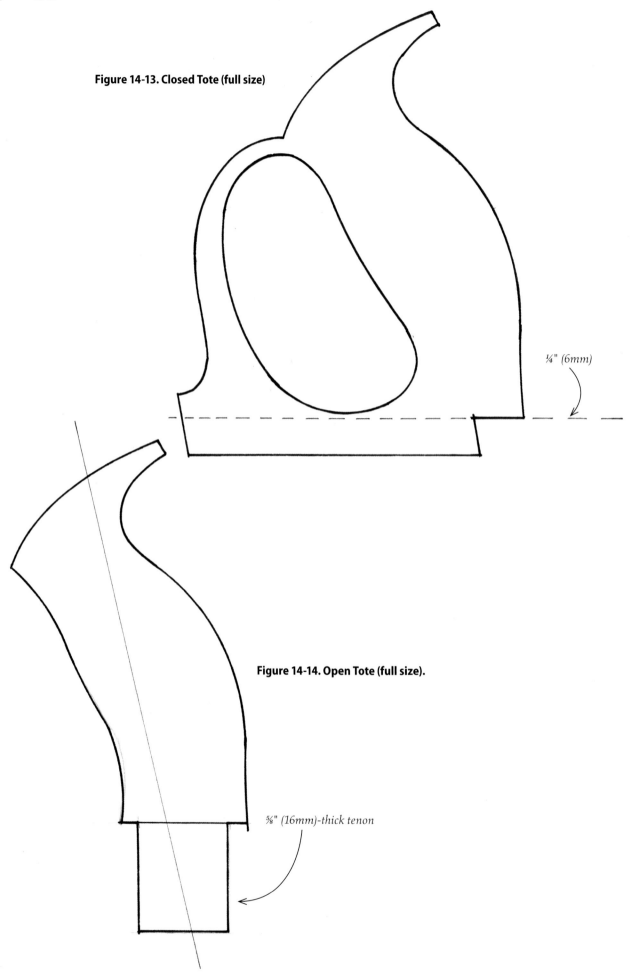

Figure 14-13. Closed Tote (full size)

¼" (6mm)

Figure 14-14. Open Tote (full size).

⅝" (16mm)-thick tenon

Figure 14-15. Profile of Wedge (full size) (width equals blade width)

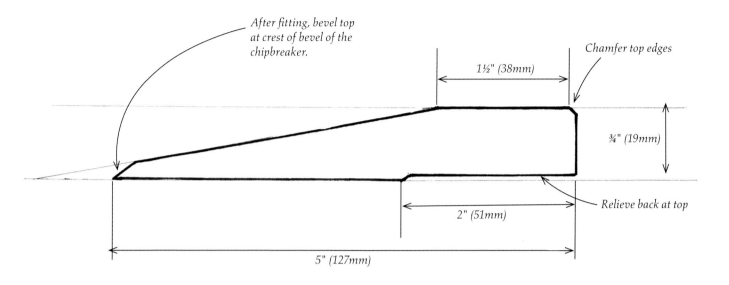

After fitting, bevel top at crest of bevel of the chipbreaker.

Chamfer top edges

1½" (38mm)

¾" (19mm)

Relieve back at top

2" (51mm)

5" (127mm)

Figure 14-16. Cross-pin Bearing Plate

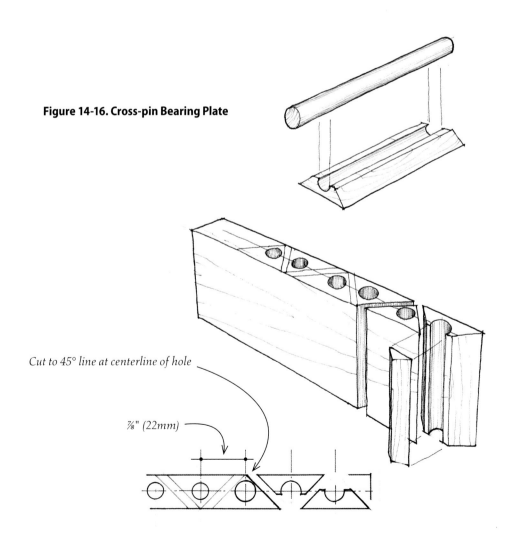

Cut to 45° line at centerline of hole

⅞" (22mm)

Figure 14-17. *Rough-milled blanks should be stickered and allowed to settle for at least a week; six months is better.*

PRELIMINARY WORK

Lay out the blade and chipwell as shown in Figures 14-19 through 14-24. Before excavating the chipwell, drill the hole for the cross pin in from both sides (to reduce errors, should the bit drift) until they meet. Drilling before excavating eliminates split-out in the chipwell

Then, make up the jigs. The sole-plate jig and the jig for the sole-plate-screw recess are described in "Fitting a Moveable Sole Plate" (pages 309-312). You will need a jig for double sole-plate screws on the wider planes, but the method is the same as for the single-screw jig.

In addition to these jigs, you will need mounting blocks for mortising the plane blocks. Glue four layers of ¾" (19mm) MDF into a block about 9" (229mm) wide by 4'

Figure 14-18. *The blocks laid out, the sole-plate blank glued up, and some of the candidates for blades that will be used (the Sta-Set chipbreaker—second from left—was not used).*

Figure 14-19.

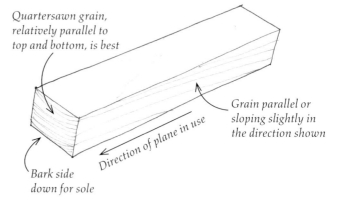

Quartersawn grain, relatively parallel to top and bottom, is best

Grain parallel or sloping slightly in the direction shown

Direction of plane in use

Bark side down for sole

Figure 14-20.
Mark blade-edge line and transfer around block.

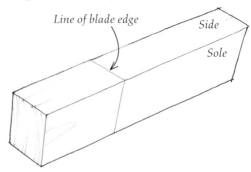

Line of blade edge

Side

Sole

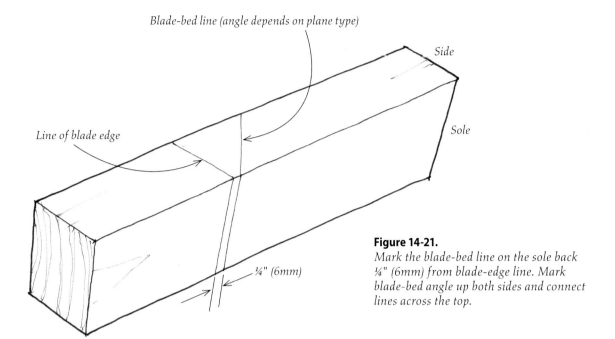

Blade-bed line (angle depends on plane type)

Side

Sole

Line of blade edge

¼" (6mm)

Figure 14-21.
Mark the blade-bed line on the sole back ¼" (6mm) from blade-edge line. Mark blade-bed angle up both sides and connect lines across the top.

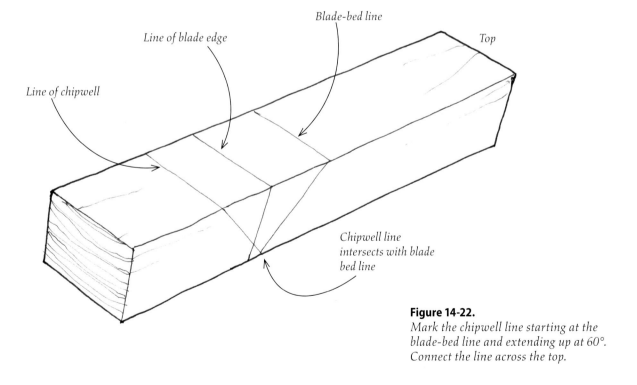

Line of blade edge

Blade-bed line

Top

Line of chipwell

Chipwell line intersects with blade bed line

Figure 14-22.
Mark the chipwell line starting at the blade-bed line and extending up at 60°. Connect the line across the top.

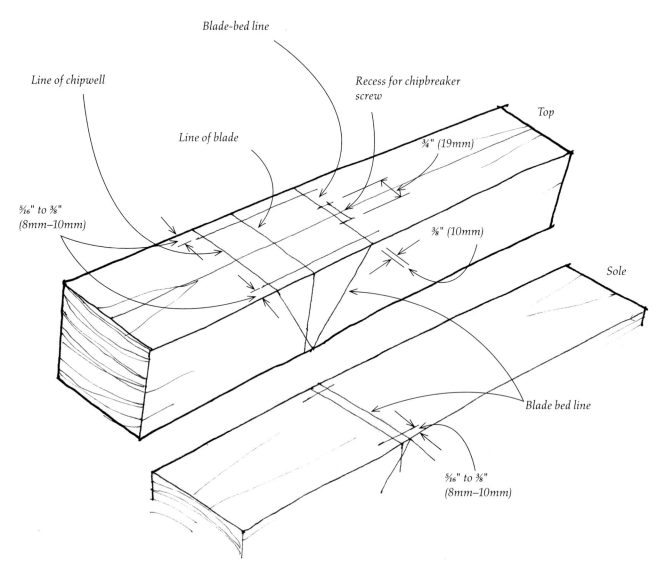

Blade-bed line

Line of chipwell

Recess for chipbreaker screw

Line of blade

Top

¾" (19mm)

⁵⁄₁₆" to ⅜"
(8mm–10mm)

⅜" (10mm)

Sole

Blade bed line

⁵⁄₁₆" to ⅜"
(8mm–10mm)

Figure 14-23. *Mark the edge of the chipwell in ⁵⁄₁₆" to ⅜" (8mm to 10mm) from the sides, top, and bottom. Verify that the resulting chipwell width matches the blade width or is no more than ¹⁄₃₂" (0.8mm) wider. Mark a centerline top and bottom, and mark the recess for the chipbreaker screw.*

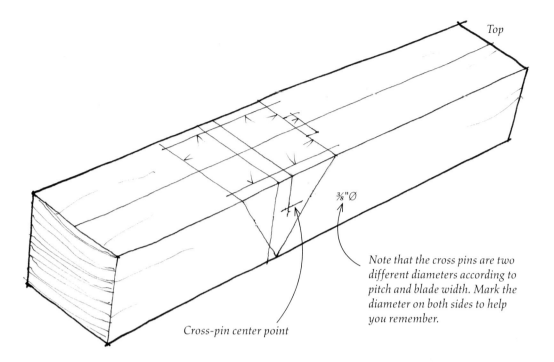

Top

⅜"∅

Note that the cross pins are two different diameters according to pitch and blade width. Mark the diameter on both sides to help you remember.

Cross-pin center point

Figure 14-24. *Mark the centerpoint of the cross pin up 1⅝" (41mm) from the sole and back from the blade-edge line according to the blade pitch. See the appropriate drawing for the plane you are making. (See Figures 14-2, 14-4, 14-6, 14-8, 14-10, or 14-11).*

(1,219mm) long. (I glued up some 1¼" (32mm) thick MDF I had in stock).

You will need one mounting block for every blade angle you intend to mortise, plus one for the chipwells. Remember, the block will be the complementary angle of the angle you want to cut. For instance, a 47½° blade angle will need a block angle of 42½°; a 50° blade angle, a block angle of 40°.

You will need some 1½" (38mm)-diameter holes drilled in the face of each mounting block for clamping (at least one for the plane block itself, plus one or two others to clamp the mounting block down, depending on the machine you are using). It is also helpful to screw a stop block on the mounting block to help keep the plane block from sliding under the pressure of the mortise chisel (Figures 14-25 and 14-26).

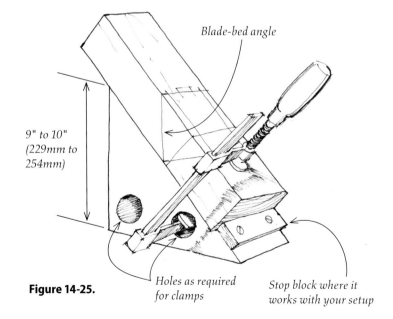

Blade-bed angle

9" to 10" (229mm to 254mm)

Figure 14-25.

Holes as required for clamps

Stop block where it works with your setup

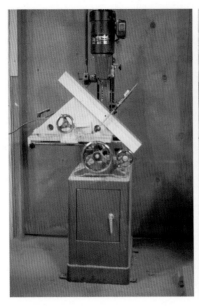

Figure 14-26. *Plane blocks and mounting blocks on the mortiser (left). Longer plane blocks may require the mounting block to be cantilevered, in order to gain enough clearance to work.*

You will have to take a good look at the capacity and limitations of your mortising setup. While I recently got a substantial stationary mortiser with good capacity, the longer plane blocks had to be positioned with one end off the table to get enough clearance under the chisel (Figure 14-26, left). I managed to get everything to clear, but just barely. With a mortising attachment on a drill press, the table can be lowered and the plane block kept entirely on the mounting block.

The mounting block on a drill press will have to be clamped and unclamped with each cut because it does not have a cross vise. Use a stack of wood or MDF pieces the same thickness as your chisel as shims behind the mounting block to the fence, and add (or subtract) one on each cut to avoid measuring and squaring after each unclamping. You may be able to mount the block in a cross vise on the drill press table, saving the trouble of clamping and unclamping

ROUGH-SHAPING THE BLOCKS

Using a ⅜" or ½" (10mm or 13mm) hollow chisel, cut the blade bed first through the mouth opening no deeper than is necessary for you to be able to finish the cut from the top. Err a little to the mouth side of the blade-bed line. Do not worry if the chisel over-cuts the mouth opening, because you will be fitting a sole plate later that will fill this. (Making this first cut through the mouth serves two purposes. First, it avoids splintering on the exit of the cut. Secondly, it allows you to complete the cut whether or not your mortising chisel is long enough to do so—and it probably is not.)

Turn the plane block over to finish the cut from the top. Cut the recess for the chipbreaker screw first; then, finish the cuts on either sides, cutting closer to the line than you did when you made the cuts through the mouth, to compensate for blade drift when cutting at an angle to the grain. Either this should result in a flush meeting of the cuts, or a small step-cut at the bottom that can be pared away later.

Cut all the blocks you are doing, changing mounting blocks as required, then change blocks, one last time, and cut the chipwell line down from the top on all the blocks. Be careful not to exceed the depth and cut into the blade bed. You can use the mortiser to cut away a lot of the waste at either side of the chipwell, being careful not to cut too deeply into the throat or blade bed. Cut away any remaining waste with a keyhole saw. Alternatively, you can cut the waste away entirely with a keyhole saw. The Fein saw, if you should happen to have one, can also make this cut (Figure 14-27).

Pare the waste and any irregularities on the blade bed away with a chisel. Smoothly pare the chipwell. Check the blade fit by holding the blade down with one finger in the center: tap the four corners of the blade with another finger (Figure 14-28). If you hear a clicking sound on any corner, that part of the blade bed is low; pare the other corners until the clicking stops. Also, visually check the bed with a straightedge, and sight down it for twist.

FITTING THE SOLE PLATE, CROSS PIN, AND WEDGE

After this preliminary blade fitting and cleanup, cut the recess for the sole-plate screwheads in the chipwell using the jigs. Drill out the slot(s) in the plane body for the sole-plate fixing screw(s). Doing this before routing out for the sole plate will eliminate any split-out in the sole-plate recess from drilling for the fixing screw. Cut the recess for the sole plate with the jig. Preliminarily fit the sole plate and tap the sole-plate screws (Figure 14-29). (See "Fitting a Moveable Sole Plate" on page 309-312).

Now make the cross pin. You can use standard dowel stock, though I would recommend oak rather than birch for the additional strength. Make sure the grain is straight and continuous. Or you can split (not saw) your own pin out of straight-grained stock. Either way you have to accurately size the dowel, either with a dowel sizer or by trial and error.

Figure 14-27. *Plane blanks at various stages of production, from back to front: the first cut through the mouth, cutting the lower half of the blade bed; top cuts completed for both blade bed and chipwell; waste cleared down both sides of the chipwell; waste removed.*

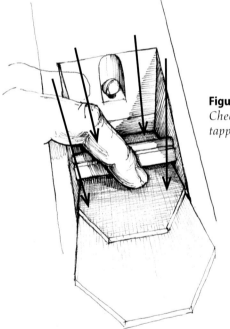

Figure 14-28.
Check the fit of the blade by tapping it on each of its corners.

Figure 14-29.
Sole plates fitted, tapped, and installed on five plane bodies. At left are three sole-plate blanks.

Make up stock for the plate that holds the cross pin out of the same material as the plane block, with the grain oriented the same way. It should be ⅝" (16mm) thick by the width of your widest blade by twice as long as you need to make the number of plates required (Figure 14-16). (You will need an end to hold it when cutting the plates free.) To drill the holes as accurately as possible on the drill press, scribe the centerlines. After drilling the holes, alternately cut the pieces free on a 45° angle until you have a few more than you need. Cut their length to the width of their matching blades and clean up the bevels. Then cut or plane the hole away on the top (narrow) side about 1/16" (2mm) shy of the scribed centerline (Figure 14-30). See if the plate can be snapped onto the cross pin. Continue planing, one or two strokes at a time, and fitting until you can snap the plate onto the pin. Carefully remove the plate, insert the cross pin into its hole and snap the

plate back on (Figures 14-31 and 14-32). Do this for all the planes.

Cut blanks for the wedges and then band saw a 10° taper over about two-thirds the length of the wedge (Figure 14-15). Clean up the cut with a plane. If necessary, cut a narrow slot in the back of the wedge for any protrusion of the chipbreaker screw. Insert the blade with its chipbreaker in the plane, and then the wedge for a trial fit. (It is easier to do this with the sole plate removed until after the wedge fitting is done.)

The wedge should descend close to the bevel of the chipbreaker before it tightens up. Remove the wedge-and-blade assembly, and fit the wedge to the shape of the chipbreaker. Carefully cross-plane the wedge until its curve matches that of the chipbreaker. Leave the underside of the wedge ever so slightly proud in the center of its length to guarantee the wedge makes solid contact at both the bottom (at the top of the chipbreaker's bevel) and the top.

Once the wedge is fit to the chipbreaker, do a trial fit of the whole wedge-and-blade assembly. Check that the blade is making solid contact with the bed, and the pressure on the wedge from the cross pin is even. You can check the pressure from the cross pin on the wedge first visually—look that there is no gap at either side—and then by pushing the wedge sideways. The amount of pressure to release the wedge should be equal from both sides. If needed, plane the high side on the top of the wedge with light strokes of a block plane until the fit is correct. Do not crown the wedge—keep it flat. Once the wedge is fitted, cut it off at the chipbreaker bevel, and bevel the end to deflect shavings. Finish shaping the rest of the wedge.

Figure 14-30. *At left, the bevel-edge shooting board is used to clean up the top faces of the cross-pin bearing plate. Next to it, the regular shooting board is used to clean up edges and ends. Cut stock for the cross-pin bearing plates can be seen between the two shooting boards, with the wedge blanks behind.*

Figure 14-31. *To assemble the cross pin and its bearing plate, push the pin home from the side and snap on the plate.*

Figure 14-32. *Then, install the blade assembly with the wedge to begin checking the fit of the wedge.*

Figure 14-33. *After installing the cross-pin assembly and fitting the wedge on the smoothing planes, the thumb piece is added.*

Figure 14-34. *The angle cut of the thumbpiece waste at the bed line is deeply scored with a hand saw, but not cut free until after the block is glued on so as to allow it to be clamped up.*

Figure 14-35. *Then cut the thumb-piece waste free and give the plane its final shape.*

Finish fitting the sole plates by planing the mouth-edge end on the shooting board until you have the mouth opening you want. You can always adjust it further, later. Screw it in place when you are satisfied. You can, for the time being, leave ⅛" (3mm) or so of the mouth edge at a 90° relief angle, relieving the throat above, or close to, the chipwell of the plane block. If you find, in use, that chips jam in this area, you can remove the sole plate and rework the mouth to a greater relief angle.

SHAPING THE SMOOTHING PLANES

On each of the smoothing planes, first mark the curve of its coffin shape on the top—it is easier now—but do not cut it. Then band saw and smooth the curve of the thumbpiece on a long piece of stock. Mark the blade angle and make a partial cut on the line all around the piece, ⅛" to ¼" (3mm to 6mm) deep. This will help keep you from marring the plane when you cut the angle after the thumbpiece has been glued on.

Cut the thumbpiece off the stock square beyond the blade line, and glue it to the

HANDLE SHAPE

Designing a tote (or other handle) for handplanes begins with understanding a few fundamentals. A handle must accommodate the hand and provide an appropriate surface area to spread the stress of planing evenly over the hand. The palm is significantly concave. The German plane's rounded end (or a coffin-sided) smoother matches the concavity pretty well, the shape of a traditional Western tote perhaps not so well. In addition, the crook of the thumb and first finger requires a properly shaped bearing area, because resistance to sliding forward up off the handle happens here. Finally, the position and angle of the handle or grip must focus the force toward the blade's edge. The implications of these considerations amount to this:

The handle or tote must be *humped*, not straight or even gently curved, if it is to fit the hollow of the palm. It should be thick in order to engage as much of the hand in the area of the thumb and first finger as well as the palm. And, the centerline of the arc of the hump must pass through the blade edge. Additionally, because the plane must be returned back to the beginning of the stroke and not only just pushed, the tote must be the right circumference to be comfortably grasped and lifted. Make sure it is big enough around that the fingers of the hand do not press upon the palm before getting a good grip, and, of course, not so big that is becomes tiresome to grab.

If you look at traditional totes from wooden planes, they follow most of these mandates. Perhaps the totes could be thicker, but I am not sure what the optimal thickness would be without significant experimentation. It would also appear that a rounded-end coffin-shape in the traditional style of plane would benefit from the addition of a *neck* for the thumb and first finger similar to that on German planes.

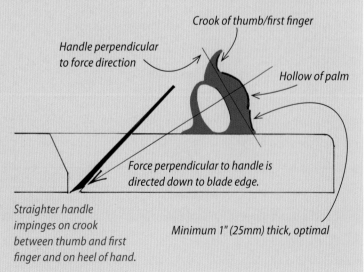

Crook of thumb/first finger

Handle perpendicular to force direction

Hollow of palm

Force perpendicular to handle is directed down to blade edge.

Straighter handle impinges on crook between thumb and first finger and on heel of hand.

Minimum 1" (25mm) thick, optimal

block with the cut you made on the blade line back about ¹⁄₁₆" (2mm) from the blade bed. After the glue has dried, finish cutting off the waste at this partial sawcut line (Figures 14-33 and 14-34).

The thumbpiece should be cut and pared back from the blade line so it does not interfere with the blade if it has shifted during glue-up. Band saw and smooth the plane's coffin shape (if you leave the back curves of the plane uncut until after you shape the front, the plane is easier to hold in a vise) and then cut, shape, and smooth the thumbpiece and the back of the plane to your grip (Figure 14-35).

MAKING AND FITTING THE TOTES

On the other planes, prepare stock for the handles, or totes (Figures 14-13 and 14-14). Sometimes it is nice to do the totes in a contrasting wood; an argument could be made that a tote from a dark wood will look better over time, as a tote from a light color wood will show grime. It all depends on your taste and the stock you have at hand.

I suggest you do not cut the totes free from their stock until you have shaped the grip (Figure 14-36). This will make it easier to maneuver on the router table, should you want to form the round part initially with a router bit, or to hold the blank in a vise in order to smooth.

After shaping the totes, mark the location and size of the recess required on the plane. On razee planes, make the back cutout of the block and smooth it before doing this.

Figure 14-36. *The totes in various stages of completion.*

Probably the easiest way to cut the recess for the closed totes, since on the razee-style planes the curve behind the blade interferes with a router jig, is to use the hollow-chisel mortiser. This leaves a rough bottom, reducing the gluing area, which can be smoothed, or adjusted if necessary, with a router plane.

Cut the recess for the closed totes to its shortest length and finish undercutting the back dovetail. Then, cut the angle of the front with a chisel. Make a template of the handle and its dovetail out of ⅛" or ¼" (3mm or 6mm) hardboard or plywood, and use it to check the fit as you work. Then finish fitting the totes. Do not glue them in until the planes are shaped and smoothed.

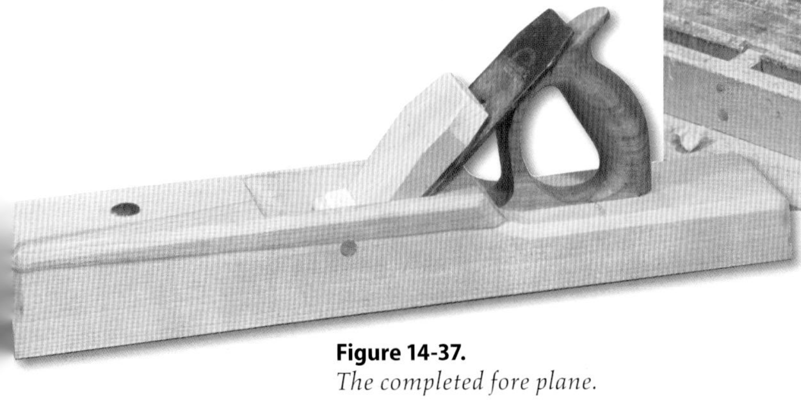

FINISHING TOUCHES

Insert the blade and wedge it securely, about ¹⁄₁₆" (2mm) shy of the bottom. Follow procedures outlined for setting up wood planes, "Configuring the Sole" on page 150, to true the bottom.

Smooth the plane's top surfaces. Check that the faces are square. Glue in the tote. Form the eyes at the chipwell, which can make it a easier for a hand working in the vicinity.

Find or make a length of hardwood dowel ⅝" to ¾" (16mm to 19mm) in diameter for the striking knob on the long planes. Drill a hole about 1" (25mm) deep, round the top end of the dowel (before gluing it in), cut it off so it will stand proud about ³⁄₁₆" (5mm), and glue it in its hole.

Apply a light coat of oil on the top surface of the plane and tote, to give protection and improve grip (Figure 14-37 and 14-38).

Figure 14-38.
The completed jack and jointer planes.

Figure 14-37.
The completed fore plane.

Making a Japanese-Style Plane

Japanese-style planes, of all the styles of planes, can be the fastest to make, and, because there is no glue to dry, they can be used the same day. Moreover, the design is versatile and can be adapted to a variety of shaping and finishing requirements.

Angles, widths, and lengths can be varied for finishing a variety of woods. Shapes can be varied for rough shaping or for finishing moldings or carvings. Anyone with good hand skills should have little problem constructing the basic plane.

First, obtain a blade of suitable width. If this is your first plane, start with a blade narrower than 55mm (2⅛"). Making planes for 60mm and 70mm (2⅜" and 2¾") blades is

more difficult, increasingly so, the wider the plane. I find that 48mm (1⅞") is a versatile size and a good one to start with.

The block must be made of dense wood. If you have ever felt the difference between the white oak used for a *dai* and common Japanese white oak (similar to our red oak in density and texture), you will realize the density required: the oak used for the *dai*, both red and white, is considerably denser than the common stock.

This is a result of trees carefully selected and cut just for the plane-making trades and involves a drying process often lasting 10 to 40 years—or more. In addition to being dense and hard, the wood must also grip the blade well, which the wood of the Japanese *dai* does very well. I like to use the Japanese *dai*, which comes pre-cut to match your blade width. In a pinch, I have used cherry, beech, rosewood, canary wood, and angico.

The last two were the most effective, though I had trouble finding pieces of cherry and beech that were dense enough. A dense piece of indigenous white oak is also a good choice. Maple is not a good choice because, even though it is hard, it does not grip the blade well.

Orient the grain as shown in (Figure 14-39). Grain orientation is important if for no reason other than resistance to the wedging action of the blade. Select a *dai* that is ⅜" to ⅝" (10mm to 16mm) wider than your blade—a 48mm (1⅞") blade should have a *dai* 2¼" to 2½" (58mm to 64mm) wide. It should

Figure 14-39. Grain Orientation

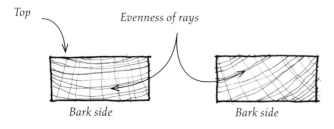

Top

Evenness of rays

Bark side   *Bark side*

End View: Either orientation of the growth rings is acceptable.

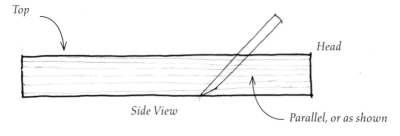

Top

Head

Side View

Parallel, or as shown

be thick enough to capture almost the entire hardened portion of the blade at the intended angle. Lengths are somewhat standardized on finish planes—the width being about three-tenths of the length—but this can be altered according to the intended use of the plane. Truing planes such as jointers are, of course, longer, but finish planes can be made much shorter to facilitate the cutting action of a very finely set blade.

The edge of the blade is traditionally set at a point about five-eighths of the length of the plane back from what we would call the front of the plane. (The Japanese call this the *back* of the plane, and the area behind the blade the *front* of the plane (Figure 14-40).) This is also not absolute, because on a shorter plane, you might not end up with enough wood behind the blade to support it, so the area in front of the blade could be proportionally shorter.

Next, select the angle of your blade (see "Blade Angles for Different Woods" on page 35). Japanese plane blades are frequently set at an angle of 8 in 10 (Figure 14-41), approximately 40°. I have made finish planes at 9 in 10 (43°), 10 in 10 (45°), 11 in 10 (47½°), and 12 in 10 (50°)

Before laying out and cutting the block, you must flatten and sharpen the blade, as well as the chipbreaker   if you are using one. (See "Prepare the Blade" and "Prepare and Fit the Chipbreaker" for Japanese planes on pages 179-180.)

Now begin the layout of the block, making sure all edges are square. (See "Laying out a Block for a Japanese Plane" on page 288.)

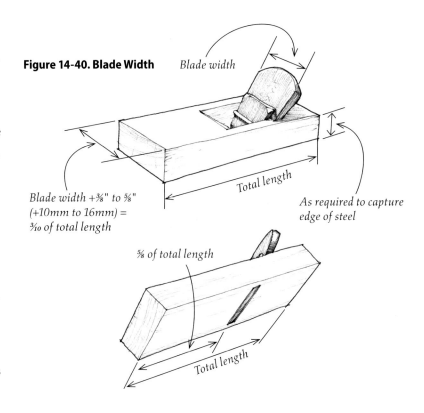

Figure 14-40. Blade Width

Blade width

Blade width +⅜" to ⅝" (+10mm to 16mm) = ³⁄₁₀ of total length

Total length

As required to capture edge of steel

⅝ of total length

Total length

Figure 14-41. Traditional Japanese Method of Establishing Blade Angles and Their Degree Approximations

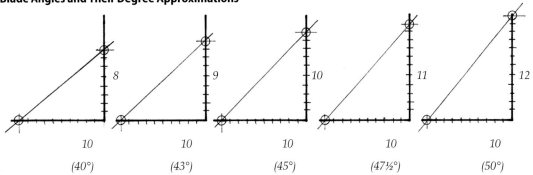

8	9	10	11	12
10	10	10	10	10
(40°)	(43°)	(45°)	(47½°)	(50°)

LAYING OUT A BLOCK FOR A JAPANESE PLANE

1 Mark a line for the blade edge.

2 Use a bevel gauge to mark the angle of the blade, beginning at the blade-edge line. Transfer all lines around the block.

3 Mark the angle above the throat— the chipwell—at 45° to 50°, starting ¼" (6mm) above the bottom. Transfer the lines around the block.

4 Lay out the relief angle of the throat at 75° to 80° (more if the angle of your blade is high), and transfer the lines around the block if you wish.

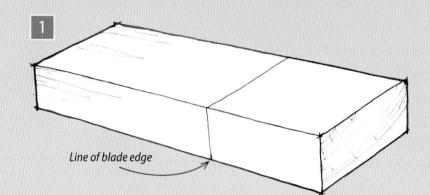

Line of blade edge

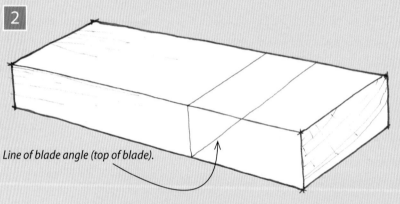

Line of blade angle (top of blade).

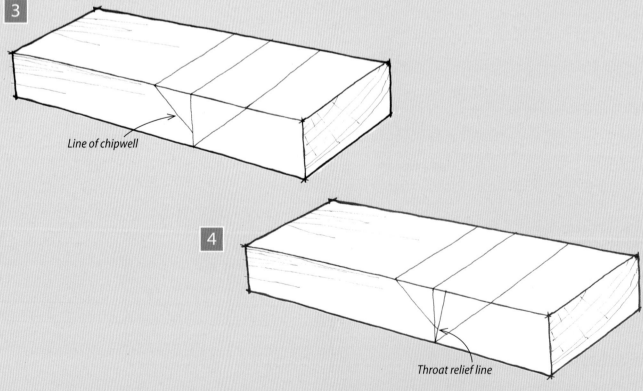

Line of chipwell

Throat relief line

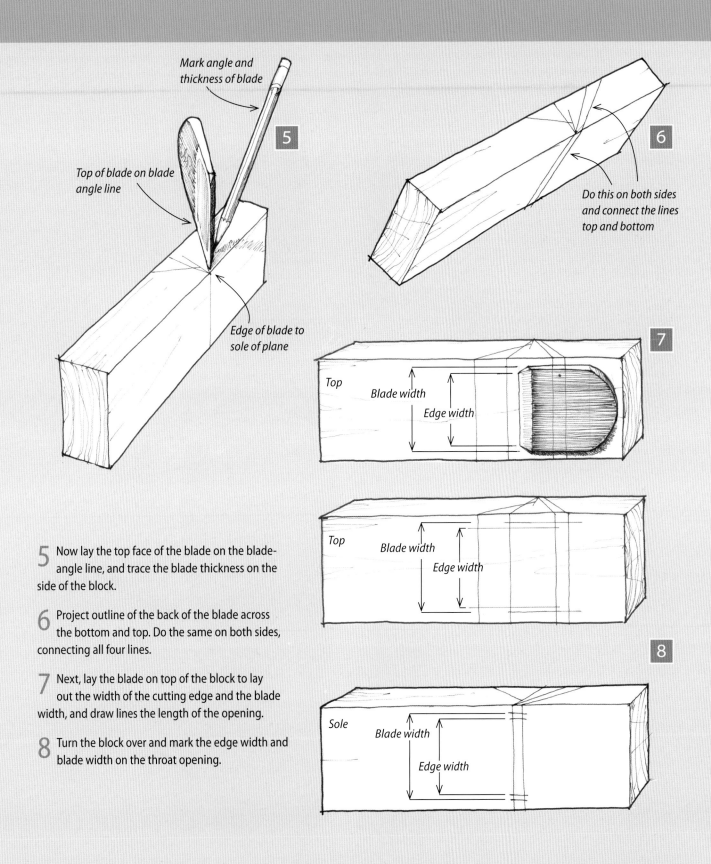

Mark angle and
thickness of blade

5

Top of blade on blade
angle line

Edge of blade to
sole of plane

6

Do this on both sides
and connect the lines
top and bottom

7

Top

Blade width

Edge width

Top

Blade width

Edge width

8

Sole

Blade width

Edge width

5   Now lay the top face of the blade on the blade-
    angle line, and trace the blade thickness on the
side of the block.

6   Project outline of the back of the blade across
    the bottom and top. Do the same on both sides,
connecting all four lines.

7   Next, lay the blade on top of the block to lay
    out the width of the cutting edge and the blade
width, and draw lines the length of the opening.

8   Turn the block over and mark the edge width and
    blade width on the throat opening.

CHISELING THE CHIPWELL, MOUTH & BLADE SEAT

1 Chisel to a clean V-shaped opening, keeping the cuts parallel to the blade-bed line and the chipwell line. You can chisel with the bevel down at first if you want, but as you progress, turn the bevel up and keep the back of the chisel at the same angle as the chipwell and blade-seat lines marked on the side of the block.

2 Do this by positioning yourself so you can sight down the back of the blade and along the lines marked on the side at the same time. It is important to maintain the proper angle of the cut, especially once you are within ⅛" (3mm) of the line. If you overcut the line at the blade seat, you will ruin the block.

3 Chisel the opening at the angles marked— approximately ⅛" (3mm) inside the front and back lines and ¹⁄₁₆" (2mm) inside the sidelines—until all lines meet.

4 Turn the block over and chisel the throat opening somewhat shy of the layout lines.

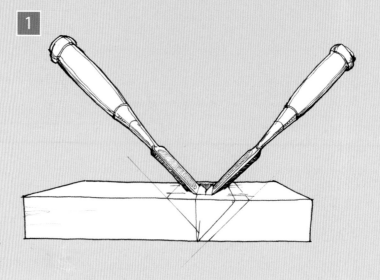

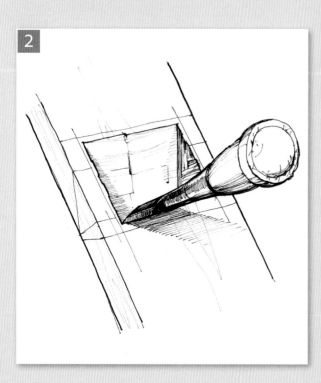

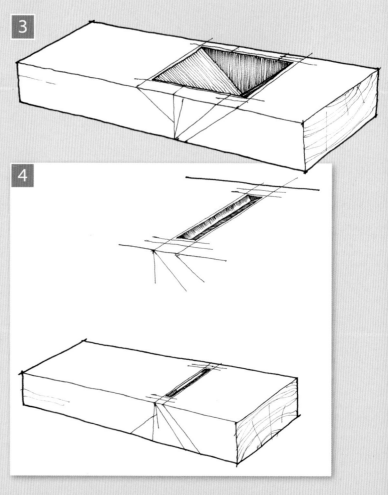

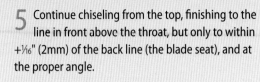

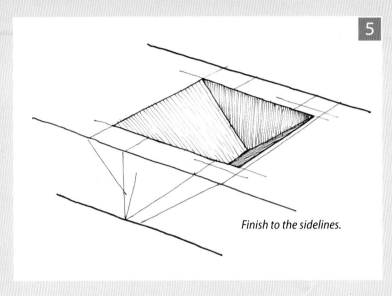

Finish to the sidelines.

5 Continue chiseling from the top, finishing to the line in front above the throat, but only to within +¹⁄₁₆" (2mm) of the back line (the blade seat), and at the proper angle.

6 Cut the throat open at its angle a little shy of the line—about ¹⁄₆₄" (0.4mm). Continue cutting until you break through. Clean up and finish from the top.

7 Pare the blade seat to a convex curve to the layout lines at either side.

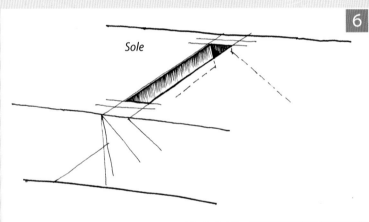

Sole

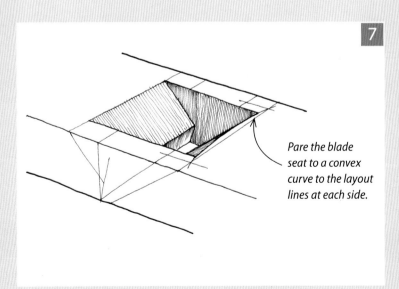

Pare the blade seat to a convex curve to the layout lines at each side.

CHISELING THE CHIPWELL, MOUTH & BLADE SEAT *(continued)*

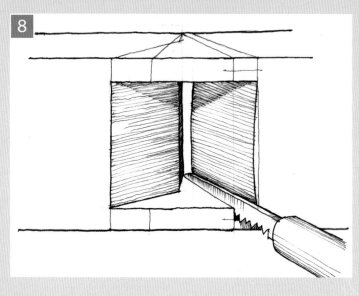

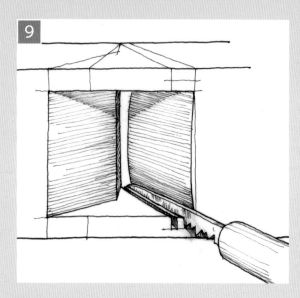

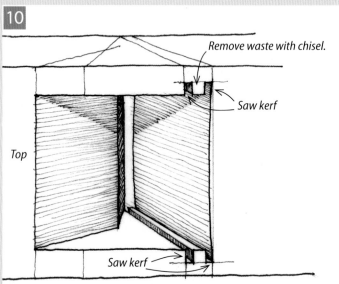

Remove waste with chisel.

Saw kerf

Top

Saw kerf

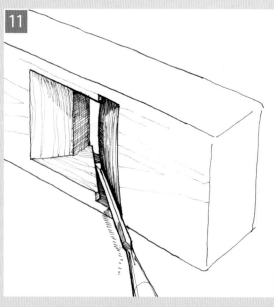

8 With a good quality keyhole saw, cut to the lines of the abutments that hold the blade. The blade-angle line (top of the blade) is critical—the cut must be straight and accurate. The cut is easier to start through the throat opening, starting the saw cut at the top of the block. Finish the cut from the top, making sure it is to its full depth.

9 Cut the blade seat line from the top by laying the saw on the blade seat.

10 After sawing, you will have a strip of waste between the kerfs on each side.

11 Clean out the cut to the lines with a small chisel.

Begin making the plane by chiseling the top opening. Since I'm right-handed, I find it easiest simply to lay the block on my bench against a stop at the left end, chisel into the stop—sighting down the back of the chisel—and then rotate the block—rather than my body position—and chisel the other side of the opening. (See "Chiseling the Chipwell, Mouth, and Blade Seat" on page 290.)

Once you have the blade seat prepared, you can trial-fit the blade. Probably it will barely go in. Sight along the back of the blade to see where it is hitting. Most likely, the blade seat will be too curved. Flatten it along its length until the blade goes in about halfway, or until it begins to approximate the curve of the back of the blade. It is important to note that the underside, or bevel side, of the blade usually is forged to a concave shape across its width.

Coat the back of the blade with ink, pencil, or petroleum jelly, and slide it into place. When you remove it, the high places of the blade seat will be marked. Pare or scrape these down carefully and repeat the operation. Continue doing this until you can push the blade in by hand up to a point equal to half the width of the blade's bevel from its final position—⅛" to ³⁄₁₆" (3mm to 5mm). (For more on fitting the blade, see "Bed the Blade Properly" on page 155.)

Hold the plane up to the light and sight between the blade and its seat; you should not see any light. If, when you begin fitting the blade, there is considerable light—a gross misfitting of the blade—you can pare down the obvious high areas before you begin the marking and paring process, thereby saving

yourself some time and tedium. If, when you are doing the final fitting, you pare away too much, you can shim the blade using paper glued to the blade seat. Try a single layer of bond paper first—you will be surprised how much difference one piece of paper can make.

Turn the block over and finish paring the throat opening to the line. If this is to be a fine finishing plane with a chipbreaker, then this may be the entire opening you need because the pressure of the chipbreaker tends to open the throat slightly.

If it is to be a coarser plane, or one without a chipbreaker, you may want to open the throat a little more. Tap the blade into its final position and look at the gap. Do this carefully—or you may drive the blade into the throat, should there not be enough opening to begin with.

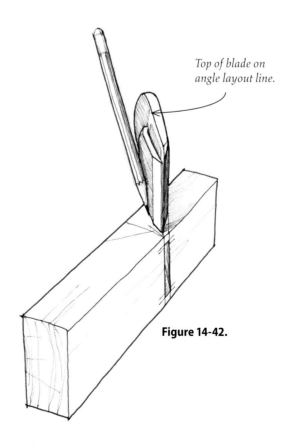

Top of blade on angle layout line.

Figure 14-42.

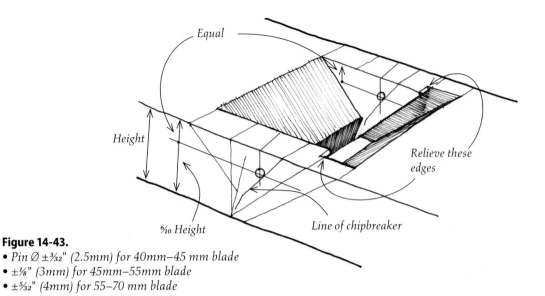

Figure 14-43.
- *Pin Ø ±³⁄₃₂" (2.5mm) for 40mm–45 mm blade*
- *±⅛" (3mm) for 45mm–55mm blade*
- *±⁵⁄₃₂" (4mm) for 55–70 mm blade*

Fitting the pin for a chipbreaker is a little tricky. Put the blade and chipbreaker together, lay the blade top on your blade-angle layout line, and mark the line of the chipbreaker in the same way you marked the blade in the beginning (Figure 14-42). Mark a line about six-tenths of the way up from, and parallel to, the bottom. The center of the pin lies on this line at a distance of one radius from the line marked for the top of the chipbreaker (Figure 14-43).

Bore carefully in from one side. Insert the blade and chipbreaker to their final position, and tap the pin in to check its fit. Hopefully, the fit will be close. If not, there are ways to correct it. Mark the line of the top face of the chipbreaker inside the plane as well as the line parallel to the bottom.

Mark the center of the pin and bore the hole—inserting the bit through the first hole. It is not necessary to bore the hole all the way through. Insert the pin, blade, and chipbreaker, and check the fit. If the fit is too loose, bend the corners of the chipbreaker more. If the pin is too tight or

not parallel, file it. If the pin is grossly off, the next larger diameter pin can be fit by using a rat-tail file to enlarge the pinhole as needed.

Flatten and relieve the bottom with scrapers to the configuration appropriate to your plane. (See "Japanese Plane Setup" on page 177.)

Lastly, finish off the rest of the plane. The leading edge of the plane and blade bed must be sharp and crisp in order to prevent loose chips getting underneath the plane while

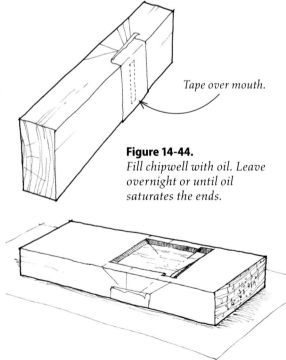

Tape over mouth.

Figure 14-44.
Fill chipwell with oil. Leave overnight or until oil saturates the ends.

working. I relieve the areas on either side of the blade (see Figure 10-50 on page 298) because these are hard to level in the course of maintaining the bottom and often become high spots that mark the work.

I also chamfer both sides of the bottom to reduce some of the areas bearing on the work and thereby lessen the friction. The top edges can be rounded all over, with the area behind the blade chamfered at an angle perpendicular to the blade and rounded a little to reduce damage when the blade is being tapped out.

You can treat your block with oil if you like (Figure 14-44), using either camellia oil to reduce friction in use or tung oil for stability, but my personal preference is to skip this step. Rub the bottom with an oiler charged with camellia oil when the plane is completed, and frequently when working, making sure to lubricate the blade as well. This will not only reduce the friction of the sole, but also, the Japanese believe, extend the life of the blade's edge by reducing the heat caused by the friction of the cut.

Set the blade and try it, making sure you have clearance at the throat. You should get a shaving. If not, or if you cannot produce as fine a shaving as you want, and you can see the blade is protruding, then the bottom is not flat. Check again; assuming the blade is sharp, you missed something.

Figure 14-45A.
Chibi-kanna *with the blades removed. All of the blades in these chibi-kanna were cut from a larger blank, two of them from the blank in the foreground.*

Making *Chibi-kanna*

Making these small planes is the same as making the larger Japanese planes, but because the blades are small, the bedded side of the blade is flat and not concave, and because they are usually made without a chipbreaker, they can be made quickly. Refer to the other sections in this chapter for laying-out and making Japanese planes, and for laying-out planes with blades having a shaped edge.

Traditionally, the blade stock for the *chibi-kanna* comes in about 4" (102mm)-wide sections (the blade length is about 2" or 51mm), and is available in different grades. It

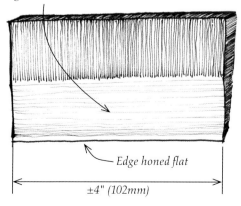

Inlaid edge steel; slight hollow ground across entire width

Figure 14-45B.

Edge honed flat

± 4" (102mm)

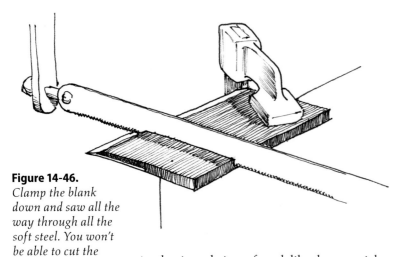

Figure 14-46.
Clamp the blank down and saw all the way through all the soft steel. You won't be able to cut the edge steel.

is a laminated piece of steel, like the material out of which the bigger blades are made, but having a gentle hollow grind from the edge to the upper portion of the blade where the lamination ends, and extending straight across the full width of the stock. This is done so that a blade of any width can be cut from the blank (Figure 14-45A) and still only the very edge has to be honed flat, rather than the entire back (Figure 14-45B). This long, gentle sweep of the hollow grind does not affect the fit of the blade in the *dai*; the blade is fitted in its tapered escapement, bevel down, much like other Japanese plane blades.

To make a blade, you mark the required width, cut through the backing steel with a hacksaw, and snap the brittle edge-steel free of the larger blank (Figures 14-46 and 14-47). Grind the edges smooth and, if you wish, shape the top edge where you will be tapping it with a hammer for adjustment (I usually don't bother). Then hone the back of the blade. Because only about the last 1/16" (2mm) of the back, at the edge, is honed, it goes fast. Then, sharpen the bevel.

Alternatively, since this blade blank is hard to find, you can buy the small blades already cut and finished to width, and sometimes

even with the edge shaped to one of various curves. These come in sizes from about ¼" to around ⅞" (6mm to 22mm) wide and about 2" to 2¾" (51mm to 70mm) long. Laminated high-quality blades hold an edge well.

Select the material for your *dai*. I often save the cutoffs from other planes I have made to use for these finger planes. The type of wood and grain orientation is the same as for the larger planes. The *dai* needs to be ¼" to about ⅜" (6mm to 10mm) wider than your blade. While you can, of course, make the planes any length, most of the time you want the plane proportionally short for the width of the blade, so it can get into restricted areas and easily shape or smooth what might initially be a less than perfectly level surface.

If this is the case, the finished length should be around 2" to 2½" (51mm to 64mm). Give yourself some extra length

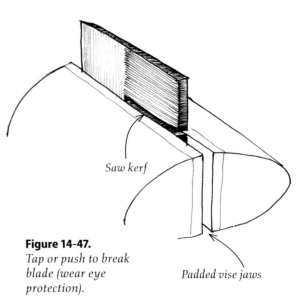

Saw kerf

Figure 14-47.
Tap or push to break blade (wear eye protection).

Padded vise jaws

when first laying out your *dai*; you may need it after determining the position of the mouth. To determine the thickness of the *dai*, decide on your blade angle; the *dai* should be thick enough to capture the laminated portion of the blade. Check your blade, but this usually results in the *dai* being ¾" to about 1" (19mm to 25mm) thick.

The *dai* is laid out as with any Japanese-style plane, but because of its shortness, there are some layout parameters to remember. You need about ¼" (6mm) or more of *dai* behind the blade at the top to properly support the blade.

Because of this, the layout of the *dai* begins at the back behind the blade to ensure you have enough wood there, rather than locating the mouth first at the usual five-eighths of the length of the *dai*. On a block longer than you think you'll need, begin your layout with a line, representing the top face of the blade, across the top back of the *dai* about ½" (13mm) in from the end. Then draw your blade-angle line from this to determine the location of the mouth.

Depending on the final length of your *dai*, the mouth may end up being far forward of where you expected it. You do not want much less than half the length of the plane in front of the blade or you will find it awkward starting a stroke. Cut the length of the *dai* after you have determined the position of the mouth (Figure 14-48).

Finish laying-out the *dai*. If you are making a plane that will have a curved blade, you may have to use the graphic projection method to cut the mouth opening. Most

chisel blades are too thick to cut open the mouth at the angle of the blade as described in the direct cutting method. (See "Laying Out and Cutting the Mouth Opening for Different Blade Shapes" on pages 302–305.)

To cut the *dai*, follow the same procedures as you would for a larger plane. If you are doing a plane with a shaped sole, first fit the blade most of the way to its final position before shaping the sole. When you are done with the sole, finish fitting the blade and adjust the mouth shape, if necessary.

Figure 14-48. Laying Out *Chibi-Kanna*

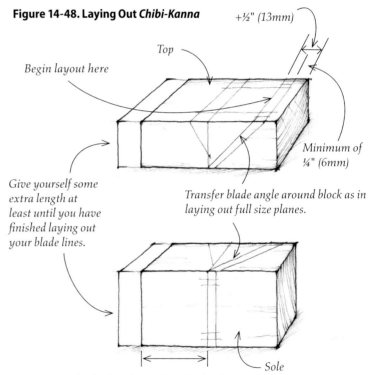

+½" (13mm)

Top

Begin layout here

Minimum of ¼" (6mm)

Give yourself some extra length at least until you have finished laying out your blade lines.

Transfer blade angle around block as in laying out full size planes.

Sole

Length of sole in front of the blade edge should be at least half the plane length.

Making a Compass Plane

If you are modifying a plane, make sure that the curve you are intending is not too severe; you do not want to remove too much wood (more than about a third of the original height of the plane body) and render the plane unworkable.

This is especially true of a plane with a concave sole, as any more than a slight curve will open the mouth too much, encroaching on the throat area, and may reduce the bed of the blade too much, as well. If you want more than a slight curve on a concave-sole plane, you may have to make a new plane with dimensions to compensate for what will have to be cut away (Figure 14-49).

Make a template directly from the work or a full-scale drawing, or use a thin batten or a compass to make the curve. The curve must be part of a circle (i.e., have a constant radius, not a varying radius, like a French curve). It is best to make a template of the curve of the work rather than the curve of the plane; that way you can use the template against the plane to check your accuracy. Transfer the curve to the plane. It is best to transfer the lines all the way around the plane (Figures 14-50 and 14-51).

If the maximum amount of material you have to remove is less than ⅛" (3mm) or so, you can use another plane to shape the bottom, working cross-wise to the length. Otherwise, band saw the waste away and fair the curve with another plane.

As the planing approaches the line, back the blade off to make lighter and lighter cuts. If the surface is particularly rough after this, you can smooth it some with a file. It does not have to be very smooth at this point. Check that the area of the sole in front of the mouth is dead straight across, as are the areas at the very head and toe, and that the sole is not twisted (Figures 14-52 and 14-53).

Figure 14-49.

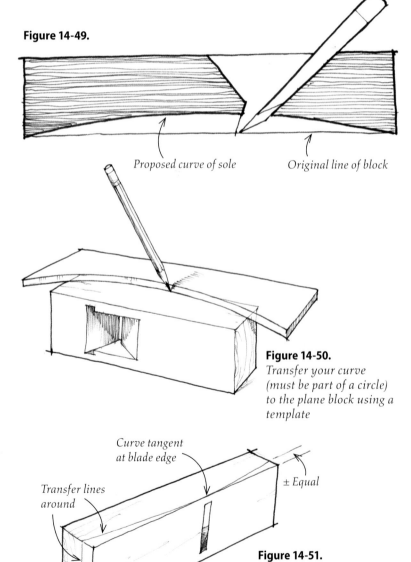

Proposed curve of sole

Original line of block

Figure 14-50.
Transfer your curve (must be part of a circle) to the plane block using a template

Curve tangent at blade edge

± Equal

Transfer lines around

Figure 14-51.

± Equal

Now here is the crucial part: the sole of the plane must contact the work only at the very front of the plane and at a small area right in front of the mouth. If other areas of the sole contact the work, the plane will ride up and you will have trouble getting a consistent cut. All the other areas of the sole must be relieved so that they do not contact the curve. The amount of relief will determine the accuracy of the curve, especially at the beginning and end of the cut, so you do not want to remove too much: just a few thousandths of an inch.

As well, make sure the area in front of the mouth follows the curve; the closer this area is in matching the curve, the finer you'll be able to set the blade (Figure 14-54). I usually use a card scraper to form these areas, perhaps assisted by some draw-filing to even things up. Give the sole a few degrees of chamfer along its length on either side of the blade; this will reduce the chance these areas will contact the work and interfere with the cut (Figure 14-55).

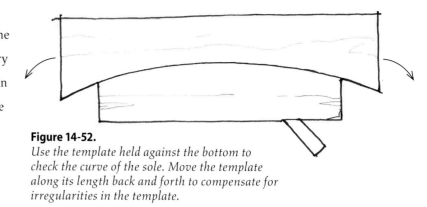

Figure 14-52.
Use the template held against the bottom to check the curve of the sole. Move the template along its length back and forth to compensate for irregularities in the template.

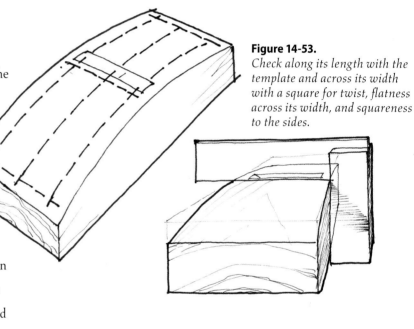

Figure 14-53.
Check along its length with the template and across its width with a square for twist, flatness across its width, and squareness to the sides.

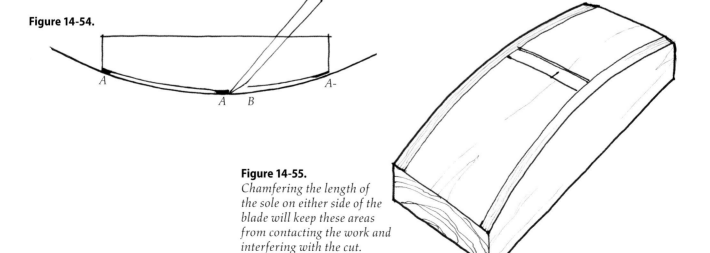

Figure 14-54.

Figure 14-55.
Chamfering the length of the sole on either side of the blade will keep these areas from contacting the work and interfering with the cut.

Figure 14-56.

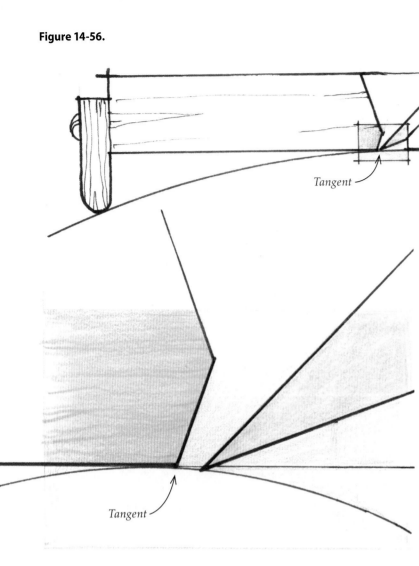

Tangent

Tangent

Figure 14-57.

For complex curves, I have been using a small Japanese-style smoother with a stop screwed to the front. How deep this stop is set determines the radius of the work. This works well except when coming off the curve, as the stop drops off losing the reference point. I have been able to work around this, but technically, you should also put a stop at the back of the plane to help stabilize the plane as the front stop comes off.

Round the bottom of the stop (Figure 8-3 on page 126). It can be screwed to the plane with machine screws (finer adjustment, greater holding power than a wood screw). Drill the holes in the plane with a drill bit sized to the shank of the screw, and let the screw tap its own threads as you drive it in.

To set the stop, position the plane on the curve of the work and adjust the stop until the blade just contacts the work. Check to see that the stop is parallel to the sole and then tighten the screws. If you also have a stop on the back of the plane, set it to just contact the surface (Figure 14-56 and 14-57).

Hollowing, Rounding & Spoonbottom Planes

If you need a hollowing or rounding plane of a specific size or curvature and are modifying a plane, pay attention to the geometry of the mouth and throat opening.

If you start with a plane with a straight blade, regrind the blade, and re-form the bottom of the plane, the mouth opening and the chipwell, as well, will no longer be parallel to the edge (Figure 14-58). This is because the throat angle is not parallel to the bed angle and so will open up the more the sole is curved. This may not be a problem if the sole is only slightly curved, or if a fine mouth is not important.

If the mouth opening is excessive for your needs, you will have to fit a sole plate or *kuchi-ire* to close the mouth down. If you are making a plane from scratch, curve the mouth opening and the chipwell to match.

While traditional Western hollow and round planes in the molding-plane style often have a casual mouth opening, formed by the angle of the chipwell that results in a mouth that does not exactly follow the curve of the blade, many times on a bench plane, you may want a tight mouth on a plane with a curved blade in order to reduce tearout.

When making such a plane, you have two ways to achieve this. The first is to graphically project the curve and cut it directly. The second is to cut the mouth opening and throat at the blade bed angle, shape the sole, and then cut the throat-relief angle to the resulting curve.

To make a spoonbottom plane, which is a compass plane with a convex curved blade, begin with the curve across the width of the plane. Cut the blade bed and mouth opening as described in "Laying-out and Cutting the Mouth Opening for Different Blade Shapes." Then form the curve across the plane's width, and grind and hone the blade to match. Lastly, form the curve along the length of the plane as described. Make a template before starting both curves, and check the work.

Figure 14-58.

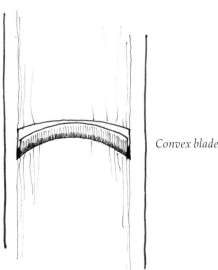

Convex blade

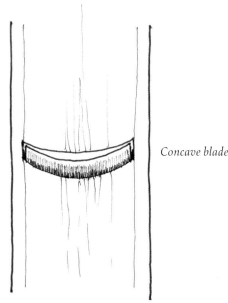

Concave blade

LAYING OUT & CUTTING THE MOUTH OPENING for DIFFERENT BLADE SHAPES

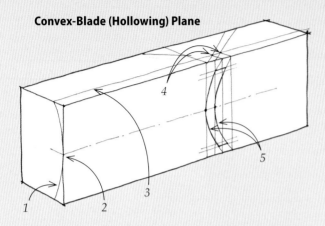

Convex-Blade (Hollowing) Plane

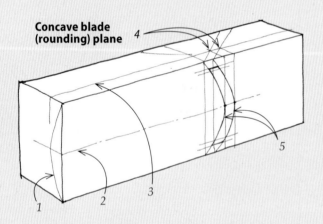

Concave blade (rounding) plane

Graphic Projection Methods for Blade Curves of Constant Radius

Convex-Blade (Hollowing) Plane

1 Mark the curve of sole on both ends of the block.

2 Mark the apex of the curve; for a symmetrical curve, this will be the centerline of the block

3 Mark the curve height line down both sides of the block. (If the curve is not symmetric, these may not be the same height.)

4 At the intersection of the curve height line and blade lines draw lines down the side and across the sole at 90° to intersect with the blade width lines and the apex line of the curve.

5 Sketch a curve from the intersection of these lines with the sides of the block to their intersection of the apex line with the mouth line. This is the line of the mouth opening. (If the curve is not symmetrical, it may be helpful to project a few more points to establish the curve.)

Concave blade (rounding) plane

1 Mark the curve of sole on both ends of the block.

2 Mark the apex of the curve; for a symmetrical curve this will be the centerline of the block

3 Mark the curve height line down both sides of the block. (If the curve is not symmetric, these may not be the same height.)

4 At the intersection of the curve height line and blade lines, draw lines down the side and across the sole to intersect with the line of the apex of the curve

5 Sketch a curve from the blade lines at either edge of the sole to the intersection of the apex line with the mouth line. This is the line of the mouth opening. (If the curve is not symmetrical, it may be helpful to project a few more points to establish the curve.)

If you cut the chipwell flat and not to a curve similar to the mouth opening, you may end up with very little support at the mouth, or even the chipwell cutting into the final mouth opening. Layout this curve before cutting to make sure you have enough material at the throat.

Laying Out the Chipwell of a Concave Blade (Rounding) Plane

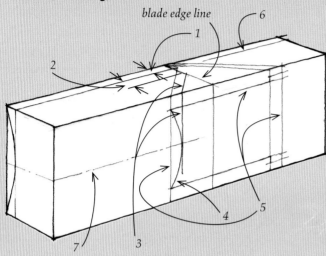

blade edge line

Laying Out the Chipwell of a Convex Blade (Hollowing) Plane

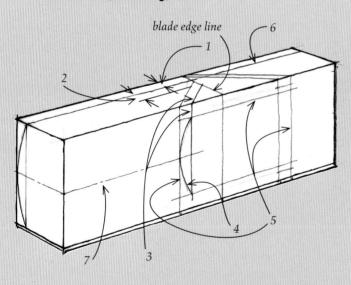

blade edge line

Laying Out the Chipwell of a Concave Blade (Rounding) Plane

1 Measure the height of the curve.

2 Transfer this dimension up from the curve height line to the blade edge line.

3 Transfer this point to the top of the block at the same angle as the chipwell, and across the top to intersect with the apex line.

4 Sketch a curve from the intersection of this line with the apex line to the corners of the original chipwell layout

5 Original chipwell layout lines

6 Curve height line

7 Apex of curve

Laying Out the Chipwell of a Convex Blade (Hollowing) Plane

1 Measure the height of the curve.

2 Mark this throat-height dimension up from the intersection of the curve-height line marked on the side with the blade-edge line.

3 Transfer this point to the top of the block at the same angle as the chipwell, and across the top to intersect with the apex line.

4 Sketch a curve from the intersection of this line with the layout line of the side of the chipwell to the intersection of the apex line with the front of the chipwell.

5 Original chipwell layout lines

6 Curve height line

7 Apex of curve

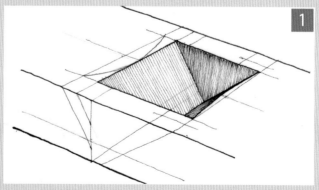

1

1 Cut open the opening for the blade as you would for a regular plane, chiseling to the high point of the curve of the chipwell.

LAYING OUT & CUTTING THE MOUTH OPENING FOR DIFFERENT BLADE SHAPES *(continued)*

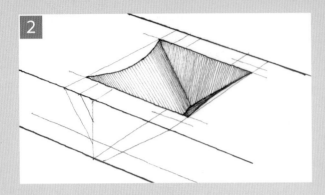

2 Form the curve of the chipwell.

3 Turn the block over and begin cutting the mouth opening. Chisel straight down—90° to the sole—on the line of the mouth, making a relief cut to free the chip back from the blade-bed line. Continue until you break through. Finish forming the blade bed.

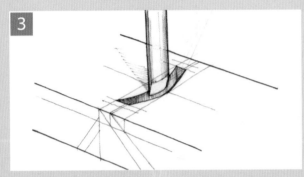

Direct Cutting Method

If your blade edge curve is a section of a circle, the Graphic Projection Method produces reasonable results. Curves that are more complex could also be projected in such a manner, but it is not practical to project very many points accurately on such a small scale. For this reason, and the fact that I often make mistakes in projecting my points, I most often use this method. You still need to graphically project the curve of the wall of the chipwell. Refer to pages 302 and 303, and Figures 1 and 2 (above) for laying out and cutting the chipwell.

4 After the chipwell and blade seat are fully excavated, make a V-cut to open the mouth on the bottom. The slope of the front cut at the mouth should match that of the top of the blade. The back cut at the blade seat is more vertical.

5 Continue cutting the mouth opening on the bottom with the front cut at the angle of the top of the blade, but the back cut (at the blade seat) increasingly undercut toward the angle of the blade seat.

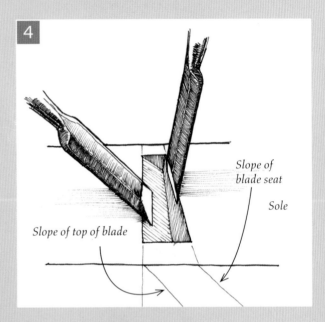

Slope of blade seat

Sole

Slope of top of blade

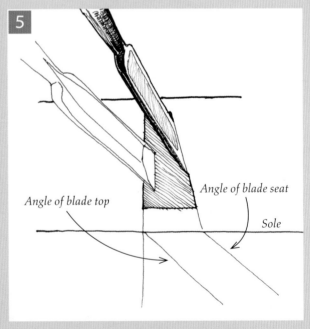

Angle of blade top

Angle of blade seat

Sole

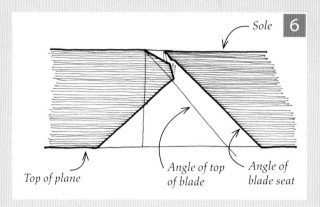

Sole

6

Top of plane

Angle of top of blade

Angle of blade seat

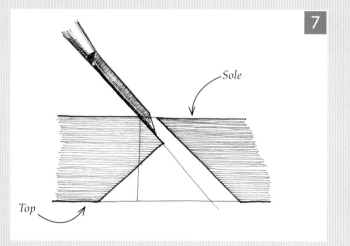

7

Sole

Top

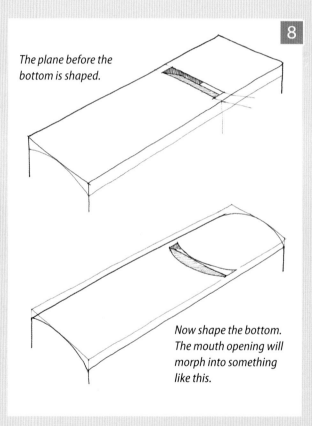

8

The plane before the bottom is shaped.

Now shape the bottom. The mouth opening will morph into something like this.

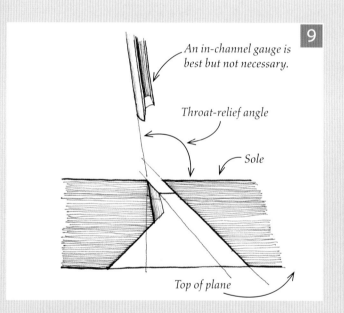

9

An in-channel gauge is best but not necessary.

Throat-relief angle

Sole

Top of plane

6 Alternate chiseling down from the top of the plane at the angle of the blade seat and from the sole, deepening the cut while opening it to the angles of the blade top and seat. Eventually you will break through.

7 Finish paring the opening down from both the top and bottom until you have a clean slot at the mouth parallel at the front to the angle of the blade top and at the back to the blade-seat angle.

8 Shape the bottom.

9 Pare the throat-relief angle back to the curve of the mouth opening.

FITTING A SOLE PLATE AT THE MOUTH OF A PLANE

Every plane should have a mouth opening sized to the task it is to perform, Or, said another way, the mouth opening should not be much larger than the thickest shaving the plane is expected to make. The performance of every plane in general—and a smoothing plane in particular—will improve if it has a sharp, properly sized mouth opening.

Fitting a sole plate at the mouth of a plane is a good way to restore an old wood plane whose mouth has worn and become too open to give the best performance. Many old wood planes are quite affordable, have good quality cast-steel blades, decent chipbreakers, and many years of service left in the bodies. Repairing the mouth opening with a sole plate will rejuvenate such planes, giving exceptional value for the effort.

Rather than chiseling an opening for the plate by hand, this technique uses a router and a custom-made template. Though time is spent making the template, I believe this is offset by the speed, and in particular, the accuracy of the router in cutting the flat bottom recess, which is difficult to do accurately by hand. Reuse the template for sole plates on planes with the same blade width.

The sole plate, the piece used to repair the mouth, should be the same species of wood as the body of the plane, with the grain oriented the same way—traditionally, flat-cut with the bark side down. It should be ½" to ⅝" (13mm to 16mm) thick, about as wide as the plane body, and long enough for several repair pieces. Do not rip it to final width yet.

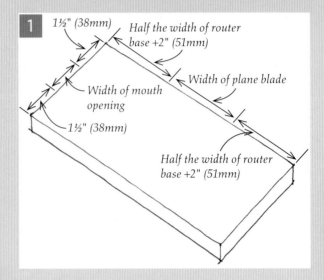

1 1½" (38mm) Half the width of router base +2" (51mm) Width of plane blade Width of mouth opening 1½" (38mm) Half the width of router base +2" (51mm)

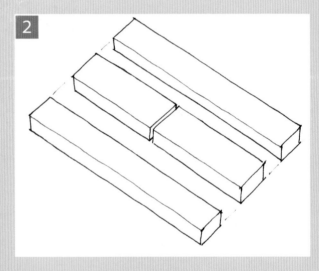

2

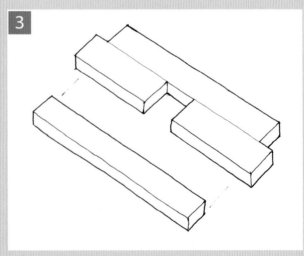

3

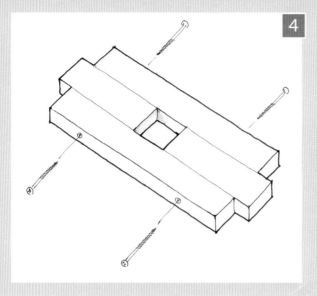

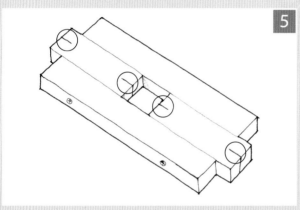

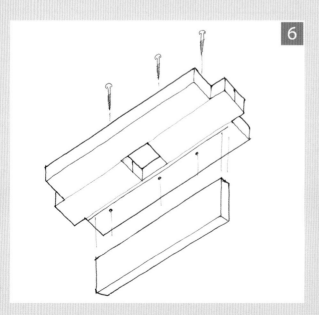

1 Prepare some ¾" (19mm) MDF to make a jig for routing the sole-plate recess.

2 Rip 1½" (38mm) off one side, then rip a piece the width of the mouth opening. With the saw still set at this width, rip the sole-plate blank to width. Having the jig and the blank exactly the same width simplifies fitting the repair. Next, cut the center piece in half

3 Mark a distance equal to or less than the blade width (this dimension is less critical—the sole plate is roughly square) at about the center of both of the sidepieces. Using isocyanurate glue (to allow hand alignment to set the pieces and reduce clamp time), glue the two centerpieces to the sidepiece at the mark. Work on a clean, flat surface to help align the faces.

4 Glue the second side to the centerpieces, reinforcing the glue with screws or dowels. Pre-drill the screws to prevent splitting. You can trim the ends of the centerpiece flush, if you want.

5 Mark centerlines on vertical faces of the centerpieces.

6 If your plane is too short to have the jig clamped without interfering with the router, clamp the jig in position and screw a fence to the jig at the side of the plane. Use the fence to clamp the jig when routing.

7 Mark a centerline down the sole of the plane. Adjust the plane blade so it just barely cuts, and mark the position of the blade edge with pencil on the sole and down the sides. Then remove the blade.

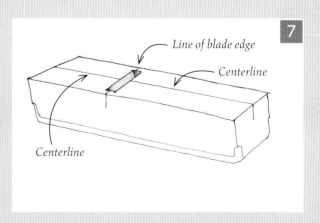

Line of blade edge

Centerline

Centerline

FITTING A SOLE PLATE AT THE MOUTH OF A PLANE *(continued)*

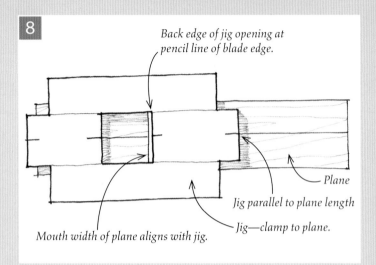

8

Back edge of jig opening at pencil line of blade edge.

Plane

Jig parallel to plane length

Jig—clamp to plane.

Mouth width of plane aligns with jig.

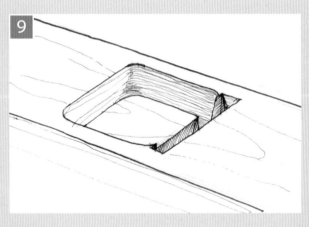

9

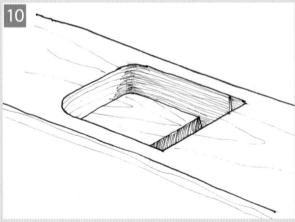

10

8 Align the jig with the centerlines of the plane, the back of the jig opening (the plane-blade end) slightly behind the pencil line indicating the blade edge. Verify that the jig opening aligns with the width of the mouth opening; this position takes precedent over alignment with centerline markings. Use the centerline markings to make the jig parallel with the length of the plane. Clamp the jig to the plane.

9 Use a ½" (13mm)-diameter by ¾" (19mm)-long pattern-routing bit with a top-mounted bearing. Set the depth and begin the cut by plunging to the full, or nearly full, depth in the center of the jig (so you do not damage it). Finish routing in the recess.

10 Square the rounded corners at the blade edge, carefully preserving the wedge abutments if they intersect. You can square up the other corners of the recess, or round the corners of the sole plate, your choice.

Cut the sole plate to the exact length of the matching opening in the jig. Fit the sole plate into the recess and insert the blade into its position. The sole plate should be slightly larger than will allow the blade to be set to its cutting position. If not, move the sole plate to its final position in relation to the mouth opening you want and glue it in place.

If the sole plate is too long, remove it and trim it on the shooting board until it just fits, establishing the mouth opening you want. If you want a throat-clearance angle less than 90° (70° or 80° is common for a plane other than a fine smoother), or, alternatively, if you want to increase the chip clearance angle for a fine smoother, plane the mouth end with the piece shimmed up on the shooting board to achieve the angle you want. This will, of course, shorten the sole plate, so be careful you have enough left. Be aware, the angle may complicate fitting at the wedge abutments. Lastly, glue the sole plate in.

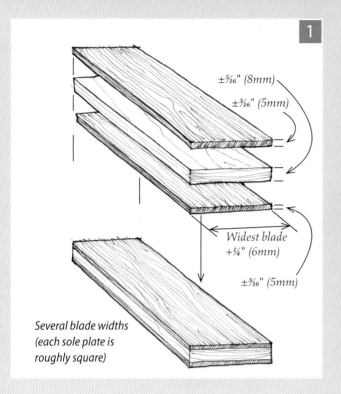

1

±⁵⁄₁₆" (8mm)

±³⁄₁₆" (5mm)

Widest blade
+¼" (6mm)

±³⁄₁₆" (5mm)

*Several blade widths
(each sole plate is
roughly square)*

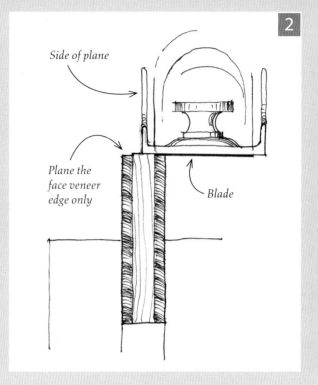

2

Side of plane

*Plane the
face veneer
edge only*

Blade

3

*Half the width of
the router base
+1½" (38mm)*

*Cut these
off; they
are fragile*

2" (25mm)

2"

2"

⁹⁄₃₂" or diameter of
collar or pattern-
routing bit

¾" (19mm) MDF

A moveable sole plate has a number of advantages. It increases the versatility of the plane, since the mouth opening can be set for fine or coarse cuts or to accommodate unruly grain. Additionally, as the sole wears and is trued, the plate can be readjusted to close the mouth, rather than having to be replaced.

The process for fitting a moveable sole plate is the same as fitting a glued-In repair. There are some additional steps, however. It is not necessary, but probably better, to laminate the sole plate for wear and stability. Also, slots must be cut for the fixing screw and screw head.

Begin by laminating up the sole-plate blank. Make it at least ¼" (6mm) wider than your widest mouth opening, and long enough for several repairs. The face material should be about ³⁄₁₆" (5mm) thick, each side, with a core (one ply) of the same wood as the plane body, about ⁵⁄₁₆" (8mm) thick, and the same grain orientation as the main body of the plane (**Figure 1).** For the wood, lignum vitae, ironbark, ipe, or pau ferro are good choices; some dark tropical woods, such as ebony, can chip and sometimes leave dark streaks on light wood.

FITTING A MOVEABLE SOLE PLATE *(continued)*

4

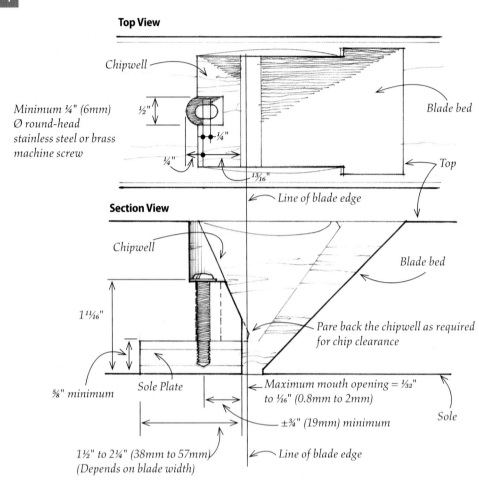

Top View

Chipwell

Minimum ¼" (6mm)
Ø round-head
stainless steel or brass
machine screw

½"

¼"

¼"

13/16"

Blade bed

Top

Line of blade edge

Section View

Chipwell

1 11/16"

Blade bed

Pare back the chipwell as required
for chip clearance

⅝" minimum

Sole Plate

Maximum mouth opening = 1/32"
to 1/16" (0.8mm to 2mm)

±¾" (19mm) minimum

Sole

1½" to 2¼" (38mm to 57mm)
(Depends on blade width)

Line of blade edge

Slot for screw head must be deep enough to allow ±¼" adjustability and bearing for the screw head's washer, and be able to use a standard length screw that does not penetrate the surface ply of the sole plate.

Cut a ½" (13mm) slot for the screw head and its washer, and a through slot for the shank of the screw. Make both long enough to give the screw about ¼" (6mm) travel.

Glue up the blank and let it sit overnight, preferably longer, before jointing one edge and then ripping it to width when the jig is made

The procedures for making the router jig for cutting and fitting the sole plate is as shown in "Fitting a Sole Plate at the Mouth of a Plane" on page 306. Do not glue the sole plate in. Fitting the moveable sole plate involves an additional step: leave the core wood a snug fit in its recess; however, plane back the width of both face veneers, one light shaving each side **(Figure 2).**

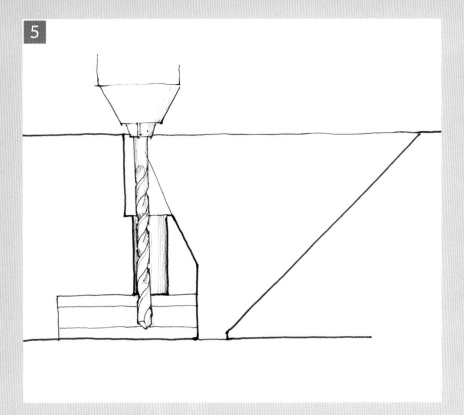

5

5 Drill a hole the diameter of the screw
shank (not the thread diameter!)
at the front end of the screw slot, to a
depth just shy of the bottom of the core
veneer of the sole plate.

Make a jig for routing the slot for the screw head similar to the jig made to route the
sole-plate recess, using the same techniques **(Figure 3).** You can make the jig to
accommodate a ½" (13mm)
pattern-routing bit with a top-mounted bearing, or you can use a
½" (13mm) diameter straight bit with a collar. Each has its advantages and
disadvantages. With the pattern-routing bit, it is easy to size the jig, but also easy
to damage it. With a straight bit and collar, you'll have to size the jig cutout to
accommodate any offset between the diameter of the collar and the diameter of the
bit, but the jig is less likely to get damaged by the bit.) You may have to use a straight
bit anyway to get the length required. Check before you make the jig **(Figure 4).**

Again, if the plane is too short to clamp on top, mount a side fence below to clamp to.

Mark the centerlines on the top of the plane and the front location of where the slot
will be (see Figure 4) for calculating the position of screw). Set the jig on the centerline
with the front of the jig opening at the mark of the front of the screw. Route the slot for
the screwhead with a ½" (13mm)-diameter router bit. If you are using a pattern-routing
bit, make sure the bit is long enough to reach while still keeping the bearing within
the thickness of the jig. Set the depth of the bit so the bearing is within the jig before
starting the router. Otherwise, you will be making another jig.

FITTING A MOVEABLE SOLE PLATE *(continued)*

Locate the centers of the screw-shank slot: drill each
end and then the center on the drill press. Clean out
the slot with the drill bit to get an unencumbered slot.
A Forstner bit is best for this, or a good brad-point.

Fit the sole plate as you would a fixed plate: if it is too
long, cut it so it gives the maximum mouth opening
you may want for this plane when it is in its far forward
position. Check that the edge of the mouth is parallel
with the blade edge when the blade edge is parallel
to the sole of the plane. Adjust the clearance angle of
the throat to your requirements, as described above for
fitting a fixed plate. Then, with the sole plate in position,
drill a hole the diameter of the screw shank at the front
end of the screw slot, to a depth just shy of the bottom
of the core veneer of the sole plate (**Figure 5**).

Remove the sole plate, clean the hole of all debris,
replace the sole plate, and screw the machine screw
(with a washer attached) into the hole in the sole plate.
This will tap threads into the wood as it goes. If you
have to remove the screw and reinsert it, be careful to
properly start the screw in the already-cut threads.

When the mouth needs to be closed down, after the
screw is loosened, sometimes the sole plate sticks and
cannot be moved with the fingers. You can cut a notch
about 1⁄16" (2mm) deep by approximately 3⁄8" (10mm)
wide at the front of the plate—first remove the plate, of
course (**Figure 6**). Then, when the plate sticks, a small
screwdriver can be gently inserted to carefully coax the
plate into position. Do not forget to lock it in place with
the machine screw.

Now, if the edge of your mouth is parallel with the blade
and its edge is clean and sharp, you are good to go.

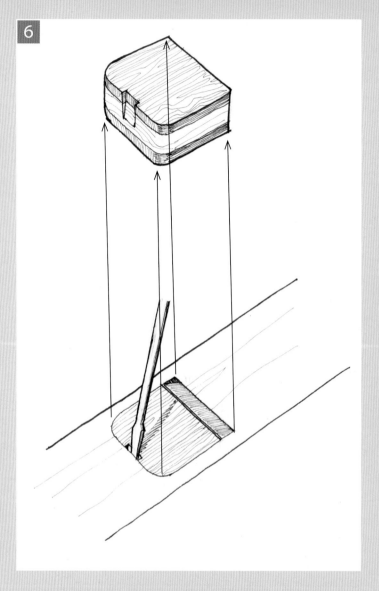

6

6 Cut a notch about 1⁄16" (2mm) deep by approximately 3⁄8" (10mm) wide at the
front of the plate so that when the sole plate sticks, a small screwdriver can
be gently inserted to carefully coax it into position.

Fitting a moveable sole plate when making a Krenov-style plane is relatively easy if done before the plane is glued up. It simplifies getting a very tight mouth, and allows increased versatility of the plane should that be required.

When making the plane, after the blade bed block is cut free, cut the front part of the center block at 90° at the throat line. Then, cut from the front block a piece that will become the sole plate, leaving a notch ¹¹⁄₁₆" deep by ±2" long overall. Cut this notch on the table saw with a tenoning jig or clamped to a miter gauge. You can then cut the line of the chipwell on the front block.

Rip the thickness of the piece that will become the sole plate to ⁵⁄₁₆" (8mm) (it should be about ½", or 13mm, before) and glue ³⁄₁₆" (5mm)-thick face veneer on each side (see "Fitting a Movable Sole Plate" on page 309). It will be safer to rip this core piece by hand: with a marking gauge, scribe a line all around the piece at ⁵⁄₁₆" (8mm), saw to one side of the line and plane it down to split the line. After it is glued up and installed, any discrepancies in thickness can be planed out when the plane's sole is conditioned. After a few days drying, trim the face veneer flush, and then a light plane stroke narrower, on each side. Proceed with completing the plane, making sure when gluing up that glue is cleaned from the recess for the sole plate.

Before shaping the plane, make the jig for routing the slot for the screwhead. Route the slot and drill the elongated holes. Try to keep the slot within the chipwell. Finish fitting the sole plate as with any moveable sole plate.

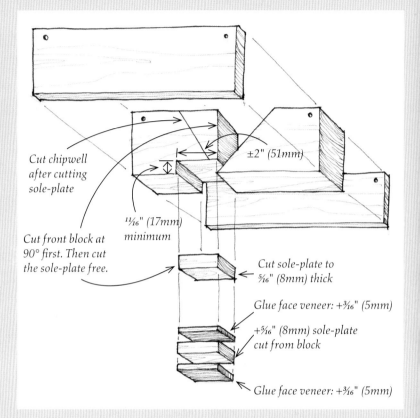

Cut chipwell after cutting sole-plate

±2" (51mm)

Cut front block at 90° first. Then cut the sole-plate free.

¹¹⁄₁₆" (17mm) minimum

Cut sole-plate to ⁵⁄₁₆" (8mm) thick

Glue face veneer: +³⁄₁₆" (5mm)

+⁵⁄₁₆" (8mm) sole-plate cut from block

Glue face veneer: +³⁄₁₆" (5mm)

INDEX

A

alloy steel, 24–29
  A2, 26, 27
  changing market for, 28
  chrome vanadium, 26
  commonly used types, 26
  cryogenic hardening process, 27
  development of, 24–25
  eliminating problems of carbon steel, 25
  forgeability of, 25
  grain structure of, 25
  high-speed steel (HSS), 29
  ingredients, 21
  01, 26, 27
  tungsten vanadium, 26
anatomy of planes, 30–57. *See also* angle of
  blade; bevel angle; chipbreakers; *specific
  types of planes*
  about: overview of, 30–32; using
    information about, 32
  common features summarized, 32
  core tactics, 32
  length of plane/width of blade, 55–57
  mouth opening, 41–44
  shape of blade edge, 54
angle of blade, 33–44. *See also specific types
  of planes*
  best, 35–38
  bevel angle and, 39–40, 52–53
  cabinet pitch, 36
  common angles, illustrated, 36
  common pitch, 36
  custom angles, 39–40
  for cutting end grain, 36
  defined, 33
  half pitch, 36
  middle pitch, 36
  plane geometry summary and, 49–51
  skewing plane and, 40
  task requirements and, 38
  traditional angles, 33–35
  by type of wood, 35, 36–38
  using lowest effective angle, 34, 35–36
  York pitch, 36
annealing steel, 20
antique planes/blades, 39, 88, 124, 163–65,
  168, 258, 259
A2 steel blades, 26, 27

B

Bailey-style planes. *See* Stanley/Bailey-style
  planes
bedding blades
  checking for custom fit, 166
  convex beds, 182–83
  Japanese planes, 181–84
  rabbet planes, 190
  Stanley/Bailey-style planes, 155–56
  troubleshooting issues, 197–98
  wood-body planes, 166–67
bench hooks, 111, 240. *See also* shooting
  boards
bench planes overview, 58. *See also specific
  types of planes*

bench work, 216–37. *See also* dimensioning
  stock
  about: overview of, 216–18
  bench dogs for, 224
  bench slave for, 223
  common tasks, 234–35
  deadmen and helper boys for, 223
  with difficult grain, 235
  handscrew clamp holding work, 222
  keeping surface flat, 201
  shooting edges, 235–37
  simple bench for, 220–21
  simple bench stop for, 218–19
  vise stops for, 219–22
bevel angle, 52–53
  chatter and, 48, 198–99
  correct, 52
  custom angles, 39–40
  factory-ground, 52, 53
  honing hollow-ground bevel, 53
  how edge dulls, 53
  microbevels and, 146, 147, 180, 206–7
bevel shape, sharpening and, 205–7
blades, 14–29. *See also* cutting edge
  adjusting, general techniques, 152. *See
    also specific types of planes*
  anatomy of steel and, 17–20
  angle of. *See* angle of blade
  basic criteria for, 16
  choosing, 16
  confusing/contradictory claims about, 14
  durability of, 16
  flattening back of, 148–49, 178, 179
  grain of steel, 17
  hardness of, 19–20
  individuality of, 16
  mouth opening and, 41–44
  preparing, 146
  sharpening. *See sharpening references*
  structure of steel, 17–19
  types of steel for. *See* steel types
  width of, length of plane and, 55–57
block planes (metal)
  adjusting blade, 152
  adjusting throat of, 76–77, 78, 79
  advantages and disadvantages, 77–78
  angle of blade, 79
  antique, 39
  custom blade angles and, 39–40
  features and functions, 70, 76–79
  as first plane to buy, 136
  market models, 77, 78, 136
  old Stanley 5 ½, 74
  recommended models, 136
  sequence of use, 136
  versatility of, 77
block planes (wood), 86–88, 194, 196
blue steel, 22
body, attending to details of. *See* inspecting
  planes; sole, details of body and
bottom of planes. *See sole references*
bridge boards, 114
bullnose/chisel planes, 112

C

carbon steel, 21–24
cast steel (or crucible steel), 22–23
chamfer planes, 124, 130, 131
chatter
  bevel angle and, 48, 198–99
  leaving parallel marks perpendicular to
    stroke, 197–98
  poor design and manufacture causing,
    199
  Sta-Set chipbreaker stopping, 48
  troubleshooting, 197–99
chibi-kanna, 39, 129, 132, 133, 295–97
Chinese planes, 98–99
  adjusting blade, 152
  anatomy of, 99
  angle of blade, 33–35, 98
  blades, 28, 98–99
  brass mouthpiece, 98, 99, 174, 175
  features and functions, 98–99
  intermediate smoother, 34
  jointer planes, 34, 64
  sizes and types of, 34
  smoothing planes, 34, 68, 98–99, 174
  sole of, 98, 174
  tearout control features, 98
Chinese planes, setting up, 173–76
  adjusting mouth, 175
  attending to details of body and sole, 175
  attending to details of grip and finish, 176
  bedding blade, 166–67
  checking brass mouthpiece, 175
  configuring sole, 174
  inspecting plane, 163–65, 173–74
  preparing blade, 146
  preparing/fitting chipbreaker, 146–50
  troubleshooting, 197–201
chipbreakers
  flat bevel-style, 45–46
  function of, 45
  Japanese planes, 45, 95, 96, 180–81
  plane geometry summary and, 49–51
  rounded-style, 46
  shapes and types, 45–47
  Stanley-type, 46
  Sta-Set, 46–47, 48
  thickness of assemblies, 47
chipbreakers, preparing and fitting
  general guidelines, 146–50
  Japanese planes, 180–81
  rabbet planes, 190
  Stanley/Bailey-style planes, 155
choosing handplanes, 134–43
  about: overview of, 3, 134
  beyond basics, 140–43
  compass planes, 143
  first plane, 136
  jointer planes, 141–42
  joint-making planes, 138
  second plane, 137–38
  smoothing planes, 139–41
chrome vanadium blades, 26
Clifton planes, 46–47, 96, 110, 112, 140, 259
compass planes, 123, 124–27, 143, 298–300,
  301

concave blade (rounding) planes, 128, 196, 301, 302, 303
configuring sole. *See* sole, configuring
contact areas. *See also* sole, configuring
    causing shiny streaks on work, 201
    flat metal soles and, 57
    flatness tolerances, 55–57
    of Japanese planes, 56–57
    relieving areas around, 56–57
    varying depending on use, 56–57
convex blade (hollowing) planes, 128, 183, 301, 302, 303
cryogenic hardening process, 27
cutting edge. *See also* angle of blade; bevel
  angle; blades; *specific types of planes*
    angle of. *See* angle of blade
    on Disston saws, 19
    how it dulls, 53
    ideal, 18
    requirements, 16, 18
    shape (curvature) of, 54
    shaping with abrasives vs., 13
    sharpening. *See sharpening references*
    types of steel for. *See* steel types
    what happens when using, 151

D
deadmen and helper boys, 223
diamond stones, 210
dimensioning stock, 225–34
    checking for parallel, 228
    continuing with jointer plane, 230–31
    examining boards, 226
    planing edges and second side, 233–34
    preparing first face (scrub and jack
      planes), 226–30
    smoothing first face, 232
    using winding sticks, 226, 227, 228, 229
dovetail, sliding, 108–9
dovetail planes, 108–9, 117
dovetailed shooting board. *See* shooting
  boards
dulling of blade, 53
dust, handplanes and, 4

E
edges (of blades). *See* cutting edge
edges (of wood)
    shooting, 235–37
    smoothing, 12–13
end grain
    cutting, 36
    shooting, 243

F
filing mouth relief, 160
fillister planes, 105–7, 193
finish of plane. *See* grip and finish, attending
  to
finishing wood
    with oil, 10
    with penetrating finishes, 10
    preparing wood before. *See* smoothing

  wood
    sanding during and after, 10, 11
    with surface finishes, 11
    with varnish, lacquer, or shellac, 11
flattening back of blades, 148–49, 178, 179
fore planes, 61, 233, 258, 259, 262–63, 285

G
geometry of plane, summary, 49–51
grain (of steel), 17
grain (of wood)
    cutting end grain, 36
    difficult, working with, 235
grinding procedures and equipment, 207–9
grip and finish, attending to
    Chinese planes, 176
    Japanese planes, 188
    Stanley/Bailey-style planes, 162
    wood-body planes, 173

H
handles (totes), making, 274, 284–85
hardness, of blades, 19–20
helper boys and deadmen, 223
high-speed steel (HSS), 29
hinge mortise, 119–21
history of handplanes
    current reality, 3
    evolution and development, 1–2
    peak of development, 1
hollowing, 301
hollows and rounds, 128–29, 194–96, 301
horned planes, 26, 62, 76, 91–94, 173

I
inspecting planes
    Chinese planes, 163–65, 173–74
    Japanese planes, 177
    rabbet planes, 188–89
    Stanley/Bailey-style planes, 154–55
    summary of setup steps and, 144
    wood-body planes, 163–65

J
jack planes, 60–62
    angle of blade, 60–61
    Bailey-style, 85
    dimensioning stock with, 230, 233, 234
    features and functions, 60–62
    fore planes and, 61, 233, 258, 259, 262–63,
      285
    making. *See* making planes
    mouth opening, 60
    setting up. *See* wood-body planes
    traditional wood, 87
    variations, 62, 97
    what to look for in, 62
Japanese planes, 95–97. *See also* Japanese
  planes, setting up
    adjusting blade, 152, 177, 187
    advantages of, 79
    anatomy of, 95

    angle of blade, 33–34, 35, 38, 73, 74, 95
    blade chatter issues, 198
    blade steel, 22–24
    blades, 95–96
    chibi-kanna, 39, 129, 132, 133, 295–97
    chipbreakers, 45, 95, 96, 180–81
    compass planes, 123, 124–27, 143
    contact areas, 56–57, 184–86
    edge-joining boards and, 64
    features and functions, 95–97
    fillister planes, 107
    hollow of blade, 95
    hollows and rounds, 128–29
    jack plane variations, 62, 97
    jointer planes, 64, 97
    making, 39, 286–97
    moving-fillister planes, 193
    pulling instead of pushing, 96, 97
    quality of blades, 38
    rabbet planes, 103, 104, 189
    reliability of, 96–97
    removing blade, 97
    simplicity of, 95
    skew-bladed rabbet planes, 104–5, 189
    smoothing planes, 35, 64, 139
    storing, 97
    tapping out blade, 178–79
    thin shaving example, 200
    Western planes compared to, 96
Japanese planes, setting up, 177–88
    adjusting blade, 186
    adjusting mouth, 186
    attending to details of body and sole, 187
    attending to details of grip and finish, 188
    bedding blade, 181–84
    configuring sole, 184–86
    inspecting plane, 177
    preparing blade, 179–80
    preparing/fitting chipbreaker, 180–81
    tapping out blade, 178–79
    troubleshooting, 197–201
Japanese waterstones. *See* sharpening stones
jig drawbacks, 204–5
joinery planes, 100–121, 138. *See also* rabbet
  planes
    about: overview of, 102
    dovetail planes, 108–9, 117
    mortise planes, 118–21
    router planes, 101, 104, 113–15
    setting up. *See* wood-body planes
jointer planes, 63–66
    Bailey-style, 85
    choosing, 65
    curvature of blade, 63, 64
    dimensioning stock with, 230–31
    features and functions, 63–66
    Japanese and Chinese, 64–65, 97
    long planes and, 63
    making. *See* making planes
    mouth opening, 63
    traditional Western, illustrated, 63
    traditional wood, 88
    trying (try) planes and, 63
    value of, 65–66

K

Krenov-style planes, 39, 258, 313

L

length of plane/width of blade, 55–57
Lie-Nielsen planes, 40, 45, 77, 78, 85, 110, 114–15, 117, 136, 137–38, 140
long planes, 55, 61, 63

M

making planes
    about: overview of, 256, 258–59
    benefits of, 39
    blades to use, 259
    chibi-kanna, 295–97
    closed tote detail, 274
    compass plane, 298–300
    cross-pin bearing plate drawing, 275
    custom blade angles and, 39–40
    detail drawings for, 260–75
    fitting sole plates, 281–83, 306–13
    fore plane, 259, 262–63
    jack plane, 259, 260–61
    Japanese-style planes, 39, 286–97
    jointer plane, 259, 264–65
    laying out/cutting mouth openings for different blade shapes, 302–5
    materials required, 259–61
    open tote detail, 274
    panel plane, 259, 266–67
    preliminary work, 276–80
    rough-shaping blocks, 280–81
    selecting stock, 259–61
    shaping smoothing planes, 283–84
    smoothing planes, 268–71, 283–84
    sole-plate fixing screw slot layout, 272–73
    totes (handles), 274, 284–85
    wedge profile, 275
metal scraper, 158
microbevels, 146, 147, 180, 206–7
Millers Falls planes, 48, 137, 138
molding planes, 35, 38, 39, 124, 301
mortise planes, 118–21
mortising for hinge, 119–21
mouth opening. *See also specific types of planes*
    chips jamming, 200–201
    features and specifications, 41–43
    filing relief, 160
    fitting sole plate at, 306–8
    going out of parallel, 162
    laying out/cutting, for different blade shapes, 302–5
    plane geometry summary and, 49–51
mouth opening, adjusting
    Chinese planes, 175
    general guidelines, 43–44
    Japanese planes, 186
    rabbet planes, 191
    Stanley/Bailey-style planes, 161–62
    wood-body planes, 170–72
moveable sole plates, fitting, 309–13

N

Norris planes, 34, 89–90

O

oilers, 153
oilstones, 209
01 steel blades, 27

P

panel planes, 64, 140–41, 232, 234, 257, 258–59, 266–67
plane geometry summary, 49–51
planing. *See* bench work
Primus jack plane, 92–93, 94

R

rabbet planes, 54, 102–5
    adjusting blade, 152
    angle of blade, 102
    basic plane, 102–3
    bullnose/chisel planes, 112
    choosing, 104–5
    defined, 102
    features and functions, 102–5
    fillister planes, 105–7, 193
    moving-fillister planes, 193
    planing V-grooves and rabbets, 104
    shoulder planes, 110–11, 138
    side-rabbet planes, 116–17, 138
    using, 103–4
rabbet planes, setting up, 188–92
    adjusting mouth, 191
    attending to details of body and sole, 192
    bedding blade, 190
    configuring sole, 190–91
    inspecting plane, 188–89
    Japanese skew-bladed planes, 189
    preparing blade, 190
    preparing/fitting chipbreaker, 190
    troubleshooting, 197–201
rabbets, planing, 104
results with handplanes, 3–4
rewards, of using handplanes, 5
ridges, plane leaving, 201
Rockwell C (Rc) hardness scale, 20
rounds. *See* hollows and rounds
router planes, 104, 113–15

S

sanding
    cost considerations, 5
    dust concerns, 4
    finishing and, 10, 11
    grit challenges, 12
    horizontal flat surfaces, 12
    how it smoothes wood, 8
    planing compared to, 4–5, 13
    scratches/torn fibers left by, 8, 9
    size of grit, 12
scrapers, for metal, 158
scraping
    finishing wood and, 9, 11
    removing mill marks by, 11
    torn fibers and tails from, 9, 11
scrub planes, 49, 54, 70, 75–76, 92, 142, 227–28, 230, 234
sequence of planes to use, 70
setup order (general guidelines), 144–201
    about: summary of steps, 144
    adjusting blade, 152
    configuring sole, 150–51
    flattening back of blades, 148–49
    inspecting plane, 144

oilers and, 153
    preparing blade, 146
    preparing/fitting chipbreaker, 146–50
setup order (specific planes)
    Bailey/Stanley planes, 153–62
    Chinese planes, 173–76
    fillister and moving-fillister planes, 193
    hollows and rounds, 194–96
    Japanese planes, 177–88
    rabbet planes, 188–92
    troubleshooting setup, 197–201
    wood-body planes, 163–73
shaping planes, 122–33
    about: overview of, 122
    chamfer planes, 124, 129, 130, 131
    compass planes, 123, 124–27, 143, 298–300, 301
    hollows and rounds, 128–29, 194–96
    little planes (*chibi-kanna*), 39, 129, 132, 133, 295–97
    spoonbottom planes, 131–32, 301
sharpening, 202–15. *See also* sharpening stones
    about: overview of, 202
    alloy steel blades, 26
    bevel shape and, 205–7
    fundamentals of, 204
    goals of, 202
    grinding procedures and equipment, 207–9
    importance of, 16, 57
    jig drawbacks, 204–5
    microbevels and honing guides, 206–7
    multiple times daily, 16
    re-sharpening vs., 16
sharpening stones, 209–15
    diamond stones, 210
    Japanese waterstones, 209, 210, 211
    listening when using, 212
    oilstones, 209
    overview of, 209–10
    recommended, 209
    techniques, 211, 212–15
    types of stones, 209–10
    using/maintaining waterstones, 211
shiny streaks on work, 201
shooting boards, 238–55
    bench hooks vs., 240
    function of, 238–40
    making, 244–53
    for miters, 240–42
    planes to use on, 241
    quick and easy, 242
    shooting edges with, 235–37
    shooting end grain with, 243
    three variations, illustrated, 224
    using, 240–43
    value of, 225
side-rabbet planes, 116–17, 138
skew-bladed rabbet planes, 104–5, 189
skewed blades, 104–5, 107, 108, 189, 190, 241
skewing planes, 40, 126
sliding dovetail joints, 108–9. *See also* shooting boards, making

smoothing planes, 67–69. *See also* panel
  planes
    adjusting mouth of, 175
    angle of blade, 68
    Bailey-style, 85
    Chinese planes, 34, 68, 98–99, 174
    configuring sole of, 150–51
    features and functions, 67–68
    horned planes, 94
    ideal edge shape, 67
    Japanese planes, 35, 64, 139
    length of plane/width of blade, 55–57
    making. *See* making planes
    mouth opening, 68
    Norris, 90–91
    reasons for narrowness, 69
    recommended models, 139–41
    setting up, 141. *See also* wood-body
      planes
    traditional Western coffin-sided,
      illustrated, 67, 257
    traditional wood, 88
    using, for dimensioning stock, 232–34
    what to look for in, 69
smoothing wood
    about: overview of what to use, 6
    edges, 12–13
    finishing after, 10–11
    horizontal flat surfaces, 12
    planing and, 10
    planing compared to sanding, 4–5, 13
    sanding and, 8
    scraping and, 9
    scratches/torn fibers and, 8, 9
sole, configuring. *See also* mouth opening,
  adjusting
    avoiding distortion, 161
    Chinese planes, 174
    gauging straightness, 159, 161
    general guidelines, 150–51
    Japanese planes, 184–86
    metal scraper for, 158
    rabbet planes, 190–91
    Stanley/Bailey-style planes, 157–61
    winding sticks for, 157, 158, 167, 185
    wood-body planes, 168–70
sole, details of body and
    Chinese planes, 175
    Japanese planes, 187
    rabbet planes, 192
    Stanley/Bailey-style planes, 162
    wood-body planes, 173
sole plates, fitting, 281–83, 306–13
spoonbottom planes, 131–32, 301
Stanley block planes. *See* block planes (metal)
Stanley/Bailey-style planes, 82–85
    adjusting blade, 152, 163
    adjusting frog, 44, 83, 84
    anatomy of, 83
    angle of blade, 33, 83
    Bailey-style jack, jointer, and smoother, 85
    blade chatter issues, 197
    chipbreakers, 46, 47–48, 51
    cutting end grain, 36
    features and functions, 82–85
    history of, 82
    jointer planes, 63
    premium grades, 84, 85
    recommended models, 136, 137, 138
Stanley/Bailey-style planes, setting up,
  153–62

adjusting mouth, 161–62
attending to details of body and sole, 162
attending to details of grip and finish, 162
bedding blade, 155–56
cast iron resting period and, 153–54
configuring sole, 157–61
inspecting plane, 154–55
preparing blade, 146
preparing/fitting chipbreaker, 146–50
troubleshooting, 197–201
working around blade-adjustment nib,
  157
steel
    anatomy of, 17–20
    annealing, 20
    drop forging, 18–19
    grain of, 17
    hammer forging, 18
    hardening process, 20
    hardness of, 19–20
    as interface between you and wood, 16
    no forging, 19
    Rockwell C (Rc) hardness scale, 20
    structure of, 17–19
    tempering, 20
steel types, 21–29
    alloy steel, 21, 24–29
    blue steel, 22
    carbon steel, 21–24
    cast steel (or crucible steel), 22–23
    changing market for, 28
    for hardwoods, 25, 37
    high-speed steel (HSS), 29
    plain carbon steel, 24
    resting period for, 153–54
    softer, for backing, 23–24
    for softwoods, 25, 37
    white steel, 22

tearout
    avoiding, 199–200
    blade angle and, 37, 38, 63
    blade depth and, 55
    blade sharpness and, 40
    Chinese planes and, 98, 99
    chipbreaker reducing, 45, 46, 48, 50, 51,
      84, 95
    Japanese planes and, 95
    jointer plane and, 230–31
    minor, removing, 11, 12
    mouth opening reducing, 41, 43, 84
    panel planes and, 72–73
    scrapers and, 9
    smoothing plane and, 232
    troubleshooting, 199–200
tempering steel, 20
totes (handles), making, 274, 284–85
tracks, plane leaving, 201
troubleshooting, 197–201
    bevel angle issues, 198–99
    blade chatter issues, 197–99
    blade leaving parallel marks
      perpendicular to stroke, 197
    chips jamming mouth of plane, 200–201
    shavings not fine enough, 199
    shiny streaks on work, 201
    tearout, 199–200
    tracks or ridges on work, 201

truing planes, 35, 55, 56–57, 64, 73, 151, 185,
  232, 287
try planes, 34, 61, 63
tungsten vanadium blades, 26

V
Veritas planes, 40, 44, 77, 78, 79, 114–15, 135,
  136, 137, 138
V-grooves, 103–4
vise stops, 219–22

W
waterstones. *See* sharpening stones
white steel, 22
winding sticks
    checking sole with, 157, 158, 167, 185, 226
    checking stock with, 226, 227, 228, 229
wood types
    angle of blade and, 35, 36–38
    blade steels and, 25, 37
wood-body planes, 163–73. *See also* Chinese
  planes; Japanese planes
    adjusting blade, 152
    adjusting mouth, 170–72
    adjusting wedged, tapered blade, 171
    angle of blade, 35
    attending to details of body and sole, 173
    attending to details of grip and finish, 173
    bedding blade, 166–67
    blade chatter issues, 197–98
    configuring sole, 168–70
    inspecting plane, 163–65
    preparing blade, 146
    preparing/fitting chipbreaker, 146–50
    twisted, fixing, 168

Colophon:

Management:

President: Alan Giagnocavo

Vice President, Sales and Marketing:
Paul McGahren

Editorial Director: John Kelsey

Creative Director: Troy Thorne

Book Staff:

Acquisition Editor: Peg Couch

Designer: Daniel Clarke

Editor: Paul Hambke

Technical Editor: Rick Mastelli

Photographers: Rick Mastelli, Scott Wynn

Illustrator: Scott Wynn

Copy Editor/Proofreader: Lynda Jo Runkle

Indexer: Jay Krieder

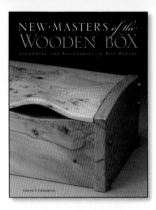
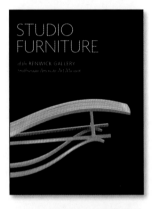
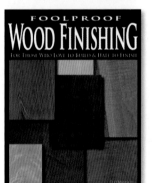

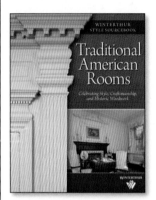
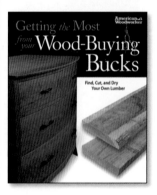